SUSAN J. WHITE is Alberta H. and
Harold L. Lunger professor of spiritual
resources and disciplines and associate
professor of worship and spirituality at
Brite Divinity School, Texas Christian
University in Fort Worth, Texas. She
earned her Ph.D. from the University
of Notre Dame in Notre Dame, Indiana.
She is the author of several books,
including *Christian Worship and
Technological Change* (1994), *Groundwork
of Christian Worship* (1997) and *The Spirit
of Worship: The Liturgical Tradition* (2000).
White lives in Fort Worth, Texas.

A History of Women
in Christian Worship

A History of Women in Christian Worship

Susan J. White

THE
PILGRIM
PRESS
Cleveland

The Pilgrim Press
700 Prospect Avenue
Cleveland, Ohio 44115-1100
pilgrimpress.com

08   07   06   05   04   03   5   4   3   2   1

Library of Congress Cataloging-in-Publication Data

White, Susan J., 1949-
    A history of women in Christian worship / Susan J. White.
       p. cm.
    Includes bibliographical references and index.
    ISBN 0-8298-1550-3 (alk. paper)
    1. Women in public worship – History. 2. Christian women – Religious life –
History. I. Title.
BV26.7.W47 2003
264'.0082 – dc22

                2003055542

For
Penelope Ruth Cracknell Jones
Sarah Ann Cracknell Daniels
Deborah Judith Cracknell Mainwaring
and their daughters

shapers of women's history
in the twenty-first century

Our dear little child has joined the angels. I dressed him and helped to make his casket. There is no minister in the whole country and I could not bear the little broken lily-bud to be just carted away and buried, so I arranged the funeral and conducted the services. I know I am unworthy and in no way fitted for such a mission, but I did my poor best, and if no one else is comforted, I am. I know the message of God's love and care has been told once, anyway, to people who have learned to believe more strongly in hell than in heaven.

— Letter from Elinor Pruitt Stewart to Mrs. Coney, August 15, 1911, in *Adventures of a Woman Homesteader: Life and Letters of Elinor Pruitt Stewart*

Contents

Illustrations follow page 80

Acknowledgments

The debts one accumulates in writing a book are among the most delightful to discharge, and I have many people to thank on this occasion. This book would not have come into being without the welcome opportunity for a year-long sabbatical from Brite Divinity School; for the additional support in the shape of a faculty research grant I am particularly grateful. The innumerable words of affirmation from my professional colleagues, both at Brite and at other institutions, have been recalled with good effect in times of discouragement. Their probing questions about the nature of this project surely helped to sharpen the analysis of the data I was collecting, and their suggestions for sources bore fruit in abundance. My friend Ulrike Guthrie has shared my enthusiasm for this project from the very beginning, and without her constant encouragement I am certain this book would never have come into being. Her incomparable editorial skill improves any text to which she turns her attention. Jill Marie Beck and Lara Blackwood, my patient and hardworking graduate assistants, have spent innumerable hours chasing down references and correcting footnotes, and my administrative assistant, Reina Rodriguez, by relieving me of many other burdens, has made it possible for me to devote more of my attention to this task. Librarian Peta Dunstan was kind and patient in inducting me into the mysteries of the new Divinity School Library at the University of Cambridge, and Rebekah Miles and Shari Gouwens, both superb teachers and scholars, were always ready to inject lavish doses of both enthusiasm and Coca-Cola when my energies began to flag.

Historians are always trying to find ways of expressing their gratitude to the dead, for without them, we would have little about which to write. The innumerable women who appear in these pages have left their footprints in the historical record, and for this I am enormously thankful. But I am no less indebted to those who have not left any trace, who lived and died quietly, remembered only by those who loved them. They, too, have been the shapers of the historical narrative. The names of scholars, both living and dead, in the bibliography at the end of this book is only a small indication of the women and men whose work has been indispensable to my research. Those whom I know personally, I have had the chance to thank already; for any others who may be reading this, please accept my deep and abiding appreciation.

The house that has two scholars at work is neither a very tranquil nor a very tidy one, and my beloved husband, Kenneth Cracknell, has borne the burdens of both neglect and chaos with his usual patient good humor. His own quest for scholarly excellence sets a high standard for all who know him, including me, and his gift for encouragement makes the attainment of that standard possible. Kenneth has read every word of this text, and, as always, his trenchant comments and suggestions have made this a far better piece of work than it would have been otherwise. Any errors and omissions in this book are my sole responsibility, but they are far fewer because of Kenneth's sharp eye for infelicity, incompleteness, and incongruity. For all of this, and more besides, I am grateful to him beyond measure.

Photo Credits

1. "Margaret of York at Prayer." From a Collection of Spiritual Treatises, Ghent, 1447–77. Courtesy of the Royal Library of Belgium, MS 9272-76, folio 182.

2. "Journal of Bathsheba W. Bigler Smith, 1847." Courtesy of Trails to Utah and the Pacific: Diaries and Letters, 1846–69 Collection, Lee Library, Brigham Young University.

3. Anonymous. "A Whore does Penance before ye Congregation in ye Church." From Drawings of Hungarian and Saxon Dresses, ca. seventeenth century. By permission, The British Library.

4. Russell Lee (1903–2000), photographer. "Group of Negro women at a revival, LaFarge, Missouri, 1938." Courtesy of the Library of Congress, America from the Great Depression to World War II: Photographs from the FSA-OWI, 1935–45, Collection. LC-USF33-011608-M3.

5. Anonymous. "Novena Cures: Women standing before lit candles and statues of saints above them on an altar inside St. Agnes Roman Catholic Church, Chicago, 1907." By permission Chicago Daily News negatives collection, Chicago Historical Society, DN-0005109.

6. Dorothea Lange, photographer. " 'Victory through Christ' Society holding a Sunday morning service in a garage, Dos Palos, California, 1938." Courtesy of The Library of Congress, Prints and Photographs Collection, LCUSF-018216-E.

7. WPA Project photograph by Dorothea Lange, photographer. "Women assembled at Wheeley's Church near Gordonton, North Carolina, to clean up church." Courtesy of The Library of Congress, Prints and Photographs Collection, LC-USF-020020-C.

8. Bernard Picard. "Communion among the Lutherans in North Germany." From *Ceremonies et Coutumes Religieuses de tous peuples du monde*, Amsterdam, 1733.

9. Master of Mary of Burgundy. "Mary of Burgundy before a window overlooking the Church." By permission National Library of Austria, Codex 1857, folio 14v.

10. Marion Post Wolcott (1910–99), photographer. "Mother and relatives at the grave of a deceased at a memorial meeting, near Jackson, Breathitt County, Kentucky, August, 1940." Courtesy of the Library of Congress, Prints and Photographs Collection, LC-USF33-031074-M3.

11. Shrine of the Virgin of Guadalupe, near Chama, New Mexico. Photograph by the author, June 2003.

12. "The Bride's Burial." From *Two Unfortunate Lovers* (Anonymous), London, 1621.

13. Embroidered Prayer Book and bag. England, 1633. By permission of the British Library.

14. "The Mother's Grave," engraving published by Kellogg and Thayer, Buffalo, 1846. Courtesy of the Library of Congress, Prints and Photographs Collection, LC-USZ62-60606.

15. Edward Dowd, photographer. "Skitwish girls in communion dresses pose on the steps, Sisters of Providence School, Desmet, Idaho, ca. 1936." Courtesy of the Library of Congress, American Indians of the Pacific Northwest Collection, LC96-109-96.

16. Anonymous. "African American women posed outside a church, Georgia, 1900." Courtesy of the Library of Congress, Prints and Photographs Collection (W. E. B. Du Bois Archive), LC-USZ62-114267.

17. Marion Post Wolcott (1910–99), photographer. "The Women's Guild leaving church after a home management demonstration by the supervisor and a baby shower they gave for Mrs. Verdon Lee, one of the members." Courtesy of The Library of Congress, Prints and Photographs Collection, LC-USF34-05419-D.

18. Marjory Collins (1912–85), photographer. "Procession and High Mass on Easter at the Corpus Christi Church in the Polish Community," Buffalo, New York, 1940. Courtesy of the Library of Congress, Farm Security Administration/Office of War Information Collection Library, LC-USW3-023738-E.

19. Gari Melchers (1860–1932), artist. "The Communion." Published by the Detroit Publishing Company, 1910. Courtesy of the Library of Congress, Prints and Photographs Collection, LC-D416-606.

20. Robert Runyon (1881–1968), photographer. "Child (First Communion)." Courtesy of the Robert Runyon Photograph Collection, courtesy of the Center for American History, University of Texas at Austin.

21. George Edward Anderson, photographer. "Mrs. Albert Mainwaring and her children, Springville, Utah, 1903." Courtesy of Rell G. Francis.

22. Marjory Collins (1912–85), photographer. "Housewife in the Polish community preparing her Easter feast for blessing by the priest on the Saturday before Easter," April 1943. Courtesy of the Library of Congress, Prints and Photographs Collection, LC-USW3-023769-D.

23. Anonymous. "Memoir of Miriam Warner, Who died at Northampton, Mass. Feb. 21, 1819 in the 11th year of her age." New York: The American Tract Society c. 1875. From the Russel B. Nye Popular Culture Collection, Michigan State University Libraries.

24. J. Knight. "Look, Bairn, at thy father once more." *The British Workman*, 1857.

25. Anonymous. "Men, women and children outside a log cabin gathered around a small casket placed on a cloth-covered bench," c. 1900. Courtesy Fred Hultrand History in Pictures Collection, NDIRS-NDSU, Fargo, North Dakota.

26. Russell Lee (1903–2000), photographer. "Singing in church, Pie Town, New Mexico, June, 1940." Courtesy of The Library of Congress, Farm Security Administration/Office of War Information Photograph Collection Library, LC-USF34-036673-D.

27. "A Mound Is in the Graveyard, or the Missionary-Mother's Lament." Lyrics by Mrs. Judson, 1851. Courtesy of Duke University, American Sheet Music Collection, 1850–59.

28. Pierre la Rue, Mechelen, ca. 1528. "Liber missarum" (mass-book) of Margaret of Austria. From the Charles Van Hulthem Collection, Royal Library, Brussels, MS 15-075, folio 2.

29. Church of San Juan, Chimayo, New Mexico. Photograph by the author, June 2003.

30. "Irene Painting a Picture." From an early fifteenth-century manuscript of Giovanni Boccacio, *De Claris Mulieribus*. By permission The British Library.

Introduction

By God, if wommen hadde writen stories...
— Chaucer's "Wife of Bath"

One summer afternoon in 1997, I stepped through a set of massive, ornately carved doors into the ancient cathedral of Sveta Sophia in Ohrid, Macedonia. The building had recently been renovated after years of neglect by Yugoslavia's communist regime; the original frescoes had been uncovered and later additions to the fabric removed in a largely successful attempt to return the interior to the way tenth-century Christians might have known it. Inside, I did what most liturgists do in a church. I tried to imagine what the experience of worshiping might have been like for those who had prayed there more than a thousand years earlier. Scholars generally agree, I recalled, that men and women would have been separated from one another during an ordinary service in the early period of this church's existence, with men praying in the nave of the church and women in the large antechamber called the narthex. So I went into the narthex, prepared to feel a sense of righteous indignation at yet another example of the second-class treatment to which my sisters in ages past were subjected. But as my eyes adjusted to the dim light, I gradually realized that I was not alone. All around the walls of the narthex were floor-to-ceiling frescoes of more than seventy female figures, standing shoulder-to-shoulder, their feet on the ground, their torsos covering the walls, and their faces looking down at me from the vaulting above. I was surrounded and overshadowed by the women saints of Byzantine Christianity. Suddenly, I knew something about women's experience of worship that I had not known before: I understood that when women gathered to pray in this place, surrounded by the presence and prayers of the great cloud of women witnesses to the faith from the past, it was an experience of solidarity and empowerment rather than an experience of segregation and repression. No amount of time sitting in my study reading scholarly accounts of Byzantine worship would have told me this.

This experience in the former Yugoslavia left me with a number of questions. Were we getting an accurate picture of women at worship when we only looked at what was stipulated in liturgical texts, rubrics, and canonical legislation? Was there a way of reconstructing women's actual worship lives and of recovering the

1

experience of women at worship? The answer to the first question now seemed to be an unequivocal "no"; the answer to the second remained a mystery.

Two years later, I found myself in a quite different setting than Sveta Sophia: a small, brightly lit parish hall in Ipswich, England, attending a submeeting of the British Methodist Conference. At that meeting, men and women were recalling their experiences on the front lines of the interfaith dialogue movement in Britain during the previous four decades. One pioneering Roman Catholic woman, a mother of five who had begun her interfaith work in the 1960s by gathering in her home women from many religious traditions to discuss common problems, spoke movingly about the opposition she had faced from members of her congregation. She had been concerned that the local bishop would share their suspicions and would prohibit her from doing the work she had begun to see as essential to the future survival of humanity. "One evening I happened to meet the bishop at a social gathering," she said, "and decided to ask him outright if he was intending to stop me from being involved with interfaith dialogue." The bishop had smiled at her with genuine warmth, replying, "Of course not, my dear. You're only a laywoman, and it doesn't really matter what you do, does it?" The audience was both shocked and dismayed, and those were my initial reactions as well. But as I thought about it, I wondered how many other women in the history of the church had been set free to explore the boundaries of faith and practice, including liturgical practice, because they were not constrained by institutional expectations.[1]

Was there a way to reconstruct women's worship lives? How might one go about it? The experience of this Roman Catholic woman seemed to indicate that looking at women's liturgical experience institutionally was not the way — that what the texts, rubrics, and canon laws were going to tell was mainly what women were "supposed to be doing" rather than what they actually were doing. But to recognize this historiographical difficulty was one thing; to do something about it was another.

The Ways and Means of Traditional Liturgical History

It is often said that "history has many mansions." In commenting on this image, historian Dominick LaCapra observed that "today social history tends to occupy many of the mansions and intellectual history a number of shacks."[2] While this

---

1. A number of women who appear in this study conform to this model. For example, Elinore Pruitt Stewart, a settler on the American frontier at the turn of the twentieth century, says in a letter home, "I have absolutely no manners, and therefore can and do ask questions, can mingle with anybody and everybody since I have no standard to support." Elinore Pruitt Stewart, *Letters on an Elk Hunt by a Woman Homesteader* (Lincoln: University of Nebraska Press, 1979 [1915]), viii.

2. Quoted in Russell Jacoby, "A New Intellectual History?" in *American Historical Review* 97 (1992): 406.

may be true of recent historiography generally, it is hardly true at all of the historiography of Christian liturgy, and this absence of attention to social history is the cause of some of the difficulties in reconstructing the history of women at worship. With very few exceptions, liturgical history has been written as the history of institutions, with official texts, pronouncements, and commentaries bearing nearly the full weight of interpretation. Because, as the experience of the Roman Catholic woman in Ipswich suggests, women have tended to be less institutionalized than men, most of this historical work has uncovered the thinking and actions of men. As a result, in virtually no survey of the history of the liturgy — from Walahfrid Strabo's *Libellus de exordiis et incrementis quarundam in observationibus ecclesiasticus rerum* ("A little book about the origins and development of certain aspects of the liturgy"), written sometime in the 840s, to Gregory Dix's *Shape of the Liturgy*, written eleven hundred years later — is any woman mentioned at all, let alone featured. The worship lives of laywomen have been, quite simply, absent from traditional liturgical history.

Of course not only women are absent from traditional liturgical history; men are as well, or at least ordinary laymen. The names we have always associated with liturgical history are, almost entirely, the names of men (or groups of men) with recognized authority within ecclesiastical structures: Hippolytus, Ambrose, Gregory the Great, Calvin, Cranmer, the Westminster Assembly, John Wesley, Alexander Campbell, the Cambridge-Camden Society, the authors of *Lumen Gentium*. This attention to those who had power over liturgical processes arises from the prevailing perception that "worship" is something prescribed, regulated, and organized from the top, rather than something experienced "from below" by ordinary men and women.[3] In other words, the focus of attention is generally on the liturgical reformers rather than on those who were being reformed, on the liturgical "police" rather than on those who were policed (or who resisted policing). Those historians who have taken account of so-called "popular liturgy" have usually seen it as inevitably in conflict with "official" rites and practices, and (as a result) less valid. While conflict did sometimes occur, both popular accommodation to official faith and practice and official accommodation to popular faith and practice occurred in equal measure. This is not to say that "with its complex of spiritual courts and its network of local churches, its bench of bishops and its army of parish priests"[4] the institutional church did not have enormous influence

---

3. This is why the "nontext" worship traditions, including the Free and Independent Churches, have been underrepresented as subjects of liturgical history.

4. Martin J. Ingram, "Communities and Courts: Law and Disorder in Early Seventeenth-Century Wiltshire," in *Crime in England, 1500–1800*, ed. J. S. Cockburn (Princeton, N.J.: Princeton University Press, 1977), 97.

over the liturgical lives of ordinary men and women. It did. But that influence has never been irresistible, nor have the lines of liturgical influence always been unidirectional.

It is also tempting to believe that the meaning of worship is solely determined by factors internal to the church: theology, sacramental practice, structures of authority, biblical interpretation. Surely, as historian Emma Mason says, in any review of the traditional church histories of the last half-century, "a casual reader might understandably gain the impression that the whole edifice of clerical personnel, finance and bureaucracy existed in a vacuum."[5] But gradually we are beginning to understand that all kinds of other factors — economics, public health, climate, aesthetics, secular power-politics, technological change, and mortality rates, for example — have also contributed to shaping worship lives of Christian people. Some liturgical scholars have recognized this, of course. Roman Catholic theologian Aidan Kavanagh talks about parishioners and their clergy who together engage in "primary theology" as they explore the mysteries of faith. But this is accomplished

> not by concepts and propositions nearly so much as in the vastly complex vocabulary of experiences had, prayers said, sights seen, smells smelled, words said and heard and responded to, emotions controlled and released, sins committed and repented, children born and loved ones buried.... Their critical and reflective discourse is not merely *about* faith. It is the very way faith works itself out in the intricacies of human life both individually and in common.[6]

To commit ourselves to paying attention to the noninstitutional factors in liturgical life is to make the liturgist's task enormously difficult. To admit that liturgical history is lived in the main by the unknown and forgotten, rather than the "heavyweights" of history, is to make the task of writing that history more difficult still. But if we are to make any headway in constructing a women's history of Christian worship, then these difficulties must be overcome.

So Why Bother?

Why is a new model of liturgical history that includes the experience of ordinary women necessary? Some might argue that the need is essentially a political one, that to reconstruct women's worship lives goes some way to redressing the imbalance that has existed in liturgical history. While this may be a valid motivation,

---

5. Emma Mason, "The Role of the English Parishioner, 1100–1500," *Journal of Ecclesiastical History* 27 (1976): 17.

6. Aidan Kavanagh, *On Liturgical Theology* (New York: Pueblo, 1984), 73.

there are several more urgent ones. Historians have become much more sensitive to the elusiveness of women in the historical record and to the fact that, as a group, women have constituted the most spectacular casualty of traditional history. While we may be exercising a form of "reverse discrimination" when we uncover the hidden history of women in worship, the more important consequence will be to give a much more adequate picture of the richness and variety of ritual expression of Christianity. The institutional history of Christian worship is only half the picture. It is not a "wrong" picture, simply a partial and inadequate one that demands revision.

The second reason for finding a new paradigm for liturgical historiography has to do with the function of history in the construction of human identity, and in this case, women's identity. Women's contemporary experience of participation in and leadership of worship is impoverished by not having an established and commonly agreed-upon historical foundation on which to ground it. Women often find themselves reinventing the liturgical wheel, without a diversity of models on which to base their choices. What would it mean for twenty-first-century women to know that their sisters in previous generations have incorporated liturgy into solutions to their problems, both social and religious; that they have used various means, both legal and illegal, to resist attempts to imprison their liturgical imaginations; and that they have found ways of satisfying their ritual needs when the church has abandoned its concern for them? All of these stories are a part of women's legitimate religious inheritance, an inheritance that has not been available to them (see fig. 1).

A Women's History of Christian Worship

The dual assumptions of most feminist liturgical scholars (which, before beginning this study, I largely shared) are, first, that men have always controlled women's liturgical lives, and, second, that "the church" was a power structure which used the historic liturgy as a technology of dominance. But, as I began to discover in writing this book, while both of these assumptions may be true, they are not invariably and wholly true. It is impossible, of course, to be a historian in the twenty-first century, and especially a woman historian, without being conscious of power: the power of one people over another, men over women, elites over nonelites, and rich over poor. These power differentials have surely come into play in the construction of liturgical history. As a result, those on the underside of the power structures — traditionally women, the poor, and the socially marginalized — appear in the literature and documents of Christian worship almost exclusively as the reflections of ideas about them held by the power elite.

As liturgists became increasingly sensitive to the power relationships that have pervaded the history of Christian worship, they began to recognize the ways in which women have not only been absent from liturgical historiography, but restricted in their liturgical participation. As one woman scholar writes, "The primary conditioner of women's liturgical history is that they have not been allowed to be ordained."[7] The information and insights we have gained about the exclusion of women from certain significant liturgical roles and practices have been enormously valuable as we begin to reconstruct the history of women at worship. But, once again, this is not the whole story. Women's liturgical history is not only the history of their exclusion. As Charlotte Methuen writes, "we need to see where women were as well as where they were not. We need to know what spaces women found for their self-expression, and how these traditions were transmitted or lost."[8]

As Methuen suggests, if we are eventually to draw an accurate picture of women's liturgical history, we must begin to discover the details of women's worship lives *beyond* their exclusion. What, in the more positive sense, were women's experiences of worship, opinions about worship, and worship practices? Is it possible to reconstruct the actual liturgical lives of ordinary women? This is primarily an exercise in women's history rather than feminist history, although both will eventually be necessary to the formation of a complete narrative of women at worship.[9] The usual focus of feminist history — that is, the ways in which gender identity is formed and understood in various periods — is not the central concern of this book. (But it is hoped that information in this book is useful to feminist historians who wish to use women's participation in religious ritual to create a more complete picture of the process of gender construction.) To the extent that the story of the church's worship has been colonized, perhaps this book can be seen as a postcolonial reading of liturgical history, in which those at the margins of traditional histories of worship appear not simply as the objects of liturgical change, of the revisions of liturgical texts and pronouncements, but rather as the center and subject of their own liturgical lives, albeit within the context of these wider theological, social, and institutional movements.

---

7. Teresa Berger, *Concilium: Liturgy and the Body* (1995/3): 112.

8. Charlotte Methuen, " 'For Pagans Laugh to Hear Women Teach': Gender Stereotypes in the *Didascalia Apostolorum*," in *Gender and Christian Religion*, ed. R. N. Swanson (Woodbridge, U.K.: Boydell, 1998), 23.

9. See Joan Scott, "Experience," in *Theorizing the Political*, ed. Judith Butler and Joan Scott (London: Routledge, 1992), 25–35; and Catherine Hall, *White, Male, and Middle-Class: Explorations in Feminism and History* (New York: Routledge, 1992).

The Plan

When I began work on this project and told people that I was attempting to write a women's history of Christian worship, many said (only half-jokingly, I think) that the result would surely be among the "Great Short Books of All Time." As it happened they were mistaken; in the end I became convinced that there was certainly sufficient material on women's liturgical lives to fill several volumes. Some of this material I have been able to locate; much still remains to be unearthed. As a result, I must issue a disclaimer. Despite its ambitious title, this book actually has a quite modest aim. Rather than attempting to map the entire geography of women's liturgical experience, the pages that follow represent something of a "programmatic statement," an outline of the kinds of information that will need to be taken into account if such a map *is* eventually to be drawn. My ardent hope is that future liturgical historians will be willing to continue this work to its completion.

One of the first tasks in making a plan for this outline was deciding on its organization. Although women have successfully resisted the complete colonization of their liturgical lives in the course of Christian history, liturgical studies has not been quite so successful. Most often organized around clerically regulated activities — eucharist, baptism, confirmation, penance, ordination, and so on — the standard curriculum looks at Christian worship from the top down, with the laity generally understood as consumers of the church's various liturgical programs and projects. Different traditions of Christian worship have been established by mapping the relationships between and among these elements in order to determine the degree to which they deviate from predetermined plumb lines, and by tracing the liturgical agenda of the founders and proponents of the traditions. Of course, within these parameters there are always choices to be made, and the subdiscipline of pastoral liturgy had been about making these choices with due attention to the ritual and devotional needs of congregations. But again, these choices, and the creation and application of the meaning structures that underlie them, are seen to be the province of clergy and others "in authority."

But if we approach the study of Christian worship "from below," the traditional categories begin to prove less than helpful for interpreting what we find. We discover that women often make sense of their liturgical experiences without reference to official interpretations; we find that women occupy liturgical space in ways that meet their own ritual needs, and take the liturgy into spaces over which they have direct control (the street and the home, for example); we find that their definitions of the how, why, where, and who of valid and efficacious liturgical practice are not necessarily the same as the definitions enforced by those in authority.

As a result, this book does not tend to follow the schedule usually adopted by standard liturgical histories. We begin by asking the question, "How do we find women in the history of Christian worship?" Are there particular sources and methods that allow us to hear what women say about their own liturgical lives, rather than what is said about them by others? Then we look at the question of space. While ecclesiastical authorities have always been quite clear about the locations in which "real liturgy" takes place, women have tended to have a more fluid understanding of sacred space. So the question is, "In what kinds of spaces have women chosen to worship?" Women have exercised their own kind of influence over the ways and means of Christian worship, and although this book is not primarily concerned with influential women, chapter 3 discusses the ways and means by which women influence the large and small structures of Christian common prayer. Women's concern for preparing themselves for meaningful participation in Christian worship is the topic of the next chapter, and then in chapter 5 we see them as they join in the common prayer of their congregation on Sundays. Finally, we discover the ways in which women have understood their houses as liturgical spaces (chapter 6) and have participated in the various liturgical arts and crafts, including music (chapter 7).

This book is about the minutiae of women's liturgical lives. Although some women here have been involved in the grand politics of liturgical change on a large scale, most have not. The women we meet are, by and large, women like Hannah Fuller Pocock. She was not a famous theologian, a religious activist, or a skilled orator, but an ordinary wife and mother and member of John Wesley's City Road Chapel in London, who "found her way to services . . . 'by help of a penny candle' and died 'with a hymn on her lips.' "[10] We meet women like the Roman Catholic mother of eight, living in a Boston tenement at the turn of the twentieth century. "I've seen her go to church when she could hardly walk," her son says. "I've seen her give money to the church when there wasn't food in the joint to feed a canary. Whenever I complained that I didn't want to go to church because I was either poorly shod or poorly dressed, she would come back at me with: 'God don't look at your shoes or your clothes, son, he only wants your soul.' "[11] These women are representatives of the great multitude of women worshipers who have spent their lives saying prayers and singing hymns, giving money and decorating altars, teaching their children and burying their dead. In doing these things with persistence, courage, and integrity, they are to be considered primary actors in liturgical history and shapers of the liturgical future of the church.

---

10. W. W. Pocock, *In Memoriam William Fuller Pocock, FRIBA, 1779–1849* (Privately printed, 1883), 9.

11. J. Callagan, *Man's Grim Justice: My Life Outside the Law* (London: J. Long, 1928), 2–3.

CHAPTER ONE

FINDING WOMEN
IN THE HISTORY OF
CHRISTIAN WORSHIP

Here lyeth entombed Marie Dudley, daughter of William Howard of Effingham, in his time Lord Admiral of England, Lord Chamberlain and Lord Privy Seal. She was grandchild to Thomas Duke of Norfolk . . . and sister to Charles Howard, Earl of Nottingham, High Admiral of England by whose prosperous direction through the goodness of God defending his lady Queen Elizabeth, the whole fleet of Spain was defeated and discomforted. She was first married to Edward Sutton, Lord Dudley and after to Richard Monpesson Esquire who in memory of his love erected this monument to her.

— Monument to Maria Dudley in St. Margaret's, Westminster, London

The words "invisible" and "silent" are all too often used to describe the position of women in Christian history.[1] While this description is surely not an invariably accurate one, it does seem that when women *do* become visible in the historical record, they tend to appear — like Maria Dudley — only in reflection: as the daughter, wife, mother, sister, or lover of a more central, male character in the narrative. But students of women's history are convinced that women are only invisible and silent because we have traditionally looked and listened for "Christian history" in the wrong places, or at least in places where women are least likely to be found — in the cathedrals and not in the kitchens, in the episcopal palaces and not the wayside shrines, in the pulpits and not in the pews. By using different methods, sources, and modes of analysis we can discover women as actors in Christian history (and for our purposes, the history of Christian worship) in their own right and on their own terms.

---

1. See, for example, the title of a volume of the theology journal *Concilium: Women: Invisible in Church and Theology* 182 (1985).

9

The Evidence for Women's Liturgical Lives •

Because the religious experience of women like Maria Dudley is so often written in the margins of traditional church history rather than in the center of the page, tracking that experience requires distinctive methods of detection. Indeed, some of the sources that are the usual mainstays of liturgical historiography — systematic theological treatises, official rites and texts, and learned commentaries, for example — reveal hardly any indications of the presence of women, and for this reason are given much less weight here than in traditional surveys of liturgical history. Conversely, various materials that are rarely cited in conventional histories of worship are given high priority in the following chapters.

As women move through history they leave multiple kinds of traces behind them, and therefore methodological flexibility is of the essence. Like all good detectives, we must take what evidence we find and allow it to speak to us about the reality of women's liturgical lives.[2] Any number of factors — denomination; temporal, geographic, and socioeconomic location; power politics — determine the kinds of sources available for reconstructing the worship lives of women. Wealthy medieval women left wills, but only rarely diaries; middle-class Methodists were prolific writers of journals, but few engaged in legal proceedings; women in the sixth century made material provision for churches and monastic houses, but few of their letters survive. The elusiveness of women in the liturgical record can be overcome, but not by the stringent application of a single, invariable methodology.

Women Speaking for Themselves

While flexibility in the use of sources and methods of analysis is necessary, some overarching principles of selection are applied throughout this study. Because women's voices have so often been muted and their experience so often recounted

---

2. In their introduction to the multivolume *History of Women in the West*, Natalie Zeman Davis and Annette Farge describe the inherent complexities involved in tracking women as historical actors: "Protestant and Catholic women approached culture and learning in distinctive ways that affected their relation to the family and community. Epidemic, famine, and war drove many women into one form or another of resistance or transgression and thus brought them into the public arena. Relations between men and women, between the 'masculine' and the 'feminine,' changed as the world changed, sometimes making the balance of power more symmetrical, sometimes not." N. Z. Davis and A. Farge, "Women as Historical Actors," in *A History of Women in the West*, vol. 3: *Renaissance and Enlightenment Paradoxes*, ed. Natalie Zeman Davis and Annette Farge (Cambridge, Mass.: Belknap Press of Harvard University Press, 1993), 3.

and interpreted by men, precedence is given here, wherever possible, to what women have to say about themselves, their own lives, and the lives of other women. What men say to women and about women plays a subordinate role.[3] Fortunately, women have left us a fair number of first-person source materials — which are discussed in detail below — including private letters, advice manuals, wills, journals, diaries, affidavits, and autobiographies.

First-person writing might be our most valuable and useful source of information on women's liturgical participation, but numerous difficulties must be overcome. The first, of course, is the relative scarcity of this type of material. Women diarists, autobiographers, and letter writers may have been prolific, but it has to be acknowledged that most of their output has been lost to us, and from some historical periods almost no personal records of women's lives have survived at all. So even though we might *wish* to give priority to women's own testimony about their worship lives, we only occasionally are able to do so.

But why is there such a dearth of women's first-person writing? Some of the scarcity can be attributed to the social disruption resulting from war, famine, and natural disaster, but for the most part, unpublished letters, journals, and diaries were lost in the past for the very same reasons they are lost today: we simply throw them out with the rubbish. (The same kinds of circumstances have resulted in a similar scarcity of first-person writing by men.) Of course, not all of the paucity of women's personal writing results from "natural causes." Some is the direct result of the type of gender politics that has marked much of Christian history, a politics in which the native ability of women was devalued and in which writing of any kind by women was discouraged. Certainly, many women have been renowned for their intellectual capacities, even in the earliest periods of Christian history.[4] But many more women have been socialized into thinking that to write, even if only of their own experience, was an audacious and unnatural thing to do. So even a woman of such noted accomplishments as Christine de Pisan (c. 1364–c. 1431) could begin her major work with the words: "I, a woman, dare...."[5]

---

3. So, for example, while there are two near-contemporary accounts of the life of St. Radegund, one written by Venatius Fortunatus (*De vita sancta Radegundis Liber I*) and one by the nun Baudovinia (*De vita sanctae Radegundis liber II*), only the latter will be drawn upon. See Simon Coates, "Rendering Radegund? Fortunatus, Baudovinia, and the Problem of Female Sanctity in Merovingian Gaul," in *Gender and Christian Religion*, ed. R. N. Swanson (Woodbridge, Suffolk, U.K., and Rochester, N.Y.: Boydell, 1998).

4. Melania the Younger and Melania the Elder, and Paula and her daughters Blesilla and Eustocium are all commended by contemporary commentators for their wide learning and facility in languages.

5. Christine de Pisan, *The Book of the City of Ladies* (New York: Persea, 1982), xi.

Not only is the autographic material skewed in terms of its historical distribution, it is also skewed in terms of its sociological distribution. Although some writers were what Margaret Spufford has described as "humble autobiographers,"[6] the majority of the women who have left us their own words come from the ranks of the well-bred and well-educated. Until the early sixteenth century, women who could read and/or write at all were probably quite rare, although more common in some social, economic, and geographical locations than others. For example, Quaker and Puritan women in the 1700s were more likely to read and write than their Roman Catholic sisters; a higher percentage of sixteenth-century Italian women were literate than their German counterparts in the same period.[7] Because women of lower social and economic standing have always been less likely to leave a record of their own experiences than their wealthier and more educated sisters, the voices of women of color, slaves, peasants, and children are only very rarely heard in first-person writing.[8]

First-Person Narrative: Journals, Diaries, Ledgers, Letters, and Autobiographies

As a way of overcoming the pervasive sense of the silence of women, historians have relied heavily on various kinds of first-person accounts, the analysis of which has been described by South African writer Alison Goebel as "the ideal feminist method."[9] From at least the year 203, when Vibia Perpetua wrote from her prison cell about her journey toward martyrdom, literate Christian women have described their experience, including their experience of worship, in journals and diaries, letters and autobiographies. Such personal memoranda provide us with details of the small, everyday occurrences that constitute the rich tapestry of women's lives, as well as contributing genuine warmth and passion usually missing from mere reportage (see fig. 2).

Given the importance of the earliest centuries of Christian history in establishing baselines for further study and interpretation, the paucity of material from

---

6. Margaret Spufford, "First Steps in Literacy: The Reading and Writing Experiences of the Humblest Seventeenth-Century Autobiographers," *Social History* 4 (1979): 407–35.

7. We return to this question of literacy in chapter 4, pp. 124–30.

8. See on this issue Amanda Vickery, "Golden Age to Separate Spheres? A Review of the Categories and Chronology of English Women's History," in *Historical Journal* 36 (1993): 383–414.

9. Alison Goebel, "Life Histories as a Cross-cultural Feminist Method in African Studies: Achievements and Blunders." Paper presented at the "Promoting Women's History: Local and Regional Perspectives" Conference, Grahamstown, South Africa, July 6, 1983. This dichotomy between rich and poor in terms of their first-person writing begins to fade in the nineteenth century. For example, Joanna L. Stratton has uncovered at least 103 autobiographies from women, both rich and poor, on the Kansas frontier in the 1850s–1880s. For her list, see Joanna L. Stratton, *Pioneer Women: Voices from the Kansas Frontier* (New York: Simon and Schuster, 1981), 271–303.

this period is a serious handicap in the study of the history of Christian women. Examples of writing of any kind by women in the first thousand years of Christianity are extremely rare, and first-person writings can be counted on the fingers of two hands:[10]

1. Vibia Perpetua's account from prison before her martyrdom in Carthage (203 C.E.) inserted into the compiled *Passio sanctarum Perpetuae et Felicitatis.*

2. A letter from sometime in the 350s C.E. written by a woman named Valeria to the anchorite Paphnutius containing a prayer for healing.

3. A travel diary by Egeria, a nun or anchorite likely from Galicia, in which she reports on her pilgrimage to the Middle East (381/384 C.E.) and describes monasticism and liturgical practice.

4. Eleven letters from Melania the Elder to Evagrius Ponticus, originally transmitted in Armenian and translated into Latin.

5. A letter from Paula Eustochium to Marcella (325–410 C.E.) inserted into the letters of Jerome.

6. Two letters from a Spanish woman ascetic to a female colleague (ca. 400 C.E.) also preserved among the letters attributed to Jerome.

7. Letters from Amalasuntha, daughter of Theodoric the Great, the Ostrogothic king of Italy. She ruled in her own right for nine years in the early sixth century, and two of her letters to Justinian and Theodora plus another to the senate of Rome have been preserved.

8. The writings of Aldegund (d. 684 C.E.), a young noblewoman who refused marriage in order to enter a convent, which recount her visions for the spiritual edification of her sisters, and describe her relationship with God in highly erotic terms.

9. A letter written by Gisla (c. 757–810 C.E.) and Rotrund (c. 775–810 C.E.), respectively the sister and daughter of Charlemagne, to Alcuin, asking him to write a commentary on the Gospel of John for them because their own studies were confounded by the complexity of Augustine. (Alcuin dedicated the commentary to Gisla when he finished it in 802 C.E.)

---

10. Jean Gerson, canon lawyer and chancellor of the University of Paris in the early fifteenth century, argues in favor of women's silence from this paucity of women's writing in the early church: "Where are the writings of most learned and pious females, like Paula and Eustochium? Certainly nothing is preserved because they did not have the presumptuousness to write." *De examinatione doctrinarium* (1423) II, 2–3 *Oeuvres* 9 (Paris, 1973), 468.

10. A manual of etiquette written by the Carolingian noblewoman Dhuoda for her eldest son sometime around 835, C.E. which treats religious as well as social concerns.[11]

Things improve considerably after the turn of the twelfth century, when the number of women from whom we have extant literature increases dramatically. For example, just in the two hundred years between 1100 and 1300 Hildegard of Bingen (d. 1179), Hadewijch (d. c. 1250), Mechtild of Magdeburg (d. c. 1282), Gertrud of Helfta (d. 1292), Mechtild of Hackeborn (d. 1299), Marguerite d'Oingt (d. 1310), and others produced letters and autobiographical narratives, as well as major works of theological, spiritual, and liturgical reflection; rules for the ordering of monasteries; and hymnody. After 1600 the number of literate women increases again, and the amount of source material written by women about their own lives continues to expand to the present day.[12]

Letters are by far the most numerous and widespread of these first-person writings. In some cases we have not only individual letters, but whole sets of

---

11. Other writing by women before 1000:
- Roman aristocrat Faltonia Beatitia Proba's Virgilian *Cento* (ca. 360), a paraphrase of biblical texts from the creation to the resurrection.
- A hagiographical account of the Martyrdom of St. Cyprian by the Byzantine Empress Aelia Eudokia Augusta (d. 460), the only remnant of six books to have been preserved. (Reportedly these books include biblical paraphrases, poetic versions of Daniel and Zechariah, and a hymn on the Octateuch.)
- The *Sayings of the Desert Mothers: Theodora, Sarra, Syncletica, and Eugenia* from the fifth century, which are preserved as a part of the *Apophthegmata Patrum*.
- A letter of instruction from Caesaria the Younger addressed to Radegund and Richild in the monastery of the Holy Cross at Poitiers and dated somewhere between 552 and 557. The letter emphasizes the importance of liturgical prayer. Three surviving *Dicta* which also seem to have been from her are concerned with the same matters.
- The completion of Fortunatus's Life of St. Radegund by the nun Baudovinia, the first woman hagiographer of Merovingian Gaul, writing between the years 609 and 614.
- A travelogue of St. Wunibald's pilgrimage to the Holy Land, produced about 760 by a nun at Heidenheim.
- A life of St. Willibald written by the nun Hugeburc in the second half of the eighth century. She later wrote a life of St. Winnebald.
- Hymns composed by the Byzantine abbess Kassia (d. sometime before 865), which remain in use as a part of the Greek Orthodox liturgy.
- A number of legends and plays showing wide knowledge of the Bible and patristic sources left by Hrotsvith of Gandersheim, a German canoness living sometime in the mid-tenth century.
- An epic poem by Jóreiðr I Miðjumdal, a sixteen-year-old female farmhand who is one of the Icelandic Skáldkonur (women poets, writers of epic poetry), from around 950 to 1000.

12. These accounts are, however, always outnumbered by those written by men. For example, of the eighty-nine known Puritan and Quaker spiritual autobiographies in English written before 1725, only twenty-four are by women (eleven Quaker and thirteen Puritan or Baptist). See Owen C. Watkins, *Puritan Experience* (London: Routledge & Kegan Paul, 1972), appendix 1 for a complete list.

correspondence covering many years, in which women writers relate all sorts of ordinary (and many extraordinary) events to their friends and family.[13] Although descriptions of some of the large-scale events in Christian liturgical history can sometimes be found in these letters, most usually they record the minutiae of liturgical participation, giving life and breath to the traditional macrohistory of Christian worship. Journals and diaries, while more scarce, often provide not only the details of the author's worship life, but also her attitudes toward and critiques of certain practices. Household accounts give evidence of the more "commercial" side of women's participation in the liturgy, recording such things as how much was spent to rent the family pew and the amount paid to the bell ringer at the baby's funeral.

Although they are among the most useful sources we have for evidence of women's liturgical participation, first-person writings do have certain disadvantages to the student of Christian worship. While some of these writings have been published, most exist only in library archives or family collections; their contents may never have been catalogued, and so each piece must be read carefully for information about liturgical involvement. As we have seen, first-person autobiographical narratives, diaries, journals, or letters usually give evidence of only one particular strand of women's experience, that of the literate, educated, and usually relatively wealthy woman. In addition, and perhaps more significantly, they only rarely provide any systematic treatment of liturgical subjects, although there are some cases — travel journals, for example — in which extended and detailed observations are made. Of course, even when we do have first-person sources from women, we must use caution in taking what they say at face value: women can be as deceptive (and self-deceptive) as their male counterparts, and we must equally apply a healthy skepticism of their credibility. As valuable as they are, if we are to make any broad generalizations about attitudes and practice from these sources, we must buttress them with other kinds of material.

Other Genres of Women's Writing

Of course, first-person narrative is not the only kind of writing women have left the historian of the liturgy. Women have also produced collections of corporate prayers and hymns, works of liturgical analysis and sacramental theology,

---

13. See, for example, James Gairdner, ed., *The Paston Letters, 1422–1590*, 4 vols. (Westminster: A. Constable, 1900); C. L. Kingford, ed., *The Stonor Letters and Papers, 1290–1483* (London: Camden Society, 1900); Thomas Taylor Lewis, ed., *Letters of Lady Brilliana Harley* (London: Camden Society, 1854); Sibylla Holland, *Letters of Mary Sibylla Lyall Holland*, 3d ed., ed. Edward Holland (London, 1907).

visionary prose, and manuals of instruction for worship, all of which are useful sources of information about the liturgical lives of women, as well as evidence of the influence of women over the liturgical lives of others. This material is usually intended for a wider public: a religious order; a particular convent, congregation, or denomination; the academic world; the community of faithful believers in general. Increasing interest in women's ecclesiastical history has placed these materials under more intensive scholarly scrutiny, and during the past thirty-five years critical editions of many of the manuscript sources have been published, making them more easily available than the more personal sources.

Although this type of material is invaluable for the study of Christian women's history, in the pages that follow it takes a subordinate place, for a number of reasons, to the first-person writing we discussed above. Its distribution is perhaps even more intensively skewed in its historical, sociological, and geographical range than the first-person material. While many different kinds of women over the centuries have been willing to pen personal diaries and letters to friends, until fairly recently only the most confident and well-educated have been prepared to write for a more general audience. Because of its public character, this type of material has often been subject to a greater degree of "external pressure" — the intervention of male editors, compilers, or transcribers, for example — than the first-person sources, and is thus often one or more steps further removed from women's direct experience of worship participation. Often, too, especially in the premodern period, the authorship of this material is contested — not only because historians have misattributed some women's writing to men, but also because women authors themselves have been known to sign their own work with the name of a male relative in the hope that their ideas would be accepted by the intellectual elite.[14]

The final reason that this important source of information must take second place is that although attention is given to "women of influence" in these pages,[15] influential women, in the ordinary sense of the word, are not the center of attention in this book. Rather, the various ways in which ordinary women have experienced the baptisms of their children, their own weddings and those of their sons and daughters, communion, rites at the sickbed, liturgical devotions, feasts and fasts are the main focus of these chapters. So again, we are left to find other sources of information about most of the liturgical lives that take shape here.

---

14. See below, pp. 36–37.
15. Especially in chaps. 3 and 7.

Women at Law: Wills and Testimony under Oath

The most prolific legal documents relating to women that we have are wills, legal documents that give instructions about the disposition after death of a person's body, tangible and intangible goods, and sometimes even his or her soul. In the Christian West, we first begin to see women's wills in fair numbers by about the thirteenth century, although wills for women in the Greco-Roman and Carolingian periods are not unknown. In most cases, wills are a part of the public record, and therefore are generally better preserved than other kinds of primary source materials written by individuals. Because of the relative stability in the form and underlying intention of wills, they are valuable sources of information for those studying human geography, historical sociology, and material culture.

For the student of Christian worship, wills yield various kinds of evidence. They provide some of the best data we have of the type and distribution of liturgical books left *by* or *to* women, and may also describe bequests by women of church furnishings; of stipends for the upkeep of church buildings, chapels, and shrines; and for their own monuments. In some cases, a woman would record her theological or liturgical motivations for making particular bequests, thus revealing something of her attitude toward the role of worship in the Christian life.

Both men and women used their wills to impose, often in meticulous detail, liturgical requirements on those whom they left behind: directives to participate in services at the time of death, to visit the gravesite periodically for prayer, to make special provisions for the feast day of a patron saint, and to engage in public almsgiving, for example. One medieval citizen of York instructed in his will that his wife go on pilgrimage both to Carlisle and to Brough in order to pray for God's mercy on his soul. Not only does this instruction give us a sense of a wealthy woman's incentive for a fairly rigorous form of liturgical devotion,[16] but it is the only extant evidence that Carlisle, famous at the time for its bejeweled statue of the Virgin Mary, was also a place of pilgrimage.[17] Modern wills, at least among Protestants, are less likely to make such demands on others, but they do show that many women continue to make bequests for additions to the church building and furnishings, for the purchase of service books and hymnals, and for the enhancement of church music.

Because testamentary documents are public indications of the deathbed wishes of their makers, they are usually quite reliable indicators of what was actually

---

16. A trip to Carlisle required negotiating the treacherous road across the Pennines, and in order to reach Brough one had to cross the English Channel.

17. Margaret Clarke, "Northern Light? Parochial Life in a 'Dark Corner' of Tudor England," in *Parish in English Life, 1400–1600*, ed. Katherine L. French, Gary Gibbs, Beat A. Kümin (Manchester: Manchester University Press, 1997), 60–61.

done. It is almost unthinkable that the widow of the deceased man described above would *not* have gone on the pilgrimages he requested, if only to avoid the censure of her neighbors. Barring financial catastrophe, bequests are usually honored, so even when the material evidence for a bequest is lost (the building has burned down or the hymnals replaced), the will gives us evidence of their previous existence. But again, caution must be used with testamentary documents. The women who made wills were invariably those with something to leave, so once again, another of our primary sources mainly gives evidence of the lives of women of substance. But often wills do mention other women — servants or poorer friends — bequeathing to them devotional items such as relics or books, or instructing them to undertake certain kinds of liturgical activities as a memorial.

Testimony in court is another kind of legal evidence for women's liturgical activities, attitudes, and, most importantly, their deviance from prevailing ritual or theological norms.[18] Given that court officials are responsible for providing verbatim reports of what is said under oath, court testimony is, in the words of Georges Duby, "one of the few places where we can catch the unadorned sound of the female voice."[19] For most American readers, steeped in the tradition of separation of church and state, it may be difficult to imagine the degree to which legal proceedings have been influential in shaping the history of the church generally, and of Christian worship more specifically. The proceedings both of civil courts, in situations where the church is established by law, and church or "consistory" courts[20] provide evidence of women's involvement in matters of dispute over the liturgy, of their compliance with changes in worship, and of the extent of their knowledge about liturgical matters.

Several different matters traditionally have come under the jurisdiction of the consistory courts.[21] Women could be brought to court for failure to attend church or to pay the tithe; for unseemly behavior in church; for working or rowdy drinking on Sunday; for neglecting to have children baptized; for adultery, fornication, incest, heresy, witchcraft; or for giving birth to illegitimate children. Matrimonial suits as well as some kinds of slander, usury, and probate were also brought before the church courts. The heresy trial is among the most grave and impassioned form of church trial, and one to which, as we shall see, women

---

18. See appendix 3.

19. Georges Duby, "Affidavits and Confessions," in *A History of Women in the West*, vol. 2: *Silences of the Middle Ages*, ed. C. Klapisch-Zuber (Cambridge, Mass.: Belknap Press of Harvard University Press, 1992), 483.

20. The consistory court was the bishop's court, which dealt with causes and offenses under ecclesiastical law.

21. See the photo of consistory court in Chester Cathedral in Jane Cox, *Hatred Pursued beyond the Grave: Tales of Our Ancestors from the London Church Courts* (London: HMSO, 1993), 13.

were regularly submitted.[22] Documents from heresy trials reveal deviations from lawful liturgical practice and in the theological interpretation of various rites and ceremonies. (Chaucer's portrayal of the much-reviled "Summoner" in the *Canterbury Tales* gives us some sense of the public apprehension engendered by the consistory court; the knock at the door by the summoner [sometimes called the apparitor], who was charged with delivering the summons to court, was much feared by people of all social ranks.)

But the church courts were not only places where women were charged with theological and liturgical deviance; women could also bring suit against others at consistory courts, or be parties to the suits brought by men. All matters related to the fabric and interior of churches, dereliction of duty by churchwardens or parish clerks, and all matters of clergy discipline were heard before the consistory court, and women could — and did — petition the court for redress if their liturgical and ecclesiastical "rights" were being violated by the clergy. So, court evidence can disclose not only women's deviation from liturgical norms, but also their reaction to clerical malfeasance in liturgical matters.

Yet more information can be gained from court records, since some of the judgments of these courts involved the imposition of public liturgical penances on those convicted. In the period leading up to the Reformation in England, for example, the usual penance ordered by the church courts required the offender to walk at the front of the Sunday procession, clad in a white sheet, barefoot and bareheaded, carrying a lighted candle, and to kneel before the altar and present the candle to the celebrant at mass (see fig. 3). If the accusation involved an offense against members of the congregation, various forms of restitution were required, and often a public appeal for forgiveness was inserted into the main Sunday service. In 1544, for example, Dionese Constable, convicted of fornication, was ordered to confess her fault publicly in these words: "Neighbours, whereas I have offended God and commonwealth, in that you have had me in suspicion of ill living with George Wakefield, I cry God for mercy, and am sorry for it; and I pray you be in love and charity with me."[23]

Finally, coroners' inquests can also aid us in finding women in the history of Christian worship, as liturgical details surface in the investigation of a death. The death of eighteen-month-old Agnes Wellester in 1385 is a good example. According to the testimony presented before the coroner, her mother, Alice, a resident of Stanford, England, had been heating water in her home on Thursday after Epiphany "when she heard the church bells ring for Eucharist. She put down

22. See pp. 163, 169, and appendix 3.
23. Susan Brigden, *London and the Reformation* (Oxford: Clarendon, 1989), 148–49.

a container of boiling water and ran to church. A dog followed her, running, and knocked the bowl over on her one-and-a-half-year-old daughter."[24] Equally interesting is the fact that Wellester defended herself by arguing that her pious intentions mitigated her responsibility for the death of her daughter.

Although it can certainly be argued that women have not always been treated equally under the law, the record of their public testimony as participants in legal proceedings of various kinds does allow us to hear women speaking in the first person about their own lives. Of course, we can never really know the extent of women's willful deceptiveness in court or the degree to which their confessions were coerced. But legal material does have certain real advantages in the reconstruction of women's history. Women of all social and economic positions are represented in legal proceedings, and the words of even illiterate and under-educated women have been preserved. The various kinds of legal evidence can usually be relied upon as having been quite accurately recorded, and because most legal systems rely on the concept of precedent, more care has been taken to conserve legal documents than almost any other kind of material, so we have evidence from a wide range of times and places. We still need, however, to exercise caution in using legal testimony as a source for reconstructing women's liturgical history, because such testimony generally records the unusual occurrence — the untimely death, the deviant practice, the heretical view — rather than the ordinary course of events.

The Material Evidence

Historically, women have been the builders of shrines and painters of pictures, the purchasers of prayer cards and Sunday hats, and the subject of innumerable photographs and engravings. Analysis of the production of, the intentions behind, and the use of these kinds of artifacts can contribute enormously to our ability to fill out the details of women's worship lives. Indeed, since the mid-1970s, scholars of religion have increasingly paid attention to the tangible, material residue of Christian devotional and liturgical practice, recognizing that we live in a "world made up not only of ideas but of things."[25]

---

24. Cited in Barbara A. Hanawalt, *The Ties That Bound: Peasant Families in Medieval England* (New York: Oxford University Press, 1986), 27. We also learn the ways churches and churchyards were used: three women selling eggs in a Lincolnshire churchyard in 1352 were killed when a gable toppled over on them (34).

25. Colleen McDannell, *Material Christianity: Religion and Popular Culture in America* (New Haven: Yale University Press, 1986), 2. Some of the historic failure to appreciate the value of the material aspect of Christian history is that it was the province of what McDannell calls "women, children, and other illiterates" (8).

The interpretation of material evidence is not necessarily easy; "meaning" is created in all sorts of locations. Each item is set within a complex social and aesthetic context, and what the creator of an object intended may or may not have been appropriated by the woman who owned and used it. Indeed, the meaning of any particular artifact can change over time. The way a woman understands and uses a family prayer book may be entirely different than the way her grandmother understood and used the very same book seventy-five years earlier. Sometimes a woman leaves us a verbal description of her relationship with the objects in her material environment, but more often we are left with only the objects themselves, which remain mute. To what extent is a posed photograph of family prayers representative of the role women actually played? Why did a particular woman embroider the Lord's Prayer onto canvas? Where did it hang in her home? What function, if any, did it serve in her private devotions?

As we go back in time, the interpretive difficulties only increase. Radical changes in stylistic and allegorical conventions, removal from the original context — ecclesial, social, and economic — and sometimes physical deterioration of the artifact itself make accurate decoding extremely difficult.[26] We can see this difficulty by looking at the example of early "Exultet Rolls," scrolls containing the text chanted by the deacon at the Easter Vigil when the paschal candle is lit. Several of these scrolls contain representations of women in liturgical garb, painted upside down in relation to the words so that, as the deacon intones the proclamation and unrolls the scroll over the back of the lectern, the images are visible to the congregation. Because some of these manuscripts show women standing behind the altar on which the communion bread and wine are placed, with their arms held in the "orans" position, the stance of the priest during the opening words of the eucharistic prayer,[27] they have provided fodder for arguments in favor of women's ordination or liturgical presidency in the early centuries. Other scholars, however, contend that the women in these manuscripts represent the church, the pure and holy Body of Christ, and are not intended to depict actual liturgical activities.[28] Most of these manuscripts exist only in fragments, and almost no supporting interpretive material is available to us; we are left to speculate not only about the degree to which they are representative of women's

---

26. For hesitancy in using painting and iconography in the West as evidence for female piety, see Caroline W. Bynum, *Jesus as Mother: Studies in the Spirituality of the High Middle Ages* (Berkeley: University of California Press, 1982), 172–73.

27. See, for an example of this image, Myrtilla Avery, *Exultet Rolls of South Italy* (Princeton, N.J.: Princeton University Press, 1986), pl. 64. In other cases she sits on a structure that doubles as both a church building and an altar, with candlesticks ranged on either side of her.

28. See Jo Spreadbury, "The Gender of the Church: The Female Image of Ecclesia in the Middle Ages," in *Gender and Christian Religion*, ed. R. W. Swanson (Cambridge: Boydell, 1998), 97.

actual liturgical roles, but about the meaning they may have held for women in the assembly.

The architectural setting of Christian worship can also be "read" for information about women's worship participation. In some cases, the church building provides the most tangible evidence of women's liturgical lives, allowing us to encounter there the gifts they have provided for the adornment of the environment for worship, the memorials to loved ones they have had erected, and the epitaphs that have marked their own final resting places. In addition, the church building can be a spark for the historical imagination. To stand in a worship setting and imagine the women who, Sunday in and Sunday out, came to participate in the ongoing round of corporate and devotional prayer can give us a palpable sense of their existence as independent actors in the historical narrative.

Often the information collected from the building needs to be integrated with information gathered from other sources about women's worship lives. If, for example, a parish history has told us that women in a particular period occupied a certain group of pews during the Sunday service, the building can tell us what they might have seen and heard from their seats. If a woman reports in her private diary that she intends to donate a stained glass window to the congregation, the window itself can speak eloquently of her religious sensibilities at the time. As we shall see,[29] the area around the building has also served as a liturgical space at various times, so when a woman writes in her autobiography of arriving at the church door bearing the lifeless body of her newborn baby boy, only to be told that she must get her neighbors to dig a grave for him far away from the consecrated ground around the church because he has died unbaptized, a walk along the path that runs away from the comfort and safety of the churchyard can give a very real sense of the utter desolation she would have felt.

To read the experience of women at worship in any given period from architectural evidence is not always easy, however. Like most elements of the built environment, churches change over time, responding to changes in taste, function, economics, and ideology. For some periods of Christian history only a very few buildings survive. What we see today in the church buildings that do survive is usually the result of a multiplicity of small, cumulative alterations; to provide a lively sense of their previous incarnations is the life work of architectural historians and archeologists. Church buildings do have important stories to tell about the liturgical lives of the women who worshiped within their walls, but often these stories are fragmentary and ambiguous.

---

29. See chap. 2.

Despite these kinds of difficulties, the material residue of women's liturgical lives must be taken into account as we try to amass our body of evidence. Perhaps one day the material reconstruction of liturgical history will be a significant study all its own, best done as a collaboration between art and architectural historians, theologians, and liturgists. Working together, they will begin to develop both a methodology and a comprehensive "material history" of women at worship. In these pages, however, the approach is to be provisional and slightly tentative about the use of material evidence, and to rely on those who have begun the process of making sense of women's worship lives through the medium of material artifacts.

The View from a Distance

Although it would be intriguing to attempt to reconstruct the history of women at worship using only what women say about themselves — their journals and diaries, their public writings, their testimony in court, and the things that they have made and used — this strategy would surely run the risk of missing certain important kinds of data. For this reason, more traditional, historiographic materials are cited when necessary, although they are always used with caution and play a secondary role to the types of first-person resources discussed above.

The more traditional sources we will be using are of diverse types: inventories and statistics,[30] canonical legislation and the minutes of ecumenical gatherings, official and quasi-official rites. Some (liturgical texts, for example) are prescriptive; others (such as parish registers) are descriptive. What they all have in common is that they are almost universally institutional documents, written for institutional purposes, usually by men to meet the aims that men have defined for themselves and others. Of course, this characteristic does not make them necessarily inaccurate or insignificant. It simply means that they are viewing the place of women in Christian worship from a distance, through a lens that tends to deflect the gaze from women's worship participation.

Finding Women in the Worship Life of the Congregation

Although we meet many women in these pages who had deep and wide influence over the macrohistory of Christian common prayer, for the most part, the primary arena for women's participation in Christian worship has been the local church.

---

30. Statistical work is always difficult when it comes to women, because in most periods it was fairly usual to count men or perhaps male heads of household when quantifying communicants at any given time. Anne Whiteman, ed., *The Compton Census of 1676: A Critical Edition* (Oxford: Oxford University Press, 1986), xxxiv–xxxvi.

(Indeed, in almost every period, women outnumber men as churchgoers by statistically significant margins; see fig. 4.)[31] The principal raison d'être of the local church has been to ensure the adequate and appropriate celebration of public worship and the proper administration of the sacraments; but from the very beginning other kinds of functions began to cluster around the parish-as-institution: social welfare, civil administration (including taxation), and community life.[32] This constellation of purposes has generally placed the parish at the center of not only the religious, but also the political, cultural, and social lives of individuals and groups. Thus, documents related to the history of congregational life can provide a sense of the liturgy's wider interpretive context and, in addition, can often reveal the various facets of that participation in intimate detail.

Local church histories as we know them began to appear in Northern Europe in the seventeenth century, and in North America about fifty years after the settlement of any particular place. In many cases these documents not only contain small insights into the place of women in the worship life of congregations, but also tell the larger stories of the role women have played in moving local churches from one liturgical situation to another. Often we find evidence in the pages of the parish history that the very existence of a given church depended upon the deep commitment of women to perpetuate Christian common prayer in the places where they lived. The history of First Baptist Church, Holly Springs, Mississippi, is uncommon only in its straightforwardness on this matter. Describing the period

---

31. To cite just two examples from the nineteenth century: in English Methodism, a reconstruction of membership rolls shows 55 percent women in rural communities and moving toward 75 percent in urban communities, and in America in the first quarter of the nineteenth century, a persistent majority of between 60 percent and 70 percent. The statistical evidence is summarized in M. M. Dunn and G. Ryan Moran in Janet Wilson James, ed., *Women in American Religion* (Philadelphia: University of Philadelphia Press, 1980), and in Richard Shiels, "The Feminization of American Congregationalism, 1730–1835," *American Quarterly* 33 (1981): 46–62. Also, having looked at the evidence for churchgoing by nineteenth-century Episcopalians, Richard Rankin, *Ambivalent Churchmen and Evangelical Churchwomen: The Religion of the Episcopal Elite in North Carolina, 1800–1860* (Columbia: University of South Carolina Press, 1993), 53, states that "Women made up the overwhelming majority of Episcopal communicants throughout the ante-bellum era." In nine Episcopal parishes recorded in North Carolina, new female communicants outnumbered male communicants by 3:1 between January 1, 1855, and December 31, 1859 (268 women to 92 men) (cited in Rankin, *Ambivalent Churchmen and Evangelical Churchwomen*, 169). The ratio for all communicants in four churches was nearly 5:1.

32. As one recent history of the development of the pre-Reformation English parish notes: "Poor relief, religious worship, neighborhood and village celebrations, the collection of taxes, and a myriad of cultural interactions and negotiations were all organized and conducted within this fundamental unit." The word "parish" refers to a geographical unit centered on a local church and presided over by clergy who are appointed for service to that church. Although this description is being applied to the situation in England in the period between 1400 and 1600, it clearly has wider application, and until the rise of the Free Churches in the early modern periods, most social contexts in the West "simply cannot be understood without taking the parish into account." "Introduction," in *Parish in English Life, 1400–1600*, ed. Katherine L. French, Gary Gibbs, and Beat A. Kümin (Manchester: Manchester University Press, 1997), 3.

just after the Civil War, when successive waves of yellow fever washed over the town, decimating the population, the history reports:

> These times tried the souls of the faithful and only seven God loving women took up the burden of holding the church together for the sake of the Lord. . . . They met, prayed, and wept, trusting the Lord to keep His promise of "two or three gathered together in His name." They met almost daily, praying and working in every way. . . . It is because of this band of saintly women, who were so consecrated and worked so valiantly to perpetuate the struggle of holding the church together, that our church is here today.[33]

Other parish histories give details of the material gifts and financial contributions women have made to churches,[34] of the role of women in the selection of clergy and the preparation of the building for worship,[35] and of the debates surrounding women's leadership. Often, and in some cases more importantly, we glean from the parish history a sense of the more general "texture" of the experience of worship for women: seating patterns, dress restrictions, disciplinary proceedings.[36]

Again, however, a number of difficulties attend the use of local histories as a source of information for the worship lives of women. These documents are not always readily accessible given that most have been published privately in very limited editions; they tend to be uneven in their scholarly quality, and facts are often undocumented and difficult to authenticate independently. In addition, the extent to which one can generalize about the place of women more widely from the particular situations described within the pages of a local history is always uncertain. But they do often provide the kind of intimate detail unavailable in many more "formal" source materials, and regularly give a genuine warmth of feeling about congregational life that adds immeasurably to the story being told.

The more "official" documents arising out of the institutional life of the local church, recorded by those who have authority over that church, can provide further evidence of the liturgical lives of women. These documents are of various types, depending upon the way churches are organized. Parish registers are the most common, recording those human events over which the church has lawful jurisdiction: baptisms, marriages, and burials.[37] From these registers we can

---

33. "A History of First Baptist Church, Holly Springs," *South Reporter*, April 24, 1986, 14, col. 2.
34. See pp. 285–87.
35. See pp. 91 and 104.
36. See pp. 174–76, and appendix 3.
37. Often parish registers give more complete details than who was married, baptized, and buried when and by whom. One records the baptism of "chrisom children," but there is debate among

determine such things as whether women were pregnant at the time of their marriage, how many children died in infancy, and who served as witness to baptisms and marriages.[38] By detailing fees paid to "outside contractors" for goods and services for the church, ledgers kept by those appointed to oversee the financial affairs of the parish (initially called churchwardens and later treasurers) give a sense of matters as diverse as patterns of bell ringing, festivities associated with saints' days or homecomings, burial costs, and the appropriation of revised service books. Beginning in the seventeenth century, as the governance of some Christian churches started to become more democratic, we occasionally find the minutes kept by oversight committees — sometimes called vestries or parish councils. Women may appear in these records as initiators of and contributors to important discussions about the direction the church's worship should take, as providers of the necessary funds for renovation of the liturgical space and its furnishing, or as instigators of parish teaching programs on matters related to the community's common prayer.

Other kinds of secondary source material are mentioned in the pages that follow. Obituaries and biographies can often provide useful information about the patterns of worship a given woman followed, and her attitudes and motivations toward the church's liturgical life. Statistical work can increase our sense of the wider social and demographic context that women worshipers inhabited. Population shifts resulting from climate change, warfare, and disease, as well as changes in the balance between the proportion of men and women, can be compared to patterns of women's influence in matters related to worship.[39] Gender divisions in churchgoing can be determined by reconstructing membership rolls.

---

historians about what kind of children this term denotes. "Clearly such children took their name from the white 'chrisom cloth' in which they were wrapped during the ceremony, and ultimately from the chrism oil used to anoint them. What is unclear is whether they were infants dying before baptism, or between baptism and their mother's churching, when the cloth was returned to the church." Will Coster, "Popular Religion and the Parish Register, 1538–1603," in *Parish in English Life, 1400–1600,* ed. Katherine L. French, Gary Gibbs, and Beat A. Kümin (Manchester: Manchester University Press, 1997), 104.

38. We begin to find parish registers in the twelfth century, but they were irregularly kept and there are large gaps in the record. In England, an act of 1538 ordered the recording of all baptisms, marriages, and burials. They were generally listed on loose sheets of paper until an act of 1597 which stipulated that in the future the registers should be bound and that only the minister and the churchwardens be allowed to make entries. These registers can be called upon as legal evidence, and genealogists have found them invaluable for tracing family ties.

39. So, for example, when we read that between 1250 and 1500 the population of Europe decreased by about one-third, with successive wars leaving more unmarried women (although death in childbirth probably evened things out), women were more necessary to the work force, and hence had more authority in both churches and homes. Records survive of a large number of women landholders, both widows and single women. R. Hilton, *The English Peasantry in the Later Middle Ages* (Oxford: Oxford University Press, 1975).

Finding Women in Traditional Liturgical Sources

For most of Christian history, the ongoing pattern of the church's liturgy was the framework within which women's religious devotion was expressed. Women may indeed have periodically pursued a radical, even anarchic, path with regard to their participation in worship, but even this was rarely undertaken without reference to the baselines of the church's liturgical life. Prayers learned in church punctuate women's diaries and advice books, liturgical symbolism infiltrates their mystical visions, and rites and gestures practiced in the pew and at the altar find their way into the kitchen and bedchamber. Although the traditional historiographical sources (official rites, learned commentaries, and canonical legislation, for example) rarely mention women directly — which is, of course, why traditional liturgical histories almost never mention women — we cannot ignore them without distorting the picture of women's worship lives.

But very real problems emerge when attempting to trace the worship lives of women in and through these kinds of documents. Written or compiled largely by those with influence over institutional life, and as a part of the exercise of that influence, official rites and texts rarely lead us directly toward an understanding of the grass roots of liturgical experience, and as often as not they lead us away from it. Did the laity actually say the words appointed for them to say in the baptismal rite? If so, did the laity give to the words the interpretation intended by theologians, liturgists, and clergy? Was a particular bit of eucharistic legislation written in Rome fully enacted in Slovenia or Wales, or was it adapted or overridden by culture, convention, and custom? Were learned treatises on the nature of the penitential rites read by people in the pews? Traditional historians of Christian worship write as if the answers to all of these questions are unequivocal yeses. But even the most superficial examination of the kinds of sources we have described in the first part of this chapter reveals that this conclusion is mistaken. (Indeed, ask yourself about the degree to which the "official" theological, liturgical, and canonical positions of your own denomination is absorbed by the ordinary person in the pew.) It seems that often the best we can say about official rites, canons, and learned commentaries on the liturgy is that they are maps of the liturgical landscape; they should never be confused with the landscape itself.

Is there a way to approach these documents that can maximize their usefulness to us? In some cases, we may need to concentrate not on what these sources say, but rather on what they do not say. For example, rubrics, canonical statutes, and treatises on the practice and purpose of Christian worship contain a variety of injunctions aimed at restricting women's liturgical role and status. We could take these at face value, as evidence of the limitations under which women were placed in a given community, or we could look for the shadow underneath the prohibition, recognizing that there is rarely a need to prohibit something unless it is actually being done. Sometimes the motive for the prohibition is spelled out clearly, as in the case of one of the famous ecclesiastical degrees of Gratian (twelfth century) in which he states that "Some priests have so little regard for the divine mysteries that they entrust the holy of holies to lay people and women who are prohibited from entering the sacrarium and approaching the altar."[40] Often, other kinds of evidence attest to the persistence of a practice that has been officially banned. In the early seventh century, for example, the wearing of amulets was forbidden by St. Eligius when he arrived in Germany, but the presence of amulets in the graves of Frankish Christian women attests to their continuing popularity during the several hundred years following the decree. It seems indisputable that throughout the history of Christianity, some women have consistently refused, in the words of ecumenist Pauline Webb, "to become simply a solid, static base, supporting pyramids of male hierarchy,"[41] and have actively resisted any legislation that limits the full expression of their religious aspirations.

The reader should not presume, though, that all traditional liturgiological sources are intrinsically misleading. Some seem to give quite straightforward descriptions of women's modes of participation in Christian worship.[42] The fifth-century church order called the *Didascalia*, for example, speaks reasonably clearly of the tasks assigned to women deacons, who are listed with bishops and presbyters as a part of the church's hierarchy. These deacons are to stand at the door of the church and regulate who is admitted, to go to women in the community to teach and pray, and to anoint women with oil at baptism.[43] Should we ignore this information simply because it comes in an "institutional" package? Surely not. But we must not be tempted to think that we have a full picture of the role of women in the early Syrian church, nor even of the role of women deacons.[44]

---

40. Gratian, *Decretum* (*Treatise on Laws*), 1–20, trans. A. Thompson (Washington, D.C.: Catholic University Press, 1993), 72. A further example comes from a letter of Gelasius to the bishops in southern Italy: "Women are performing services at the holy altar, doing what has been ascribed to the ministry of men alone" (Letters 14 and 21). Another letter to three bishops in northern Gaul in the sixth century issued a warning to Breton priests who were traveling with women assistants "who raised the chalice containing the blood of Christ in the manner of the Pepudian sect."

41. Pauline Webb, *She Flies Beyond: Memories and Hopes of Women in the Ecumenical Movement* (Geneva: WCC, 1993), 12.

42. And of course it must be recognized that some of these kinds of documents are written by women themselves: revival leaders, abbesses, preachers, sect leaders. But even these partake of the "institutional" character of official documents and must be treated in the same class as those written by men.

43. R. H. Connolly, *Didascalia Apostolorum: The Syriac Version, Translated and Accompanied by the Verona Latin Fragments* (Oxford: Oxford University Press, 1929).

44. See, on the interpretation of early rites, Paul Bradshaw, *The Search for the Origins of Christian Worship* (Oxford: Oxford University Press, 1993).

Challenging the Dichotomies

One by-product of taking women's experience seriously in reconstructing the history of worship is that many of the dichotomies which traditionally have been used to define and describe the church's liturgical life begin to break down. The first to be dismantled is the distinction made between "official" and "popular" ritual practice. For most of Christian history, women have interpreted and participated in both institutionally sanctioned forms of worship (Sunday services, baptism, marriage rites) and popular liturgical celebrations (household prayers, street processions, shivaree), with equal devotion and intensity, finding redeeming grace within a wide range of practices with very little regard to their relative degrees of canonical authority. Although we generally find some priority given to the importance of the sacramental life, the various unofficial ritual accompaniments to the rites have tended to form a seamless whole with the official ceremonial.

Because of this blurring of the traditional boundaries of ritual practice, the second dichotomy that is invalidated by the evidence gathered about women's liturgical lives is the sharp distinction between religious ceremonial that takes place "inside the church building" and that which takes place "outside the church building." As we shall see,[45] throughout Christian history much of women's liturgical practice has taken place in contexts not traditionally defined as "liturgical spaces": in kitchens and bedrooms, roadways and pilgrimage places, and churchyards.[46] Although women have clearly felt at home in churches, these alternative, more egalitarian contexts often give women enormous freedom to organize and direct their own liturgical lives, and to participate creatively in religious ritual-making.

The sharp demarcation we tend to make between the home and its environs ("private space") and the workplace and its environs ("public space") does not have a long history, dating only from the mid-nineteenth century in the West, and may not be useful in our understanding of the ways in which women have organized their liturgical experience. Surely what Mary Claire Martin argues for the period from 1740 to 1870 in England and Karen E. Smith for a slightly later period in Baptist history is probably true of domestic space generally during most of the Christian past: as the setting for regular business transactions, open meetings for religious instruction and church administration, and various degrees

---

45. See chap. 2.

46. In sixteenth-century London, for example, "there was in every corner a cross set." Each one was adorned by local women with images, the virgin and child, Christ's resurrection, angels, and for each great occasion of public ceremonial in the city, the crosses were regilded. Susan Brigden, *London and the Reformation* (Oxford: Clarendon, 1989), 6–7.

of hospitality, a busy household becomes "a quasi-public space, more in the nature of a small office."[47] As we shall see, even a woman's bedroom was generally accessible to a quite wide range of people, even to those outside the immediate family, until the modern period.[48]

If the study of women's liturgical lives tends to smudge the sharp line between public and private liturgical space, it does the same to the sharp line between "public" and "private" prayer. Scholars of the liturgy have used various terms in making this distinction, opposing "liturgical" and "devotional" prayer, "communal" and "individual" piety. But these categories are rarely adequate to describe the complexities of women's religious experience; their diaries, journals, and autobiographies record that liturgical prayer was routinely the context for interior devotional activity while private prayers were consistently informed by participation in communal rites. In many periods most Christians, including women, participated in various forms of what historian Joel Rosenthal has called "an individualized form of institutional religion."[49]

More difficult, perhaps, is the usual distinction made between "magical" and "religious" ritual.[50] At many points, the ritual activities described in these pages look very much like magic: the concocting of charms and countercharms, the wearing of protective amulets, the discernment of signs and omens. As historian Joseph Goering reminds us:

> In recent years, we have become increasingly aware of other strata of religious experience besides the familiar sacraments and the sermon. These strata, less influenced by changes in doctrine or practice outside the local village, illustrate the strength and adaptability of traditional customs, and the continuity of village religious life with the distant, even pre-Christian past. There are, for example, a number of religious activities that we have ignored because they occur outside, or on the fringes, of official church institutions.[51]

But the problem of sources increases when considering these activities,

---

47. Mary Clare Martin, "Women and Philanthropy in Walthamstow and Leyton 1740–1870," *London Journal* 19 (1995): 119; Karen E. Smith, "Beyond Public and Private Spheres: Another Look at Women in Baptist History and Historiography," *Baptist Quarterly* 34, no. 2 (1991): 79–87.

48. See the description of Lady Culross's prayers at the Scottish Revivals of 1630, below p. 204.

49. Joel Rosenthal, *Nobles and the Noble Life, 1295–1500* (London: G. Allen & Unwin, 1976), 49. Of course this is very likely also true of laymen, but their liturgical experience has yet to be evaluated in this way.

50. See below, pp. 64–65 and 150–54.

51. Joseph W. Goering, "The Changing Face of the Village Parish II: The Thirteenth Century," in *Papers in Medieval Studies*, ed. J. A. Raftis (Toronto: Pontifical Institute of Medieval Studies, 1981), 2:324–25.

... since by their nature these kinds of things are handed on by oral tradition, by experience, rather than through texts. Some we have because they were, almost by accident, written down — priests putting field blessings in the margins of the missal, or in diaries or collections [for example].[52]

If we are willing to accept the blurring of the usual divisions made by historians of Christian worship, then it is likely that the distinction between "liturgical participation" and "liturgical leadership" also will be lost when attempting to describe women's involvement in worship. Although it has sometimes attended to the presence or absence of lay participation, traditional liturgical history has largely been concerned with what the "leaders" of worship say and do in any given rite, and with the meaning of these words and actions. But perhaps the clerical bias of this approach has set up definitions of leadership that do not hold up under close examination. For example, is the woman who stands beside her pew in the Sunday service to give her testimony of the workings of God in her life a "worship leader"? Not if a leader is defined as one who stands facing the congregation reciting the words contained in the officially sanctioned book. But if we were to define a leader as someone who sets the pace of the service, who regulates its temperature and establishes its direction, then the woman giving her testimony surely qualifies to carry that title.

Perhaps there are no sharp bipolarities that are helpful for the historical analysis of women's religious experience. Certainly this conclusion is the trend among those who are thinking seriously about the nature of historiography in general. While in the 1960s and 1970s, for example, historians of women's experience commonly enforced the rigid distinction between men's definition of women and women's roles on the one hand, and women's own self-definitions on the other, more recently it has become clear that in order to understand fully the situation of women in any given time and place, both of these need to be taken into account. Similarly, the model of "elite" versus "popular" culture (originally developed by Peter Burke[53]) has come under recent criticism for failing to do justice to the infinite gradations of society that can be discovered at any historical moment, and for ignoring the large number of interpretations, values, and meanings that are shared over a wide social spectrum. Surely this kind of critique can help us appreciate that meaning is made in many different social

---

52. Ibid.
53. See Peter Burke, *Popular Culture in Early Modern Europe* (London: Temple Smith, 1978, and New York, 1983), and Natalie Zeman Davis, "From 'Popular Religion' to 'Religious Cultures,'" in *Reformation Europe: A Guide to Research*, ed. S. Ozment (St. Louis: Center for Reformation Research, 1982), 321–46.

locations, which holds true as well for the meaning of liturgical symbols, texts, and rituals.[54]

The Parameters of Women's Liturgical History

It is increasingly acknowledged that nothing is more fatal to the study of history than the idea that human nature is constant and universal. Wilfred Cantwell Smith, the late, great historian of religions, was insistent that being a Christian is a different experience in different social and historical situations, and the same is true for being a woman. Neither "Christian" nor "woman" is a monolithic category or state of being. The meaning of "being a woman" (and for our purposes, a woman worshiper) differs according to the time and place in which she lives, the social and economic circumstances into which she is born, the wider religious and intellectual milieu within which she lives, and even her state of health.

Some of these variations in women's experience involve differences in the wider sociocultural arenas within which women have operated and differences in their relationship to existing institutions. For example, Frankish women had much higher status under law than their Roman or English sisters. After 800 C.E., the Frankish woman had some legal responsibility for both her husband's family and her father's; she could hold and administer land, defend herself in the courts, make donations on her own behalf, and free her slaves if she wished. The higher her social rank, the likelier that she would carry many other social responsibilities than the care of her immediate family. Indeed, the Frankish queen was, in law, an "honorary man."[55] But women under Roman and English law were much more likely to be regarded as the chattel of a husband or father.[56] Thus, an English or Italian woman's participation in worship was subject to different kinds of constraints than that of a Frankish woman of the same period, and the transgression of those constraints might therefore take different forms and have different sorts of social and economic implications.

The woman's role within her own domestic sphere has also changed over time. The modern romantic view of women as devoted mothers, as their husband's helpmeet and companion, and as the managers of the privatized home was only

---

54. See Martin J. Ingram, "From Reformation to Toleration: Popular Religious Cultures in England, 1540–1690," in *Popular Culture in England, c. 1500–1850*, ed. Tim Harris (New York: St. Martin's, 1994), 95–123.

55. Celtic woman had similar legal authority.

56. See John Michael Wallace-Hadrill, *The Frankish Church* (Oxford: Oxford University Press, 1983), 404. The equality of women under Frankish custom can also be seen in the fact that in Roman law the dowry was what the woman brought to the marriage; in Frankish law it was what the husband brought.

gradually developed between 1700 and 1850.[57] As feminist historian Catherine Hall observes, "the pre-industrial family was a self-sufficient economic unit and consequently domestic work had a much wider definition than it does now."[58] For most of Christian history the household was the center of a number of different kinds of activities — commercial, domestic, and religious — and therefore women who may be described as "housewives" in the historical record had real responsibility not only for family nurture, but for a multiplicity of economic and devotional decisions as well.

Differences in social status also determined what roles and occupations women might appropriately undertake. Hall reminds us that every society has rules about which activities are suitable for which sex, but also that these rules are not constant; the sexual division of labor is not a rigid division. "The activities of men and women are always patterned," she says, "and the patterning always reveals relations of domination and subordination in relation to the major productive spheres."[59] For example, relatively few trades in feudal society were forbidden to women, and the labor of poor women was absolutely vital to the survival of the household. But the activities of aristocratic women were much more rigidly circumscribed. Wealthy women were simply not economic necessities in the same way that poor women were, except when it came to their marriageability. Although we may have more extant evidence about the lives of aristocratic women, this evidence may not be a fair representation of the fullest range of women's activities; their less influential sisters likely had more freedom, if not the privilege and power.[60]

Was there ever an "ideal" time to be a woman, a time when her religious, social, and economic options enhanced the probability that she would be able to fulfill her deepest needs and desires, whatever her social and economic standing? Some historians argue for a brief Golden Age for women of all social ranks in the fourteenth century, when the aftermath of the Plague created a new range of opportunities. Others maintain that the advent of Protestantism, when women's role as helpmate was elevated to the status of a vocation, marked the high point of women's autonomy. But ambiguities persist; as one historian of the Reformation

---

57. Anthony Fletcher characterizes this shift as "the gradual internalization of social roles as inherent personality traits." See his "Beyond the Church: Women's Spiritual Experience at Home and in the Community, 1600–1900," in *Gender and Christian Religion*, Studies in Church History 34, ed. R. N. Swanson (Woodbridge, U.K.: Boydell, 1998), 189.

58. Catherine Hall, *White, Male, and Middle-Class: Explorations in Feminism and History* (New York: Routledge, 1992), 44.

59. Ibid., 43.

60. Of course, as the professionalization of work increased, there was an increase in male dominance of economic production. See Alice Clark, *The Working Life of Women in the Seventeenth Century* (New York: A. M. Kellogg, 1968).

period argues, "the subversive potential in these reforms led to an Act of 1543 prohibiting Bible reading by women, apprentices, servants, and others of low degree, leaving in doubt the 'liberalizing' impulses of reform."[61] However we evaluate this conflicting evidence, it is true that the decisions women have made about their lives can only be fully understood by taking into account the time, place, and sociocultural situation in which they find themselves, which includes their decisions about their various modes of participation in Christian worship.

Given what we have said about the fluidity of women's experience, we are left with the vexing problem of the most accurate way to divide the various epochs of women's liturgical history. The reader will notice that, like most histories of worship, the standard methods of periodization are used in these pages, with distinctions made between early (to c. 700), medieval (sometimes subdivided into early and late medieval, c. 700–1250 and c. 1250–1500, respectively), Reformation (c. 1500–1650), early modern (c. 1650–1900), and modern (c. 1900 to the present) periods of ecclesiastical history.[62] This approach is difficult to avoid, because these categories are used in most of the secondary sources on which this study has relied. But many scholars have begun to question whether this typical division applies to women's history in general, and by extension, to women's liturgical history. Joan Kelly-Gadol, for example, argues that while women may have had a renaissance they did not have it during "The Renaissance," as traditionally defined by historians. Indeed, "The Renaissance" represented a period of the restriction of women's scope and power.[63] So while we continue to use the traditional categories, we do it with the understanding that the material we uncover in the course of this study may ultimately result in undermining them, as we see the various ways in which the defining characteristics of each period fail to describe women's experience accurately.

The Persistent Elusiveness of Women

Even though we have become sensitive to the elusiveness of women in the historical record, and have settled on the strategies best suited to locating them,

---

61. Claire S. Schen, "Women and the London Parishes, 1500–1620," in *The Parish in English Life, 1400–1600*, ed. Katherine L. French, Gary Gibbs, Beat A. Kümin (Manchester: Manchester University Press, 1997), 251.

62. Different historians use different dates to demarcate these periods, and many subdivide the individual periods for further specificity.

63. Joan Kelly-Gadol, "The Social Relation of the Sexes: Methodological Implications for Women's History," *Signs* 1 (1976): 810–22; and her "Did Women Have a Renaissance?" in *Becoming Visible*, ed. Renate Bridenthal and Claudia Koonz (Boston: Houghton Mifflin, 1977), 139–64; and "Notes on Women in the Renaissance and Renaissance Historiography," in *Conceptual Frameworks for Studying Women's History*, ed. Marilyn Arthur et al. (Bronxville, N.Y.: Sarah Lawrence College, 1975).

some difficulties remain. One is the temptation of, as one historian says, "revert-ing to over-reliance on notable or notorious women at the expense of their more ordinary and typical sisters."[64] Certainly many historians of women's religious ex-perience have yielded to this temptation, producing very important studies on, for example, women Gnostics,[65] Waldensians, Lollards,[66] Ranters,[67] and Shakers.[68] There is good reason for this, of course. Because such movements emphasized the priority (and urgency) of seeking God's will over the compliance with existing ec-clesiastical norms and jurisdictions, they were particularly attractive to women and often gave them enormous scope for active involvement and, in many cases, leadership. It would be fairly straightforward to follow the example of the schol-ars of sectarianism and to write the history of women's participation in Christian worship as simply the history of these more radicalized women. But if we fail to include less exceptional women within the frame, would we be drawing an accurate picture of the history of women's worship lives?

The problem of the historical obscurity of most ordinary women is not an easy one to overcome. In many periods, even aristocratic women remain anonymous; wives, sisters, and daughters are all too often remembered only by reference to their male relatives, as we saw in the epitaph of Maria Dudley above. But even

---

64. Amanda Vickery, "Golden Age to Separate Spheres? A Review of the Categories and Chro-nology of English Women's History," *Historical Journal* 36 (1993), 383. "Historians are now sensitive to the elusiveness of women within the political record, the strategies needed to locate them, and the dangers of reverting to over-reliance on notable or notorious women at the expense of their more ordi-nary and typical sisters." Historians of all periods of women's history make this point. In her afterword to B. M. Kienzle and P. J. Walker, *Women Preachers and Prophets through Two Millennia of Christian-ity* (Berkeley: University of California Press, 1998), 340, Karen L. King claims that the connection between women and religious dissent has been overemphasized by church historians. Claire Cross, writing about the religious ferment that precipitated the English Civil War, makes a similar point, arguing that the historical record has become distorted by attending to women in radical movements, obscuring the importance of "more sober protestant matrons" (Claire Cross, "'He-Goats before the Flocks': A Note about the Part Played by Women in the Founding of Some Civil War Churches," in *Popular Belief and Practice*, ed. G. J. Cuming and Derek Baker, Studies in Church History 8 [Cam-bridge: Cambridge University Press, 1972], 195). For the early period of Christian history see also Paul McKechnie, "Women's Religion and Second Century Christianity," *Journal of Ecclesiastical History* 47, no. 3 (July 1966): 409.

65. See Elaine Pagels, *The Gnostic Gospels* (New York: Random House, 1979). Paul McKechnie, "Women's Religion and Second Century Christianity," is particularly puzzled by the degree to which the Gnostic tradition is attractive to feminist scholars when so many Gnostic texts are antipathetic to women. He cites especially the *Gnostic Dialogue of the Saviour*, in which Jesus admonishes his followers to "Pray in the place where there is no woman."

66. See Margaret Aston, *Faith and Fire: Popular and Unpopular Religion, 1350–1600* (London: Hambledon, 1993).

67. See J. C. Davies, "Fear, Myth, and Furor: Reappraising the Ranters," *Past and Present* 129 (1990): 160–69; see also Jerome Friedman, *Blasphemy, Immortality, and Anarchy: The Ranters and the English Reformation* (Athens: Ohio University Press, 1987).

68. See Marjorie Procter-Smith, *Women in Shaker Community and Worship* (Lewiston, N.Y.: Edward Mellen Press, 1985).

then, the wealthy retain some degree of individual identity as actors in the historical drama. If a medieval noblewoman donated a length of cloth to her parish church, for example, it would be identified and recorded according to its value and the kind and amount of ornament it contained; because it could be thus identified, it would be properly listed as a donation and the woman's name would be recorded in the list of those to be included in the church's intercessory prayer. But her poorer sister would very often leave only the cheapest sort of cloth, with no embroidery or other means of distinguishing it. Therefore, it would not ordinarily appear on the bede-roll of a church, rendering the contribution of this ordinary woman benefactor historically invisible. She, too, becomes invisible. Only those who actually knew the woman and could identify the particular cloth as having belonged to her would know the donor's identity.[69]

The actual influence of women is disguised in other ways, often even by women themselves. Identifying women preachers and worship leaders, for example, is made more difficult because so many women were unwilling to describe their exercise of their calling to proclaim the Word of God as "preaching" and the services they organized as "worship." The early Methodist women preachers Mary Fletcher (1739–1815) and Phoebe Palmer (1807–74) are cases in point. When Mary Bosanquet married John Fletcher in 1781 "she had already been preaching for several years, though she usually called it 'speaking.'"[70] Phoebe Palmer also insisted that she was not preaching, but only "talking," and not conducting services but "holding meetings."[71]

Women have also tended to diminish or dismiss the importance of those liturgical actions performed by other women. In her description of worship of the Fire Baptized Assemblies of God Church, an African American congregation in the Chicago area, Brenda Eatman Aghahowa distinguishes men's and women's roles, saying that, "women worship assistants handle *minor* tasks at the altar, like draping cloths over women who fall under the power of the Spirit. But they do not serve communion or take up the offering."[72] In the Renaissance and Tudor periods, men were often given credit for writing that women produced, and the rightful author rarely challenged the error. Italian philosopher Laura Cereta (1469–99), for example, was positively pleased when her work was attributed to her father,

69. See Judy Ann Ford, "Art and Identity in the Parish Communities of Late-Medieval Kent," in *The Church and the Arts*, ed. Diana Wood (Oxford: Basil Blackwell, 1992), 236.

70. Earl Kent Brown, *Women of Mr. Wesley's Methodism* (New York and Toronto: Edwin Mellen Press, 1983), 150.

71. The psychosocial reasons for this are complex, and feminist scholars use this evidence in attempts to untangle the dynamics of male power and female submission. But that is not our purpose here.

72. Brenda Eatman Aghahowa, *Praising in Black and White* (Cleveland: United Church Press, 1996), 123. Emphasis added.

because such attribution was indisputable evidence of its quality. When Sir John Harrington declared Mary Sydney's (1561–1621) *Psalmes* to be the work of her chaplain because, as he said, "it is more than a woman's skill to express the sense so right as she hath done in her verse,"[73] she never publicly disputed this mis-attribution. Some women did defend their own authorship, however. Marie de France was so conscious of this tendency to deprive a woman of her own work that the epilogue to her *Fables* reads:

> Marie is my name,
> I am from France,
> It may be that many clerks
>   will take my labor on themselves —
> I do not want any of them to claim it.[74]

One can see that there indeed may be fairly large numbers of writings important for reconstructing the history of women's participation in and influence on Christian worship that have yet to be credited to their proper authors. Unfortunately, many works by women will very probably never be uncovered.

Fortunately, during the past century or so, ordinary women have become much more historically visible; as the mass media began to report everyday events in women's lives, oral histories began to be recorded,[75] and artifacts of daily life gathered and preserved by individuals and institutions alike. Because we are increasingly attentive to the necessity of including the testimony of ordinary women to the processes of history, we have begun to search more actively for the footprints they leave. In assembling our data, we are increasingly mindful of the inherent bias in the evidence toward both the unconventional and the privileged, and we recognize the infinite variety of concrete female circumstances that lie between the milking stool and the throne. As a result, the historical elusiveness of women is beginning to be overcome.

In the months following September 11, 2001, the *New York Times* published daily a series of "Portraits of Grief," minieulogies gathered from the family and friends of each of the victims of the World Trade Towers' collapse. The portrait of Robert Andrew Spencer, a securities broker at Cantor Fitzgerald, appeared exactly four months after the day of his death and poignantly described his love for his wife Christine, for their two young daughters and newborn baby boy, and

---

73. Quoted by Margaret Hannay, "Introduction," in *Silent but for the Word: Tudor Women as Patrons, Translators, and Writers of Religious Works*, ed. Margaret Hannay (Kent, Ohio: Kent State University Press, 1995), 4.

74. Ibid.

75. These include those recorded by the Works Progress Administration in the 1930s and interviews of the women of the Grange four decades later.

for the life they shared. But in a single paragraph at the end of the tribute to her husband, we discover Christine Spencer not simply as a grieving widow, but as an actor in the narrative of liturgical history in her own right:

> In what she called a celebration of life, Mrs. Spencer decided to have the baby's baptism and her husband's memorial service on the same day.[76]

With this simple decision, Christine Spencer joins twenty centuries of Christian women who have taken responsibility for shaping their own liturgical lives and the liturgical lives of others. Most of these women are anonymous, and even in the pages that follow, many remain unnamed. But their small decisions about the baptisms of their babies and the burials of their husbands are as much a part of the history of Christian worship as the story of the decisions of theologians and popes and ecumenical councils. This book attempts to tell these women's story.

---

76. *New York Times*, January 11, 2002, 15, col. 2–3.

CHAPTER TWO

THE PLACES OF WOMEN'S WORSHIP

Is there a pulpit needed? Down goes the top and here is the car for a pulpit. Is there a stand needed? The windshield opens to hold Bible and song book. An altar needed where the penitent may weep his way to Calvary? The running board does good service, ever ready to receive the copious tears of seeker and worker as they kneel together.

—Aimee Semple McPherson describing her "Pentecostal Gospel Car"

The Fluidity of Women's Worship Space

In the previous chapter we saw that traditional surveys of liturgical history have usually confined their attention to what occurs within the four walls of the church building, but that this approach may not adequately describe women's worship experience. Certainly women have worshiped in church, and much of the material in the chapters that follow relates to this more formal definition of liturgical practice. But there has also tended to be a fluidity about women's attitude toward worship spaces and a resistance to drawing sharp lines of demarcation between the ritual-making that they undertake in church and that which they undertake in other kinds of settings. Women's ritual words and actions have been highly portable, carried from location to location as they have sought to meet their religious needs; women have worshiped God in the parlor and the wayside shrine, the nave of the parish church and the cloister, the private chapel and the cemetery and the brush arbor. Like revivalist Aimee Semple McPherson quoted above, they have been masters of improvisation, adapting the spaces available to them for use as the settings for Christian worship.[1]

---

1. The "Pentecostal Gospel Car" was used by McPherson during the period of the First World War instead of a tent because the tentmakers had been commandeered for government work. Aimee Semple McPherson, *This and That* (New York: Garland, 1985 [1919]), 178.

39

The boundary between church and home is perhaps the most difficult one to draw in the case of women's worship history. From the New Testament period onward, communities of Christians met in the houses of influential women: Chloe,[2] Lydia,[3] the unnamed mother of Mark,[4] Nympha,[5] Priscilla.[6] Women recited daily liturgical prayer in the home, and instructed children and servants in the intricacies of the Christian liturgy. Later, they established and furnished private chapels in their houses and they employed clergy to serve the various liturgical needs of the household. In their domestic kitchens, sectarian women hosted clandestine meetings, Catholic women prepared feasts and enforced fasts according to the liturgical calendar, and Orthodox women baked communion bread. At one time or another, the Christian home has been the setting for the baptism of babies, the betrothal of young couples, the anointing of the sick, the laying out of the dead.

But other worship settings in addition to the home have been important to women, and the boundaries between the ritual activity that takes place in these settings and that which takes place in the church have also been less than well-defined. Indeed, in the lives of many women the liturgical "axis" can shift from one location to another depending on her life circumstances. For the newly professed nun, the convent or hermitage may become the hub of her devotional world; for the pioneer woman, the revival tent may supplant the church as the most meaningful worship setting; for the rural peasant, the center of devotional gravity may be the shrine within which the relics of her patron saint are housed; for the African American slave, the brush arbor may allow a fuller degree of prayerful integrity than the master's Presbyterian church. As we shall see, the evidence suggests that women have historically resisted attempts by others to define and limit the places where God could be met. Indeed, perhaps because of such restrictions, women have sought alternative worship settings outside the church.

The Church Building

Having noted the exceptions, the church building has generally been the principal gathering place for the Christian community, and at Sunday services and other liturgical occasions women have been in church, and usually in larger numbers than men. Church attendance has played a significant role not only in women's

---

2. 1 Cor. 10:11.
3. Acts 16:14–15, 40.
4. Acts 12:12.
5. Col. 4:15.
6. Although the house is described as belonging to Priscilla and Aquilla, it is notable that the name of Priscilla comes first. Rom. 16:3; 1 Cor. 16:19; 1 Cor. 16:15–17.

religious lives, but in their social lives as well.[7] Attending church has offered women the opportunity, in the words of English church historian William M. Jacob, "both to make sense of their lives in relation to God in the context of the liturgy, and to identify themselves in relation to each other in the context of local society."[8] While this potent combination of the religious and the societal has been present in other settings in which women worship, the church building has been the predominant place where women's social and religious lives intertwined and have been expressed in public ritual.[9]

Women have claimed and occupied space in the church building in various ways (see fig. 5). Some parish churches actually belonged to women.[10] Historian Ulrich Stutz coined the term "Eigenkirche"[11] to refer to the church that a noble family builds on its lands as a private holding, which yields both profit to the family through tithes and other, more spiritual, benefits. Before the year 1000, most churches in England, France, and Germany could be described in this way, and many were owned by women. Early in the eighth century, for example, the German noblewoman Regimond and her daughter Vrederune established seven churches in different farms on the family territory.[12] Many other European parish churches began as private chapels in feudal households; others were built by feudal landholders at crossroads and served neighborhoods, and still others were

---

7. Partly as a result of this interpenetration of the religious and social, only rarely has regular attendance at church been required of women. Cases of required attendance include sectarian and communal groups such as the Amish and the Shakers; in the medieval and Reformation periods, the help given to the poor and orphaned by almshouses and charities was often conditional upon being in church for services.

8. William M. Jacob, *Lay People and Religion in the Early Eighteenth Century* (Cambridge: Cambridge University Press, 1996), 53.

9. Of course, until after the Reformation, the only powers of the parish were to gather the whole community at the compulsory Easter service and to oblige its members to pay tithes for the support of the church. Unlike the guild, the parish was not intended primarily for the mutual assistance of its members. Members of a parish might possibly act on some common interest and sympathy toward one another, but it was certainly neither expected nor required until fairly recently.

10. The term "parish" has had different meanings at different times. The Greek adjective *paroichos* meant something like the modern term "resident alien," a foreign resident in a Greek city; it was taken over by the Greek fathers to describe the church — resident in the temporal world but alien to it. It was Latinized to *parochia* and used synonymously with *diocese*. When Christianity spread north, the term was used the same way: Bede uses *parochia* to describe a diocese in the *Ecclesiastical History*, and Boniface carried the term to the continent. But in Gaul, *parochia* was a smaller ecclesiastical unit, and by the early ninth century, *parochia* had come almost everywhere to mean a rural or village church with resident clergy subject to the authority of a bishop. More recently, especially in North America, the term "parish" is synonymous with a local congregation.

11. Stutz first used this term in his inaugural lecture at the University of Basel, October 23, 1894. The lecture has been translated into English by Geoffrey Barraclough, *Medieval Germany* (Oxford: Oxford University Press, 1948), 2:35–70.

12. Later, in 792, a bishopric was established, and the canonesses who had served the churches founded by Regimond and her daughter were regularized at St. Mary's Überwasser, although they did not live in community nor take vows.

collectively owned by early craft guilds.[13] In the centuries that followed, even though almost everywhere parish churches became part of larger ecclesiastical institutions, we can find many occasions when women took it upon themselves to see that a conveniently located church building was provided to the community and staffed with competent clergy.

This self-appointing was particularly true of women during the period of westward expansion in the United States. Groups of African American women, for example, were responsible for building great numbers of churches in the South immediately after the Civil War. In describing a group of Methodist former slaves in Natchez, Mississippi, who raised the money to build their church, historian William Montgomery writes that: "It would not be an exaggeration to say that the securing of property, the construction of buildings, and the expansion and maintenance of these buildings were the direct result of the vital role that women played in the development of the church."[14] A similar story is told of the women of Memphis's Beale Street Baptist Church. In 1865 they organized the Baptist Sewing Society in order to raise money to erect a permanent church building:

> Their power as fundraisers was evident when within nine months they had raised more than $500, and within two years they had generated enough revenue to enable the congregation to pay off a $1000 mortgage on a building site and put away another $1000 in a savings account in the Freedmen's Savings and Trust Company.[15]

In the absence of a purpose-built church building, women have often been willing and able to improvise (see fig. 6). Gristmills, schoolhouses, stables, general stores, railroad depots, and even jails have served as the setting for Christian common prayer.[16] Kansas pioneer Cordelia McDowell reports in her diary that "Meetings were held wherever convenient, sometimes in a carpenter shop, with Mother Earth for a floor, and shavings and carpenter tools for ornaments."[17]

---

13. John Schofield, "Medieval Parish Churches in the City of London," in *Parish in English Life, 1400–1600,* ed. Katherine L. French, Gary Gibbs, and Beat A. Kümin (Manchester: Manchester University Press, 1997), 36.

14. William E. Montgomery, *Under Their Own Vine and Fig Tree: The African American Church in the South, 1865–1900* (Baton Rouge: Louisiana State University Press, 1993), 95.

15. Ibid., 95–96.

16. In Savannah, the fledgling Ezra Presbyterian Church held its first services in an old gristmill; in the town of Richmond, Lumkins Jail, "a notorious antebellum slave market," served as the setting for worship; "Bethel Church in Adel, Georgia, conducted its services in an abandoned railroad boxcar; a Baptist congregation in Austin, Texas, met in a barbershop and the Metropolitan AME Church there occupied a local opera house on Sundays," ibid. See also Joanna L. Stratton, *Pioneer Women: Voices from the Kansas Frontier* (New York: Simon and Schuster, 1981), 174–75.

17. Cited in Stratton, *Pioneer Women,* 175.

Over and over again frontier women record in their journals and memoirs their deep appreciation for these simple worship spaces. In early Hays, Kansas, a union of mixed denominations met for weekly worship in an old courthouse. There Catherine Cavender, the daughter of an army officer stationed at the fort nearby, attended her first service in the summer of 1877. "It was a simple, beautiful service," she explained,

> No gilded trappings, no blazing candles, sweet odor of flowers or tang of incense. Just the dusty old court room, but the presence of God was there with the few gathered together in His name. . . . Hays has many beautiful churches today and the people tread different paths to "meeting" now . . . [but] those old union meetings bound hearts together with bonds no religious dogma can sever.[18]

Some women carefully and passionately argued for the kind of simple worship spaces that others occupied by necessity. Often this self-conscious simplicity was part of a larger program of eschatological preparedness. Mother Ann Lee (1736–84), for example, founder of the United Society of Believers in Christ's Second Appearing (usually called the "Shakers") guided her followers in developing an airy and unadorned meetinghouse style that has served the Shaker community throughout the more than two hundred years of its history.[19] Some more radical women took this eschatological stance even further and advocated abandoning church buildings altogether. As Anna Trapnell (d. c. 1670), Fifth Monarchist prophet, proclaimed, "The Lord is building his Temple; it is no time now for them to build Tabernacles."[20]

Although the admiration for the simplicity of improvised worship spaces is heartfelt among many women, others have been deeply concerned with the ornamentation of the church interior. The roots of women's contributions to the furnishing and adornment of church buildings are probably too deep in the Christian past to uncover, but a few landmarks can be noted. As we shall see when we look at the question of women's benefaction and patronage,[21] from at least the fourth century in both East and West, in addition to building and endowing new churches, wealthy women gave important gifts of vestments, relics, altarware, and statues for the enhancement of the worship space. In England, legislation

---

18. Ibid.

19. Julie Nicoletta, *The Architecture of the Shakers* (Woodstock, Vt.: Countryman, 1995).

20. Anna Trapnell, *Cry of a Stone* (1654), cited in A. Gibbory, *Ceremony and Community from Herbert to Milton* (Cambridge: Cambridge University Press, 1998), 27.

21. See appendix 2.

enacted in the thirteenth century formally transferred the responsibility for the upkeep of the nave of each parish church to those who used it: the congregation. Later in the century, "parishioners were also assigned the responsibility for providing and maintaining the requisite complement of liturgical equipment within their church."[22] From then onward, there is hardly an extant parochial record that does not include women among the donors of items for the adornment of the worship environment. Sometimes women banded together to make donations for the furnishing and decorating of the church. At St. Mary's, Sandwich, England, in 1509–10, the largest single donation for the gilding of the rood loft was from a group referred to only as "the Wives," which gave eight shillings to the project.[23]

The adornment and upkeep of the parish church was also a source of paid employment for poor women. In England, for example, both before and after the Reformation, "menial tasks... — like washing linen, sweeping out the aisle or street, hanging up holly at Christmas, or even whipping dogs out of the church — gave suitably remunerated employment to a small army of parish poor, especially women."[24] Other churches paid women for washing and mending the "church clothes" and for making tapers and for "scouring."[25] In 1675, North Parish Church, North Andover, Massachusetts, employed Widow Rebekah Johnson as its sexton "for sweeping ye meeting house and ringnge ye bell" each night at nine o'clock, a position she held for eight years.[26] Women volunteers, however,

---

22. "The first of these obligations meant that congregations were obliged to raise and dispose of considerable sums of money; the second, that valuable utensils and equipment, if not donated, had to be purchased, kept and, as necessary, replaced by parishioners.... Simultaneously, in response to the obvious need for permanent — or at least permanently renewable — lay superintendents, churchwardens emerged to assume an increasingly responsible role in parish life." C. Drew, *Early Parochial Organization in England: The Origin of the Office of Churchwarden* (London: St. Anthony's Press, 1954), 76–77. See also Clive Burgess, "'A Fond Thing Vainly Invented': An Essay on Purgatory and Pious Motive in Later Medieval England," in *Parish Church and People: Local Studies in Lay Religion, 1350–1750,* ed. Susan. J. Wright (London: Hutchinson, 1988), 56–80. Burgess argues that "occasionally" women filled the office of churchwarden in this period, though he does not cite his evidence for this statement.

23. See Judy Ann Ford, "Art and Identity in the Parish Communities of Late-Medieval Kent," in *The Church and the Arts,* ed. Diana Wood, Studies in Church History 28 (Oxford: Basil Blackwell, 1992), 232.

24. Nick Alldredge, "Loyalty and Identity in Chester Parishes, 1540–1640," in *Parish Church and People: Local Studies in Lay Religion, 1350–1750,* ed. Susan. J. Wright (London: Hutchinson, 1988), 91.

25. Claire S. Schen, "Women and the London Parishes, 1500–1620," in *Parish in English Life, 1400–1600,* ed. Katherine L. French, Gary Gibbs, Beat A. Kümin (Manchester: Manchester University Press, 1997), 258–59.

26. "It was during her employment at North Parish that she would be accused of witchcraft, and jailed for 8 months, her good name and perhaps her life, saved only through the intervention of Andover's courageous elder minister, the Rev. Francis Dane." Juliet Haines Moffard, *And Firm Thine Ancient Vow: The History of North Parish Church of North Andover, 1645–1974* (North Andover, Mass.: Naiman, 1975), 24.

have been the most numerous and enduring group responsible for the adornment of the worship space. Women's "altar guilds," "sacristy teams," and "flower rotas" in the contemporary church care for the worship space in exactly the same way as generations of their sisters before them (see fig. 7).

Their motivations for the adornment of the worship space, however, have undergone some changes. For some women, the placing of flowers, herbs, and evergreen branches around the interior of the church building has been considered more a practical necessity than a decorative enhancement. The large assemblies of (frequently unwashed) parishioners, not to mention the occasional presence of animals and of decaying bodies under the floor, made the smell of early and medieval churches, for example, something of a problem. Expenditures for fresh straw to be placed on the floor and herbs around the church are regularly recorded in ledgers and churchwardens' account books of the period immediately before and after the English Reformation.[27]

For other women the proper adornment of the church interior was clearly seen as a stimulus to the spiritual regeneration of worshipers. The example of Margaret Hallahan, founder of the Third Order of Dominicans during the 1840s, is a case in point. In a letter to her sisters, she reveals her sense of the intimate link between doctrine and décor:

> We went yesterday to the Chapel at Stoke, and oh, my Sisters! I cannot tell you what I have felt since! A total want of all things! Our Lord and God in a *pewter* ciborium, gilt a little on the inside! and not one decent thing in the place. How can we expect the people to be converted? they have nothing to attract them; and how can they believe us when we instruct them in the Real Presence? They may well doubt the faith of Catholics — the Lord of heaven and earth in *pewter* for the love of us, and his creatures using silver for the meanest purposes![28]

(Hallahan promised that when she built her own convent chapel she would use only the best-quality materials.) But in most cases, churches were adorned in the past for the very same reason they are adorned today: the simple desire to highlight certain festal occasions, to add color and texture to the setting as a

---

27. For example, "Officials at St. Margaret's Pattens scattered 'herbs' around the church on the occasion of an episcopal sermon in 1573." Gary Gibbs, "New Duties for Parish Communities in Tudor London," in *Parish in English Life, 1400–1600*, ed. Katherine L. French, Gary Gibbs, Beat A. Kümin (Manchester: Manchester University Press, 1997), 165.

28. *Life of Mother Margaret Mary Hallahan* (London, 1869), 200, cited in Susan O'Brien, "Making Catholic Spaces: Women, Décor, and Devotion in the English Catholic Church, 1840–1900," in *The Church and the Arts*, ed. Diana Wood, Studies in Church History 28 (Oxford: Basil Blackwell, 1992), 456.

means of encouraging the sense of celebration, and to honor God. To these needs, women have always been highly sensitive. Throughout Christian history we find women like those at Staining (England), who each year from 1470 onwards are recorded as having decked the interior with garlands of flowers, birch branches, and pennants for the feasts of Corpus Christi and Midsummer, and with "holly, ivy and other evergreens" for Christmas.[29]

If enhancement of the worship environment can be attributed to women, so can its despoliation. Many women, for example, were active in ensuring that the interiors of churches conformed to Reformation principles, by removing "super-stitious" objects and furnishings. For example, Mrs. Whittingham, the "diehard wife of the diehard Dean of Durham" took it upon herself to burn the famous banner of Saint Cuthbert in the Cathedral church, which she considered a temp-tation to idolatry. In addition, the records of the Cathedral report that "two holie waterstones was taken awaie by Deane Whittingham and caryed into his kitch-ing and put into profayne uses; and ther stoode during his liffe in which stones thei dyd stepe ther beefe and salt fysh."[30] After her husband's death in 1579 Mrs. Whittingham followed his example, removing one of Cathedral's holy water stoups for her kitchen, and installing gravestones that had lined the interior of the building into her house as flooring.[31]

Sometimes women resorted to supernatural means to remove perceived impro-prieties in church buildings. In her journal, Lavinia Gates Chapman, a stalwart Presbyterian, remembers the building of the church at Linsey, Kansas, in the last years of the nineteenth century. The building project was the combined effort of the town's Methodists and Presbyterians, who would occupy the church on alternate Sundays, and as it was nearing completion the members of the two con-gregations ran out of funds. "So they nailed boards to the windows," Chapman recalls

and decided to raise what was needed by giving a dance and had all in readiness when I told them I would pray to the Lord to blow the building down rather than to dedicate it with a dance....And I said, "Lord, Lord, will you let them dedicate it with a dance?" Just before dark a storm came and some of the church went east, some went north, some west and some

---

29. Gibbs, "New Duties for Parish Communities in Tudor London," 180.

30. J. T. Fowler, *Rites of Durham* (Durham, U.K.: Surtees Society, 1903), 26–27. Cited in Margaret Aston, *Faith and Fire: Popular and Unpopular Religion, 1350–1600* (London: Hambledon, 1993), 295, n. 13.

31. Ibid. In his commentary on this episode, Fowler describes Mrs. Whittington's action as a "happy combination of dogma and domestic convenience."

south, the ground where the church had stood was swept as clean as if it had been swept and they never got the pieces together again.[32]

(In a display of conflicting religious sensibilities, Chapman concludes this journal entry with the words: "A piece of one of those boards would be a relic to me now.")

Throughout the history of Christianity, women have clearly felt at home in the church building; they have built churches, furnished and maintained them and, when necessary, have taken steps to ensure that the fittings of the church adequately reflect doctrinal norms. Women are found volunteering their time and their energy, donating money and making bequests of the furnishings and accoutrements necessary to the various rites of the church. Banners, kneelers, altar cloths, communion bread, shrouds, baptismal gowns, and vestments made by women's hands have been used in almost every Christian church in the world. Perhaps more important, over and over again in women's first-person writings we find eloquent testimony to the degree to which women have loved the places in which the congregation gathers for public worship, and the lengths to which they have been willing to go to protect it and to preserve its beauty and integrity.

Limitations

Nonetheless there have been restrictions, some quite stringent, on women's behavior in and around the church building. At the simplest — but at the same time most intimate — level, there have been limitations on what women could wear when inside the church building. Head covering for women in the Christian liturgical assembly has a history dating back to the New Testament (1 Cor. 11:5–16), and in many places during the centuries that followed, this requirement has been restated (presumably because of women's persistent noncompliance). Some canonical legislations and episcopal directives narrow the circumstances under which the veil was to be worn: the *Apostolic Constitutions* (latter half of fourth century) stipulate that any woman wanting to receive communion should approach the altar with her head covered.[33] Tighter restrictions still are imposed by *The Penitential* attributed to Cuminius (c. 650 c.e.), the abbot of the monastic center of Iona (off the Scottish coast), which declares that "women shall receive the Holy Communion under a *dark* veil" and cites the authority of St. Basil for

---

32. Cited in Stratton, *Pioneer Women*, 178.

33. Book ii: chapter 57. This was also the custom of the early Gallican church, where a head covering (called a "dominicale") was ordered to be worn by women at the time of communion, by the second canon of the Council of Auxerre (578 or 585).

this undoubtedly Eastern custom. (The same direction appears in the *Penitential of Theodore* [c. 750].)

The Protestant counterpart of the practice of veiling in Roman Catholic and Orthodox churches is a strong "Sunday hat" tradition, which has been enforced by common consent if not by statute.[34] Roman Catholic women continued to wear head coverings at mass at least until after Vatican II (that is, the mid-1960s), but more recently, as social sanctions requiring women to wear head covering in any sort of public situation have been relaxed — first in North America, and later in other parts of the West — Sunday hats have disappeared among Protestant and Catholic women alike. Some sectarian groups still insist that women cover their heads while in services of public worship. Among the Amish, Old German Baptists, Mennonites of the "Old Order," and the Plain Brethren, for example, white or black caps are worn, not only during worship, but at most other times as well, using the New Testament passage cited above as justification.

In some cases, women have been denied access to certain parts of the church and prohibited from touching certain objects. One set of seventh-century Irish canons forbade any woman from going near the altar or taking the chalice in her hands,[35] and the Gallican Constitutions of Theodulf, bishop of Orleans (802–11) ordered "ut feminae ad altare non accedat" ("women are not to go up to the altar"). In a tenth-century collection of Anglo-Saxon laws we find the following injunction: "We also command that when the priest sings mass, no women draw near the altar, but stand in their places, and let the mass priest there receive from them the offerings which they are ready to make to God."[36]

Some of these restrictions were enforced not only by statute but also by elements of church architecture. At Durham Cathedral in England, for example, women were not allowed to cross a line of blue marble set into the floor at the entrance to the chancel. At times these impediments were supported by local legend as well. Somewhere around 1150 C.E. we hear the tale of a certain church

---

34. See Michael Cunningham, *Crowns: Portraits of Black Women in Church Hats* (New York: Doubleday, 2000). We return to this question of appropriate dress when we talk about the issue of liturgical propriety in chap. 4 and appendix 3.

35. "Nulla femina ad altrare Domini accedat, nec calicem Domini tanget" (Leabhar Breac., f. 248, col. 1).

36. See Thomas Frederick Simmons, *Lay-Folks Mass Book* (London: Early English Text Society, 1879), 233–36. Beginning in the ninth century, efforts were made in the Frankish church to limit women's exercise of power, enclosing them more securely and regulating their action and conversation. In the tenth century, several books of instruction by clerics further defined the demands of the Christian life for women. Women were told not to approach the altar, but to remain in their places where the priest would accept their offerings. They were not to touch the sacred vessels or vestments, nor to carry incense to the altar. Frankish nuns were ordered by the Council of Friuli (c. 796) not to go on pilgrimage, nor to wear male attire.

in North Munster (Germany): any woman (or indeed any animal of the feminine gender) who dared to cross the threshold was immediately struck down dead.

Some of these kinds of restrictions were imposed by craft and devotional guilds. In 1218–36 a Bristol guild warned its women members not to "walk about in church during services" but to "stand or kneel in the chancel as an example to other laity."[37] Indeed, "keeping of good order" and "providing a model of behavior for others" are very common rationales for restricting women's movements in church, found in manuals of ecclesiastical discipline well into the modern period. Again, such limitations were very likely stated over and over again because women refused to keep their places. At the very least, as we shall see,[38] transgressions of these prohibitions on access to certain spaces within the church often appear as themes in women's mystical visions. For example, in Hildegard of Bingen's famous eucharistic vision, she sees what she calls "the image of a woman" who "frequently approaches" the altar and there "devotedly offers her dowry, which is the body and blood of the Son of God."[39]

Claiming Their Place in Church: Seating

We have seen that where laywomen stood or sat in church has often been regulated by statute, but it has also been determined by local custom and by the sometimes minute gradations in social status and economics. As a result, the analysis of where women have situated themselves in the church building (and how they have responded to being situated by others) illuminates the relationship between women's place in the assembly and their place in the wider society, as well as changing attitudes toward their liturgical contributions.

Prayer has traditionally been considered among the most intimate of all human activities, and so that the segregation of men and women in public worship has a long history is not surprising. The *Didascalia* (early third century) and *Apostolic Constitutions* (late fourth century) both say that the congregation should be divided "by species, men, then women, with each age group in its proper place within these two groupings," and that the female deacons are to enforce this seating plan.[40] In the East, this gender separation during common prayer seems to

---

37. Nicholas Orme, "Children in the Church," *Journal of Ecclesiastical History* 45, no. 4 (October 1994): 571.

38. See below, chap. 4.

39. See Hildegard of Bingen, *Scrivias*, trans. Columba Hart and Jane Bishop (New York: Paulist, 1990), ii, vision 6, 237, illus., 235.

40. Throughout the early period, in Eastern Rite and Orthodox churches, women were relegated to the *gynaikeia*, the "women's section" in the galleries, or to the narthex, and were instructed that on no account were they to join the men in the nave during services. In the Byzantine church, the narthex was used for certain hourly liturgies, the washing of the feet on Maundy Thursday, and the blessing of the waters at the beginning of each month. In addition to Ohrid, which was mentioned in

have persisted well into the nineteenth century, and perhaps later, but in small rural churches it was probably less likely to have been enforced, if only because their architectural configuration did not support it.[41] In the West, at least until the fourteenth century, the mixing of men and women during services was probably more common than in the East, where the social segregation of the sexes was more strictly enforced. Women and men were in close proximity to one another in European churches because they were in close proximity to one another in the street, the marketplace, and at home.

But change was brewing in the West, and this change was almost wholly due to the introduction of fixed seating, which was without a doubt among the most significant and innovative elements in liturgical furnishing in the history of church architecture. Pews dating from the thirteenth century survive in some parish churches, although they were common only from the early fourteenth century, and usual only by the early 1500s. While pewing can be understood as a method of social control (one commentator describes pews as part of a "brave and often frustrating endeavour to impose discipline by making people sit and listen attentively to the pastor's sermon"[42]), it was also a means of enforcing gender segregation and increasingly complex congregational hierarchies (see fig. 8).

But only rarely did women make any challenge to being separated from their husbands, sons, and brothers during worship, and occasionally we find them making donations for the installation of pews in a gender-segregated plan, specifying at the same time who would be seated there. In Grantham (Lincolnshire, England) parish church, for example, "Madm Sarah Ellys built ye Lofts in ye North Ile at her own charge for Batchelors to Sit in."[43] The more usual complaint made by

---

the introduction to this book, the Church of Haggoi Anargyroi in Kastoria, Greece, and the church of Hagios Strategos in the Mani also have full-length female saints around the narthex. "The depiction of female saints in the narthex is intimately linked to the ritual use of that space." Sharon E. J. Gerstel, "Painted Sources for Female Piety in Medieval Byzantium," *Dumbarton Oaks Papers* 52 (1998): 98. See also Thomas F. Matthews, *Early Churches of Constantinople: Architecture and Liturgy* (Philadelphia: Pennsylvania State University Press, 1971), 130–32.

41. This was certainly the case in the seventeenth century, when Leo Allatios made his tour of the Greek countryside, describing the churches he found and the place occupied by their congregations in the following manner: "In rural churches, often quite small and scattered here and there among the fields, there is no difference between choir and narthex. Rather everyone, both men and women, is enclosed in one little place." (But note Allatios's evident surprise at this state of affairs.) Cited in Gerstel, "Painted Sources for Female Piety in Medieval Byzantium," 94.

42. Raymond A. Mentzer Jr.,"The Reformed Churches of France and the Visual Arts," in *Seeing beyond the Word: Visual Arts and the Calvinist Tradition*, ed. Paul Corby Finney (Grand Rapids, Mich.: Eerdmans, 1999), 212. Schen ("Women and the London Parishes, 1500–1620," 258–59) also credits the maintenance of "good public behaviour" as responsible for the segregated seating arrangement established at St. Michael's London in 1576.

43. Schen, "Women and the London Parishes," 259. Sometimes gender separation could be a positive enhancement to women's participation in the worship service. In the Dorchester (Massa-

women was that all too often the seats they were allocated were not of the same quality as those for the men. William Nicolson (1655–1727), bishop of Carlisle, responding to the protests registered by women parishioners in advance of his annual visitation of the parishes in his diocese, observed that at Askham "the women's seats in the Body of the Church are without Backs, but those for men [are] well enough." At Udale, "Half of ther Seats are good; and the rest (for the women) look a little mean," and at Melmerby, "the seats appropriated to ye Men are back'd and good; but those for the women are low and mean."[44]

Objections to gender segregation in church may have been rare, but the frequency and "breathtaking ferocity"[45] of pew disputes on other grounds is evident in a review of court proceedings, parish histories, and personal memoranda. The most vitriolic arguments over seating were invariably those surrounding the allocation of pews according to the social rank of the individuals and families who would occupy them. Although a given church's "pew map" can be read as a diagram of the infinite gradations of the parish's social hierarchy, rank was a matter of subjective interpretation, and any given pew map was always subject to dispute. As one commentator has described the problem, "Place was never determined by an individual's rank alone, but by a broader concept of respect or 'honour' in which a number of considerations were balanced against each other."[46]

Some parishioners claimed precedence "as by reason of their houses"; others "according to any fitting degree of magistracy . . . which they should be advanced to within the said city." One Chester woman, disputing the right of her neighbor Henry Harpur to precedence in seating in church, appealed bluntly to the amount of money she had paid in church rates. But on this point the church wardens

chusetts) meetinghouse, men sat on the left and women on the right in order of social rank. Elders sat at the communion table, and deacons sat in a group on the left. The pulpit faced the women's section of pews and when the church grew and new seats were installed, a "double seat for women" was built "at ye right hand of ye Pulpit," and a "second seat to ye Double seat" also for women was later added alongside. Amanda Porterfield, a historian of Colonial women's piety, argues that "This new seating arrangement effectively nestled the pulpit in the laps of the women, representing and encouraging a closeness in the preacher's relationship to his female listeners and a relative distance in his relationship to their fathers, husbands and sons." Amanda Porterfield, *Female Piety in Puritan New England: The Emergence of Religious Humanism* (Oxford: Oxford University Press, 1992), 92. A similar arrangement prevailed at Lausanne, Switzerland, in about the same period. After a stay in Lausanne for seven months in the mid-1550s, Catholic commentator Antoine Carthelan likened the new arrangement to that of a "college or school," and made the observation that in the Reformed church there the women and children sat near the pulpit, the men a little further back. See Mentzer, "The Reformed Churches of France and the Visual Arts," 212, n. 49.

44. Cited in Jacob, *Lay People*, 217.

45. Judith Maltby, *Prayer Book and People in Elizabethan and Stuart England* (Cambridge: Cambridge University Press, 1998), 102.

46. Alldredge, "Loyalty and Identity in Chester Parishes, 1540–1640," 117.

could defend their decision: "Henry Harpur hath paid and doth pay more than you...and almost double as much."[47]

Exchanges of verbal abuse and physical blows, even during church services, were not uncommon among women who believed themselves to be slighted in the allotment of seating in church. A mother and daughter, members of a prominent family in Aimargues (France), "rudely shoved and insulted" the minister's wife, whom they believed responsible for having relocated them to a less desirable place in the church, and were accused of "pulling her hair and scratching her throat and upper chest."[48] And sometimes women resorted to demolition work. Several men reported to the consistory court of Saint-Jean-du-Bruel in February 1596 that someone had "hacked to pieces the pew belonging to their wives." Upon investigation, ecclesiastical officials learned that the bench, which had only recently been built and installed in the temple, deeply offended Madame de Capluc, a prominent member of the congregation. Her pew stood immediately to the right of the new one. More to the point, the carpenter had moved the bench on which Mme. de Capluc's daughters sat in order to accommodate the notaries' wives. The perceived slight led to "highly passionate" exchanges and considerable murmuring around town.[49] So enraged were Mme. de Capluc and her daughters at being displaced from their rightful pews that they arranged for the destruction of the newly installed seats.

Disputes over precedence were undertaken not only over the matter of seating in church but over the ranking to be observed while receiving communion or processing to the altar at the offertory. In one English parish in the sixteenth century women were often in contention during processions "by reason of fond courtesy and challenging of places."[50] Chaucer's Wife of Bath was certainly prepared to defend her rightful place in the procession to make the Sunday offering:

> In al the parisshe wif ne was ther noon
> That to the offerynge bifore hire sholde goon;
> And if ther dide, certeyn so wrooth was she,
> That she was out of alle charitee.

47. B. Beresford, "The Churchwarden's Accounts of Holy Trinity, Chester 1532 to 1633," *Journal of the Chester Archeological Society*, n.s., 38 (1951): 126. For other examples of disputes over seating, see A. J. Pollard, "Richard Clervaux of Croft: a North Riding Squire in the Fifteenth Century," *Yorkshire Archeological Journal* 1 (1978): 162; and Martin J. Ingram, "Communities and Courts: Law and Disorder in Early Seventeenth-Century Wiltshire," in *Crime in England, 1500–1800*, ed. J. S. Cockburn (Princeton, N.J.: Princeton University Press, 1977).
48. See Mentzer, "The Reformed Churches of France and the Visual Arts," 216.
49. Ibid., 215–6.
50. Susan Brigden, *London and the Reformation* (Oxford: Clarendon, 1989), 38.

Women did not always resort to acts of violence when deprived of their pews or allocated pews in an inferior position. Two women from the Nîmes municipal elite in the mid-sixteenth century simply went into the church when no one was there and nailed several benches together to create a larger, more splendid pew for themselves. Some women also attempted to use the various legal structures available to them to maintain their places in church.[51] In 1627 Mademoiselle de la Rouvière, the daughter of a local burgher at Durfort, complained to the consistory court that she had nowhere to sit because impertinent townspeople had taken over her father's bench. The court agreed to provide her a small portable bench on condition that it be removed during times other than the worship service.[52]

In the complicated matter of seating, keeping track of who rightfully occupied which seat was clearly of the utmost importance for maintaining good order. Most often, social control was enforced by parishioners themselves. Lady Charlotte Guest reports in her journal (August 18, 1839) that "the Chartists went to church at Merthys in a body this morning. They were perfectly quiet and orderly, not attempting to get into anybody's pew without being invited."[53] Pew owners often furnished their seats elaborately in order to mark their place. Noble families might install family coats of arms and damask draperies, but ordinary women also found means of staking out their territory, as exemplified by two women in post-Reformation Montauban who nailed cushions to their favorite benches.[54] In all but very large urban churches, however, most members of the congregation — like Lady Charlotte — would have known immediately had a usurper intruded on another's pew. Unfortunately, this self-regulation seems to have been insufficient to maintain peace within many churches, and congregations were often forced to apply external pressure to the matter of keeping people in their proper pews, including the imposition of fines and other penalties.[55] In many cases, older women

---

51. In his famous book *The History of Myddle* (Harmondsworth: Penguin, 1981 [1834]), Richard Gough cites a petition dated from the last decade of the seventeenth century in which women joined with men to request that the diocesan bishop enforce their right to have seats provided for them in the main parish church after the resident priest refused to conduct services for them in the smaller chapel nearer to their homes. Unfortunately, they were unsuccessful in their petition. Although the bishop acknowledged the validity of their case, he refused to interfere with the autonomy of the minister of the parish church, and declared that since the seats had been officially renounced, the thirty families represented in the petition would have to manage without services of worship until either seating became available in the parish church or the minister changed his mind about providing clergy for the chapel (36–37).

52. Sometimes women used difficulties with seating as a reason for failing to attend church. About a decade after de la Rouvière's difficulties with the elders, she was questioned about her repeated absence from services, and she replied that the "sole cause" was other people's use of "her bench." R. A. Mentzer, "The Reformed Churches of France and the Visual Arts," 215.

53. Earl Bessborough, *Lady Charlotte Guest, Journal, 1833–1852* (London: John Murray, 1950).

54. Mentzer, "The Reformed Churches of France and the Visual Arts," 216.

55. On February 2, 1680, the "seating committee" of North Parish Church in Andover, Massachusetts, decreed that "If any person, either male or female, shall sit in any other place in ye meeting

were appointed to ensure that their female neighbors, particularly young girls, occupied the proper pews and behaved in a manner befitting the public worship of God.[56]

Except among the Society of Friends, seating was also used to impose racial segregation in churches almost universally until the 1960s. Even among the traditionally Black churches, a sort of "unofficial segregation" could be observed in the years after the Civil War, with lines of separation drawn between former free Blacks and former slaves and between light-skinned and dark-skinned worshipers. In a church in Tougaloo, Mississippi, after the Civil War, "the mulatto women students from Tougaloo College refused to sit with ordinary people from the town."[57] Because where seating was planned it was usually allocated, at least in part, according to the occupant's income (or, as one parish describes it, "in dignity according to the taxes they bear"), African American Christians were almost always at some disadvantage in the allotment of seats, if only by reason of the economic disparity between themselves and their Anglo neighbors.[58]

Indeed, very wealthy women were rarely at the mercy of the seating plan. In many medieval parish churches the Lord and Lady of the Manor erected an elaborate, enclosed pew in or very near the chancel, and furnished it with draperies, small stoves, and other appurtenances designed to increase their comfort during services. Some women benefactors of monasteries and collegiate chapels set themselves up in a small room, separate from the church (either above the church porch, in the rood loft, or over the sacristy), from which they could hear the

---

house than where they are appointed by ye aforsd Committee they shall forfeit for every such offense to ye use of ye townce 20 shillings to be forthwith gathered by ye constables by order from sd Committee and if the constable faileth to doe as aforesd, to pay sd sum himself." Cited in Moffard, *And Firm Thine Ancient Vow,* 31. See also Chester Historical Society, *"Att a Society Meeting": The Records of the Fourth Ecclesiastical Society of Old Saybrook, 1741–1808* (North Chester, Conn.: Chester Historical Society, 1980).

56. "In St. Botolph Aldersgate beginning in 1571–72 a blind woman and another living in 'greate necessitye and wante' oversaw the young men's and maiden's galleries to enforce orderly and regular church attendance." Schen, "Women and the London Parishes, 1500–1620," 258.

57. Montgomery, *Under Their Own Vine and Fig Tree,* 260.

58. Of course, economic disadvantage has also generally applied to women in comparison to men, and this too had implications for seating. Although the preponderance of church members were always women, men generally held ownership of the pews. For example, ninety-six of the ninety-nine pew owners in the Hartford (Connecticut) First Congregational Church were men, but only twenty were church members at the end of 1808. One of these was a man named Daniel Wadsworth, who, in 1807, purchased "the most expensive pew in the new church," a large box in the corner to the left of the pulpit. For $1,100. He also purchased eight other pews and slips valued at over $1000 additional, either as an investment or to support the building project. It was only in February 1815 that Daniel Wadsworth became a covenanted member of Hartford's First Church. See Gretchen Townsend Buggeln, "Elegance and Sensibility in the Calvinist Tradition: The First Congregational Church of Hartford, Connecticut," in *Seeing beyond the Word: Visual Arts and the Calvinist Tradition,* ed. Paul Corby Finney (Grand Rapids, Mich.: Eerdmans, 1999), 434.

service being sung in church, while being separated from the rest of the congregation.[59] At Nimes after the Reformation, wealthy women built so-called "cabinets," small rooms attached to the outside of the walls of the church, within which the occupants sat in relative comfort and isolation, watching and listening to the service through a window cut into the wall (see fig. 9). The semidetached booths quickly became the places of choice for members of the aristocracy and municipal elite, who undoubtedly saw these "luxury boxes" as stunning reinforcement of their own status and recognition.[60]

While formal pew allocation grew increasingly rare after 1900, designated seating for women of the highest rank in any community was probably the last to disappear, and was enforced — at least by convention — well into the modern period in many churches.

Other Means of Claiming a Place in Church

Of course seating was not the only way in which women found places for themselves in churches. Perhaps a more predominant (and permanent) way in which women "claimed" space in the church building was by being buried there. Sometime before 750 C.E., cemeteries were moved from the village outskirts into the parish churchyard, and the tombs of the privileged began to be moved inside the building. Historians Peter Jupp and Clare Gittings describe the social consequences of this move: "The faithful stood on the bodies of their loved ones as they prayed. The world of the living and the world of the dead were united, separated only by a symbolic divide, the church floor, and sharing the same sacred space."[61]

While the earliest burials in churches were probably those of the nobility, we begin to find burials of other prominent citizens inside the church buildings in the middle of the fourteenth century. Sometimes the tombs of women were a central feature of the worship space, and were the setting for important rituals at the most significant times in the liturgical calendar. The fifteenth-century tomb of Joanne Alfrey of London is a case in point. Until the Reformation it was used as an "Easter sepulcher," the place where the crucifix and sacrament were deposited between Good Friday and Easter Sunday.[62]

---

59. The room Lady Margaret Beaufort built off the Chapel of Christ's College, Cambridge, is a good example.

60. Mentzer, "The Reformed Churches of France and the Visual Arts," 213.

61. Peter Jupp and Clare Gittings, *Death in England: An Illustrated History* (Manchester: Manchester University Press, 1999), 28.

62. Architectural historian Bridget Cherry suggests that "table-like tombs on the north side of the chancel would commonly have had this dual function." She says "that the popularity of this form [of tomb] may have reflected a change in religious attitudes, a rejection of the private chantry chapel in favour of a commemorative monument in a prominent position, which would at the same

Although burials inside the church declined after the Reformation, monuments to deceased women parishioners who are buried outside the church in
the graveyard (or elsewhere) continued to be installed in churches throughout
the centuries which followed, in both Europe and North America. Beginning in
the last quarter of the twentieth century, the movement to install columbaria in
churches — niches within which the ashes of deceased members are placed —
has again allowed women to claim space in the church building by being buried
there. (Indeed, in many churches the establishment of columbaria has been the
direct result of women's initiatives.)

For medieval women there was another important means of establishing a
place in the church building: the endowment of a "chantry." The founder of
a chantry, either within a parish church (at the high altar or in a separately
endowed side chapel), in an existing monastery, or, as we shall see, in a household
chapel, provided funds to ensure that a chaplain would remember the donor in his
prayers at mass.[63] In this way, women donors claimed both space and authority in
churches, because "the founder of a chantry . . . had quite wide latitude in setting
the rules under which the chaplain operated, and most founders laid down strict
requirements for the number and kind of masses to be celebrated, the specific
intentions for which they were to be made, the number of Offices to be said,
which prayers should be used."[64]

When a woman endowed a side chapel as a chantry, she not only had authority
over the services to be performed there, but also over the appurtenances and
ornamentation that would adorn the chapel.[65] So it was with Mechtild Erin who,
with her husband Johan, came before the burgermeister of Rottweil in southern
Germany in 1349, declaring her intention to build an altar in the parish church

---

time have formed part of the ritual at the most important ceremonies of the year." Bridget Cherry,
"An Early Sixteenth-Century London Tomb Design," in "Design and Practice in British Architecture:
Studies in Architectural History Presented to Howard Colvin," ed. J. Newman, *Architectural History*
27 (1984): 89.

63. K. L. Wood-Legh, *Perpetual Chantries in Britain* (Cambridge: Cambridge University Press,
1965).

64. Ibid, 304. Wood-Legh continues: "Indeed, chantries were so much expressions of individuality,
that Wycliffe condemned their founders, whom he assumed to be rich in the goods of this world, for
believing that they could obtain special divine grace for themselves and their families, adding that
they were seldom if ever free from the pride of Lucifer in wishing to perpetuate their name in the
world."

65. In Scotland, the transfer of property to a chantry was made in the presence of the provost and
baillies. At Irvine in 1446, Lady Alice Campbell gave five marks annual rent to endow a chantry at
the altar of the parish church of St. Michael. She appeared in person and placed in the hands of the
baillie, "a silver penny together with 'the hesp and stapill' of the tenements from which the rent was
to be paid to give sesein and hereditary right to the said St. Michael, whose image had been brought
in procession. Then at the insistence of the Lady Alice, the baillie invested the image 'nomine et loco
eiusdem sancti' with the said five marks of rent and, in token of the transfer of sesein and hereditary
right, gave to the saint the aforesaid silver penny." Ibid., 63.

of the Holy Cross, and to endow a priest to celebrate masses there perpetually "for the praise of God, the honour of St. Martin and the weal of the souls of their ancestors and themselves." With the Black Death raging, Mechtild swore before the saints that if Johan should die first, she would, within the two months immediately following his demise, build the altar and would contribute "all his clothing and armour and horses that he had at home for the purchase of a chalice, vestments, and all the ornaments necessary for the altar."[66] Like many of her medieval sisters, Mechtild established for herself a place in the Church of the Holy Cross, where she herself would be buried six years later.

The House As a Ritual Space

From the earliest days of Christianity, the domestic community has served as a unit of worship. The New Testament letters of Paul and the writings of such early theologians as Augustine and Jerome "assume that religious training and celebration was based on the household."[67] In the centuries that followed, the house became the setting for a wide variety of ritual activities, which centered on the human rites of passage, the liturgical calendar, and the ordinary round of daily and weekly prayers. For women, whose primary sphere of influence has traditionally been the household, the home has often rivaled the church in importance as a setting for Christian common prayer.

Of course, the meaning of "house" and "household" has changed significantly over time, along with the place of the domestic dwelling in the wider life of the community. Our present notion of the house as a building subdivided into self-contained units, each with a specific purpose — eating, sleeping, food preparation, study — would have been entirely foreign to many if not most of the women represented in this volume. For most of Christian history, the houses of ordinary people probably looked very much like the one Fuller Pocock saw in Ireland in June 1846: "The woman, fowls, pig and cow, [were] all in one room. The bedstead and straw mattress without covering stood against the wall opposite the entrance, the fireplace was at the right hand end of the house, the pig was littered at the head of the bed near the fire, and the cow at the foot."[68] The lack of privacy this woman experienced inside her house was mirrored in what

---

66. Ibid., 30.

67. R. G. Mertes and K. A. Mertes, "The Household as a Religious Community," in *People, Politics and Community in the Later Middle Ages,* ed. Joel Rosenthal and Colin Richmond (Gloucester, U.K.: Alan Sutton, and New York: St. Martin's, 1987), 123.

68. W. W. Pocock, *In Memoriam,* 56, cited in Clyde Binfield, "Architects in Connexion: Four Methodist Generations," in *Revival and Religion since 1700: Essays for John Walsh,* ed. Jane Garnett and Colin Matthew (London: Hambledon, 1993).

historian Michael MacDonald calls the "relentless intimacy" of village life. Until fairly recently, people living outside urban settings knew almost everything about their neighbors. Young Mercy Mallett, living in an ordinary English village in the mid-seventeenth century, is a case in point. The parish priest reported that she had gone to him for advice in a state of genuine desperation: "[She was] disturbed because her village thought that she was pregnant. She remarked that she had not menstruated since her father's suicide, and the neighbors knew it."[69]

For those of higher social rank things were quite different, in terms of both the house itself and the relationship with the wider community. Wealth allowed the building of multicelled houses, and both the differentiation of rooms by function and the limitation of access to the house to those with specific business with the members of the household gave the well-to-do much more control of their domestic circumstances.

But when viewed as a ritual space, even the most modest house was the setting for women's authority over the worship activities that took place inside. This is largely because so much domestic worship surrounded events over which women have traditionally presided: childbirth, sickness, and death. One description of the feudal period in France could apply to most places and times until the late-nineteenth century, when (in the West at least) the medicalization of these crucial life events became more routine: "Masculine power ended on the threshold of the room in which children were conceived and brought into the world and in which the sick were cared for and the dead washed. In this most private sanctum, women ruled over the dark realm of sexual pleasure, reproduction, and death."[70]

As time went on, ritual events such as death were anticipated in the design of houses. In 1875, for example, the Abbé Chaumont wrote to a women seeking his advice that the master bedroom was a "sanctuary" that someday would be the scene of the final agony, and should therefore be equipped with a "soothing

---

69. Michael MacDonald, *Mystical Bedlam: Madness, Anxiety, and Healing in Seventeenth-Century England* (Cambridge: Cambridge University Press, 1981), 106.

70. Georges Duby, Dominique Barthélemy, and Charles de la Roncière, "The Aristocratic Households of Feudal France," in *A History of Private Life*, vol. 2: *Revelations of the Medieval World*, ed. Georges Duby (Cambridge, Mass.: Belknap Press of Harvard University Press, 1988), 82. Even after hospitals were available to women who were giving birth, sick, or dying, the bedroom remained the choice for women of means. In childbirth, for example: "its theater was the family bedroom and men were excluded, except for the doctor who, thanks to the medicalization of childbirth, assisted more and more frequently at the bedsides of relatively wealthy clients.... Giving birth in a hospital was a sign of poverty or, even worse, shame and solitude; unwed country girls came to the city to give birth in the hospital before abandoning their babies." Michelle Perrot, ed., *A History of Private Life*, vol. 4: *From the Fires of Revolution to the Great War* (Cambridge, Mass.: Belknap Press of Harvard University Press, 1990), 136. The same was true of sickness and death. the well-to-do were ill and died at home, the destitute in hospitals. This is not to say that the bedchamber was not, until perhaps as late as the early nineteenth century, a quasi-public space. Over and over we see that women receive callers in their bedchambers, and that, in wealthy households particularly, business is conducted there as well.

and instructive image" of Saint Joseph.[71] In some periods, women also believed that the physical character of the entire house and its furnishings would encourage the liturgical piety of the family. Between 1840 and 1870, for example, the Gothic Revival was applied to the design of church and home alike, and "Gothic-style furniture, which looked like it belonged in an Anglican church, could be purchased by the well-to-do."[72] Not even kitchen utensils were exempt from this principle. A patent for a silver tea set with the twelve apostles in a Gothic Revival style was registered by Charles Meigh of Hanley, Staffordshire, and later copied in porcelain for American women with more modest budgets.

We can see how the linking of the iconography of church and home operates by looking at one prominent twentieth-century example, Warner Sallman's famous "Head of Christ," which was (and in many places remains) a fixture in both church and home, a stable part of the visual culture of Protestantism since it was painted in 1940. The same firm (Kriebel and Bates) that provided religious goods for the church, such as church bulletins and funeral announcements, made accessories for the home such as the "Inspira-clock" and the "Inspira-lamp" with Sallman's "Head of Christ" glowing within.[73] In commenting on Sallman's place in the Protestant home, David Morgan observes that

> The home constitutes the most sacred site in the faith of many Protestants, because it is the seat of the marriage and the place where children are raised and where relatives and friends are entertained.... Sallman's image often serves as the centerpiece of the room and the focal point for family devotions and prayer. Further, owners become so attached to the images they received as confirmation, wedding, and anniversary gifts that the pictures subsequently accompany them from home to home and into retirement. Not infrequently the images pass from generation to generation.[74]

In most middle- and upper-class American households, both Protestant and Catholic, the trend toward pious decoration weakened beginning in the 1920s, with the encouragement of designers who advocated either elegant simplicity in décor (a home "free of superficial application of ornament") or the Colonial Revival (as a response to the perceived threats of immigration and pluralism). But those women less concerned with fashion continued to bring images and stylistic

---

71. Perrot, *History of Private Life*, 4:332.
72. Colleen McDannell, "Marketing Jesus," in *Icons of American Protestantism: The Art of Warner Sallman,* ed. David Morgan (New Haven: Yale University Press, 1996), 99.
73. David Morgan, ed. *Icons of American Protestantism: The Art of Warner Sallman* (New Haven: Yale University Press, 1996), 130–31.
74. Ibid., 291.

conventions associated with the public worship setting into the home to establish it as a "worshipful environment" for the household.[75]

In the same way that the visual iconography of the church found its way into home décor, the aesthetics of the drawing room also set the standard of style for the church interior. In the second volume of *The Victorian Church*, Owen Chadwick draws the parallel between the Victorian drawing room and the church, noting the accumulation of "elaborate furniture," "clutter," "little ornaments," and "colour," and concluding that "the taste of the middle class housewife" had somehow influenced the furnishing of churches. He does not elaborate on this, and he does not cite any examples of active women's involvement in this process, although others since then have begun to explore what so-called "parlor culture" has meant in the design and furnishing of churches.[76]

Worship in the Christian Home

The religious rituals that have taken place in the home represent a wide variety of forms and intentions. Some, such as daily prayer and festal meals, have always been the preserve of the laity; others, such as baptisms, were ordinarily presided over by clergy, but could in certain situations be performed by laywomen. For still others (for example, a domestic eucharist or the blessing of the house) women typically called upon the services of clergy. In each of these cases, however, women have taken all or part of the responsibility for deciding when and where these rites were performed, procuring clergy when necessary, and managing any associated costs. In addition to the more "formal" elements of the Christian liturgical system, other related rituals also have occupied women's attention: the decoration of the family Christmas tree, prayers at the sickbed, washing and clothing the body after death, maintaining fast days, baking Easter bread, helping children open

---

75. Much of this falls under the general term "kitsch," used by Paul Tillich: "I use the untranslatable German word kitsch for a special kind of beautifying, sentimental naturalism, as it appears in disastrous quantities in ecclesiastical magazines and inside church buildings. The word kitsch points not to poor art, based on the incompetence of the painter, but to a particular form of deteriorised idealism (which I like to call 'beautifying naturalism'). The necessary fight against the predominance of such art in the churches...leads to the frequent use of the term kitsch." Paul Tillich, "Contemporary Visual Arts and the Revelatory Character of Style," in *Paul Tillich on Art and Architecture*, ed. John Dillenberger and Jane Dillenberger (New York: Crossroad, 1987), 132–33, n. 3. Morgan and McDannell argue that women have often used so-called kitsch to create a sacred environment in the home (David Morgan, *Icons of American Protestantism* [New Haven: Yale University Press, 1996] and Coleen McDannell, *Material Christianity* [New Haven: Yale University Press, 1996]).

76. Owen Chadwick, *The Victorian Church*, 3rd ed. (London: A. & C. Black, 1971). See also R. L. Bushman, *The Refinement of America: Persons, Houses, Cities* (New York: Random House, 1993), chap. 10.

the windows on the Advent calendar, and setting up and decorating a household shrine in honor of a patron saint.

A number of religious movements have made use of the house as the setting for more intimate gatherings than were possible in the church building. While John Wesley's class and band meetings are probably the most well-known examples, these were hardly the only such gatherings, nor the earliest. From Waldensians and Lollards (in the twelfth and fourteenth centuries, respectively), to the nineteenth-century Millerites, to those who have worked to reinvigorate "house churches" in the twentieth century, all those who have sought a more intense religious experience or greater intimacy among members have made use of domestic settings for worship. Often these meetings have been related to the church in their intention. John Newton (1725–1807) describes the beginnings of his own experiment with class meetings (an idea borrowed from the Moravians and Methodists) during the summer of 1767, which grew out of an existing group meeting in the house of a young woman parishioner: "Some of the younger and more lively sort began in the spring of 1765 to meet at six o'clock on Sunday mornings to pray for me and the services of the day."[77] Newton was not alone among clergy who promoted the interpenetration of domestic and church worship. "The clerical promotion of family worship also asserted the ability of the members of the family to aid each other in the mission of salvation."[78]

In some cases, women of means could establish and furnish more elaborate settings for household worship, and could pay clergy to officiate under their direction. In the later Middle Ages, the English and Continental aristocracy acted on the principle that their households should be religious as well as domestic communities, and they installed private chapels staffed with clergy to meet the religious needs of the inhabitants of the house and those who were tied to the family by ties of blood or fealty. Indeed, it has been argued that "one would be hard-pressed to find a gentle or noble establishment devoid of a building or room for worship."[79] These could be anything from a small room or closet to a building rivaling the size of a parish church, and often there was more than one chapel in

---

77. "It was at one of these morning prayer meetings that Cowper famously found his heart overcome with feelings of sweetness as one line from a hymn the poor folks were singing seized his attention all in a moment. Cowper later recalled that these meetings lasted until about 1772 and were attended chiefly by the lacemakers; there would always be forty or fifty poor folks present." D. Bruce Hindmarsh, *John Newton and the English Evangelical Tradition: Between the Conversions of the Wesleys and Wilberforce* (Oxford: Clarendon, 1996), 201.

78. Colleen McDannell, *Material Christianity: Religion and Popular Culture in America* (New Haven: Yale University Press, 1995), 98.

79. Mertes and Mertes, "The Household as a Religious Community," 124.

any given manor house.[80] Technically, all private chapels required a license from the local bishop before mass could be celebrated there (although it seems that in many cases this license was not actually obtained, or, at any rate, recorded in the Episcopal Register);[81] and women often applied for such licenses in their own right as the head of a household. For example, Robert Mascall, bishop of Hereford, granted licenses for private chapels to four women between December 10, 1404, and February 19, 1405; some of these were temporary licenses.[82] (During this same period ten men were granted similar licenses.)

Most noble households, which often could employ over one hundred people, retained a domestic chaplain to oversee their liturgical needs, and perhaps also several additional clergy and musicians to assist the chaplain in his duties. The Stonors, for example, had six priests in their employ in 1349 to serve their Chapel of the Holy Trinity, as did the Fifth Earl of Northumberland, who in the early sixteenth century had one priest designated a "Ladymessepriest," employed solely in the saying of masses to the blessed virgin, as well as a full choir. Lady Margaret Beaufort's (1443–1509) choirmaster, Thomas Farthing (d. 1521), was a significant figure in the development of English church music and left many compositions that were written under her patronage.

The patron had an extraordinary amount of control over the worship in the chapel. In many cases, patrons would adapt and adjust the liturgical calendar or designate the particular rite to be used at mass to meet their particular religious needs. In the Stonor chapel, for example, the feasts of St. Anne (July 26) and St. Katherine of Alexandria (November 25), the patron of many Stonor women, were raised to the level of major solemnities.[83] In the noble household, as in the monastery, the liturgical calendar was more intensely experienced. Easter was celebrated with a High Mass and a banquet. Christmas, the season as well as the day, was the most important holiday of the year, and feasting and other festivities of the household were extensive. On Candlemas, candles were issued to every member of the household so that they could participate in the feast. Patron saints' days, dedication memorials, and feasts with special meaning for the family were given special attention.[84]

---

80. Castle Heddingham had at least four fully equipped chapels in use in 1513. V. Anderson, *The deVeres of Castle Heddingham* (Lavenham: Terence Dalton, 1993), 27.

81. For instance, the Luttrells had two active chapels within the walls of Dunster Castle, but no license for either is traceable in the near-perfect set of registers for the diocese of Exeter. Mertes and Mertes, "The Household as a Religious Community," 127.

82. Ibid. For example, the Episcopal register notes that "Feb 10 Margaret Vale, alias Chippenham, [for a chapel] in her house at Hereford, till Michaelemas."

83. See ibid., 134.

84. Ibid., 131.

Letters written by the Stonor women between 1290 and 1485 give explicit directions for the conduct of baptisms and funerals, including who is to attend and in what order of precedence they are to process into the chapel. Noblewomen also instructed their domestic chaplains on the appointment of godparents, the services to be held during their absences from the house, the dress expected of clergy, the rites to be used on particular days, and the intentions for which specific masses were to be said. The letters of Lady Margaret Cely, for example, give directions that the following services should be offered in the chapel: "On Sunday the mass of the day; on Mondays the Requiem; on Tuesdays the Mass of St. Stephen, on Wednesdays, the Requiem; Thursdays the Mass of the Holy Spirit; Fridays of the Cross; Saturdays, of Mary."[85]

While few modern-day families have had the inclination to set up private chapels inside their homes, many Roman Catholic women continue to devise portable altars and shrines to patron saints, while their Protestant sisters decorate their "prayer closets" with pictures, tapestries, and statues that serve as aids to their devotion. In such places they keep the form of the liturgical calendar that has meaning for them, with attention to wedding anniversaries, birthdays, and dates which are remembered as landmarks on the journey toward mature faith.

Churchyards

Places where the faithful are laid to rest have been liturgical spaces almost since the beginning of Christian history. In the first centuries of the church's life, Christians were buried in public cemeteries, and women mourners often preceded the funeral procession and prepared the commemorative meal (the *refrigerium*) held at the gravesite. When cemeteries were established in the church precincts sometime in the eighth century, women not only attended burial rites, but tended graves and prayed over the bodies of the departed on anniversaries of the death and at other times. The churchyard was often also the assembly point for processions on feast days, and the setting for preaching services led by traveling evangelists. At least until the nineteenth century, when burials were removed to cemeteries at some distance from the church, women regarded the area immediately around the church as a sacred space and were responsible, at least in part, for the various subsidiary rituals that sanctified it.

The sanctity of the burial ground has not always been strictly maintained. For centuries, the churchyard was a public gathering place (often the churchyard

---

85. H. E. Malden, ed., *The Cely Papers, 1475–1488* (London: Camden Society Publications, 1900), 282.

contained the only public well) and was used for open-air meetings, fairs, markets, and other kinds of "secular" activities. Sporadic (and usually unsuccessful) attempts were made to curtail these activities. In the early fourteenth century, for example, Bishop William de Pagula (1290–1332) instructed parish priests in his diocese not to allow "markets and fairs in church yards, or games or stone-throwings, or those 'dissolute dances' and 'inhonest songs' customarily performed on the vigils of certain feasts."[86] The very lack of success of these restrictive efforts can be attributed, in large measure, to women, who were often responsible for establishing and sustaining the delicate balance between such mundane activities as drawing water and buying potatoes and the spiritual obligation to those who had preceded them in death.

As we saw in the case of the church building, women have not always been granted free access to burial places, and in some periods attempts by church authorities to regulate their behavior in graveyards have been common. Fears that women's mourning might tend toward the excessively emotional seem to be most often cited as the rationale for these prohibitions, especially in the early period of Christian history. Sometimes these exclusionary rules are the result of wider efforts at maintaining gender segregation. At the monastery of St. Mamas, for example, "aristocratic women were vouchsafed permission to attend the burial or memorial rites of relatives of the founder; they were admitted only to the church and had to leave as soon as the ceremony was ended,"[87] thus being prohibited from further contact with the gravesite. Later, among the Reformed churches in the sixteenth and seventeenth centuries, especially in Scotland and among Puritans in England and America, women customarily did not attend burial rites, but remained at home, preparing the communal meal that followed the interment. But some of these attempts to bar women from graveyards had another motivation: the perennial fear of witchcraft.

The connection between women, cemeteries, and magical rites has a long history, and through the centuries many women have harnessed the peculiar power associated with the graveyard to meet religious needs that the official liturgy of the church was unable to meet.[88] Often these "alternative" rituals respond to life events of particular concern to women; for example, the pregnant woman who has suffered previous miscarriages is instructed by her female relations to step over a dead man's grave, a symbolic transference of death away from the living child

---

86. See Susan J. Wright, ed., *Parish, Church and People: Local Studies in Lay Religion, 1350–1750* (London: Hutchinson, 1988), 133.

87. Alice-Mary Talbot, "Women's Space in Byzantine Monasteries," *Dumbarton Oaks Papers* 52 (1998): 114.

88. For more on the matter of magic as alternative ritual, see pp. 150–54.

in her womb to the world of the dead. Women unable to conceive were given particular incantations to say while burying a cloth soaked in their own menstrual blood in a corner of the cemetery. Often these rituals were interlaced with prayers from the official liturgy and given added potency and meaning by women's own keen sense of the persistence of the link between the dead and the living.

Toward the end of the nineteenth century, as death and mourning became increasingly romanticized, and as burials were removed from the church precincts to parklike cemeteries on the outskirts of town, the connection between women and cemeteries was strengthened in some places. "During the 1890s," says one historian of the period in France, "the illustrated weekly *Le Soleil de Dimanche* used the occasion of All Souls Day to show young women paying their respects to the dead; but in these images the moralizing and faithful element has been effaced, and instead artists emphasize sensuality and coquettery. On the cover of the issue of November 5, 1899...the woman swoons on the cross with an expression that could easily be interpreted as one of sexual arousal."[89] (One can see similar images — if perhaps more ambiguous in their sexual connotations — on the stylized memorial pictures given to the families of the deceased in the United States from 1830 onwards, and which typically portrayed women draped over the gravestone of the dead loved one, surrounded by weeping willow trees.) While the artistic imagination may have magnified the degree of emotional release women experienced during a visit to the cemetery, many Victorian era women did increasingly spend time in the cemetery, which became the venue for recreation (strolling among the monuments, painting the carefully contrived vistas), meditation, and even for the solicitation of funds for worthy causes.[90]

At the same time, women have continued to be responsible for various quasi-liturgical rituals at the gravesites of the departed family and friends. The anniversary of the date of death, birth, or marriage; Memorial Day; and Veterans' Day are now the principal occasions on which women return to the graves of family and friends to plant flowers, say prayers, or leave flags, toys, or other items of significance to the deceased (see fig. 10). In many churches around the United States, as well as in England and Northern Europe, women have worked to revive the notion that the church building might become the repository of the remains of members of the congregation. As we have seen, the establishment of columbaria

89. Thomas A. Kselman, *Death and the Afterlife in Modern France* (Princeton, N.J.: Princeton University Press, 1993), 217.

90. Ibid., 219–20. In Angers, an association of upper-class women collected money at the Cemetery of the East on Good Friday, All Saints' Day, and All Souls' Day for masses to be said for the intentions of the dead; young girls from the group volunteered to seek the donations of visitors at their stations in the cemetery. Although the practice declined after World War I, "as late as 1943 members were still requesting donations at the gates of the cemetery on All Saints' Day."

has very often been the result of women advocates, who have been converted to the ancient notion that the living and the dead continue to participate in one communion of faith and friendship, and that they should not be separated during the community's common prayer. In some cases the graveyards surrounding old churches have been extended and reopened for occupancy, again often as a result of women's commitment and labor.

On the Road: Pilgrimage Sites, Shrines, Processional Pathways, Brush Arbors, and Revival Tents

When women have traveled, they have often claimed liturgical spaces away from the familiar settings of home and church. On pilgrimage, at the shrines of the saints, in festival processions, and at camp meetings women have made liturgical spaces their own, both by participating in established rituals and by devising their own worship patterns. From the late fourth century onward, women's diaries and memoirs are filled with descriptions of their ritual activities in these varied settings, and the testimony of onlookers and critics alike attests to the importance of these subsidiary worship places to women's sense of liturgical identity.

Christians seem always to have a desire to visit the places where Jesus walked and where the heroes of the faith were martyred. One of the earliest women's first-person narratives we have is the travel diary of Egeria (sometimes spelled Etheria), who went from Spain on pilgrimage to Jerusalem in about the year 384, in order to follow the path Jesus took in the last week of his life.[91] Three centuries later, some royal women were choosing to go to Rome to die, in imitation of St. Paul, and in the eighth century, "a sufficient number of women were subscribing to the tourist trade for Boniface to ask archbishop Cuthbert whether matrons and nuns could possibly be restrained from making frequent trips to Rome."[92] Evidently they could not be so restrained, and descriptions of and by women pilgrims only increase as the centuries go by. Guides to the important Christian sites in both Rome and Jerusalem were common, with many (like the one written for Margaret of York in 1474, describing the churches of Rome) designed to highlight the special interests of women pilgrims.

Women rarely traveled alone; like Chaucer's Wife of Bath they sometimes joined mixed groups sharing a single destination. Sometimes whole parishes or guilds, led by the parish clergy, would go on pilgrimage together. Those women

---

91. See E. D. Hunt, *Holy Land Pilgrimage in the Later Roman Empire A.D. 312–460* (Oxford: Clarendon, 1982), passim.

92. Joan Nicholson, "Feminae Gloriosae: Women in the Age of Bede," in *Medieval Women*, ed. Derek Baker (Oxford: Basil Blackwell, 1978), 27.

who had taken monastic or quasi-monastic vows usually needed permission from a religious superior to make the journey. At the end of the fourteenth century, for example, "a London woman, Catherine Kelsey, who had taken a vow of enclosure in Rome and had promised to live on alms alone, was permitted to leave her place of residence near St. Peter's and go on pilgrimage."[93] It must be admitted that these communal journeys were not only religious events but forms of popular entertainment; when the group stopped at the end of the day, the pilgrims would occupy their time gambling, dancing, eating, and drinking.

Women had various reasons for making pilgrimage. We saw earlier[94] that some were responding to wishes expressed in the wills of relatives; others simply took it upon themselves to go to a place of known spiritual potency in order to pray for the souls of deceased family members, or for other pious intentions. The various collections of miracle stories from the High Middle Ages tell us that women with serious physical illnesses, disabilities, or deformities (including mental problems) might visit a number of shrines seeking relief, traveling first to places close to home, and then to larger, more famous sites: "The miracle book of Our Lady of Prado in Ciudad Real [Spain] gives a case of this kind, a woman who had worked out an annual itinerary of shrines seeking a cure. Others went essentially as vagrant tourists for whom the shrines were a means of livelihood and spiritual entertainment."[95] This last observation is of some importance, because at pilgrimage sites women clearly found sources of revenue enhancement as well as sources of spiritual nurture. At the very least, women were often hired to see to the upkeep of pilgrimage sites. In the Basque country and the Spanish mountains, for example, single women (called *beatas*) have been employed as shrine keepers for at least seven centuries, collecting donations, managing the accounts, paying the priest, and taking responsibility for general maintenance.

Women's ritual activity at places of pilgrimage has been regulated largely by the custom of the individual shrine (see fig. 11). Prayers were said, candles were purchased and lit, and other offerings were made in order to enhance the efficacy of those prayers. Often instructions on the "proper" prayers and rituals to be said (both on the journey and at the site itself) were passed from one woman pilgrim to another, along with information about the particular relics housed in the shrine. Some relics were known to have miraculous power over problems of particular concern for women. Among the most potent of these for medieval women were

---

93. John A. F. Thomson, "The Well of Grace: Englishmen and Rome," in *The Church, Politics, and Patronage in the Fifteenth Century,* ed. Barrie Dobson (Gloucester, U.K.: A. Sutton, 1984), 107.

94. See above, pp. 17–18.

95. William A. Christian Jr., *Local Religion in Sixteenth-Century Spain* (Princeton, N.J.: Princeton University Press, 1981), 123.

the "girdles" of Mary the mother of Jesus and her cousin Elizabeth, which women pilgrims used to touch or wear as a means of relieving the pain of childbirth.[96] Of course, not only relics produced miraculous effects. The New Mexico church of Chimayo is widely known for the healing properties of dirt found there, and women still leave tokens of their afflictions at the shrine — crutches, prostheses, bandages — as both an oblation and a testimony to others of the restoration of health. Very often the testimony of women, passed from household to household, gave these shrines their authority and widened their reputation as sources of spiritual and physical healing.

As we have seen before, attempts at restricting women's behavior in worship spaces were common. Shrines were no exception. In addition to the intemperate behavior of pilgrims while making the journey to the site, the principal difficulty cited was the indiscriminate mingling of men and women at the shrine itself, especially during the all-night vigils that preceded the saint's day. "At the Kosmidion shrine in Constantinople the pilgrims established themselves under shaded porticos. They brought their own bedding with them: curtains were sometimes used to partition off private space, but often men and women pilgrims lay right next to each other."[97]

We catch a glimpse of the problem from another direction in the canonical decrees from Spain that proliferate in the fifteenth and sixteenth centuries. The Council of Badaloz (1501) counseled men and women to keep their clothes on while they slept in the shrine. The councils of Burgos (1411), Avila (1481), Cuenca (1531), and Jaen (1511) explicitly mention the "fornications and adulteries" taking place at shrines, and express the concern that the presence of large numbers of unencumbered women was leading to "the profanation of sacred places by dancing, feasting and drinking, farces and plays, and secular, dirty, and lewd songs."[98] In 1565, vigils at shrines were forbidden altogether by the Council of Toledo. In other places there is some evidence that children acted as chaperones when women and men traveled together. In England, when two priests accompanied Margery Kempe on pilgrimage to the church at Mintling

---

96. In 1535 the chronicler Charles Wriotheseley described the virgin Mary's girdle among other relics removed from churches during the early Reformation: "Our Ladies girdell at Westminster, which women with chield were wont to girdle with, and Sanct Elizabethes girdell, and in Poules a relixque of Our Ladies milke, which was broken and founde but a peece of chalke, with other reliques in divers places which the used for covetousness in deceaphing the people." W. D. Hamilton, ed., *A Chronicle of England during the Reign of the Tudors, from A.D. 1485 to 1559* (London: Camden Society, 1875), 31.

97. Alice-Mary Talbot, "Women's Space in Byzantine Monasteries," *Dumbarton Oaks Papers* 52 (1998): 116.

98. Christian, *Local Religion in Sixteenth-Century Spain*, 166.

near Kings Lynn in the fifteenth century they "took with them a child or two and went to the said place together."[99]

For much of Christian history, the street was also a place of ritual importance, particularly for women of lower socioeconomic standing. As one commentator observes: "Workers' rituals were situated differently [than those of the bourgeoisie] with respect to both time and space. Their theatre of choice was the street, the café, the outdoors."[100] While some of these street processions were a part of the more formal ritual of the church, others were a creative blend of Christian and pre-Christian elements. We can see this in the "candle processions" of pre-Reformation England, which combined the spiritual power of lights, virgins, and festal processions into one:

> In some parishes girls accompanied their mothers when they processed to church with a candle at Candlemas.... On "Frick Friday," just before Whitsun, the women and youths of St. Thomas' Salisbury gathered to dance and carry lights into the church, and the "virgins" at Leicester carried an image of Mary during the Whitsun processions.[101]

Women have also taken a leading role in liturgical processions to calvaries and in setting up wayside crosses, which commemorate God's deliverance from disaster or mark the location of an accidental death.

Not only bourgeois women participated in street processions. In the late fourth century, the Byzantine Empress Eudoxia led a spectacular nocturnal procession carrying the relics of martyrs from the great church to a suburban church she had built nine miles away. The inhabitants of the city carried torches and candles so numerous that John Chrysostom likened them to a "sea of fire." In a sermon on reaching the church, Chrysostom refers to magistrates and the homeless, nuns and priests and ordinary workers gathered together to accompany the relics, and women "usually softer than wax" emerging from their seclusion to join the procession.[102]

---

99. Cited in Orme, "Children in the Church," 570.

100. Michelle Perrot, ed., A History of Private Life, vol. 4: From the Fires of Revolution to the Great War (Cambridge, Mass.: Belknap Press of Harvard University Press, 1990), 136.

101. Susan J. Wright, "Catechism, Confirmation and Communion: The Role of the Young in the Post-Reformation Church," in Parish Church and People: Local Studies in Lay Religion, 1350–1750, ed. Susan J. Wright (London: Hutchinson, 1988), 207.

102. "But why," he concluded, "speak of women or magistrates when she who wears the diadem and purple mantle [Eudoxia] would not abide the slightest separation from the relics through the whole distance but attended the saints like a handmaid, clinging to the relic box and to the linen that covered it?... Through the whole distance they saw her, holding tightly to the bones, not flagging or giving way to weariness." Her husband had stayed at home. (John Chrysostom, Homily 2. "On the empress coming into the great church in the middle of the night..." PG 63, 467–72; cited in Kenneth G. Holum, Theodosian Empresses: Women and Imperial Dominion in Late-Antiquity [Berkeley:

Some medieval guilds were almost wholly dedicated to the enactment of street rituals, and many if not most of these had women members.[103] The flagellant guilds of Italy, France, and Spain are an example.[104] Flagellation is thematically related to Christ's passion; one flails oneself "thinking and contemplating how the docile and humble lamb Our Lord, son of the True God, chose to be crucified on that most blessed tree and shed his precious blood; and deserving in memory of the Sacred Passion of Our Redeemer Jesus Christ in remission of our faults and sins to shed our human blood." . . . [105] The members of the flagellant guild regularly participated in Holy Thursday and Good Friday processions, as well as in petitionary processions at other times, gaining indulgences for their service.

Again, church authorities had some difficulties with the unregulated nature of these occasions. One of Bishop John Buckingham's (d. 1398) early challenges was a wayside cross that had been erected in the town of Rippingale in his diocese. "A serious complaint has reached us," the bishop writes,

> that many of our subjects have made for themselves a pretended statue vulgarly known as a Jurdon Cros, in the fields of Rippingale, and have begun to adore it, and to report that many miracles are done there. They are preaching and ringing bells and holding processions, for the deception of the people and the increase of gain, and laymen are said to be converting the offerings to their own uses.[106]

In larger cities, processions could become the occasions for acrimonious disputes among different guilds over which one of them would take precedence in the procession.[107] Street processions have also often been a means of promoting particular theological agenda; the "dueling processions" between the Nicene and anti-Nicene parties in the fourth century or the anti-Wycliffite Corpus Christi processions eight hundred years later are two examples.[108]

University of California Press, 1982], 70–71). This was the apex of the bishop's relationship with the Empress. A few years later he would regularly compare her with Herodias and Jezebel, "the embodiment of queenly evil," 72.

103. For guilds, see pp. 90–94.

104. After 1520, the Spanish and Italian flagellant guilds (usually formally dedicated to the True Cross) certainly included women. Of the French guilds there is less certainty about women's status.

105. "Constitution of the Guild of the True Cross at Caceres," cited in Marie-Claude Gerbet, "Les Confreries religieuses a Caceres de 1467 a 1523," *Melanges de la Casa de Velasquez* 7 (1971): 96n.

106. Cited in Dorothy M. Owen, "Bacon and Eggs: Bishop Buckingham and Superstition in Lincolnshire," in *Popular Belief and Practice*, ed. G. J. Cuming and Derek Baker (Cambridge: Cambridge University Press, 1972), 141.

107. "Even today, anyone who goes to Seville will hear the most outrageous insults hurled at the images of other brotherhoods or barrios." Christian, *Local Religion in Sixteenth-Century Spain*, 150.

108. On the Corpus Christi processions as a way of combating Wycliffite objections to worshiping the host, see Emma Mason, "The Role of the English Parishioner, 1100–1500," *Journal of Ecclesiastical History* 27 (1976): 17–29.

But on the whole, street processions were festive occasions, in which women from a wide range of social stations took part in a variety of ways. In the little Spanish town of Cuenca, with a population at the turn of the sixteenth century of less than seven hundred, the Chapel of St. Anne was a popular shrine, and an early description of the procession which took place on her feast day probably applies to similar processions in other places throughout the Middle Ages. The procession began at the parish church,

> accompanied by many clergy, crosses, pennants, and musicians — all that can be gathered together, and sometimes flageolets and sackbuts, cornets, and flutes; many dancers come and different kinds of instruments. There are many skits performed. On arrival at the shrine mass is said with the maximum dignity. There is a sermon, and the most learned preacher that can be found is chosen to speak. Bulls are run, the best ones available. So many people come from far away, that... for each person one meets from this town, one meets many from other towns.[109]

A similar intertwining of the religious and the social can be seen in the nineteenth-century frontier revivals. Usually arranged in the weeks just after the lonely work of planting and cultivating crops, the revival was a time for neighbors to come together, not only for spiritual renewal, but for socializing, gossip, communal meals, and (if evidence from the peak in the birth statistics that generally followed nine months after a revival in any given place is anything to go on) other, more intimate forms of entertainment. The descriptions women have left us of these occasions give equal attention to the social and religious aspects of revival meetings, to the rituals of eating together and praying together, to the delicate balance between the public confession of sins and the restoration of vital human connections with neighbors, friends, and enemies alike. Dorothy Howard remembers her girlhood in Sabine Bottom, Texas:

> One by one the sinners marched down the aisles to kneel in a long line before the preacher, who prayed aloud, his voice rising above a gathering "Amen" from the congregation, until finally, a sinner arose to shout "Praise God" or "Hallelujah" above the voices of the congregation. Other saved sinners arose one by one to join him, and the families of the shouters went

---

109. Eusebio Julian Zarco Bacas y Cuevas, "Relationes de pueblos del obispado de Cuenca hechas por orden de Felipe II," in *Biblioteca Diocesana consequense*, II (Cuenca, 1927), 21, cited in Christian, *Local Religion in Sixteenth-Century Spain*, 113. J. J. Scarisbrick, in his famous reevaluation of the Reformation, argues that in the post-Reformation parish the suppression of these kinds of nonparochial foci of worship where lay representation and control had predominated caused a marked shift of power in favor of the clergy.

forward to hug and kiss their repentant kin while the preacher lined out the song "Amazing Grace."[110]

The worship which took place in the "brush arbors" and "praise houses" that American slaves established as sacred spaces away from the oversight of the plantation masters, was, by necessity, a more secretive affair. Women slaves often report having had difficulty in restraining the free expression of their religious fervor. One young girl recollected how the elders would go among the people and "put dey han' over dey mouf an' some times put a clof in dey mouf an' say 'spirit don talk so loud or de patterol break us up.'"[111]

Because women have been, at least until the Victorian period, at home in the street, the market, and the public square, where ecclesiastical sanctions were less likely to be imposed or enforced, they could often meet their deepest religious and liturgical needs in these kinds of places more fully than in the more controlled circumstances of the church building. To say that any or all of these ritual activities are not Christian worship because they take place away from the church building is to discount the testimony of generations of faithful women who persist in describing and interpreting them in much the same terms as the officially authorized rites. But one last category of women's liturgical space represents both the quite narrowly ecclesiastical and the ability of women to exercise a measure of control over their liturgical lives. From the early centuries of Christianity to the present day, life in religious communities has given women enormous scope for liturgical self-expression and authority.

Monasteries

Women were very probably the first Christians to live in community under a disciplined way of life. These original communities were not monastic foundations in the strict sense, but simply groups of women attached to urban cathedrals, who were elected and set apart for special service to the church, and who, for convenience, lived together under a Rule.[112] The date of the widespread establishment of women's monasteries in the narrower definition of the term is more difficult to pinpoint for any given location. Generally we find communities of Christians

---

110. Dorothy Howard, *Dorothy's World: Childhood in Sabine Bottom, 1902–1910* (Englewood Cliffs, N.J.: Prentice Hall, 1977), 281–83.

111. Timothy E. Fulop and Albert J. Raboteau, *African American Religion: Interpretive Essays in History and Culture* (New York: Routledge, 1997), 76–77, cited in David Hempton, "Methodist Growth in Transatlantic Perspective," in *Methodism and the Shaping of American Culture*, ed. Nathan O. Hatch and John H. Wigger (Nashville: Kingswood Books, 2001).

112. The rule by which these so-called "canonesses" lived was later adapted for male canons with similar responsibilities.

living an intentional Christian life soon after the conversion of a particular population. In France, for example, the first monasteries appear just after conversion of the Franks in the sixth century, with the number increasing throughout the sixth and seventh centuries. With the conversion of the Anglo-Saxons at the end of the sixth century, a similar flourishing of monasteries took place, and in Saxony, conversions at the end of the eighth century led to the founding of many nunneries of great sociopolitical significance.

The women who established and had oversight of these early communities were of prominent families, and "their entrance into monastic life effectively broadened rather than limited their secular influence by giving them control over the material assets of the nunnery."[113] Royal women not only gave the organization of the monastic house its shape, but also determined the monastic Rule under which a given convent would operate, and many times designed the space within which the community gathered for worship. Before the tenth century, especially in England, an abbess might have oversight not only over the liturgical affairs of her own sisterhood, but also of a male community amalgamated with the convent into a so-called "double monastery."[114]

Patterns of women's monastic life vary from period to period and from place to place, and their motivations for entry into the religious life differ as well. In early Irish society, for example, where family relations were all-important and no major decision could be taken without the agreement of all, whole families might enter a monastery together.[115] In other parts of Europe, royal women entered and founded convents not only as a way of seeking holiness, but as a way of removing themselves from the power-political arrangements over marriage, dowry, and childbirth that were being made for them by their male relatives. Indeed, only relatively late in monastic history, perhaps near to the dissolution of the monasteries that attended the sixteenth-century Reformation, could women outside the aristocracy and merchant elite enter the monastic life, not least because a "dowry" was required, much the same as if she were entering a marriage.

---

113. Penny Schine Gold, *The Lady and the Virgin: Image, Attitude, and Experience in Twelfth-Century France* (Chicago: University of Chicago Press, 1985), 78.

114. There were also such double monasteries during the early period (550–787) of the Byzantine, but they all were closed in 810, having been forbidden by Canon 20 of the Second Council of Nicaea.

115. "The *Life of Samson* tells how the saint's father and mother, five brothers and sister, his father's brother and his wife and three sons all dedicate themselves to the monastic life, making over the family property to church foundations. Adammnán's *Life of Columcille* refers to what seems to be a family monastery. It is called 'Clocher of the sons of Damien,' and the story it tells is about the daughter of Damien who lived there as a holy virgin, presumably alongside her kinsmen. When a sizeable family property was converted into a monastery did everyone living on the land follow the same kind of ascetic life, sharing the work and supporting the rest with their labour and produce?" Kathleen Hughes, "Sanctity and Secularity in the Early Irish Church," in *Sanctity and Secularity: The Church and the World*, ed. Derek Baker (Oxford: Blackwell, 1973), 30.

Aristocratic nuns could be a bit of a problem, however. Clothild, daughter of the sixth-century Frankish king Charibert, was unhappy with conditions in the monastery to which she had been sent (St. Radegund at Poitiers) and organized a revolt against the abbess, whom she accused of various personal debaucheries and laxity in monastic discipline. When the abbess objected, Clothild threatened to throw her over the precinct wall. The sisters asked the bishop to intervene, and he excommunicated Clothild and ordered her expelled from the convent.

> But she did not leave things there. She gathered around her "a band of cut-throats, evil-doers, fornicators, fugitives from justice, men guilty of every crime" and at the beginning of Holy Week together they attacked the nunnery, planning to take the abbess prisoner. The abbess . . . took refuge in the convent chapel in front of the reliquary. When the men found her, they began to fight among themselves for the honor of capturing her, during which time the prioress blew out the candle and tried to smuggle the abbess away under the altar cloth.[116]

While Clothild may have been overzealous in her reaction to her abbess' perceived failings, this episode does reveal that the exercise of power was not the only reason that noblewomen entered convents. At the trial following this episode, Clothild defended her actions by claiming that because the spiritual life of the house was in such a state of disarray, her own higher aspirations (and thus her eternal destiny) were in jeopardy. For women, the monastic space was not only a place within which they might have some measure of control over their personal and liturgical lives, but also was a staging ground for their salvation.

Convents have varied in size but through most of Christian history they have been quite small. Shaftesbury Abbey, the largest and richest of the English female communities in the Middle Ages, housed 120 nuns in the early fourteenth century; Wilton and Romsey numbered 80 and 90, respectively. But most were considerably smaller, like Lacock, with numbers between 14 and 17.[117] Often, and in part because of its multiple uses as burial place and shrine, as well as the equivalent of a local church for members of the community, the convent chapel was larger than these numbers would indicate. But large or small, the convent chapel

---

116. Throughout the Easter period, Clothild's gangs rioted and looted the monastery until finally routed by the king's armed retainers. "When the bishop arrived, Clothild attacked him. At the trial which followed, Clothild made various accusations against the abbess, . . . but failed to persuade the judges (who were said to be relatives of the abbess, and thus biased toward her cause)." Pauline Stafford, "Sons and Mothers: Family Politics in the Early Middle Ages," in *Medieval Women*, ed. Baker, 98–99.

117. Mary Martin McLaughlin, "Looking for Medieval Women: An Interim Report on the Project 'Women's Religious Life and Communities, 500–1600 A.D.,' " in *Monastic Studies: The Continuity of Tradition*, ed. Judith Loades (Bangor, Wales: Headstart, 1991), 274.

is always the principal worship space for women's monasteries, and the pattern of worship is determined by the particular rule under which the community is organized. Daily prayer chanted in common[118] has been the most frequently observed form of worship. Sometimes the lesser offices (especially None) have been sung in the dormitory rather than the chapel.

Other women besides professed nuns have often claimed their place within the walls of a convent. Families founded monasteries and used them in lieu of the parish church as a repository for the bodies of their deceased relatives, and indeed, "once such a necropolis was begun, everyone in the family had to be buried there, arranged in order of rank...."[119] Members of the family would come to the convent to celebrate anniversaries not only of the death but also of the birth of the deceased. Various laywomen — patrons, founders, beguines, boarders, novices, students, hospital patients, and servants — were also present in the convent precincts.

By 1150, nearly ten thousand women were living permanently in convents, but the ability of these women to establish these places under their own jurisdiction was increasingly under threat; from the turn of the thirteenth century onwards, attempts were made by the established male religious orders (especially the Cistercians and Premonstratensians) to bring them under discipline. In 1215, the Fourth Lateran Council limited the number of nuns in any given establishment and ordered that they be strictly enclosed (that is, forbidden to receive visitors or to venture outside the convent grounds). Although these kinds of decrees are good evidence of the anxiety church leaders felt about women claiming their own space, their actual severity was more apparent than real. If the women's communities could support themselves economically they could usually continue as they were.[120]

But restrictions on women's movements in and around monastic spaces were also common. In the early and medieval periods, menstruating nuns were often expected to refrain from entering the convent chapel, and to stand in the narthex

---

118. This round of eight services marking times of the day is also called the Daily Office, the Liturgy of the Hours, and the Opus Dei.

119. Georges Duby, *A History of Private Life*, vol. 2: *Revelations of the Medieval World* (Cambridge, Mass.: Belknap Press of Harvard University Press, 1988), 83. "On the birthday of a departed family member, the family shared its dinner, as in the monasteries, with the dead — or, more precisely, they ate for the loved one, in his stead, in order to secure his blessing."

120. R. W. Southern has argued that the restriction of women's monasticism is the direct result of the increased emphasis on continuous and exact liturgical performance, which it was believed could most effectively be accomplished by monks. With each new wave of monastic foundation, the pattern is the same: Women are accepted and fully integrated in the early phases of development, but as the structures get more firm and the organization more elaborate, women are increasingly excluded, and the surge of women wanting to participate is left unprovided for. R. W. Southern, *Western Society and the Church in the Middle Ages* (London: Penguin, 1970).

during prayers.[121] Most of the restrictions on women's access to spaces in their own convents, though, were related to the presence of men. In double monasteries, men and women would alternate saying the Hours so that they did not occupy the same space at the same time, although some texts seem to imply that men and women attended the liturgy together, perhaps separated by a screen.

The rule of the *abaton* (literally meaning "inaccessible") "describes the principle that a male monastery was off-limits to women and vice versa."[122] There were various legitimate reasons that women would want to enter male monasteries (as well as some illegitimate reasons). Feast days of special importance to women might draw those living near the monastery for devotions.

> At Kosmosoteira [in Constantinople] women were admitted for worship three times a year, on the Marian feast days of the Annunciation (March 25), the Birth of the Virgin (September 8) and the Dormition (August 15). On these occasions they were to wait until the monks had left the church after the conclusion of the liturgy and to enter only by the east gate of the monastery. There they could make their devotions to the Virgin.[123]

Women pilgrims might also come to the gates of male monasteries to receive food, or to visit healing shrines within the monastic precincts.[124] In some places, such as Mount Athos, the *abaton* was very strictly enforced, including not only the monastery buildings themselves, but also a wide area surrounding it, and prohibiting not only female human beings, but female animals as well. It is not surprising, then, that the theme of a woman entering a male monastery in disguise was common in both Western and Byzantine writing.[125]

Because not all worship in the convent chapel could be conducted by women, the *abaton* was more difficult to enforce in women's monasteries. The demands of eucharistic worship and confession made male priests indispensable, and attempts to restrict their presence to particular spaces within the convent were common.

---

121. Talbot, "Women's Space in Byzantine Monasteries," 126.

122. Ibid., 114.

123. Ibid., 115.

124. "Some monasteries, though, forbade women from coming to healing shrines, and women got around this prohibition by sending male servants or relatives to obtain for them some holy oil or water that has been in contact with the shrine." Ibid., 117.

125. The only problem that arose was in the headgear, because men and women alike wore long tunics and a pallium (cloak). Women would have kept their head covered, men would have had bare heads. "When the gender of St. Matrona for Perge was revealed, the abbot asked her how she, a woman, dared to approach the holy eucharist with her head uncovered (as men would do), and Matrona described to him the trick she used to avoid discovery and at the same time comply with the prohibition imposed on women: she claimed to suffer from a headache and raised her pallium over her head." Alexander Kazhdan, "Women at Home," in *Dumbarton Oaks Papers* 44 (1990): 15.

Nuns have frequently been required to make their private confessions either in the narthex of the church or, when it was cold, in a special heated building just inside the convent gate; the frequency of the confessor's visits varied according to the custom of the convent, from daily to two or three times a month. On certain feast days, male choristers were also called upon to sing the mass, although some abbesses thought these an unnecessary breach of the *abaton*:

> Irene Doukaina [founder of the Kecharitomene convent in Constantinople] …was adamant about refusing entrance to male singers or psaltai even on special feast days or days of commemoration. At the Lips convent, Theodora Palaiologina also normally prohibited admission of the singers…but she was willing to make an exception on the birthday of the Theotokos.[126]

Laymen might also enter the convent church, especially if it housed the tombs of relatives, but then only after the nuns had finished singing the Office and had returned to their dormitory. Various others necessary to the functioning of the life of the community — carpenters, field hands, and physicians, for example — also have had limited access to various places within the walls of the convent. Although in the modern period some of these restrictions have been relaxed, they remain in place for fully enclosed communities.

Despite these seemingly complex rules, the convent, and for our purposes especially the convent chapel, is essentially women's space. Men, even bishops and priests, usually have had to obtain permission from the Superior (or her designate) to enter the monastic precincts, and while there they operate largely under her direction. Women founders and benefactors have determined its design and decoration, abbesses have negotiated changes in the Rule (and, by extension, the forms of common prayer) under which the community lived, and professed nuns have been able to integrate prayer and work without continual reference to male demands and expectations.

Beguinages and Hermitages

The places that perhaps allowed women the highest degree of freedom to claim their own liturgical space were beguinages and hermitages. Women hermits probably joined their male counterparts in the Egyptian and Syrian deserts sometime in the fourth century, setting themselves up in small cells or caves. Our direct information about the worship lives of these early women hermits is limited, although the overarching principle was ceaseless prayer and the performance of various

---

126. Talbot, "Women's Space in Byzantine Monasteries," 122.

ascetic disciplines. Within the hermitage, women ascetics in this early period seem to have had considerable autonomy in the forms of prayer they adopted, the times of prayer, and the spiritual and physical disciplines undertaken. The seventh-century description of Shirin of Syria provides a good example:

> Her unremitting labor consisted in the Office of the Psalms and in heart-felt prayers intermingled with groans, to such an extent that she would spend most nights without any sleep, being occupied with continual singing of the Psalms and with prayer. During the daytime, however, she would divide her time between this and reading the Scriptures, the lives of upright men, and uplifting works written for the guidance of the monastic life and for instruction in true religion.[127]

Women like Shirin usually maintained contact with the worshiping community, and in their cell received both men and women who sought them out for advice, exorcisms, blessing, and healing. The tradition of women hermits continues but has never been attractive to great numbers of women, and today most women hermits are associated with one of the existing monastic communities, with their hermitages set up somewhere on the grounds.

The Beguine movement, which began in the late twelfth century, allowed a woman who was not drawn to (or not eligible for) the life of a professed nun to dedicate herself to holiness and service. Lambert le Bègue (nicknamed "The Stammerer") was ordained priest in Liége, France, in the early 1160s and appointed to a ruined rural church. He began his work by repairing the church building with his own hands and then provided everything necessary for holding services. A poor man himself, he preached against priests who charged fees for baptizing, administering the sacrament to the sick and the dying, and burying the dead. (He also disapproved of pilgrimages, arguing that the time and money would be better spent on the care of the poor, the consolation of the bereaved, and the comfort of prisoners.)

The women of Lambert's congregation were particularly inspired by him and responded to his increasing calls for devotion to the eucharist. Many of these women began to stay at church after the service on Sunday in order to sing hymns and to pray. Imprisoned by the bishop in 1175 on false charges of heresy, le Bègue died two years later. But his vision lived on in the corps of women he had inspired, who in the generation after his death came to be called the Beguines by their enemies. The Beguine movement spread from France to the

---

127. Sebastian P. Brock and Susan Ashbrook Harvey, trans., *Holy Women of the Syrian Orient* (Berkeley: University of California Press, 1987), 180.

Low Countries and north to Germany, giving women an opportunity to live an ordered life dedicated to the sacramental and vocational vision that le Bègue had represented. Beguines lived in ones and twos, in small houses attached to or near their parish church. The house of Julian of Norwich (c. 1342–after 1413) is a good example of a Beguinage: a single room attached to the Church of St. Julian with a window into the church that allowed her to see and hear the mass being celebrated at the altar.

Various manuals, such as the tenth-century *Ancrene Wisse*, gave general instructions for the ordering of life, but the genius of the Beguine movement was that it was flexible in its arrangements and moderate in its demands. Women who wished to live the life of a Beguine were to dress modestly, refrain from gossip, keep only one servant, and do good whenever and wherever they could. Many middle-class women found this creative blend of discipline and freedom attractive, but eventually persecution by those who misunderstood their vocation (and probably mistrusted their freedom) forced them under the discipline of monasteries, or into hermitages in the wilderness.

Neither hermits nor Beguines fit the stereotype of the passive, subservient, and unobtrusive women who were usually acclaimed as saints by the church. Indeed, in John of Ephesus's (c. 507–86) hagiographical account of the heroes of the early Syrian church, he "feels compelled to apologize every time he tells a woman's story."[128] Their own spiritual authority allowed these holy women to turn their cells into worship spaces over which they alone had jurisdiction, and within which they exercised the pastoral-liturgical roles of blessing, exorcising, and healing others. Like the women who entered convents, the ability of Beguines and hermits to establish and claim worship places for themselves was in some measure related to their ability to claim independence from male control.

Conclusion

Despite persistent efforts to limit their access to worship spaces, to regulate their behavior while in worship spaces, and to define which spaces could be legitimately considered worship spaces, women have in a variety of ways made places of Christian common prayer their own. Women have felt comfortable in church buildings and passionate about the degree to which their place in church accurately mirrored their place in society. They have used their resources to furnish the liturgical environment and to memorialize themselves and their loved ones

---

128. Ibid., 23.

after death. They have established convent chapels and have supervised the liturgical patterns followed there. In their own homes, women have overseen feasting and fasting, family devotions and clandestine prayer meetings, and worship at the sickbed, the deathbed, and in the birthing room.

At the same time, women have been willing and able to transform different kinds of open-air places — streets and churchyards and brush arbors — into functional and potent liturgical settings. Poor and marginalized women especially have claimed authority over worship in these environments, and, perhaps more importantly, in worshiping there they have challenged the barriers between church and world that the ecclesiastical establishment has persistently attempted to erect. Indeed, the ability of women to adapt the spaces in which they are most comfortable into worship settings is surely one explanation for the continued strength of Christianity in women's lives, despite generations of officially sanctioned repression and subjugation.

A Gallery of
Women's Worship

"We need to see where women were as well as where
they were not. We need to know what spaces
women found for their self-expression, and how
these traditions were transmitted or lost."
– Charlotte Metheuen

Figure 1. Most women of means in the Middle Ages set up private chapels for their liturgical and devotional use, like this one built by Margaret of York.

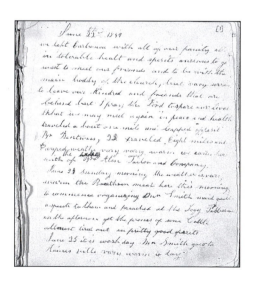

Figure 2. Women's diaries provide invaluable evidence for ordinary worship life. This is a page from the diary of Bathsheba Smith, written during her westward migration, 1847.

Figure 3. For most of the church's history, women's penance has been public. Here, a Saxon prostitute asks for the congregation's forgiveness, seventeenth century.

Figure 4. Demographically, the highest percentage of worshipers has always been women. These women gather for a revival, La Farge, Missouri, 1938.

Figure 5. Women have traditionally found their own ritual space within the church building. These women gather to pray in St. Agnes Roman Catholic Church, Chicago, 1907.

Figure 6. In the American West, before the establishment of purpose-built churches, women arranged makeshift worship spaces, such as this garage, Dos Palos, California, 1938.

Figure 7. These women at Wheeley's Church, Gordonton, North Carolina, gather to clean and decorate the church for worship on the following Sunday, ca. 1935.

Figure 8. The segregation of men and women in the worship space was common in Reformed congregations until the seventeenth century and persists in some traditions to the present day.

Figure 9. Many women of means set up private rooms adjacent to the parish church from which they could watch the liturgical proceedings in comfort.

Figure 10. The cemetery is a significant liturgical space for women, where mourning rituals and grave decoration provide for the ceremonial expression of grief.

Figure 11. Outdoor shrines have provided a focus for women's devotion and an arena for freedom of liturgical expression.

Figure 12. Often girls carried the coffin at the burials of friends. This sixteenth-century woodcut shows young women in "funeral aprons."

Figure 13. Prayer books served as both devotional aids and fashion accessories for wealthy women. Here is an elaborately embroidered seventeenth-century example.

Figure 14. Women have been aware that the decorative arts could provide instruction in proper ritual behavior and often included pedagogical pieces in the furnishing of their homes.

Figure 15. For women, the various ritual moments of the Christian life have been marked by the wearing of special clothing, such as these communion dresses worn by residents of an Indian school, Desmet, Idaho, ca. 1936.

Figure 16. Dressing for church takes on ritual significance for women, particularly for African American women like these, gathered outside a Georgia church, ca. 1900.

Figure 17. Members of a mid-week Women's Guild leave the church after a meeting. For women, the church is a space in which multiple rituals take place.

Figure 18. Young girls find their place in worship from an early age. These children form the procession at Easter Mass in Buffalo, New York, 1940.

Figure 19. Women have found their place at the Communion table, but not always without controversy. The matter of precedence often led to acrimony.

Figure 20. A girl's first communion has often been seen as a rehearsal for her wedding. This Texas girl in bridal attire poses for a formal photograph ca. 1910.

Figure 21. Like Mrs. Albert Mainwaring, Springville, Utah (1903), generations of Christian women have taught forms of liturgical and devotional prayer to their children.

Figure 22. The preparation of special foods marking the liturgical year transforms the family kitchen and dining room into liturgical space over which women have traditionally had control. This woman prepares the Easter feast, ca. 1943.

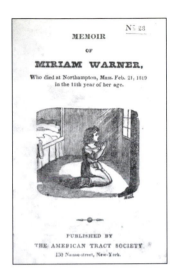

Figure 23. Women learned the choreography of the "beautiful death" through publications such as this, which describes the last hours of a pious young girl in great detail.

Figure 24. Until the funeral industry took over, women were the directors of household mourning rituals and of the preparation of the body for burial.

Figure 25. In all periods of Christian history, high infant mortality rates have meant that women often have had to superintend the burials of their children.

Figure 26. Women, like these in Pie Town, New Mexico, ca. 1940, have often taken leadership roles in providing music for congregational worship.

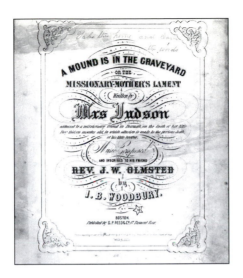

Figure 27. Women hymn writers set the tone for much of the Victorian attitude toward death and the proper forms of mourning.

Figure 28. Wealthy women in the Middle Ages were patrons of the various liturgical arts, especially music. This choir book was commissioned by Margaret of Austria, ca. 1528.

Figure 29. Women have often been given freedom to embellish subsidiary ritual spaces within churches, places within which to memorialize deceased friends and family members.

Figure 30. Throughout the centuries, women artists have contributed to the decoration of the worship space. Here in a fifteenth-century illumination, St. Irene paints an image.

CHAPTER THREE

Women of Influence

We have anew to repeat our deep regrets that Her Majesty is so ill-advised as to set so evil an example to her loyal subjects. The Opera till the morning of the Lord's Day. In the morning attendance at public worship. In the afternoon Her Majesty presenting herself as the leader of that worldly show which the parks exhibit on the Sabbath. —*London Record*, June 21, 1838

Calculating Influence

It is difficult to deny that women have often been subject to restraints of various kinds throughout the history of Christian worship. Attempts to define proper dress and postures for prayer, to ban access to particular areas within the church building, to prohibit women from assuming certain liturgical roles: all of these are a part of the story of women at worship. But women's liturgical history is more than just the story of the restrictions placed upon them by others. Moreover, when we begin looking beyond the restrictions, we find that all kinds of women have had not only considerable freedom in the matter of worship, but also considerable influence over both the large and small structures of Christian common prayer.

Influence, however, is a rather slippery category. Because of the way in which most historiography has been presented, we have become accustomed to thinking about influence almost entirely in terms of the large-scale structures and processes of history. The general who leads the charge in the decisive battle, the scientist who discovers the vaccine against a deadly epidemic, the diplomat who negotiates a treaty between warring nations: These are the people — typically men — to whom we have applied the term "influential." As we have seen, though, we are beginning to recognize that influence may be more complicated than that, and that meaningful change takes place not only as the result of momentous events and heroic individuals, but also as the result of the accumulation of small decisions, small acts, small shifts in attitude and perception. In tracking this kind of incremental historical influence, we are as likely to find women as men as actors and change agents.

Some women have also had influence in the more traditional sense of the word, and indeed we shall meet several of these women. But such "influential" people are not the only ones who are historically significant. In this chapter we look at the kind of influence women have had, and the kind of women who have had influence in the course of liturgical history. Some of this influence has only been exercised within the local parish, monastery, or household; some resulted in significant liturgical change within a denomination, a religious movement, or the church as a whole. To track this influence, we look at the lives of abbesses and scholars, missionaries and revivalists, sectarians and noblewomen. We find through our search that the women who have had the widest and most persistent influence in the shaping of the history of Christian worship have been ordinary laywomen living out their liturgical lives in Christian congregations.

Ordinary Laywomen

Laywomen have had influence over worship in diverse and sometimes surprising ways. In churches they have compelled the clergy to perform the authorized rites and to introduce liturgical reform. They have been generous benefactors — founding congregations, adorning church interiors, and providing the various materials necessary for worship. Women's drawing rooms have been the settings for prayer meetings and, as a result, for the establishment of sectarian worship patterns. By extending hospitality to traveling preachers, women have assisted (or impeded) reform by promoting sermons, thereby spreading and encouraging certain views on worship.[1] Women have rallied for the excommunication of their neighbors, challenged the social order by breaking Sabbath, and supported the civil government by fasting on occasions of national calamity. In all of these seemingly small ways, women have shaped the worship of their local congregations and their denominations, and of succeeding generations as they have trained their children in the patterns of Christian common prayer.

Fee Payers and Fund-Raisers

The work of the church, including the worship of the church, requires money. At various times, parishioners have been responsible for paying church rates,[2]

---

1. See Susan Wabuda, "Shunamites and Nurses of the English Reformation: The Activities of Mary Glover, Niece of Hugh Latimer," in *Women in the Church*, ed. W. J. Shiels and Diana Wood (Oxford: Blackwell, 1990), 335–44.
2. In England, tithes provided income and maintenance of the minister, while rates raised the funds necessary for normal repairs to the church and also for the paraphernalia needed to perform the liturgy: vestments, bread and wine, books. The rate system was well-established by the fourteenth century, but was more or less voluntary until after the Reformation, when a compulsory church

tithes, fees for clergy services, annual charges for Easter communion (usually called "Easter Books"),[3] and special collections for particular liturgical needs. From about the thirteenth century onwards the laity were expected to contribute to church building and maintenance throughout Western and Central Europe, although in England there was some distinction between the chancel and the nave of the building, with the chancel regarded as the priest's freehold property and thus his own financial responsibility. In France parishioners and clergy divided responsibilities equally, and occasionally we find "communally owned" churches where the entire building was kept up by the parish. In all of these cases, not only did women pay the normal charges, but often in poor parishes, where tithes may not have met expenses for the ongoing liturgical life of the church, women made special efforts to raise money.

In cities, both before and after the Reformation, tithes were usually assessed according to the value of the house in which the parishioner lived — if she rented the house, on the amount of the rent, and if she owned the house, on its value. In the countryside careful calculations were made on the economic output of the household, and tithes were levied accordingly. A woman would also have paid a personal tithe of 10 percent on her income, but often these charges were left unpaid until death, even though preachers warned against such delay. Tithes were intended to pay the salary, housing, and maintenance of the clergy, and so were only indirectly for the support of worship. But many women were refused burial until their past-due tithes were paid, and others were refused communion if the calculation made by the priest did not match the householder's estimate. Clergy were criticized because "they look so narrowly on their profits that the poor wives must be countable to them for every tenth egg, or else she getteth not her rights at Easter and shall be taken as an heretic."[4] But while money was one of the things that often caused difficulties between clergy and their congregations, the laity did not in principle object to the paying of tithes.

Fees paid to clergy for performing liturgical services were another matter, however. Throughout much of Christian liturgical history, money has been an integral component of the spiritual transaction between clergy and laypeople, which has

---

rating system was established under Elizabeth I. Rates were set by churchwardens, with the consent of the parish meeting, and assessed according to their ability to pay, usually determined by the house the parishioner lived in. See Judith Maltby, *Prayer Book and People in Elizabethan and Stuart England* (Cambridge: Cambridge University Press, 1998), 188–90. There were also special community-wide collections to pay for particular items needed, especially collections for wax, because large numbers of candles were needed.

3. The "Easter Books" was an annual fee for communicants that was usually intended to supplement the priest's income. See Susan J. Wright, "Easter Books and Parish Rate Books: A New Source for the Urban Historian," *Urban History Yearbook* (1985): 30–31.

4. Simon Fish, *Supplicacyon for the Beggers* (London: 1529), 2.

had profound consequences for women's liturgical lives. Fees required at their marriage, at the birth and the baptism of their children, at the burial of their husbands, and as a prerequisite for admission to communion at Easter strengthened married women's dependence on husbands and left single women liturgically insecure, given that they have always been at a statistical disadvantage in terms of disposable income. Many poor women went without their most basic ritual needs being met, simply because they did not have the means to pay for them. At the same time, we often find women objecting to the paying of fees to priests who were indolent, undeserving, immoral, or negligent.

We get an idea of the degree to which fees in the medieval and Reformation periods were a part of women's liturgical lives by looking at the fee schedule for one London parish just before the Reformation:

> At weddings: a fee for the curate's services, a fee for candles, an offering for the Mass. . . . At burials: each priest in the church receives a fee, or else he will not sing the funeral. At each month's anniversary of the death a fee is paid to each priest who participates, or else no commemoration will be made, an additional fee for candles, for the corpse to be brought into the church, for the ringing of the bells. . . . For any who wish to be buried in the choir or in the chancel, additional money is paid.[5]

The fees required of women at the rite of Purification of Women after Childbirth (commonly called "churching") gave medieval and Reformation women particular difficulty. A part of medieval custom and enshrined in successive editions of the *Book of Common Prayer* of the Church of England, churching was usually performed forty days after a woman gave birth and marked her reentry into society. This transparent link between the religious and the social made churching a ritual of profound significance to women.[6] The same London parish described above required not only a fee for the churching itself, but for special Gospel readings in the weeks during which she was confined and another for remembering her in the prayers at the altar.[7]

---

5. Cited in Susan Brigden, *London and the Reformation* (Oxford: Clarendon, 1989), 50.

6. In some places in the English Midlands, churching is still performed according to the rite in the 1662 *Book of Common Prayer*. See appendix 1.

7. "When women do lie in childbed, the curate has every Sunday of some women for the saying of the Gospel one penny or 2d, and at her purification they demand of custom 1d, with the chrism over, and besides the offerings at Mass." Fish, *Supplicacyon for the Beggers*, 51. Similar charges are reported at the turn of the nineteenth century by Richard Gough in *The History of Myddle* (New York: Penguin, 1981), 46–47: "Easter tithes: 'For every Milch cow the Rector is to have 1d; for every calfe between Easter and Easter, yearley, an half-penney; for every colt, 4d; for every stall of bees that are put down, 2d; a garden, 1d; a smoake [fireplace], 1d; for everyone that receives, or that is of age to receive the sacrament, 2d yearely, which wee call offerings. Easter eggs are paid (viz) three for the cocke, two for every hen, and soe for ducks and turkeys. . . . For christenings in the church, nothing;

But women have often provided financial support for the church without the motivation of this kind of *quid pro quo,* and they have been remarkably innovative in their efforts to secure funds for the maintenance and enhancement of the church's public worship. Groups of medieval women engaged in fundraising schemes that sound surprisingly modern: the sale of extraneous church furnishings, special collections at festival meals, "church ales," and communal entertainments. Some of these were remarkably successful. In the year 1493, records from one Somerset (England) parish show that the Maidens' Guild employed several of these methods and raised nearly 30 percent of the church's total income.[8] Women in rural parishes were usually more active in these kinds of activities than urban women, largely because urban parishes were, on the whole, more wealthy; but women in parishes with an important shrine or wonder-working relics always found pilgrims a ready source of revenue enhancement.[9]

Clergy were not always ardent supporters of these fund-raising schemes, and conflict between women and the clergy sometimes resulted from attempts to impose restrictions on women fund-raisers. Often these disputes were part of larger liturgical and theological differences between clergy and people. In St. Albans, Hertfordshire, in 1589, for example, a "Lady Bacon" was a sponsor of the Puritan cause and had brought a number of evangelists into the parish in an attempt to convert the inhabitants to a purer form of religious practice. One of these preachers, William Dyke (who had already been suspended from his ministry in Essex for refusal to conform to the established church), "immediately set about condemnation of one of the few survivors of the county's church ales, held annually at nearby Redbourn. Dyke did not attempt to claim that it was badly behaved, but averred that it was 'abused' by piping, dancing, and the custom whereby a Maid Marian came into the church to kiss parishioners and make them laugh."[10] The women of Redbourn, clearly sensing that he would inhibit their fund-raising

---

for Churchings, 4d; for Banns with a certificate, two shillings; For Banns without a Certificate, 1s; for marriage with license, 5s; for marriage by Banns, 2s 6d; for burying a Corpse in the Churche yeard, in a coffinn, 1s; without a coffin, 6d; for burying a Corpse in the Church in a Coffin, 2s; without a coffin, 1s; for registering, 4d....'" "The Clerke is to have...christenings, his dinnere and 2d; burialls in the Church yard, with coffin, 2s; without coffin, 1s; in the Chancell, 2s, 6d; marriages by license, 2s; by banns, 1s."

8. The parish referred to here is the parish of Crosscombe, Somerset. K. French, "Parochial Fundraising," 125. See also Claire S. Schen, "Women and the London Parishes, 1500–1620," in *The Parish in English Life, 1400–1600,* ed. Katherine L. French, Gary Gibbs, and Beat A. Kümin (Manchester: Manchester University Press, 1997), 250–68.

9. Parishes also rented out items needed for religious activities: funeral palls, vestments, linens, and also ordinary items, an anvil, weights and measures on market days, pots and pans on feast days. Later they would lease church premises, including bakehouses and breweries.

10. Ronald Hutton, *The Rise and Fall of Merry England: The Ritual Year, 1400–1700* (Oxford: Oxford University Press, 1994), 140.

efforts, reported him to the bishop of London "for preaching against the church hierarchy and liturgy, and he was promptly silenced again."[11]

In churches organized under a more congregational polity — where the congregation itself rather than some higher ecclesiastical body has responsibility for its own maintenance — women's fund-raising activities have been even more necessary to the financial support of public worship. In the United States, Australia, and Canada particularly, anxiety about where the money for the preacher or worship leader's salary would come from has been felt by more than one rural congregation. Mary Keller, who grew up on the Kansas frontier in the early twentieth century, remembers the difficulty her church had in raising remuneration when the circuit preacher came to her town. Often she had to take matters into her own hands:

> In the early years it was no easy task to keep a preacher. Collecting the salary was very different from the present time. I have had to help get it by taking a team and a farm wagon and riding over the sparsely settled country and gathering up meat, corn meal, some flour, chickens, eggs, sorghum molasses and anything that people could spare. For there was but little money.[12]

Finding money for the worship leader's salary was not the only concern for these women. As settlements were established and new Christian congregations were formed, finding a suitable building for worship was also important. Although, as we have seen, these early communities worshiped in a wide variety of settings,[13] the goal for each congregation was invariably to have its own church building.

Sometimes the realization of this goal was wholly due to the fund-raising efforts of women. "Hicks Chapel," an African American Baptist church in the Brazos River Valley in Texas, is a case in point. Immediately after the Civil War, the women of the congregation banded together to solve the problem of the lack of a church building, as a preacher who served Hicks Chapel recalls:

> So when freedom come in a bulge before you could say, "Amen" and they start the Baptist church down to Wild Hoss Slew, they appoint Sister Milly to help raise money to build the church house; so she calls a meeting of the sisters and asks them what can we do to raise some money to help build the church house? She say, "I ain't no woman for dancing; we don't want to do that." Then she say, "I knows what; everybody can get some hens and we'll

---

11. Ibid.
12. Cited in Joanna L. Stratton, *Pioneer Women: Voices from the Kansas Frontier* (New York: Simon and Schuster, 1981), 180.
13. See pp. 42–43.

have a hen barbecue and sell them to the white people down Calvert." So the sisters pay heed to Sister Milly and they sells a hundred dollars worth of chickens and raises the first hundred dollars on this church down to Wild Hoss Slew, and they calls it to this day "Hicks Chapel" after Sister Milly.[14]

In the former European colonies, the power and energy of women was released by the new religious situation that the settlement of the frontiers presented, and women working together to support the churches financially is one mark of this power. Indeed, the mid-nineteenth century was the high-water mark for women's fund-raising fairs, for both the church and for other "good causes," and women of every denomination[15] seem to have organized them in order to raise money for the various necessities related to Christian worship — from the church building and the minister's salary to new vessels, books, and choir vestments.[16] Although there was another peak in women's fund-raising in the 1950s, corresponding to the increase in new church building and the renovation of worship space after the Second World War, gradually, as women's time has become a more valuable commodity in the wider marketplace, fairs and bazaars have begun to decline in favor of personal donations from individual women.

It is often difficult to calculate the degree to which women's fund-raising has contributed to the worship of any given congregation. What did it mean for congregational worship that a wider range of music was available because the women of the congregation raised money for an organ? Was a congregation's eucharistic theology changed because women raised money to replace the trays of individual communion cups with a chalice (or vice versa)? Even more difficult is the task of gauging the impact of women's fund-raising on the history of worship in the wider sense. But once the question has been asked, further research might make it possible to give some credit to women fund-raisers that clergy and scholars have traditionally claimed. Perhaps, for example, we would find that the extension throughout a denomination of certain key liturgical principles embodied in a new denominational hymnal or service book can be credited to the women fund-raisers who made the purchase of those books possible in innumerable small congregations, rather than to the intrinsic theological appeal of the principles themselves.

---

14. Cited in John Mason Brewer, *The Word on the Brazos: Negro Preacher Tales from the Brazos Bottoms of Texas* (Austin: University of Texas Press, 1953), 63.

15. The Roman Catholic counterpart to the Protestant "church bazaar" was the "cathedral fair." One of these in the 1870s lasted nearly a month and raised over $160,000.

16. For further material on women's fund-raising, see Beverly Gordon, *Bazaars and Fair Ladies* (Knoxville: University of Tennessee Press, 1998), passim.

Temperance Workers

In one case, however, the influence of women on this wider history of Christian worship is not only clear, but profound and deliberate. The impact of women temperance workers on the eucharistic practice of most Protestant churches in England and America, including all Baptists and Disciples of Christ, and most Methodists, Congregationalists, and Presbyterians, cannot be overestimated. In rallies and pledge drives, in petitions and in hymnody and boycotts, temperance women convinced not only vast numbers of their fellow citizens but, more important, many of the churches that the use of alcohol was wholly incompatible with the living out of the Christian faith.[17]

Although originally aimed at restricting the opening hours of saloons and the indiscriminate sale of drink, the temperance cause soon shifted to the thorny matter of fermented communion wine. "Shall the cup of Christ be turned into the cup of demons?" was the cry, and women were soon waging the war on communion wine on various different fronts, both local and national. Typical of these women was Zerelda Wallace, a prominent member of Central Christian Church (Disciples of Christ), Indianapolis, and the wife of David Wallace, governor of Indiana. Mrs. Wallace "... assumed a militant role in the fight against the liquor traffic, even stomping out of the morning worship service one Sunday because wine instead of unfermented grape juice was used in the Holy Communion."[18] Other women rallied within their churches for the excommunication of those who would not take the teetotal pledge. Although this sort of action was a significant source of pressure, it was not only women acting independently that turned the tide toward unfermented communion wine.

The Women's Christian Temperance Union, founded in 1874, arguably the most powerful women's organization in history, put enormous effort into the campaign to banish wine from the communion table as a part of its national platform. Individual members put pressure on Protestant churches at every level (and of course many members, like Zerelda Wallace, abstained from partaking in

---

17. This connection was not immediately self-evident to the churches, and in some cases seemed to present serious theological problems. "Among women surveyed, most took the abstinence pledge to 'give encouragement to others.' In the earliest days of teetotalism, those who took the pledge were sometimes charged with religious 'infidelity'; according to some religious leaders they emphasized man's ability to change himself in opposition to the Christian doctrine that God's grace was necessary. The teetotal pledge was said to replace the Baptismal vow in the lives of teetotalers." Lillian Lewis Sutton, "'Changes Are Dangerous': Women and Temperance in Victorian England," in *Religion in the Lives of English Women, 1760–1930*, ed. Gail Malmgreen (Bloomington: Indiana University Press, 1986), 211, n. 7.

18. Louis Cochran and Bess White Cochran, *Captives of the Word: A Narrative History of the Christian Church (Disciples of Christ), the Christian Churches (Independent), and the Churches of Christ* (Joplin, Mo.: College Press, 1987), 85.

the rite of Holy Communion until their congregations fell into line). At its second national convention, the WCTU established a subcommittee to investigate the propriety of using wine in celebrating the sacraments.

> This committee reported back in 1876, citing a plethora of biblical schol-arship to show that fermented wine was not condoned by the scripture or necessary for the sacraments. The committee argued that the word *wine* was actually a mistranslation which referred to an unfermented grape juice in common use among Jews in the first century, and that the Bible taught total abstinence from alcohol except when used as medicine.[19]

The report was adopted by the convention, and the battle against communion wine began in earnest.

As a buttress to this effort, many women saw to it that temperance hymns were included in denominational and privately issued hymnals, and many such hymns were composed by women for use in church. The following hymn appeared in several hymnals from 1841 to 1888, designated as a closing hymn:

> Heavenly Father, give thy blessing,
> While we now this meeting end;
> On our minds each truth impressing
> That may to thy glory tend.

> Save from all intoxication,
> From its fountain may we flee;
> When assailed by strong temptation,
> Put our trust alone in thee.[20]

Used in both congregational and family worship, these temperance hymns linked church and home, and focused attention on the relationship between the purity of the altar and the purity of individual believers. At the same time, they enhanced the eucharistic piety of Christians who were not ordinarily noted for the frequency of their reception of communion.[21]

---

19. "Report of the Commission on Unfermented Wines" Minutes, 1879 Convention, 81–86, cited in Ruth Bordin, *Woman and Temperance: The Quest for Power and Liberty, 1873–1900* (Philadelphia: Temple University Press, 1981), 54. Bordin says that "There was considerable general discussion in temperance circles about the Greek translation of the three Hebrew words for wine, and sanction only of *tirosh* (which meant unfermented wine), but this position received little support from the more respectable Biblical scholars."

20. Cited in George W. Ewing, *The Well-Tempered Lyre: Songs and Verse of the Temperance Movement* (Dallas: SMU Press, 1977), 31.

21. The Christian Church (Disciples of Christ), practicing weekly communion, is one exception.

The success of the women's campaign against fermented wine at the Lord's Supper was rapid and widespread, and in the thirty years following 1840 (when only 7 percent of Protestant congregations used unfermented wine), mainline Protestant churches began to legislate the exclusive use of grape juice at the Lord's Table.[22] By 1872, for example, the members of New York Annual Conference of the Methodist Church passed a resolution which said that "the use of intoxicating, that is, fermented wines in our communion service is incompatible with the teachings of our Lord Jesus Christ," and committed themselves to do "the utmost to secure the general introduction of unfermented wine for Sacramental purposes in all our charges."[23] The role of women temperance workers, hymn writers, and ordinary "teetotal" parishioners in this massive sacramental shift cannot be overestimated.

Guildswomen

One subset of women is worth special consideration, because it had considerable influence over worship in an age in which one might think that all liturgical decisions were invariably imposed from the top down. Medieval guildswomen claimed not only a fair degree of autonomy and social equality with their fathers, brothers and husbands,[24] but also wielded power within the church, by virtue of their ability to raise large sums of money and to act as a body to press for liturgical change. The principle behind a guild (sometimes spelled "gild") was simple: Guilds were voluntary associations of individuals bound by oath to some common purpose or purposes. Widespread throughout medieval Europe, the guilds not only supported particular crafts and professions, but also had distinctly religious purposes as well. "Guilds were universally characterized, on the one hand, by a concern for the swift salvation from purgatory of the souls of dead members through rites of intercession and, on the other, by some form of commensality among the living."[25] Most were founded and run by laity, at least before 1500,[26] and membership crossed and transcended parish boundaries, and could thus easily accommodate the increased mobility of its members. One could be a member

---

22. Presbyterians were quite resistant to the change and Episcopalian, Lutheran, and Catholic churches were unmoved by the WCTU arguments. See Joseph Timberlake, *Prohibition and the Progressive Movement, 1900–1920* (Cambridge: Harvard University Press, 1963), 10–11.

23. *Minutes of the New York Annual Conference of the Methodist Episcopal Church* (New York: Methodist Publishing, 1872), 86.

24. In guilds, sisters had more or less the same status as the brothers. In some, women served as officers, and in most they joined as full members in their own right.

25. Gervase Rosser, "Communities of Parish and Guild in the Late Middle Ages," in *Parish Church and People: Local Studies in Lay Religion, 1350–1750*, ed. Susan J. Wright (London: Hutchinson, 1988), 32.

26. Italian guilds were something of an exception to this general rule. Clerical control over guilds in Italy was asserted sometime in the mid-fifteenth century.

of several guilds at the same time. Family members often joined the same guild, and there were also children's guilds that, like their adult counterparts, had devotional and philanthropic aims.[27] Often guilds have been portrayed as institutions in conflict with parishes, as "quasi-churches," "extra-parochial parishes," "alternative models of the church," but at least until the Reformation, churches and guilds worked together in a situation of mutual dependence.

Because they were a part of the fabric of an increasingly prosperous merchant class, guilds had a great deal of disposable income. Usually a guildswoman paid an entry fee and an annual subscription, and also made periodic donations for particular named purposes during the year. At her death, a bequest to the guild was also expected.[28] This money was used, in part at least, to ensure the eternal destiny of the members of the guild, past and present. To this end, "each [guild] had its focus on the Christian altar, and it was common, where funds permitted, for a guild to employ one or more chaplains to celebrate intercessory masses on behalf of the society."[29] These chaplains operated within designated guild chapels, sometimes set apart from the parish church, sometimes incorporated within it.

The Guild of St. Peter, a mixed guild of men and women that operated in the Northampton area, is a good example. Guild members employed a priest for work in the parish church of St. Peter, who "was kept busy almost hourly throughout the year upon the task of offering a plethora of memorial masses and prayers for the brothers and sisters of the fraternity, living and dead." This was no less onerous work than that undertaken by the priest hired by the Guild of St. Mary, a women's guild in Northampton, who provided a mass each day at dawn (for merchants who must be at their business early:[30] *qui mane in negociis suis devillare voluerunt*), another at eleven o'clock in the morning (for those who must travel into town on business[31]), and a third at one o'clock in the afternoon, for laborers before they returned to their houses.[32]

For our purposes, the most important aspect of the guild system is that the lay memberships of guilds (men and women equally in mixed guilds and women alone in women's guilds) not only exercised the power to elect priests of their choice to serve the guild chantries, they also determined the shape and character of

---

27. In 1502, St. Mary's Church at Hill, London, received 6s 8d "of the gadryng of maydens of Sainte Barnabas." Nicholas Orme, "Children in the Church," *Journal of Ecclesiastical History* 45, no. 4 (October 1994): 583.
28. "All these groups collected money, kept lights on the church, and sometimes contributed to parish finances." Ibid., 584.
29. Rosser, "Communities of Parish and Guild in the Late Middle Ages," 32.
30. "Pro oportunitate ut utilitate extraneorum et aliorum."
31. "Quam extranei laborantes et tarde villam venientes poterunt audiere quando omnes aliae misse in eadem villa finiuntur."
32. Rosser, "Communities of Parish and Guild in the Late Middle Ages," 42.

liturgical practice. Decisions were made by women about which masses would be said by the chaplain on which days and what sort of calendar he would be obliged to keep. Guildswomen also determined suitable devotional practices and imposed them on fellow members,[33] and many new liturgical feasts and devotions were initially spread by guilds, which took them up as special disciplines. One scholar traces the spread of the Feast of Corpus Christi, declared a feast of the church in 1264, to the efforts of lay guilds. "These bodies organized processions surrounding the liturgy of the festal day and fostered understanding of the doctrine; the early fifteenth century text of the ordinances of the York guild of Corpus Christi is preceded by a sermon on *Hoc est corpus meum*."[34]

Because guilds placed a strong emphasis on the public behavior of their members, many times guildswomen took over the function of the parish clergy in setting penitential disciplines for moral transgression. A persistent offender might be struck off the guild register (as one Lichfield guild ordinance says, "even as that of the malefactor from the Book of Life") without possibility of readmission.[35]

Guilds gave members a number of other liturgical advantages in addition to masses said for the repose of their souls and control over the guild's worship life. If a guildswoman couldn't come to church because of the nature of her work, the guild would ensure that candles would be lighted at the elevation of the host at mass for her pious intentions. When the parish clergy went to offer a sick member communion at home, the guild might provide a candle to be carried in procession in front of the priest.[36] But perhaps the most significant ritual benefit members derived from membership in a guild was the guild funeral, at which the entire guild would be present, and money for singers, candles, processions, and anniversary masses would be provided (see fig. 12).

Guild events were always showy, but the high point of guild liturgical activity was the annual festival, celebrated by all members of the guild as a ritual of social solidarity with one another, with deceased associates, and with God. Usually marking the feast day of the guild's patron saint, these ceremonial occasions gave guilds the opportunity to use their extensive financial resources to stage elaborate processions, feasts, and open-air dramatic performances.

---

33. "Each brother and sister of the Virgin Mary's guild at Maldon in Essex was bound to say three times a year the psalter of the Virgin for the living and dead members of the fraternity and for all Christian souls." Ibid., 43.

34. Ibid., 45.

35. *The Guild of Saint Mary and St. John the Baptist, Lichfield: Ordinances of the Late Fourteenth-Century* (Stafford: Staffordshire Record Society, 1988).

36. This seems to have been the practice in Great Yarmouth and very likely in other guilds as well. Rosser, "Communities of Parish and Guild in the Late Middle Ages," 41.

In the march sponsored by the Gild of St. George in Norwich . . . church bells
rang, priests chanted, and poor men carried candles and banners before a
parade of gild members outfitted in colorful red and white liveries. The
event culminated in a dramatic confrontation between a man dressed as
St. George and another who played a fire-breathing dragon. Gild processions
usually ended at a church where a special mass was said for the assembled
members of the gild. After the service, many gilds held sumptuous feasts
that featured mountains of roasted meat, barrels of ale, and entertainment
by minstrel groups. . . . [37]

On these occasions, guild members usually wore a common livery, brightly colored
and embroidered with the guild's insignia, and processed from the guildhall to the
church via the home of the master or mistress of the guild. Such guild festivals
afforded guildswomen a high degree of public visibility, serving as a "signal that
they had reached the pinnacle of urban society and now enjoyed the prestige and
valuable social connections that membership conferred."[38]

Guilds also served the liturgical needs of their nonguild neighbors in various
ways. Some guilds committed themselves to the increase in liturgical literacy.
The Pater Noster Guild of York, founded in 1389, is a good example. Its "primary
declared aim was the explication to others of the Lord's Prayer," and to this end
it set up in York Minster a board on which was displayed "the whole meaning and
use" of the prayer.[39] In some situations the guild itself might trace its origins to a
particular liturgical need. When the town of Baldock experienced a precipitous
decline in population in the middle of the fifteenth century and was no longer able
either to afford repairs to the parish church or to pay the priest a living wage, the
women parishioners founded the Guild of the Name of Jesus. Explicitly dedicated
to raising funds related to the maintenance of public worship in the town, the
guild was authorized to grant an indulgence to any members who contributed to
this work.[40]

Most of the sixteenth-century reformers were committed to stamping out the
guilds, for their promotion of the cult of saints, indulgences, mass intentions,
and for — as the Act of Edward VI dissolving the fraternities puts it — "devising

---

37. Ben R. McCree, "Religious Gilds and the Regulation of Behavior in Late Medieval Towns,"
in *People, Politics and Community in the Later Middle Ages*, ed. Joel Rosenthal and Colin Richmond
(Gloucester, U.K.: Alan Sutton, and New York: St. Martin's, 1987), 116–17.

38. Ibid.

39. For the illiterate, the guild regularly performed a play "setting forth the goodness of the Lord's
Prayer," with each phrase of the prayer linked to combat against one of the seven deadly sins. Rosser,
"Communities of Parish and Guild in the Late Middle Ages," 46.

40. Ibid., 29.

and phantasisnge vayne opynions of Purgatorye."[41] For women this was a serious blow, depriving them of "potential patrons, role models, intercessors, and opportunities for memberships of sometimes very important voluntary associations."[42] Historian J. J. Scarisbrick and others have argued that by destroying guilds and lay confraternities, the Reformation brought about a major power shift out of the hands of the laity and into the hands of the clergy.[43] There was some gain for lay control in the development of various church offices — churchwardens, treasurers, sidesmen — but these posts were only very occasionally held by women.[44] In addition, with the abolition of mixed-sex voluntary associations, "the pious participation of men and women in the ritual life of the parish had become more marked by gender lines. . . . Men had grander funerals, and older or widowed women moved to lesser places within the church."[45] This diminution of women's liturgical roles was a prominent feature of the post-Reformation churches, at least until the seventeenth century when women prophets and sect leaders came into prominence.

The Power of the Dead

At times, dead women have had more influence over Christian worship than living women. A very saintly woman might have power over worship through the medium of her mortal remains and other tangible remnants of her life. When the relics of a saint are known to be associated with miraculous events, worshipers visiting her shrine are likely to perform particular rites as a means of connecting with the saint's spiritual energy, and if she is incorporated into the liturgical calendar as a feast of the church, the designated propers (prayers stipulated for that specific occasion) have the highest ecclesial authority. In addition, from very early in the church's history, pious women have been the most ardent promoters of the cult of relics and the liturgical devotion that has surrounded them, and by publicizing cures and other benefits among their family

---

41. I Edward VI, c. 14.

42. Schen, "Women and the London Parishes, 1500–1620," 254.

43. He admits, though, that wealthy lay people gained influence in the church through the acquisition of ecclesiastical lands. See J. J. Scarisbrick, *The Reformation and the English People* (Oxford: Oxford University Press, 1984), 39, 162–70.

44. See William M. Jacob, *Lay People and Religion in the Early Eighteenth Century* (Cambridge: Cambridge University Press, 1996). "Women as well as men were elected overseers and churchwardens. At St. Benedict's in Lincoln women served as churchwardens in six years between 1720 and 1739. In 1739, both the churchwardens were women" (10). The vestry, which managed the affairs of the parish, was composed of ratepayers of the parish (i.e., those who owned property), which on this basis would also have included women.

45. Schen, "Women and the London Parishes, 1500–1620," 267.

and friends are often responsible for the promotion of the cultus surrounding a particular saint. The liturgical devotion to the Veil of Veronica is one
example.

In 1216, the image of Veronica was being carried in a papal procession and
miraculously reversed itself so that it could be seen by those following the procession. To mark this event, Pope Innocent III composed a prayer in Veronica's honor
attached an indulgence of ten days for each time the prayer was said. An early
convert to the power of devotion to the Veil of Veronica, the visionary German
nun Mechtild of Hackeborn (c. 1241–1298?) records a revelation confirming the
power of the relic.[46] Mechtild's revelations normally followed the course of the
liturgical year, but on the day of the exposition of the Veil of Saint Veronica she
reports having had a vision in which she saw Christ enthroned in majesty, with
those who honored Veronica's image with the special prayer approaching him,
carrying their sins. These they placed at his feet where they immediately turned
into precious jewels. It is difficult to deny that Mechtild's vision was clearly aimed
at arousing piety toward, and confirming the religious status of, the image and
selling the indulgences associated with saying the prayer of Pope Innocent, and
that it was effective in spreading liturgical devotion to the Veil of Veronica across
Northern Europe.[47]

Women have also been active in procuring relics for veneration. The Empress
Eudocia (d. 460) and her friend and spiritual guide Melania the Younger (c. 383–
438) were dedicated to the hunt for relics in the Holy Land as a part of their quest
for both personal sanctity and public acclaim. Following in the footsteps of an
earlier Imperial woman, Helen the mother of Constantine, who was credited with
discovery of the True Cross (and hence the inauguration of the Feast of the Holy
Cross, September 14), Eudocia is said to have brought the bones of St. Stephen to
Constantinople, and to have built and furnished a basilica dedicated to his name
in which to house them. Indeed, Helen becomes the prototype for many women
relic-hunters. St. Radegund (518–87), an avid collector of relics for her convent
in Gaul, inaugurated a mission to procure the True Cross from the Imperial Court
at Constantinople. Her biographer, Baudovinia, says of her: "What Helena did in
oriental lands, Radegund the blessed did in Gaul."[48]

---

46. Mechtild of Hackeborn, *Book of Ghostly Grace of Mechtild Hackeborn*, ed. Theresa A. Halligan
(Toronto: Pontifical Institute of Medieval Studies, 1979), 30.

47. Flora Lewis, "Rewarding Devotion: Indulgences and the Promotion of Images," in *The Church
and the Arts*, ed. Diana Wood (Oxford: Basil Blackwell, 1992), 179–80.

48. *Vita Radegundis* 2, c. 16, 387–89; ed. and trans. Jo Ann McNamarra and John E. Halborg
with E. Gordon Whatley, *Sainted Women of the Dark Ages* (Durham, N.C.: Duke University Press,
1992), 97.

As time went by and relics increasingly became extremely valuable commodities (in the financial as well as the spiritual sense),[49] medieval women were influential in preserving and guarding them, establishing for them a proper setting within the worship space, and ensuring that they were treated with the proper respect and care. In 1249, Thomas de Cantimpré composed the *Life* of Lutgard of Aywières (1182?–1246) — a woman known for wisdom, sanctity, and miracles — and dedicated it to Hawide, abbess of Aywières, in order to obtain from her a relic of Lutgard's body that was displayed in the abbey chapel. "There seems to have been a dispute as to which part of [Lutgard's] body would be suitable. Hawide thought a finger would be sufficient but Thomas de Cantimpré replied that he wanted her head and her hand. The abbess was adamant."[50] In this kind of negotiation over the relics of female saints, which was quite common before the Reformation, women often stood toe-to-toe with men, and equally often had the last word, asserting and claiming not only their own authority but the authority of the saint in question.

Of course more ordinary women could also have a profound influence over the shape of parochial worship after they were dead. After the eleventh century, the incidence of directives in women's wills for masses to be said for the repose of their soul increases, until by 1500 they are a standard feature in the testamentary documents of middle- and upper-class women. After the Reformation, Protestant women often direct their executors to ensure that sermons be preached in their memory, replacing the endowment previous generations would have set up for the mass-priest with an endowment for the preacher. Typical is Elizabeth Stevyns, who leaves a sum of money to be given to "her preacher, or another learned one, to make one sermon at her burial and four on the following Sundays in St. Mary Woolnoth [London]."[51]

Sanctity and money often allowed women to reach out beyond the grave and to continue to shape the worship of parishes, monasteries, and sometimes entire religious traditions after their death. Because the whole question of women's legacies is so important to understanding their liturgical interests and sensibilities, we shall devote further attention to them below.[52] Suffice it to say that women who could afford to leave money and other property after their death to build

---

49. See Patrick J. Geary, *Futura Sacra: Thefts of Relics in the Central Middle Ages* (Princeton, N.J.: Princeton University Press, 1978).

50. Brenda Bolton, "Vita Matrum: A Further Aspect of the Frauenfrage," in *Medieval Women*, ed. Derek Baker (Oxford: Basil Blackwell, 1978), 259–60.

51. Schen, "Women and the London Parishes, 1500–1620," 258. Schen directly relates the practice of requesting sermons on various days after the burial to the pre-Reformation pattern of asking for masses to be said after death. She continues, "Even in 1579 a woman asked for thirty sermons in the year following her death, a nod toward the former practice of trental of masses."

52. See appendix 2.

and furnish churches, to endow clerical appointments, or to buy or have made liturgical books could influence worship for generations to come.

Sectarians

In a study of the influence of women on Christian worship, it is very tempting to devote disproportionate attention to women sectarians. Not only is there a great deal of extant secondary literature on their life and work,[53] but they also serve as illustrations of the important part that worship played in programs of religious and social reform. Even those radical groups not led by women often exhibited a particularly high degree of tolerance for women's participation and control, because they were so often driven by an eschatological and millennial zeal in which gender distinctions were subsumed to the more subtle gradations of spiritual fitness for eternity. Indeed, a religious group's degree of deviance from the mainstream has often been determined by assessing its attitude towards women. In an anonymous 1642 pamphlet, twenty-nine London "sects" are described, and the author says that they all have three things in common: indulging in free love, speaking out of turn and in strange tongues, and encouraging "the unseemly display and power of women."[54]

It must be admitted that women sectarians are atypical, and while their influence on their immediate circle of followers (and, of course, on those who opposed them as well) is often profound, it is difficult to find patterns or to make general observations from their activities that apply across a wide range of women's worship history. But they are a part of the historical narrative, and to exclude them entirely because they are exceptional would be to distort the record.[55] Indeed, some of these visionary and passionate women are key to understanding

---

53. See, for example, Rebecca Larson, *Daughters of Light: Quaker Women Preaching and Prophesying in the Colonies and Abroad, 1700–1775* (New York: Knopf, 1999).

54. Anonymous, *The Discovery of 29 Sects Here in London* (London, 1642), 4, cited in Norma McMullen, "The Education of English Gentlewomen, 1540–1640," *History of Education* 6 (1977): 92.

55. This is Claire Cross's argument. In reviewing the literature on sixteenth-century English Puritanism, especially the work of Keith Thomas, "Women and the Civil War Sects," *Past and Present* 13 (1958): 42–62; E. M. Williams, "Women Preachers in the Civil War," *Journal of Modern History* 1 (1929): 561–69; and R. L. Greaves, "The Ordination Controversy and the Spirit of Reform in Puritan England," *Journal of Ecclesiastical History* 21 (1970): 225–41, Cross says that each of these authors has stressed the opportunities provided by the disruption for women to exercise new roles for themselves. But in focusing on radical sectarian groups, Ranters, Quakers, Shakers, e.g., they have obscured the importance of "more sober protestant matrons." "For them the Civil War did not mark a new period of spiritual awakening or intellectual enlightenment: rather it brought to fruition a tradition of independent action by laywomen which can be traced back at least to the days of the Henrician Reformation." Claire Cross, " 'He-Goats before the Flocks': A Note about the Part Played by Women in the Founding of Some Civil War Churches," in *Popular Belief and Practice*, ed. G. J. Cuming and Derek Baker (Cambridge: Cambridge University Press, 1972), 195.

the liturgical dynamics of particular periods, especially periods of transition between one understanding of worship and another. The story of the remarkable
Dorothy Hazzard, for example, who in 1640 led a group of five men and women
who covenanted together to form a separatist church meeting in her own house
in Bristol, is critical to understanding, as historian Claire Cross puts it, "the continuity between popular protestantism of the later sixteenth and early seventeenth
centuries and the congregational churches of the 1640s."[56]

In any kind of religious and political disruption, women often find niches for
exercising influence over Christian worship, as well as for raising questions about
the theological underpinnings of the various forms of Christian common prayer.
Again, Dorothy Hazzard is a good example. While still a faithful member of the
Church of England parish in which her husband was minister, she began having
serious doubts about the godliness of the services in the *Book of Common Prayer.*
At the grocery store she inherited from her first husband, she kept hours on
Christmas Day in order to demonstrate her disdain for "superstitious feasts," and
at home she provided a refuge for women giving birth, so that they might avoid
the offensive ceremonies (including the Sign of the Cross) required at the baptism
of their children.[57]

In church, however, Hazzard's scruples about the legitimacy of worship led to
a crisis. One Sunday morning, agonizing about whether to attend or to stay away,
she picked up her Bible and read Revelation 14:9–11: "If any man worship the
beast and his image ... the same shall drink of the wrath of God." She resolved
never again to hear the Church of England service. With four men, three other
merchants like herself and a minister of religion, she formed the Broadmead
Church, which grew rapidly to a membership of 160. She saw to it that ministers
of suitable theological principles were hired to preach, and when the town was
taken over by Royalists during the Civil War, she moved the congregation to a
house in London for the duration.

Katherine Chidley, another founder of separatist churches, was an almost exact
contemporary of Dorothy Hazzard, but chose a more "intellectual" form of protest
against the liturgical status quo. In her 1641 book *The Justification for the Independent Churches of Christ,*[58] she gives her views on the authority of the laity within
the church: "I tell you," she writes, " ... such honest souls (though they are not
of the clergy, but of those whom you call the laity) are the fittest men on earth to
make churches, and to choose their own ministers ... though they be tradesmen,

---

56. Cross, " 'He-Goats before the Flocks,' " 195.
57. Ibid., 196.
58. The book was a response to Thomas Edwards's *Reasons against the Independent Government of
Particular Congregations.*

and such as these have dependency on Christ alone, whose way is properly the sincere way of God."[59] Chidley's biographers also tell us that she once disputed with the parish priest at Stepney on the question of "whether an ecclesiastical building which had once been dedicated to a popish saint could ever be used for the reformed service of God."[60]

Other sectarian women used the power of the written word to influence the liturgical status quo. Two Quaker women, Priscilla Cotton and Mary Cole, leveled bitter accusations against England's clergy in their mid-seventeenth-century pamphlet *To the Priests and People of England, We Discharge Our Consciences*[61] particularly for their part in restraining the speech of women in church:

> thou tellest the people, Women must not speak in a Church, whereas it is not spoke only of a Female, for we are all one both male and female in Christ Jesus, but it's weakness that is the women by the Scriptures forbidden.... Indeed, you your selves are the women, that are forbidden to speak in the Church, that are become women.[62]

(Just after this pamphlet appeared, Cotton and Cole were imprisoned in Exeter jail.)

Women without literary skill might use their resources to finance the sectarian literature of others. In 1588–89, Martin Marprelate relied on the support of women for the publication of secret, anonymous pamphlets agitating for Puritan worship reform:

> One important member of this network of secrecy was a wealthy widow, Elizabeth Crane, who permitted the Martinist press to remain alternately at two of her homes between April and November 1588. From May to August of the next year, the press was housed by Mrs. Roger Wigston, who "deliberately" kept her husband uninformed of the presence to protect him from arrest as an accomplice.[63]

Although many other women sectarians participated in this type of pamphlet warfare directly, they often did it anonymously so that their gender would not be used as ammunition against the principles they were espousing.

---

59. Katherine Chidley, *Justification* (London, 1641), 32.

60. Cross, "'He-Goats before the Flocks,'" 200.

61. London, 1655. Collected in G. K. Fortescue, ed., *Catalogue of the Pamphlets, Books, Newspapers and Manuscripts . . . Collected by George Thomason, 1640–1661*, 2 vols. (London: British Museum, 1908).

62. Fortescue, ed., *Catalogue*, 5. For another example of a tract encouraging women's liturgical participation, see also Margaret Fell's *Women Speaking Justified* (1666).

63. Retha M. Warnicke, *Women of the English Renaissance and Reformation*, Contributions to Women's Studies 38 (Westport, Conn.: Greenwood Press, 1982), 146.

Sectarian women could also be more actively disruptive influences in services of public worship in their efforts to "purify" the existing practice. In 1524 Eleanor Higgs in Burford (England), a follower of the Lollard cause, was removed from church for exclaiming that she would burn the sacrament of the altar in her oven, and Eleanor Godfrey from Great Marlow ridiculed a fellow parishioner who showed reverence to the priest during mass.[64] Another Lollard, one "Mistress Castle" of London, was described in court documents as "a meddler and reader of scripture in the church," implying that while the prayers were being read, she was engaged in loudly declaiming portions of the Bible. At about the same time, London matron Elizabeth Sampson stopped the distribution of communion by exclaiming that she herself "could make as good bread as that was; and that it was not the body of our Lord, for it is but bread, for God cannot be both in heaven and on earth."[65] More than one hundred years later, Quaker Ann Audland (c. 1627–64) was imprisoned in Banbury near Oxford in 1655 for assaulting the local minister and using "blasphemous words" in a service of public worship.

Other women were even more radical, taking over the appointed roles of the ordained and presiding over the existing ritual in unauthorized services of worship. For example, the mid-thirteenth-century Guglielmites believed in a female incarnation of the Holy Spirit, Guglielma of Milan, who would presently establish a new church ruled by a female pope and female cardinals.[66] Assuming the office of priest, Guglielma's women disciples "consecrated hosts on Guglielma's grave, and with sectaries as acolytes recited the mass according to Roman ritual."[67] Unfortunately, most of the descriptions of women's illicit liturgical activity comes from accusations made by men as part of wider attempts to discredit sectarian views and practices, and as such their accuracy is open to some question. Many are similar in tone to Roger Dymoke's accusation from about 1390, describing Lollard conventicles in London and Oxford "where *women* (whom they call virgins, but are in fact their whores) have, I cannot say celebrated, but rather profaned masses, of which they are publicly and manifestly convicted."[68]

One thing that even this cursory look at sectarian women reveals is the wide variety of ways and means by which women have exerted influence over the

---

64. Claire Cross, " 'Great Reasoners in Scripture': Women Lollards, 1380–1530," in *Medieval Women*, ed. Derek Baker (Oxford: Basil Blackwell, 1978), 373.

65. Ibid., 376.

66. "Only with the advent of this female church would worldwide salvation be possible. And without it, according to the Guglielmites, there would be complete destruction." Stephen E. Wessley, "The Thirteenth-Century Guglielmites: Salvation through Women," in *Medieval Women*, ed. Derek Baker (Oxford: Basil Blackwell, 1978), 289. See p. 291.

67. Ibid.

68. Roger Dymoke, *Liber* (London: Early English Text Society, 1912), 63–64.

public worship of the church: from mild rebuke to formal disputation, from passive resistance to public disorder. Of course, women sectarians have also paid a heavy price for this kind of activity. They have been imprisoned, excommunicated, reviled, and publicly humiliated. Some have paid with their lives, not only because of the radical content and subversive potential of their religious views, but also because these women were so often working out of situations of limited social and economic power. Powerful women had other means of influencing the church's worship, and their wealth and prestige usually protected them from the more serious consequences of any challenge they might make to the liturgical status quo.

Royalty

All too often in Christian history, the extent of women's influence over worship has been in direct proportion to their personal affluence and social standing. As a result, royal women have had particular opportunities to influence Christian worship, not only locally and nationally, but in some cases globally as well. Like their sectarian sisters, these women are hardly typical, but because their wealth and social prestige have afforded them a peculiar power over clergy and ecclesiastical institutions, when they have chosen to act in matters of worship, their actions have often had almost immediate, and sometimes very long-lasting, consequences. Queens and empresses — ruling in their own right, as coregents with their husbands, and as regents for minor sons or brothers — have been able to appoint and depose church officials, to legislate on liturgical matters in both ecclesiastical and civil courts, to convoke local and general church councils, to build and furnish private chapels and parochial churches, and to found monastic communities and determine the Rule under which they operated. Indeed, the fact that a given people might engage in any form of Christian worship at all is often the direct result of the efforts of an empress or queen to convert her husband.

Margaret of Scotland (1046?–1093) is a good example of this kind of royal influence over national religious life. Hungarian by birth, Margaret very likely spent her childhood in the newly Christian court of St. Stephen and her formative years in the Anglo-Saxon court of her aunt and uncle, Queen Edith and Edward (the Confessor). After her marriage to Malcolm, king of the Scots, she encouraged him to strengthen links — religious as well as political — with the south; as a part of this effort, she attempted to stamp out a number of local liturgical customs. She was also committed to the reform of monastic life in Scotland. Although she respected the native Scottish hermits, at this time there was no regular Benedictine house north of Ely, and in about 1089 she approached Llanfranc of Canterbury

and asked that he send "Goldwine and two other brethren" to Scotland in order
that a Benedictine monastery might be founded at Dunfermline. This was done,
and even though after her death there was a strong popular reaction to the mod-
ification of local religious custom (and a strong reaction among court officials to
the "Anglification" of court custom), many of her liturgical programs established
themselves and Benedictine monasticism continued to flourish.[69]

Sometimes the liturgical influence of imperial women was more subtle in its
effect, if perhaps more ruthless in its execution. So it was with Irene the Athenian
and iconoclasm in Byzantium. When the great iconoclastic emperor Constantine
V was choosing a wife for his son Leo, Irene would seem to have been a peculiar
choice, coming as she did from the Greek peninsula, a well-known hotbed of
image worship. As long as Constantine was alive, Irene could not give expression
to her views on images, but he died in 775, and her husband was crowned Emperor
Leo IV. Leo shared his father's liturgical opinions and managed to appoint staunch
iconoclasts to key imperial posts, while at the same time Irene was trying to fill
the palace with those who sympathized with her own views. But Leo's health was
poor, and when he died in 780 Irene named herself regent for the next emperor,
Constantine's ten-year-old son.

Irene was a shrewd and able politician, and although various conspiracies
against her on account of her iconophile tendencies followed Leo's death, she
eluded them all and soon began actively to work toward the restoration of image
worship to the Byzantine Church. After the death of her staunchest opponent, the
patriarch, Paul, Irene chose his successor and sent a letter to the pope, Adrian I,
asking him to convene an ecumenical council in order that the matter of images
might be decided. The council was convened in Constantinople on August 17,
786, with both Eastern and Western churches represented. Among the delegates
there were still some staunch iconoclasts who managed to enlist regiments from
Irene's own imperial guard to wreck the proceedings. When the council assembled, Irene was present, sitting with her son; the guard rushed in with drawn
swords threatening death to all image worshipers.

The council broke up and the delegates threatened to abandon the process,
but Irene was not defeated. After rounding up the traitors, she saw to it that the
council was reconvened in the spring of the next year, this time in Nicaea rather
than the politically turbulent capital. By this time, however, Irene had managed
to replace or force the retirement of the most stridently iconoclastic bishops, and

---

69. For the debates about Margaret's influence in Scotland, see Derek Baker, "'A Nursery of
Saints': St. Margaret of Scotland Reconsidered," in *Medieval Women*, ed. Derek Baker (Oxford: Basil
Blackwell, 1978), 119–41. See also Joan Morris, *The Lady Was a Bishop: The Hidden History of Women
with Clerical Ordination and the Jurisdiction of Bishops* (London: Macmillan, 1973), passim.

by enforcing a system of precedence, she ensured that those of her own opinions were dominant. As a result, the doctrine of reverence to holy images was restored and defined, and the document that was approved at the eighth and final session of the council was signed by Irene as empress, who made a speech to the delegates on the critical importance of what they had done.[70]

If any one royal woman stands out in the history of English-speaking Christian worship it is Elizabeth I (1533–1603). Caught up in the center of the liturgical debate between Anglicans and Puritans, and in questions about the degree of official toleration that would be accorded to the worship practices of Roman Catholics, Baptists, and Quakers, Elizabeth gave her name to an era of religious, sociocultural, and political ferment that would, fifty years after her death, result in English civil war and the overthrow of the monarchy. Much of her influence on worship was indirect, through the appointment of bishops of reforming tendencies, the authority she added to a set of homilies to be preached in churches (many of which were designed to shape liturgical sensibilities of the hearers), and her mandates on the disposition of church funds.

Other royal women are often left out of the "official" story of the worship of a particular nation and church and can only be found with diligent attention to the sources. Liturgical scholars are fond of telling the tale (apocryphal though it may be[71]) of the Russian Tsar Vladimir's (c. 954–1015) "Examination of the Faiths"[72] at which representatives from the major faith traditions were invited to Kiev in order that they might try to persuade him of the merits of their particular religious path for the Russian situation. Unable to come to a decision on the basis of their formal presentations, Vladimir allegedly sent emissaries to observe the worship of the competing traditions, who reported back that Muslim prayers were "dour and nasty," the Latin mass was ugly, but that what they saw in Constantinople among the Orthodox was of such splendor that they did not know whether they were on earth or in heaven. Hearing this, the story goes, Vladimir immediately declared Orthodoxy the religion of Russia and mass baptisms began the following year.

The person who is usually excluded from this tale, of course, is Olga (c. 903–69), Vladimir's grandmother, who ruled Russia as regent from 945 to 962. Olga's spiritual and liturgical home had been Constantinople long before Vladimir sent his emissaries there. At her baptism in c. 957 she had taken the name Helen (after the mother of Constantine), and had built and furnished a church in Kiev

---

70. See, for an analysis, Steven Runciman, "The Empress Irene the Athenian," in *Medieval Women,* ed. Derek Baker (Oxford: Basil Blackwell, 1978), passim. Irene's story is told in the *Chronicle* of Theophanes, who is thought to be a reliable, if sympathetic, recorder of the facts of Irene's reign.

71. The story seems to be a Greek interpolation inserted at a later date into the part of the *Russian Primary Chronicle* that gives details of Vladimir's reign.

72. This event is usually dated somewhere in the years 986–87.

with the same dedication as the main basilica in Constantinople, St. Sophia. Clearly she must be taken into account in shaping Vladimir's commitment to Orthodoxy.[73] "Indeed, in their argument in favor of Orthodoxy, the emissaries used her as a weapon: 'If the Greek religion were bad, our grandmother Olga, that wisest of mortals, would not have embraced it.' "[74] Another woman is also a possible factor in this story. Vladimir's consort at the time was Greek, a former nun in an Orthodox convent, and she likely exercised her own influence in his decision in favor of her form of worship.[75]

Abbesses and Religious Superiors

It can be argued that the abbess or prioress of a large and important convent was the most powerful of all medieval women, with a scope of authority that even royal women did not possess. Because the life of a monastery centered on the regular and exact performance of Christian common prayer, much of her power was exercised over worship. In the early period of women's monastic history at least, abbesses generally had a quasi-clerical status: They governed their own convents, heard confession, undertook the benediction of their nuns,[76] preached, and had jurisdiction over the parish churches in their lands (including the appointment of clergy).[77] Certain convents were officially exempt from the oversight of bishops and the jurisdiction of secular authorities;[78] in some places — such as Jouarre,

---

73. Of course there were political reasons for his choice also, including the need to negotiate with increasingly Christianized Slav states.

74. A. P. Vlasto, *The Entry of the Slavs into Christendom* (Cambridge: Cambridge University Press, 1979), 250.

75. There is a similar story told of King Wenceslas of Poland and his queen Ljudmila.

76. See Suzanne Fonay Wemple, "Women from the Fifth to the Tenth Century," in *A History of Women in the West*, vol. 2: *Silences of the Middle Ages*, ed. Christiane Klapisch-Zuber (Cambridge, Mass.: Belknap Press of Harvard University Press, 1992), 189.

77. Migne, *PL*, 216 (1855), col 356. See also Wemple, "Women from the Fifth to the Tenth Century," 189. For example, in a charter issued between 1239 and 1341 by the prioress and convent of Ankerwyke, we can see not only the preference for the Requiem as the principal mass for the convent, but also the recognition that the requirement to say the Requiem mass daily might be quite burdensome on the clergy. In this charter, the nuns agreed to maintain a chaplain who, on all days when this was lawful, should celebrate the mass of Requiem. It is added, however, that "lest the sameness of the celebration should seem tedious to the celebrant, the said chaplain shall be permitted to celebrate a mass of the Blessed Virgin on one day each week, and a mass of the Holy Spirit or of any saint of his choice on another. But if on those days, or either of them, the chaplain can have the help of another priest, who would celebrate the aforesaid mass for the dead, he is diligently to procure its celebration. If, however, he has no means of [doing] this, he is to be released from this care." Cited in K. L. Wood-Legh, *Perpetual Chantries in Britain* (Cambridge: Cambridge University Press, 1965), 285–86.

78. In the case of Ely, the bishop himself went to Rome to seek an exemption during the time of Etheldreda. She had died by the time he returned with permission in 679. Convents in Thanet, Folkestone, Lyming, Sheppey, and Dover were exempt, with their abbesses signing the decree of exemption after the archbishop, but before the other clergy present.

Chelles, and Faremoutiers in France — abbesses had a license to strike their own coinage, with an image of their own head on the obverse.[79]

Sometimes medieval abbesses were not simply exempt from political or epis-copal jurisdiction; they functioned *in loco episcoporum*. The German abbesses of the period, for example, had great secular and ecclesiastical power, and a num-ber were given the title *Sacerdos Maxima* ("high priest"). One of them, Abbess Matilda of the community of German canonesses called the Quedlinberg Insti-tute, who at her election as abbess was wife of King Hendrich I, is referred to in contemporary documents as "Metropolitana." Other German canonesses seem to have had the title *sacerdos, praepositos, decana,* and *custos,* indicating that, at least in some of these communities, there were ordained women.[80] Even well into the Victorian era in some places, certain abbesses retained this kind of power. When Lady Herbert visited Spain in 1866, she went to a Cistercian convent at Las Huelgas and records her surprise that "Here the Mother Abbess was a Princess Palatine with feudal power over all the lands and villages around. She appointed her own priests and confessors and was in charge of the hospital a mile from the convent."[81] Even the Quedlinberg Institute seems to have retained its ancient

---

79. Abbesses of exempt monastic houses had jurisdiction over their often-large districts in both civil and ecclesiastical matters, including the management of parish churches within the boundaries of the monastic territories. This jurisdictional power was not undermined until the Council of Trent. Exemptions dated from as early as 455 released the abbey from both paying taxes and from the oversight of the bishop; the abbey was subject only to the pope and later to the superior generals of the order to which they adhered. In the case of the Cistercian abbey of Brindisi (Italy) some thirty-six parishes came under the abbess's direct control, in which both Greek and Latin rites were allowed. In Spain certainly, and in other places very probably, the abbess of an exempt monastery had the power to confer benefices on clergy; to transfer clergy from one parish to another and to examine them for suitability; to create, dissolve, or unite parishes in her district; to approve confessors; to summons and punish any priest preaching heretical views or irregular rites; and to punish laity for transgressions. She was charged with rebuilding dilapidated churches and to hear cases in the consistory court for ensuring that the sacraments were duly celebrated. She could dispense clergy from their obligation to say the Hours, and license bishops to officiate at pontifical services in her diocese, and priests to say mass in her churches. She had the right to hear the confessions of her nuns and to preach in the house chapel. Among the signatories to the Synod of Cambrais in 1565 are those of Margaret de Hinkaert, abbess of Malbodio, and Margaret of Noyelles, abbess of Nivelles.

80. One can see the degree of influence this community exercised in a story told by Joan Morris. In 1021, Bishop Arnolphus of Halberstadt began the custom of a Palm Sunday procession to the cloister on Mount Sion, where the institute was situated. Clergy and laity "swarmed up the hillside and feasted at the top at the expense of the nuns, who supplied quantities of fish to the crowds." But by the beginning of the next century, the community had fallen on hard times and was no longer able to afford this kind of hospitality, and Abbess Sophia stopped the procession from coming. The occupant of the episcopal seat at the time "considered the refusal of the procession an imposition on his rights, and he excommunicated the abbess and all those dependent on her." Abbess Sophia, on the strength of her exemption, considered she had the right to refuse, and appealed to Rome. Innocent III sent two bulls to the bishop of Halberstadt upholding the abbess and insisting on her being reinstated.... He mentioned that the abbess had authority over both the clergy and the laity belonging to her." Morris, *The Lady Was a Bishop,* 61.

81. Lady Herbert, *Impressions of Spain in 1866,* 29, cited in Madeline Beard, *Faith and Fortune* (Leominster, U.K.: Gracewing, 1997), 30.

rights of exemption after the Reformation, with the abbess continuing to exercise authority in liturgical matters. In 1539, Abbess Ann called a convocation, and the decision was taken to adopt the Lutheran rites. The Institute continued as a sisterhood, with a school for girls attached and jurisdiction still held by the abbess, until it was secularized by the Prussian government in 1803.

The Reformation was a period of particular testing for abbesses and their communities. Sister Jeanne de Jussie, a Swiss Franciscan nun, wrote a history of the Reformation in Geneva[82] in which she describes the attempts by the nuns of her convent to keep their liturgical life intact in the absence of priests and with constant harassment by civil magistrates. In many of these cases, abbesses took over sacerdotal duties; for example, on Ash Wednesday 1533 the abbess of Sr. Jussie's community placed ashes on the heads of the sisters and led them in the penitential prayers. As Holy Week approached, the sisters joined with the remnant Catholic population in procession around the city, while Protestant women "stood by and ostentatiously continued to do their clothes mending and washing, thereby destroying the validity of that ritual behavior."[83]

When abbesses were also the founders of their order, and perhaps of peculiar sanctity as well, they claimed additional liturgical prerogatives. The revelation to found an order of nuns came to the future St. Bridget in 1346 along with details of the rule to be adopted, the pattern of prayer to be followed, and even the exact measurements of the chapels to be built for her communities.[84] She was also given in a vision by Christ that an angel would dictate to her the lessons to be read by the sisters at Matins throughout each week.[85] The angel is also

82. Jeanne de Jussie, *Le Levain du calvinisme, ou Commencement de l'heresie de Geneve*, ed. Ad.-C. Grivel (Geneva, 1865 [1535]).

83. Thomas Head, "The Religion of the Femmelettes: Ideals and Experience among Women in Fifteenth- and Sixteenth-Century France," in *That Gentle Strength: Historical Perspectives on Women in Christianity*, ed. Lynda L. Coon, Katherine J. Haldane, and Elisabeth W. Sommer (Charlottesville: University Press of Virginia, 1990), 156.

84. See *Revelationes Extravagans*, chap. 28 (J. B. Holloway, *St. Bride and Her Book: Birgitta of Sweden's Revelations* [Woodbridge: D. S. Brewer, 1997], 138–41); see also *Regula S. Salv* (Rules of Saint Saviour), cap. xii, xxi, xxv and Revel. I: 18, III, IX, 28, 29, 31, 34, 38. See also *The Bridgettine Breviary of Syon Abbey* (London: Henry Bradshaw Society, 1963). From the additions to the Regula, cap. X, viii: " 'Of Dyuyne seruyse and observaunces ther in': sethe euery religion is therfor ordeyned principally that dyuyne servyse schold be dewly contynued in holychirche, therfor it is acordyng that it be performed in suche wyse, that not only the doers therof, but also the herers be edyfyed ther by. Wherfor, that dyuyne seruyse may be contynued in this religion after a dewe order and forme, the sustres schal haue ther matens after the brethres matens, ther evensong after the brethres evensonge, complen after complen, so that nerhande ther neuer cesynge; ther somge schal be sadde, sober, and symple, with out brekyng of notes, and gay relesynge, with alle mekeness and deuocion; but organs schal thei neuer have none; ther psalmody schal be dystyncte and open, and althynge schal be mesured and moderyd after discreecion. In the quyer all schalle be as angels enclynynge together, rysynge together, knelynge togyder, stondynge, turnynge and syttyng togyder, all after one forme goynge and comynge togyder."

85. The twenty-one long lessons are collectively entitled "Sermo Angelicus," and the story of their communication to Bridget, who day by day awaited the angel in her chamber pen in hand, was

said to have given Bridget a parting command after dictating the lessons: "Loo I haue now shape a kyrtel to the quene of heuen modir of god ye therfor as ye may sew it up to geddir." ("Lo! I have now shaped a garment for the Queen of Heaven, the Mother of God. You, therefore, as you may, sew it up together.") In other words, Bridget was to provide the rest of the Office, thus completing the "garment" designed by the angel.[86]

But few abbesses had this kind of supernatural assistance, and most had to rely on their personal charisma and political savvy to maintain their liturgical influence. Abbess Hilda of Whitby (614–80) is a good example of this combination of gifts and the use of those gifts in an attempt to influence the liturgical life of the English church. The great-niece of King Edwin of Northumbria, Hilda was among the first converts in the far north of England to receive baptism in 627; she soon went on to found several monasteries including Whitby,[87] a double monastery of men and women over which she had oversight as abbess.[88] The importance of Hilda and the convent she headed is seen in the fact that it was chosen to host the church synod that was called to settle the thorny question of whether the Celtic liturgy should be abandoned in favor of the new Roman rites, a synod at which Hilda was doubtless a full and vigorous participant.[89] The Celtic party resisted any change directed by "some remote man in Rome" on the matter, but those from the south believed that St. Peter would be more likely to open the gates of heaven to those who followed the Roman pattern. Although Hilda threw her considerable weight on the side of the Celtic representatives, royal prerogatives prevailed, and Whitby and the Celts were obliged to change their calendar. But she continued to oppose the decision to the end of her life, petitioning the pope a number of times for redress.[90]

Again, although abbesses and other religious superiors are atypical, like royal women their influence on the liturgy, both inside and outside their convents, is often overlooked by historians of worship. In the present day, they continue to oversee the worship life of their communities and to provide for the wider community places of retreat and refreshment where the daily round of conventual prayer serves as a model for good liturgical practice. Many religious superiors have been

---

related by Alfonso de Vadaterra (d. 1388) in his "Prologus in Sermonem Angelicus de Eccellentia Virginis Mariae...." *Bridgettine Breviary*, xxvii.

86. It is said that her confessor, Brother Peter, completed this task under Bridget's direction.

87. The abbey was then called Streanaeshalch.

88. She was also responsible for the training of local clergy as well.

89. Her successor, Aelfleda, took an equally significant role at the Council of Nidd (705).

90. See Joan Nicholson, "Feminae Gloriosae: Women in the Age of Bede," in *Medieval Women*, ed. Derek Baker (Oxford: Basil Blackwell, 1978), 17–18.

active promoters of the twentieth-century liturgical movement[91] and continue to explore the boundaries of common prayer in ecumenical and interfaith situations.

Revivalism and Women's Public Prayer

Although most usually associated with the First and Second Great Awakenings, the Moravian and Methodist revivals, and the American Frontier revivals of the nineteenth century, attempts at the revival of "true religion" have punctuated Christian history since the very beginning. Religious revivals have almost always been accompanied by renewal and reform of worship practices, and to the extent that women have promoted and guided revival they have also influenced revivalist worship. But many liturgical scholars argue that revivalist worship is a separate tradition of Christian worship in its own right, with a specific character and its own internal integrity,[92] and if this is so then key women revivalists have also contributed to shaping that character.

At the most basic level, some revivals have been ignited and spread by the religious experiences of women, as was certainly the case in the remarkable 1727 revival at Herrnhut, a Moravian religious settlement in Saxony.

> It began with the personal crisis of an eleven year old girl, Susanne Kühnel. Shortly before, she had been present at her mother's death bed [and] had been deeply moved by the evident joy with which she had surrendered her life to her Lord. The girl perceived that her mother had something which she lacked, and a powerful conversion struggle was added to her natural distress at personal loss.[93]

At a dramatic communion service a few nights later, the spiritual renewal spread to other young girls in the community and, as one observer reports, "There was to be heard in the night of 29 August from ten at night till one in the morning a heart-rending praying and singing by the girls of Berthelsdorf and Herrnhut upon the Hutberg... a spirit of prayer prevailed among the children as is beyond words to express."[94] Soon, the whole community was in a state of religious ecstasy, resulting in a renewed depth and fervency in prayer that would attract John Wesley to the Moravians several years later.

---

91. See pp. 114–17.
92. See James F. White, *Protestant Worship: Traditions in Transition* (Louisville: Westminster/John Knox Press, 1989), 45–57.
93. W. R. Ward, *The Protestant Evangelical Awakening* (Cambridge: Cambridge University Press, 1992), 127.
94. Beyreuther, *Zinzendorf und die sich althier...finden*, 206–7; cited in ibid.

Other women provided financial support for revival meetings, enabling them to flourish and to influence wide segments of the population. In 1630, Anne Cunningham, Dowager Marchioness of Hamilton, asked the local minister of Shotts in Scotland if she might be allowed to nominate the preachers who would take part in the next summer communion at the kirk. Money was no object, and word soon went out that a number of the most notable orators in Scotland had accepted Cunningham's invitation to preach.[95] "The presence of this distinguished band of Scottish churchmen drew an immense crowd to the Kirk O'Shotts that weekend, and all the way through Sunday night the services were charged with deep solemnity and power."[96] So great was the enthusiasm among those gathered from all over Scotland that "the unprecedented decision was taken to hold an additional service Monday afternoon — this, like the others, of course, to be out of doors, in the kirkyard surrounding the Church."[97] In order to accommodate the overnight visitors, the women of Shotts offered hospitality in their homes, and that Sunday evening domestic prayer meetings all over the village increased the fervor of revival. A whole series of Scottish revivals in that year was sparked by this three-day meeting, an occasion inaugurated by the philanthropy of one woman and the welcome of others.

Very soon women would be taking more public roles in religious revivals and would find a freedom to act in worship in often unprecedented ways. The Methodist revival of the eighteenth century is but one example. Historian Diane Lobody has suggested that it was the "very subversive spirituality of Methodism" that "coaxed women into speech."[98] This speech took many forms, the most basic of which was public prayer, often described in biblical terms. It was said that a Mrs. Crosby, an early Methodist class leader, "used to begin prayer with the simplicity of a little child, and then rise to the language of a mother of Israel. Thus she prayed with the Spirit and with the understanding."[99] In the earliest

---

95. Among these were David Dickson, Robert Bruce, John Livingston, and William Rigg, whose names were household words in Scotland.

96. David P. Thomson, ed., *Women of the Scottish Church* (Skinnergate, Perth: Munro and Scott, 1975), 38.

97. Ibid.

98. Diane H. Lobody, "'That Language Might Be Given Me': Women's Experience in Early Methodism," in *Perspectives* (December 1992): 134; and "Lost in the Ocean of Love': The Spiritual Writings of Catherine Livingstone Garrettson," in *Rethinking Methodist History: A Bicentennial Historical Consultation*, ed. Russell Richey and Kenneth Rowe (Nashville: Kingswood Books, 1985), 175–84.

99. Joseph Sutcliffe, *The Experience of Frances Pawson* (London: Cordeau, 1813), 104–5. This is Pawson's description of her friend, Mrs. Crosby. Freeborn Garrettson reports in 1784 that the class meeting of young women he met with had a "mother in Israel to be their leader." Garrettson's *Journal*, Saturday, February 28, 1784, cited in Freeborn Garrettson, *Freeborn Garrettson, American Methodist Pioneer: Life and Journals of Rev. Freeborn Garrettson, 1752–1857* (Rutland, Vt.: Academy Books, 1984), 237. This seems a common phrase, and is used also by John Wesley, Thomas Ware, and others.

American revivals, public prayer by women was quite common. In his seminal study of revivalist religion in nineteenth-century New York state, Whitney Cross claims that questions about the suitability of public praying by women arose quite late:

> One witness believed that "in *all instances,* where they [women] were most active, revivals were most powerful." No evidence has appeared to support the notion that either Charles Finney or Thomas Weld made any bold innovation in allowing feminine prayers in "promiscuous assemblies." No one in Oneida County thought the matter worthy of mention until the practice had to be defended before shocked New Englanders at New Lebanon.[100]

For many Christian women, public prayer was their first experience of any sort of public speaking, let alone worship leadership, and it could be initiated in various ways. Charismatic clergy wives were sometimes given permission to conclude services led by their husbands. "My method, as you know," writes a Mrs. Holder in 1825, "was to give a word of exhortation after my dear husband had finished his sermon, or to pray, as I felt led by the Spirit of God."[101]

Many women were astonished at the religious power public prayer released in them. Hester Ann Roe Rogers was a Methodist class leader in 1782 when Elizabeth Richie came to help lead her class. She reports in her journal feeling "quite small and insignificant until Miss Ritchie called on her 'to help out,' i.e., to lead in prayer."[102] She continues, "I dared not refuse. I was astonished to feel in a few moments my every word fill with power. Nancy Andrews, who had been in chains of unbelief soon melted into tears . . . and while I was praying, the heavens indeed were opened — I was full of faith, and the power of God rested on all."[103] Because it fell under the category of charismatic gift, prayer was more difficult to challenge as a form of women's religious activity. Although for some any sort of

---

100. Whitney Cross, *The Burned-Over District: The Social and Intellectual History of Enthusiastic Religion in Western New York, 1800–1850* (Ithaca, N.Y.: Cornell University Press, 1982), 177. Women also preached the Millerite millennial Adventism in the 1830s and early 1840s (304).

101. Zechariah Taft, *Biographical Sketches of the Lives and Public Ministry of Various Holy Women,* 2 vols. (Volume I, London: Kershaw, 1825; Volume II, Leeds: Cullingworth, 1828), 2:128.

102. Hester Ann Roe Rogers, manuscript journal entry for June 25, 1782. Cited in Earl Kent Brown, *Women of Mr. Wesley's Methodism,* Studies in Women and Religion (New York and Toronto: Edwin Mellen Press, 1983), 49.

103. Ibid. Rogers describes her discovery of the power of public prayer: "I opened the Hymn book on that precious hymn 'O for a Heart to Praise my God' etc — and in singing it, was filled indeed with the Divine Presence and love unprintable. Prayer was as a Gate of Heaven, and I sensibly felt the words given me to speak were not my own. I think I never was so entirely led out of myself and influenced by a divine power — while the dear people seemed as melting wax before the fire." Cited in Brown, *Women of Mr. Wesley's Methodism,* 48.

public speech by women in "promiscuous assemblies" had immoral connotations, "women who prayed publicly could be argued to be protected from the Pauline prohibitions by I Corinthians 11:5."[104]

Some women, however, moved from public praying during periods of general religious awakening to the leadership of wholesale revivals in their own right. One woman's flair for dramatic self-promotion would make her not only an important innovator in revivalist worship methods, but a genuine national celebrity in 1920s–1930s America. Aimee Semple McPherson (1891–1944) was founder of the Foursquare Gospel Church and builder of the Angelus Temple in Los Angeles, where she presented what she termed "illustrated sermons." Full of light and sound and theatricality, these revival meetings were certainly the direct antecedent of today's multimedia "contemporary worship" events. Never far from public controversy (much of which she herself encouraged in a bid for publicity) Semple McPherson recognized that conversion is a dramatic experience, and that if worship is to lead to conversion, it must be an equally dramatic experience. Liturgist Nathan Mitchell remarks on why her contribution to the history of Christian worship has been so thoroughly ignored:

> Liturgy "professionals" of today might accuse her of manipulative sensationalism, but it is clear McPherson understood instinctively that public worship "is symbolic, aesthetic, ascetical, and sapiential...." But because McPherson did her work in ways and in places that many (male) religionists disdain as outlandish, heretical and disgusting, her creative contributions as preacher and liturgist are neglected.[105]

Semple McPherson is perhaps the best example of the way in which revivalism released women to exercise liturgical influence. Millennial zeal and the eschatological urgency of seeking God overcame the myriad social and cultural constraints on women, empowering them to contribute their gifts to the leadership of Christian common prayer.

Missionaries

Another result of the millennialist tendencies in eighteenth- and nineteenth-century Christianity was the heightening of missionary activity, both at home

---

104. See ibid., 21–22.

105. Nathan Mitchell, "The Amen Corner," *Worship* 73, no. 3 (1999): 70. (The internal quotations are from Aidan Kavanagh, *On Liturgical Theology* [New York: Pueblo, 1984], 147.)

and abroad.[106] Often, women missionaries have become responsible for the worship lives of those among whom they work, the best of them contributing to the
evangelization effort through a deep knowledge of the Christian liturgical tradition, sensitivity to the problems of inculturation, and their own brand of pastoral
creativity. This kind of combination is clearly seen in Grace Young, who worked
in the Methodist mission in Ulu, Duke of York Islands, Papua New Guinea, in
1946. Describing her approach to the missionary enterprise, she says:

> What we planned to do was not to take out anything from their culture
> that was good but if something was bad that wasn't part of their lives, if
> it was really bad, then we would try.... We didn't want to change things,
> that was up to them to want to change, not for us to introduce. We didn't
> build a church for ages; we always had open air church, because we wanted
> them to build the church. It was to be theirs, and they wanted it, even if
> we infiltrated a few ideas.[107]

It seems unlikely that Young would have taken a substantially different attitude
to the matter of Christian worship.

Women have been, on the whole, remarkably aware of the serious social consequences of dislodging the established worship patterns of other people, particularly
other women. An inscription in Winchester (England) Cathedral dated 1864 describes Harriette McDougall as the one who "first taught Christ to the Women of
Borneo." In her autobiography, McDougall describes the opposition to Christianity among the Iban women in Sarawak, who at the coming of the missionaries
had had a high degree of social, political, religious, and economic equality with
the men.

> Christianity had strong opponents in the women of all the Dayak tribes.
> They held important parts in all the feasts, incantations and superstitions.
> ...For many years the women were opposed to a religion which cleared
> away the superstitious customs which were the delight of their lives, their
> chief amusement and dissipation, and a means of influencing the men.[108]

---

106. See on this Lillian Lewis Shiman, *Women and Leadership in Nineteenth-Century England* (New
York: St. Martin's, 1992), 61–62.

107. Cited in Chilla Bulbeck, *Australian Women in Papua New Guinea: Colonial Passages 1920–1960*
(Cambridge: Cambridge University Press, 1992), 177.

108. Harriet McDougall, *Sketches of Our Life in Sarawak* (London, 1882), 73–75; cited in Brian
Taylor, "Gender in Sarawak: Mission and Reception," in *Gender and Christian Religion*, ed. R. N.
Swanson (Woodbridge, U.K.: Boydell, 1998), 467.

Many women missionaries have instinctively understood, often in ways their male counterparts could not, that native women's essential roles in traditional cere-monies might make them reluctant to embrace the religious practice offered by the missionaries. "Even if they were attracted by the Gospel, they would find no comparable role in the sober Anglican worship of the nineteenth century."[109]

Women missionaries often carried current debates over worship with them into the liturgical laboratory of the mission field, sometimes with permanent re-sults for the future of Christian worship in a particular place. For example, in 1910 when Alice Luce was serving as the Anglican missionary principal of the Queen Victoria High School in Agra, India (1905–12), she became convinced of the reality of baptism in the Holy Spirit. Leaving her assignment, she moved to America and obtained missionary ordination in the Assemblies of God. Preach-ing the "Bible evidence" doctrine of Pentecostal tongue-speaking, Luce "began to evangelize Latinos and train them for the ministry. Her students carried the clas-sical Pentecostal view of Spirit baptism . . . across North America and throughout Spanish America."[110] At the same time, an influential book by Minnie F. Abrams (1859–1912) on the nature of the 1905–6 Pentecostal revival,[111] which delib-erately omitted any reference to the necessity of speaking in tongues, was also having a profound impact on the Christian mission in Latin America, causing a rift between those influenced by Luce who insisted on tongue-speaking in wor-ship and those influenced by Abrams who did not. Although this conflict in Pentecostal teaching soon resolved itself at home, it continued to divide Latin American Pentecostal worshipers for many decades.

Women on the homeland mission fields also had opportunities to influence worship. In the mills and back streets, on Native American reservations and among migrant workers, women have shaped the worship lives of new Christians. Sarah Martin (1791–1843) was an English working-class woman, a dressmaker by trade, working among women prisoners at Great Yarmouth, visiting and speaking to inmates about her faith, as well as organizing gainful employment for them during their incarceration. Because no clergyman would volunteer, she led the prison congregation in Sunday services for nearly twenty years from 1819 to 1837.[112] A window in the parish church at Great Yarmouth is erected in her memory, and portrays the poor women of Joppa displaying garments strewn out

---

109. Ibid., 468.
110. Gary B. McGee, "'Latter Rain' Falling in the East: Early Twentieth-Century Pentecostalism in India and the Debate on Speaking in Tongues," *Church History* 68, no. 3 (September 1999): 648–64.
111. *Baptism of the Holy Ghost and Fire* (1906).
112. F. K. Prochaska, *Women and Philanthropy in Nineteenth-Century England* (Oxford: Oxford University Press, 1980), 167.

of love and piety for their dead friend Dorcas. "It was a fitting tribute to the dressmaker turned philanthropist."[113]

There is much, much more to be learned about the influence of women on Christian worship as a part of the process of evangelization. As missiologists and liturgists begin to revisit the journals and diaries of missionary women, and to look there for evidence of worship attitudes and practices, the reconstruction of missionary women's liturgical influence can begin.

Women and the Liturgical Renewal in the Modern Period

During the past century, an explosion of liturgical renewal has taken place within most every mainline Christian denomination, culminating in revised rites for Roman Catholics, Lutherans, Methodists, Presbyterians, and others. Although many women have actively agitated for the reform of worship in the course of Christian history, the increasing expansion of the social and educational status of women has allowed them to be extensively influential in this process. As apologists, scholars of ancient texts (on which many reformed rites have been patterned), artists, and liturgical musicians, these women have given depth and energy to the various reform movements. At the same time, other women have worked diligently in opposition to liturgical reform, and in some cases have been the most articulate voices against the replacement of traditional rites.

The modern Roman Catholic liturgical reformation had its origins at the turn of the twentieth century in the monasteries of Europe, where scholarship into the early history of Christian worship was provoking a concern about the degree to which extraneous accretions had adhered to the liturgy over time, distorting its essential shape and purpose. The influential *Jarhbuch für Liturgiewissenschaft* (Yearbook for the study of liturgy) was edited by Odo Cassell, OSB, for nearly two decades. But it was Sr. Agape Kiesgen from the Abbey of the Holy Cross in Herstelle who maintained the index to that work, extending its usefulness to scholars all over the world.[114] In the 1930s, a nun of the same abbey, Aemiliana Löhr, wrote a series of "the most moving...and historically accurate"[115] meditations

---

113. Ibid., 168.

114. See Teresa Berger, "The Classical Liturgical Movement in Germany and Austria: Moved by Women?" *Worship* 66 (1992): 234.

115. Nathan Mitchell, "The Amen Corner: 'A Mansion for a Rat'" *Worship* (1993): 64–72. Mitchell cites the following example: "With marvelous insight, [the early church] chose the Paschal Night for her great baptismal solemnities. Together with the newly baptized she celebrated a true and holy Passover from the...night of sin...unto the Promised Land of grace, the bright day of Christ. Her children, washed in the holy waters of baptism, were now sprinkled with the blood of the true Lamb; and their lips (which St. Ambrose calls doorposts and portals for the entry of the divine Logos) empurpled with the eucharistic wine of both new life and the wondrous food by which it is sustained

on the liturgy for Sundays and solemnities in order that laypeople might claim for themselves the riches of the calendar.

With the Second World War, much of the energy for Roman Catholic liturgical renewal transferred to North America, and women found numerous outlets there for exercising influence. Many were laywomen: Ade Bethune (1914–2002), artist and founder-owner of the St. Leo Shop in Newport, Rhode Island, which became a national resource for the liturgical arts; Dorothy Coddington (b. 1912), editor of the *Catholic Worker* and with her husband founder-editor of *Liturgy and Sociology Journal* (1936–39), who was vitally concerned with teaching families (and particularly children) the meaning of the liturgy; Justine Ward (1879–1975), who was convinced of the spiritual value of Gregorian Chant and who devised a simple method for teaching it to young people.[116]

Although justly famous for her labors in support of Christian socialism through the Catholic Worker movement, Dorothy Day (1897–1980) deserves equal credit for her support and encouragement of the Roman Catholic liturgical movement, and for connecting it to the principles of social justice espoused in the *Catholic Worker* magazine. She insisted that each issue of *The Worker* contain an article on some aspect of the liturgy. Equally intriguing is Day's encouragement of the daily recitation of the night prayers of Compline at the various Worker Houses around the country, where homeless and marginal people were fed and given other forms of support. Describing Compline at the Catholic Worker House in New York City, Day writes:

> Smokey Joe knows [all the chants and hymns] by heart — though he is not very tuneful. Some sing *basso profundo* and some sing *recto tono*, and . . . it does not help matters that two or three of the older women who are tone deaf delight in singing too. But they enjoy themselves and it is the night prayer of the church, and God hears. . . . Our singing prepares us for another day. Early tomorrow morning work will start again, and so our life. . . . The surroundings may be harsh. But where love is, God is.[117]

This practice was not universally accepted by the Worker staff, however. Mary Sheehan, for example, was skeptical of the whole idea of Compline: "Who ever

---

and nourished; and the pure flesh of the Lamb, sacred unleavened bread of the Eucharist." *The Year of Our Lord*, trans. a monk of St. Benedict (New York: P. J. Kenedy and Sons, 1937), 159. See Kathleen Hughes, *How Firm a Foundation: Voices of the Early Liturgical Movement* (Chicago: Liturgy Training Publications, 1990).

116. See below, p. 263.

117. Dorothy Day, *Loaves and Fishes* (San Francisco: Harper & Row, 1963), cited in Hughes, *How Firm a Foundation*, 81.

heard of lay people saying these prayers?" she asked. "If they want to be monks then they should go to monasteries."[118]

The Grail Movement, founded in 1929 as a women's renewal movement in the Netherlands, was brought to the United States by Lydwine van Kerssbergen and Joan Overboss and centered on a farm in Libertyville, Illinois (near Chicago). It began its work by offering retreats there, guided by the most influential leaders of the liturgical movement and aiming to make the liturgy come alive for women, and especially to make the eucharist the center of the Christian spiritual life. In some of their literature, the Grail spoke of laity and clergy "celebrating the Holy Mysteries together," which brought the women into conflict with the local bishop, who insisted that laypeople only assist at mass, "but they do not celebrate Mass, which essentially consists in Acts of exclusively priestly power."[119] In 1944 the Grail transferred its base to Loveland, Ohio, where it provided a setting for experimentation with new forms of liturgical prayer and committed itself to exploring the relationship between liturgy and social justice.

When liturgical renewal began to spread to the Protestant churches in the 1960s, women also began to make important contributions to liturgical reform, both within their own denominations and ecumenically. As scholars of liturgical history, members of liturgical revision committees, and pastors of churches that tested new rites, women's work was indispensable both to the revision of service books and to the engendering of enthusiasm for the new forms of worship. The influence of women on the liturgical life of churches expanded still further as the first Protestant women graduated from programs in liturgical studies at traditionally Roman Catholic institutions such as Notre Dame (Indiana), Catholic University of America (Washington, D.C.), and Louvain (Belgium), and took up seminary teaching posts. Protestant women also began teaching in doctoral programs, contributing to the education of future scholars of the liturgy.

One of the earliest and most visible recent changes in the English-speaking liturgy was the shift from traditional Elizabethan English to contemporary language in the new services. On this matter we can find women not only as promoters of the change, but vocal opponents as well. In 1981, one year after the promulgation of the Church of England's *Alternative Service Book* with its contemporary language rites, Helen Gardner preached the University Sermon at Cambridge University, taking the occasion to criticize the new book. A scholar of T. S. Eliot and John Donne, Gardner complained that the prayers lacked poetic resonance and that the new biblical translations were unsatisfactory for reading aloud in public worship.

---

118. Keith F. Pecklers, *The Unread Vision: The Liturgical Movement in the United States of America, 1926–1955* (Collegeville, Minn.: Liturgical Press, 1998), 110.

119. Cited in ibid., 119.

The language, she says, "divides the generations and prevents the sense that in worship we enter into a communion with the dead and the unborn." She concludes her sermon by saying that "I think if I were in great distress or trouble of mind I should find it difficult to bring my sorrows to the most modern of the rites."[120]

English novelist P(hyllis). D. James (b. 1920), for a time a member of the Church of England Liturgical Commission, has been a staunch and vocal advocate of the retention of the *Book of Common Prayer* (1662). Active in the "Prayer Book Society" (formerly the "Society for the Preservation of the Book of Common Prayer"), she writes:

> We have to ask ourselves whether we really want a philistine Church whose services will be repugnant to those who seek to worship God in the beauty of holiness, a Church in which dignity, excellence of word and music, quietude and good order are all sacrificed to the demands of fashionable social, theological, sexist and liturgical theory including, God help us, inclusive language.[121]

On this issue, which is perhaps debated more publicly in England and other places where the church is established by law, the influence of royalty on worship sometimes continues as well. England's Princess Alexandra and the late Princess Margaret have both spoken out strongly in defense of the 1662 *Book of Common Prayer* at meetings of the Prayer Book Society, adding their voices to that of the Prince of Wales, another noted opponent of change.

"Women Church"

Probably the most radical attempt to give women full control over Christian worship is the "Women Church" movement of the twentieth century. Although usually thought of as a recent phenomenon, the first experiment in a women-only church was made during the early years of the First World War at Wallasey (near Liverpool), England. Begun in March 1914 by the Women's Social and Political Union, the "Woman's Church" had no premises of its own, but met in a concert hall. Two Sunday services a week were held, one in the afternoon for women and one in the evening for a mixed congregation. The church aimed to recruit both women who, finding the traditional Church "like a cage...had come away in sheer disgust at the attitude of the clergy to the things which to them are dearer than life," and also those unattached to any church "who would...be eager and

---

120. *Cambridge Review*, June 1, 1981, 219–22.
121. In M. Perham, ed., *The Prayer Book Tradition Today* (London: SPCK, 1993).

anxious to attend a service where the real needs of women were sympathetically understood."[122] As one contemporary report stated:

> Women are to preach the sermons, offer the prayers, provide the music and take the collection...unthinking people will probably smile, but, after all, there is nothing novel in the idea of a Church governed by *one* sex only: the novelty...lies in the fact that it is the sex usually governed which is to govern.[123]

This early Woman's Church initiative was supported both by suffragettes and the first wave of Christian feminists, but it did not outlive the war years. It would take seventy years for the vision to be renewed.

In her 1984 book *Bread Not Stone*, biblical scholar Elisabeth Schüssler Fiorenza coined the term "ecclesia of women" or "Women Church,"[124] and during the next decade, the concept of an ecclesial community in which the liturgical and pastoral gifts of women could be fully exercised caught the imagination of women across North America. The movement also produced its own rites, some specifically designed to celebrate the specifics of women's life cycles — including childbirth and menopause — and enacted these rites at national conferences held in Chicago (1983) and Cincinnati (1987).[125] Especially important to Roman Catholic women, for whom existing male-dominated, highly clericalized structures were particularly confining, the Women Church movement allowed women "to define both 'church' and the terms of their own inclusion in that church."[126]

> The second half of the 1980s saw an increasing globalization of feminist liturgical communities, whether or not the term Women-Church is adopted to express this reality. In England, Holland, Germany, and Scandinavia, Christian feminists typically develop feminist liturgies as their way of expressing the vision of the celebration of women's spiritual and social redemption from patriarchy at their gatherings.[127]

---

122. Krista Cowman, " 'We Intend to Show What Our Lord Had Done for Women': The Liverpool Church League for Women's Suffrage, 1913–1918," in *Gender and Christian Religion*, ed. R. N. Swanson (Woodbridge, U.K.: Boydell, 1998), 484.

123. *Free Church Suffrage Times*, April 1914, cited in ibid., 485.

124. Elisabeth Schüssler Fiorenza, *Bread Not Stone* (Boston: Beacon, 1984), 1ff.

125. See Rosemary Radford Ruether, "The Women-Church Movement in Contemporary Christianity," in *Women's Leadership in Marginal Religions: Explorations outside the Mainstream*, ed. C. Wesinger (Urbana and Chicago: University of Indiana Press, 1993), 196–210; also Rosemary Radford Ruether, *Women Church: The Theology and Practice of Feminist Liturgical Communities* (San Francisco: Harper and Row, 1985).

126. Ruether, "The Women-Church Movement," 199.

127. Ibid.

The original dream some leaders of the Women Church movement entertained of an extended network of women-only churches has not been realized, and it is perhaps yet too early to assess the impact of the movement on the liturgical life of the mainline churches. The ordination of women in the Reformed, Lutheran, Methodist, and more recently, Anglican families of churches has diminished the urgency of an ecclesia of women in Protestantism; and among most Roman Catholic women, the conviction has grown that if change is to come, it must be generated from inside the church.[128] The reaction of churches and clergy to the ritual activities of the movement has often been strongly negative, and women clergy and seminary teachers of liturgy who have attended Women Church and other feminist convocations have sometimes been censured by their denominations. But the understanding of the distinctive liturgical needs of women and the distinctive contributions of feminist liturgical scholarship has surely increased since the movement began.

Conclusion

As we have seen in this chapter, throughout the history of Christianity the influence of individual women and groups of women has been extensive. On one level this is quite surprising, because so often restrictions have been placed on women's public activity and on their public *religious* activity in particular — restrictions against speaking, acting independently of men, serving in leadership roles in church and civic life. But at the same time, prayer in common with others has been at the heart of women's devotional lives, and in case after case women have determined that the demands God makes on them to speak out and to act in liturgical matters has superseded the demands society makes on them to keep silent.

This combination of demand and restriction has meant that women have had to be particularly creative in the ways and means by which they influenced the worship of the church. It has also often meant that women's attempts to control their own liturgical lives have been accompanied by a high degree of risk, and have sometimes had terrible consequences. Quaker women have been imprisoned for speaking out in church; women revivalists have been beaten in the street for leading public prayer meetings; Catholic, Lutheran, Reformed, and Anglican women have been excommunicated. These dramatic and courageous stories need to be collected and analyzed as we seek to discern patterns of women's influence and patterns of response to that influence.

---

128. The topic of women clergy and their relation to worship, which is a topic for investigation in its own right, will have to be left for another study.

Chapter Four

The Forms of
Women's Liturgical Piety

I can never rightly know the meaning o' what I hear at church, only a bit
here and there, but I know it's good words — I do.... For what you talk
o' your folks in your old country niver saying prayers by heart nor saying
'em out of a book, they must be wonderful cliver; for if I didn't know "Our
Father," and little bits of good words as I can carry out o' church wi' me, I
might down o' my knees every night, but nothing could I say.

— Dolly Winthrop in George Eliot's *Silas Marner*[1]

The Processes of Women's Liturgical Formation

In any study of the history of women at worship, it is important to ask not only
how women participated in worship, but also how they prepared for participation
in worship, how they interpreted that participation, and how they linked that
participation to the other aspects of their lives. In other words, how was women's
liturgical piety shaped and what shape did it take? The answers to these questions
may not be as straightforward as it first appears. Women have been socialized for
learning in different ways in different times and places, and although we know
quite a lot about the ways and means of men's learning, women's learning and
men's learning have often taken different forms and have been oriented toward
different ends. Further difficulties arise because so much of women's formation for
meaningful participation in worship has been done informally, in undocumented
conversations between and among women, and because so much of their liturgical
piety has been expressed privately, in letters, journals, and diaries that have been
lost to the historian. If scholars have only rarely attended to women's liturgical
lives in general, tending to focus instead on their deviation from liturgical and
theological norms, they have given even less attention to the piety that undergirds

---

1. George Eliot, *Silas Marner* (Oxford: Heinemann, 1989), 142.

and shapes women's liturgical lives. For this reason, secondary sources for this aspect of the study of women at worship are scarce.

Still, there are ways to begin to map the geography of women's liturgical piety. By looking at the circumstances under which women were formed for meaningful participation in worship, at the kinds of worship resources they had at their disposal (and who had access to them), and at the ways and means by which they expressed their understanding of worship, some sense of the shape of the meaning of worship in the lives of women should emerge. Further help comes from looking at the processes by which women expressed and transmitted other forms of knowledge, such as magic and folk wisdom. If our dreams and visions are in any sense windows onto the soul, and in this case onto our deepest liturgical aspirations, then the part worship plays in women's mystical experiences should also increase our understanding.

Social Contexts for Liturgical Formation

In every period of Christian history, the family home has been perhaps the most significant setting within which girls have been formed for participation in the worship of the church. There they have learned (generally from their mothers or other female relatives) to say the prayers of the liturgy, to enact the appropriate rituals, and to keep the liturgical day, week, and year. In addition, the preparation women have received in their households for baptism, confirmation, and the first reception of communion has surely been an indispensable adjunct to the preparation they have received from the clergy. Family letters, journals, and diaries have also been essential to the formation of young women for participation in worship. Handed down from mother to daughter to encourage the development of an appropriate liturgical piety across the generations, these documents have been essential devotional reading for many Christian women. Because the household has been such an important center of women's liturgical preparation and action, we give it sustained attention later in this book.[2]

The Christian congregation has also been responsible for women's liturgical for-mation, both as an aspect of the ongoing teaching office of the church and in the natural interchange among members of the community. In forms of preparation for the rites of initiation, in sermons and meditations on the liturgy, in conversa-tion with fellow parishioners on the meaning of the various prayers and rituals, women have absorbed both the piety and the practices of Christian worship. Dur-ing those periods in which the role of godparents (sponsors) had pedagogical as

---

2. See chap. 6.

well as social functions, godmothers taught young girls their prayers and encouraged diligence in daily and weekly worship, as well as the link between Christian hospitality and Christian worship.[3] At one time or another in Christian history, deaconesses, widows, and consecrated virgins have taken on the role of forming women for meaningful participation in the liturgy; at other times it has been the work of clergy and lay elders.

We have already seen the ways in which participation in guilds and pious confraternities afforded opportunities for women to have a great deal of influence over Christian worship in their local churches,[4] but guilds were also an important social context for the liturgical formation of women. The Confraternity (or Sodality) of the Blessed Sacrament is one good example. Established in March 1650 in Aquitaine, France, the Confraternity was designed to promote frequent communion and to stimulate individual piety through regular confession of sin, daily prayer, communion on major feast days, and participation in processions, all highly unusual liturgical activities for lay people at the time. Although many such guilds were established during this period,

> the real innovation of the solidarity of the Holy Sacrament was that it encouraged female participation.... The Confraternity of the Blessed Sacrament was, therefore, the first official body to mobilize women and to channel devotional energies into a visible and practical manifestation of them — that is, by means of processions and charitable works.[5]

In 1654, only four years after its founding, thirty-nine women belonged to the organization, under the joint leadership of Paule de Bigos, daughter of a prominent judge, and Françoise Depau.

Other guilds of this type encouraged their members to devote pious attention to the objects associated with the liturgy, most often the images of the saints and the infant Jesus. The members of these guilds saw their service to the image as a preparation for an eternity of service to the holy personage represented. "One confraternity was even created in seventeenth-century Italy to care for, wash, swaddle and cradle the newborn Christ. Here the effigy was not only clothed and adored, but handled, coddled, and taken for walks...."[6] This kind of women's

---

3. See Christine Pohl, *Making Room: Rediscovering Hospitality as a Christian Tradition* (Grand Rapids, Mich.: Eerdmans, 2001).

4. See pp. 90–94 and 261–62.

5. Gregory Hanlon, *Confession and Community in Seventeenth-Century France: Catholic and Protestant Coexistence in Aquitaine* (Philadelphia: University of Pennsylvania Press, 1993), 191–92.

6. Robin Briggs, *Communities of Belief: Cultural and Social Tensions in Early Modern France* (Oxford: Clarendon, 1995), 324.

religious guild[7] persists in the Roman Catholic Church to this day (the Guild of the Infant of Prague is one good example), continuing to focus specific attention on the promotion of liturgical piety among women members.

Various other forms of intentional societies — convents, communities of widows, parachurch organizations, and Sunday school classes — have also played a significant role in preparing women for meaningful participation in Christian worship. In England, for example, voluntary religious societies appeared in many urban parishes from 1680 onwards, just as industrialization, urbanization, and social mobility had begun increasingly to disrupt traditional patterns of family life (and, hence, the liturgical formation it afforded). Particularly associated with the "class" and "band" system of the Methodist movement,[8] these groups were made up of devout laypeople who gathered together regularly for purposes of mutual encouragement and sacramental, charitable, and devotional discipline. The charter of the Society at Old Romney, founded in 1734, gives us a sense of what these societies were about and the way in which they encouraged and shaped the liturgical sensibilities of women participants. The members of this society were to pray daily morning and evening, to fast, to visit and pray with the sick, to "read the Scriptures with attention, reflection, and application," to attend the public services of the Church, to "make a diligent improvement of the Sermons heard and delight in the Conversation of devout persons," to be constant and well-prepared in attending "the Most Holy Sacrament at all Publick opportunity," and to keep the Sabbath strictly.[9]

With the development in the nineteenth century of organized Sunday-school education for children, some of the socialization of young women into the liturgical life of the churches was transferred to that setting. More recently, Sunday school curricula in many denominations have followed the lectionary, in order that the course of instruction for children should mirror the ongoing worship of the community week by week. After Vatican II, the Roman Catholic Church, recognizing the increasing numbers of unchurched adults and looking to ancient patterns of initiation in response, developed a series of staged rituals that make up the Rite of Christian Initiation of Adults (RCIA).[10] Because its central concern is the formation of Christians for participation in worship, the RCIA has

---

7. This type of group is to be distinguished from the craft guilds that had largely died out before the Reformation.

8. John Wesley's "Holy Club" was modeled on a similar society established by his father at Epworth.

9. Cited in William M. Jacob, *Lay People and Religion in the Early Eighteenth Century* (Cambridge: Cambridge University Press, 1996), 77.

10. *Rite of Christian Initiation of Adults: Approved for Use in the Dioceses of the United States* (Collegeville, Minn.: Liturgical Press, 1988).

been adapted for use in adult catechesis in certain of the mainline Protestant churches. More recently, women participants in congregational renewal groups such as "Disciple" bible studies, Emmaus Walks, and Alpha Courses have found themselves better prepared for meaningful participation in worship.

Women's Formation and Women's Literacy

Although most women have historically absorbed the principles and practices of Christian common prayer and have transmitted them to others without the necessity of reading, the question of literacy does impinge on the issue of women's liturgical preparation and formation. To what extent could women read for themselves the texts and rubrics of the rites? Did women read learned treatises on the liturgy? Could women communicate their understanding of worship to those at a distance and to future generations in and through the medium of writing? As difficult as these questions may be to answer for any given period, only through attention to patterns of women's literacy can we have any hope of understanding the degree to which written material related to worship was available to them.

Separating competency in reading from competency in writing is important here. Until the seventeenth century, while reading was a skill that most aristocratic women would have sought to master, writing was considered a more technical craft — like bricklaying, thatching, and carpentry — and noble and middle-class women who had not mastered the skill of writing would have employed scribes to take down what they dictated. Often, as in the case of the *Book of Margery Kempe*,[11] the role of amanuensis was undertaken by clergy. For this reason among others, the question "Who was literate?" is so difficult to answer, because sometimes we mean "Who could read?" and sometimes we mean "Who could read *and* write?"

Getting hold of women's literacy is difficult for several additional reasons. Those social historians who have attempted to determine literacy rates in a given period or region have only recently begun to include women in their calculations, and geographical and sociological variations in literacy rates are wide. For example, in 1800, 68 percent of men and 20 percent of women could read and write in Scotland, while south of the border in England both the percentages and proportions are quite different: 60 percent for men and 40 percent for women. Religion is also often a factor. In France, historically Roman Catholic, only 48 percent of men and 27 percent of women could read and write in 1800, while in

---

11. See *The Book of Margery Kempe, A New Translation*, trans. John Skinner (New York: Image/Doubleday, 1998).

largely Protestant Holland, 83 percent of men and 43 percent of women were literate. Even in America there were substantial differences, especially between north and south. At the turn of the nineteenth century 88 percent of New England men and 46 percent of New England women were literate, but only 70 percent of Virginia men and 42 percent of Virginia women could read and write.[12]

Variations in literacy between rich and poor are still more difficult to calculate, and broader, less specific descriptions are commonly employed to describe the impact of social and economic divisions on the likelihood that any given person is able to read. For example, in describing the changes in rates of literacy in England over a period of one hundred years, Keith Wrightson can only say that "in 1580 illiteracy was a characteristic of the vast majority of the common people. By 1680 it was a special characteristic of the poor."[13] Sometimes the difference in literacy between the rich and others was in the ability to read and write in two languages rather than one. In the Middle Ages, even though many middle-class laypeople were literate in both English and French, "the ignorance of Latin was typical among less privileged lay folk."[14] But by no means could all wealthy women read Latin. The reading skills of Lady Margaret Beaufort (1443–1509), perhaps the wealthiest and most influential of all medieval women, were described by her chaplain:

> Right studious she was in bokes which she hadde in grete nombre bothe in Englysshe & in Frensshe/ & for her exercyse & for the prouffyte of others she dyde translate dyuerse maters of deuocyon out of Frensshe into Englysshe. Ful often she complayned that in her youthe she had not gyuen herself to the understondynge of latyn, wherein she had a lytell perceyuynge specyally of the rubryshhe of the ordynall for the sayeng of her seruyse whiche she dyde wel understande.[15]

This question of the ability of women to read Latin certainly impinges on their liturgical formation in those periods of Christian history when treatises on worship, devotional books, and official rites were written in Latin. (One begins to wonder, for example, how women used the most significant of medieval devotional books, the Latin *Primer*, or *Book of Hours*.[16])

---

12. P. L. Smith, *The Written Life in America* (Chicago: University of Chicago Press, 1973), 13–15.

13. Keith Wrightson, *English Society 1580–1680* (London: Hutchinson, 1982), 220.

14. Martha W. Driver, "Pictures in Print: Late Fifteenth- and Early Sixteenth-Century Books in English for Lay Readers," in *De Cella in Seculum: Religious and Secular Life and Devotion in Late Medieval England*, ed. Michael G. Sargeant (Cambridge: Brewer, 1989), 233–34.

15. From John Fisher's eulogy of Lady Margaret, *A Morning Remembrance* (London: de Worde, 1509).

16. Margaret Beaufort's daily services as described by Fisher certainly seem to mirror the contents of the Book of Hours, from the "matyns of our lady" to the "dryges and commendacyons" which typically were included at the end of the Book of Hours. Driver, "Pictures in Print," 135.

Clearly the act of reading itself has had different meanings in different periods. As one commentator says, "Perhaps in the pre-print era, the laity could ponder Books of Hours, read the rubrics, study the pictures. But in an age of vernacular literacy, stress began to be placed in comprehension of text."[17] The translator of *The Arte for to deye well* (1505) underscores the importance of reading for comprehension in his preface:

> I haue loked on this boke,
> & consyderyng that to all people of goodnes it is profitable,
> & that all people understondes not the latyn,
> I haue wyll to translate it...
> in to englysshe... to thende that al good crystens may read.[18]

This emphasis on the need to understand and profit from what one reads colors the process of women's liturgical formation from the sixteenth century onwards, if perhaps more emphatically among Protestant women than among Roman Catholic and Orthodox women.

The mechanics of reading has also changed over time. For most of Christian history, to "read" meant to read aloud, and only between the sixteenth and eighteenth centuries did silent reading gradually begin to take over, thus enabling the reader to engage in private reflection on what was read. Indeed, silent reading can be considered one of the major cultural developments in the early modern era. The technique of silent reading spread from one group to another in the Middle Ages, first among those working in the monastic scriptoria;[19] then around the middle of the twelfth century scholars in the universities learned the skill, followed nearly two centuries later by the lay aristocracy. Although by the time of the Continental Reformation silent reading was more or less the norm (at least for readers who also knew how to write), as late as the nineteenth century those who were only newly literate and for whom books were strange continued in reading aloud. (This fact also has interesting implications for attempts to reconstruct the *sound* of worship services, during which — until relatively recently — congregants were very likely not as reverently silent as we might imagine.)

Finally, it must be recognized that women who could write used their private diaries and journals as mechanisms for reflecting on and deepening their own liturgical piety. Over and over again we find women not only writing about their liturgical experience, but meditating on their past writing in order to trace the

---

17. Ibid.
18. Cited in ibid., 142.
19. It was certainly a most necessary skill in the scriptoria, where transcribers working on different texts would have been distracted by others in the scriptorium reading aloud.

course of their relationship with God. The diary of Grace Brown Elmore, written during the American Civil War, gives a sense of this interplay between writing and participation in worship:

> (September 28, 1862) Next Sunday is Communion, oh that I could separate my soul from the cares, pleasures, and vanities of the earth, and fix my thoughts on heaven! If I could but dwell upon the woes of my Redeemer's life instead of considering the trials of my own. I must examine my heart this week, lay it bare before my self, and in knowledge of its wickedness cast myself upon God, and rejoice in his mercy that redeems me. I must struggle against that suspicious temper, that irritability, uncharitableness, envy and self love that consumes me, *and I must write these struggles, that I may know and not forget my wickedness and weakness.*[20]

Elmore goes on in this vein at some length, and on each significant liturgical occasion throughout the year — a baptism, a funeral, or communion Sunday — she returns to questions of her devotional fitness for participation in the liturgy and the spiritual benefits she has derived from it.

The Question of Book Ownership

While reading potentially gave women the ability to reflect on the meaning of liturgical texts and commentaries, not every woman reader owned or had continuous access to books. (For a more complete picture of women's liturgical reading, literacy statistics need to be more carefully correlated with statistics on book ownership.[21]) Most of our information on the kinds and numbers of books owned by women is derived from wills, library inventories, and the mention of books in women's first-person writing and court testimony. So, for example, to get some sense of who owned copies of the *Book of Common Prayer* in the mid-seventeenth century, we might look to a petition to Parliament in 1641 from parishioners in Chester. The petitioners, including several women, assert that

> scarce any Family or Person that can read, but are furnished with the Books of Common Prayer, in the conscionable Use whereof, many Christian hearts have found unspeakable joy and Comfort; wherein the famous Church of

---

20. Marli F. Weiner, ed., *A Heritage of Woe: The Civil War Diary of Grace Brown Elmore, 1861–1868* (Athens: University of Georgia Press, 1997), 41 (emphasis added).

21. This process of analysis can be seen in, for example, David N. Bell, *What Nuns Read: Books and Libraries in Medieval English Nunneries* (Kalamazoo, Mich.: Cistercian Publications, 1995).

England our dear Mother hath just cause to Glory; and may she long flourish in the Practice of so blessed a liturgy.[22]

Because, for most of Christian history, an "inexpensive book" was a contradiction in terms, books often appear as special bequests in women's wills. Sometimes they are left by one woman to another, giving us a double dose of evidence for book ownership.[23] In her will dated 1459, for example, Agnes Bedford of Hull leaves one primer to her friend Agnes Swan and another ("the one I daily use") to one of the latter's children.[24] (This tells us not only that Agnes owned more than one Book of Hours, but that her devotional pattern included daily reading.)

Accounts books and the inscriptions on the flyleaves of books also help to fill out the picture of women's book use. So, for instance, the copy of the devotional book *The Orchard of Syon* in the Spencer collection at the New York Public Library was, according to the inscription on the front flyleaf, owned first by a "Syster elyzabeth Stryckland professed in Syon" (in other words, a nun of Syon Abbey). A second entry on the flyleaf states that "Ryc[hard] Assheton off Mydlton knyght executor unto my lady Stryckland deceased have gyffen thys boke unto my lady wyfe . . . in the xxiii yere off the Reyne of our sufferan kyng henre viii" (that is, in 1542). The book then passed to the Sacheverell family, to one "Katherin Sacheveerell" who added her name to the others.[25] But in addition to owning books themselves, women also had access to books in libraries, first private and convent libraries, and later public institutional libraries. So, not only did "Syster elyzabeth Stryckland" retain her own personal books in Syon,[26] but the Syon convent library contained over fourteen hundred volumes at the time of its dissolution in 1539. Good evidence also survives that women were often loaned books on liturgical topics by others.[27]

---

22. John Nalson, *An Impartial Collection of the Great Affairs of State*, 2 vols. (London, 1682); cited in Judith Maltby, *Prayer Book and People in Elizabethan and Stuart England* (Cambridge: Cambridge University Press, 1998), 27.

23. See Carol M. Meale, " ' . . . alle the books that I have in latyn, englische, and frensch': Laywomen and Their Books in Late Medieval England," in *Women and Literature in Britain, 1100–1500*, ed. Carol M. Meale (Cambridge: Cambridge University Press, 1993), 72.

24. Peter Heath, "Urban Piety in the Later Middle Ages: The Evidence from Hull Wills," in *The Church, Politics, and Patronage in the Fifteenth Century*, ed. Barrie Dobson (Gloucester, U.K.: Sutton, 1984), 226.

25. Driver, "Pictures in Print," 132.

26. The *Rule* for Syon states that the nuns shall not keep books simply in order to retain their personal property, "thoo bookes they shall haue as many as they wyll in whiche ys to lerne or to studye." See Ann M. Hutchinson, "Devotional Reading in the Monastery and in the Household," in *De Cella in Seculum: Religious and Secular Life and Devotion in Late Medieval England*, ed. Michael G. Sargeant (Cambridge: Brewer, 1989), 217.

27. In his court testimony John Grossar confessed "that he received such a book of Thomas Tykill, morrow-mass priest in Milk-street, and afterwards lent the same book to Thomas Spencer,

But problems remain. Even the most detailed calculations of women's literacy and book ownership should not necessarily lead us to conclude that women were internalizing the book's subject matter. At least one contemporary scholar has suggested that primers and other such devotional books functioned for medieval women as much as fashion accessories as evidence of personal piety (see fig. 13).[28] (This assertion sheds a slightly different light on the interpretation of the iconographic evidence usually cited for the importance of reading to women, leading us to question the meaning of such images as the effigy on the tomb of Eleanor of Aquitaine in the Abbey Church of Fontevrault, in which she is depicted reading a book, and the various formal portraits of women reading.) Fortunately, many women do leave evidence of their interaction with the content of the liturgical books they read or owned. In 1514, Anne Watts of Dogmersfield (Hampshire) was brought before the consistory court along with her husband Thomas Watts for possessing certain forbidden books, and she confessed that she had hidden them in a ditch. These books included a "treatise of the sacrament of baptisme al translate into English," which she had read.[29] Indeed she was tried and convicted for her views on the nature of baptismal regeneration.

It is not only the content of the books that women read which is a matter of interest to students of women's liturgical formation. Annotations that women left in their books also provide useful evidence of women's interpretations of worship practices. In the mid-sixteenth century, Elizabeth Kensam made notes in the endpapers of her Book of Hours which seem to suggest that the change from Latin to English in the Sunday services ranked in importance alongside the birth of her children.[30] At other times, women can be overheard talking about the significance of books in their formation and the formation of others for participation in Christian worship. In 1641, for example, widow Margery Price of Chester testified that "minor canon, William Clarke, had said in the cathedral that 'Puritans were about to take away the booke of Common Prayer' and added in her own words 'whereby Ignorant people [have] found comfort as well in Church as at home.'"[31] (Interestingly, Margery herself seems to have been unable to read. In her deposition to the court she made her mark instead of signing her name.)

which Thomas Spencer with his wife used to read upon the same." John Foxe, *Actes and Monuments* (London: The Company of Stationers, 1877), 124.

28. Patrick Collinson, "Windows on a Woman's Soul: Questions about the Religion of Elizabeth I," in *Elizabethan Essays*, ed. Patrick Collinson (London: Hambledon, 1994), 87–118.

29. Margaret Aston, *Faith and Fire: Popular and Unpopular Religion, 1350–1600* (London: Hambledon, 1993), 257.

30. For a description of this manuscript, see Consuela Dutschke and Richard Rouse, *Medieval and Renaissance Manuscripts in the Claremont Libraries* (Berkeley and Los Angeles: University of California Press, 1986), 44–47.

31. Maltby, *Prayer Book and People in Elizabethan and Stuart England*, 27.

Overall, rates of literacy and book ownership have tended to be higher among Protestant women than among their Roman Catholic and Orthodox sisters. Not only were the early reformers particularly adept at exploiting the new print technology for the spread of their liturgical principles; some Protestant women were the daughters of clergymen, giving them an advantage in their learning about religious matters from childhood. Statistics from the seventeenth century indicate that the number of private libraries belonging to individuals was three times higher in Protestant cities than in Catholic ones, which probably held until the late nineteenth century. Certain subsets of Protestantism were particularly known for being bookish — literacy was particularly high among Puritans (including Puritan women), a characteristic that transmitted to North America with the seventeenth-century Puritan immigration.

Books and Women's Liturgical Piety

Various types of books related to Christian worship have been available to women throughout the centuries. Some have outlined appropriate liturgical disciplines for use at home and in church; others have suggested devotional preparations for worthy participation in common worship; still others have instructed women in the proper attitudes and behavior to be observed when in church. During periods when the church's official rites were celebrated in some language other than the vernacular (Latin, Old Church Slavonic, Old High German, or Greek, for example), treatises offering theological interpretations of the service and annotations to or translations of the various rites were important to women's active participation in the liturgy. Sometimes women carried these kinds of books with them when they attended church services; one fifteenth-century devotional manual told women to find portions of the book that might be useful in worship, "such as the manner of attending Mass and the preparations for receiving the Lord Jesus Christ," and to copy them out onto a piece of paper and place it "inside the Book of Hours which you bring to Church."[32]

Evidence for women's book ownership before the twelfth century is quite scarce, but certainly every wealthy Christian woman would have owned at least one primer (Book of Hours) as her primary devotional aid. Elaborately decorated, those primers that survive are among the great artistic treasures of the world. The first *printed* Book of Hours is generally agreed to have been published in

---

32. Cited in Thomas Head, "The Religion of the Femmelettes: Ideals and Experience among Women in Fifteenth- and Sixteenth-Century France," in *That Gentle Strength: Historical Perspectives on Women in Christianity*, ed. Lynda L. Coon, Katherine J. Haldane, and Elisabeth W. Sommer (Charlottesville: University Press of Virginia, 1990), 164.

1486, with blanks for the pictures that would be painted in by hand. Hundreds of others followed, often with woodcuts replacing the illuminations, and soon after vernacular glosses began to be inserted into the Latin text. But the primer was not the only liturgical book available to women in the Middle Ages. Manuals to assist women in intelligent participation in the full round of liturgical rites were also common.

The *Myroure of oure Lady* is one good example of this kind of manual. Written sometime after 1408, the *Myroure* provides for the nuns at Syon Abbey who used it a general theological rationale for the Divine Office, translates and explains the various Hours as they are said on each day of the week, and translates the texts of the masses and Offices for special feasts.[33] The author intends the manual as a supplement to, rather than a replacement for, the Latin texts of the Office and the mass, however, and urges prudence in its use. Should a nun wish to have the English text available to "fede her mynde therewyth," she may do so, but, he cautions, this is only to be "understonde of them that haue sayde theyre mattyns or redde theyre legende before. For else I would not counsell them to leue the herynge of the latyn, for entendaunce of the englysshe."[34] Psalters, which contained not only the Psalms of David but also the liturgical calendar (and often visual representations of the events commemorated in the calendar), pious legends illustrating the devout life, and the Creeds, the litany, the Lord's Prayer and other prayers, were also common.[35]

Other kinds of books shaped the liturgical piety of women, especially books that described the liturgical and devotional lives of the saints, on whom the reader was encouraged to model herself. The story of the varied liturgical accomplishments of two eighth-century nuns, Herlinda and Renilda, for example, told by their ninth-century biographer, is probably exaggerated, but doubtless was intended to inspire readers to new heights of commitment to the worship of the church. Herlinda and Renilda were said to know by heart not only the prayers of the Divine Office and the mass, but the entire psalter as well. They also were

---

33. The only surviving manuscript copy of this book is from the fifteenth or early sixteenth century, copied by Robert Tailour for Sister Elyzabeth Montoun, a Bridgettine sister at Syon. See Hutchinson, "Devotional Reading in the Monastery and in the Household," 222–23.

34. Ibid., 224.

35. Christina of Markyate's psalter, for example, probably made at the scriptorium at St. Albans somewhere around 1140, contains all of these elements, and others beside. After the calendar and the scenes from the life of Christ is "a brief extract from a letter of Pope Gregory I defending the use of images, first in Latin then in French, and lastly, before the psalter, three whole-page drawings illustrating Christ's appearance to the disciples on the road to Emmaus: in this case a shortened form of the account in St. Luke is written within the frame of the first picture." See Christopher J. Holdsworth, "Christina of Markyate," in *Medieval Women*, ed. Derek Baker (Oxford: Basil Blackwell, 1978), 189–90.

expert in the various liturgical arts: reading and singing, copying and illuminating, "as well as the usual feminine tasks of spinning and weaving, making and interlacing gold designs, and silk flower embroidery."[36]

In the period leading up to the Reformation, the increasing concern for meaningful participation in the liturgy led some women to produce their own manuals of instruction and to translate the work of others. Nineteen-year-old Margaret More Roper (1509–44), a daughter of Thomas More and a scholar in her own right, translated Erasmus's treatise *Precatio Dominica* from the Latin within a year of its publication.[37] Written in a simple, graceful, and unpretentious style, the translation is "as much Margaret's work as the *Precatio Dominica* is Erasmus',"[38] full of her own emendations and asides ("Would to God we might also do this...!").[39] Roper also wrote a treatise on the Lord's Prayer and a series of meditations on the "Four Last Things." During the reign of Edward VI, certain women translators were responsible for making available the work of the Continental reformers to English readers, and often adapted it to the special needs of Christian households. Anne Locke, for example, translated John Calvin's *Sermons upon the Songe that Ezechias [Hezekiah] Made after he had been Sicke* (1580), restructuring it for use in family prayer.

Three remarkable English sisters, Anne Cooke Bacon (1529–1610), Elizabeth Cooke Hoby (1528–1609), and Mildred Cooke Cecil (1526–?), were prolific and diligent translators of texts related to the liturgy. Anne translated the *Apologia Ecclesiae Anglicanae* ("Apology for the Church of England"), an official document of the Church of England which was required by the Convocation of 1563 to be placed "in all cathedral and collegiate churches, and also private houses."[40] When the *Apologia* appeared, it raised heated controversy over the question of how Christ's presence in the eucharistic bread and wine was to be understood; in an attempt to shed light on the question, Anne's sister Elizabeth Hoby made a translation of another work that would prove to be essential to the stability of the Church of England: *A Way of Reconciliation Touching the True Nature and*

---

36. S. Wemple, "Women from the Fifth to the Tenth Century," in *A History of Women in the West*, ed. Christine Klapisch-Zuber (Cambridge, Mass.: Harvard Belknap, 1992), 199–200.

37. A woodcut of Roper with a large book headed the title page of the translation and is reproduced in *Moreana* 9 (1966): 65.

38. Vera Verbrugge, "Margaret More Roper's Personal Expression in the Devout Treatise on the Pater Noster," in *Silent but for the Word: Tudor Women as Patrons, Translators, and Writers of Religious Works*, ed. Margaret Hannay (Kent, Ohio: Kent State University Press, 1995), 34.

39. The *Precatio Dominica* was published without her name, and if it were not for the censorship brought about by the Lutheran controversy of the 1520s we would never have known who the translator was.

40. Although this treatise is generally attributed to John Jewel, it is also possible that Mildred's husband William Cecil, Elizabeth's principal secretary (over whom she had a great deal of influence) was a party to the writing of the text.

Substance of the Body and Blood of Christ in the Sacrament. The editorial asides in Elizabeth's translation attempt to placate those readers of the *Apologia* who objected to its willingness to equate transubstantiation with heresy: "Neither would wee strive so much about the terme of Transubstantiation . . . [it is] a sacramental alteration . . . a spiritual not a carnal, eating of Christ's flesh."[41] Mildred (described by the Spanish ambassador to the Court of St. James as a "tiresome bluestocking"[42]) was particularly interested in translating patristic treatises touching on liturgical subjects, especially those of John Chrysostom and Gregory Naziansus.

As we move into the seventeenth century, the popularity and influence of these kinds of books of liturgical instruction increase. Manuals such as Edward Lake's *Officium Eucharisticum* (1673), the anonymous *A Week's Preparation towards a Worthy Receiving of the Lord's Supper* (1678), and *The Common Prayerbook: The Best Companion in the House and Closet as Well as in the Temple* (1685)[43] are regularly mentioned in the diaries of middle- and upper-class women as important elements in their devotional preparation for worship. Women themselves increasingly appear as the authors of these kinds of manuals, often writing specifically for other women. Susannah Hopton's *Devotions in the Ancient Way of Offices*, for example, which appeared in eight editions between 1700 and 1765, aimed at encouraging women to restore the monastic pattern of daily prayer in their households. Elizabeth Burnet's *A Method of Prayer*, which "presupposed a knowledge of the more advanced states of prayer as well as a broad knowledge of the spiritual classics,"[44] was widely read by women during the half century after its posthumous publication in 1709.

Gradually, as book production costs continued to fall, the audience for these kinds of books widened to include women of nearly all social and economic circumstances, even very poor women as they became the objects of various philanthropic efforts. The Society for the Promotion of Christian Knowledge (SPCK), which was established in 1698 in order to provide spiritually edifying reading material for those who might not otherwise have access to books, supported the printing of "Common Prayer Books and the Singing Psalms for the use of the

---

41. Cited in Mary Ellen Lamb, "The Cooke Sisters: Attitudes toward Learned Women in the Renaissance," in *Silent but for the Word: Tudor Women as Patrons, Translators, and Writers of Religious Works*, ed. Margaret Hannay (Kent, Ohio: Kent State University Press, 1995), 110.

42. Ibid., 111.

43. *A Week's Preparation towards a Worthy Receiving of the Lord's Supper* was in its fifty-second edition in 1764. *Officium Eucharisticum* went through thirty editions between 1673 and 1753, and *The Common Prayerbook: The Best Companion in the House and Closet as Well as in the Temple* went through seventeen editions between 1685 and 1734.

44. Jacob, *Lay People and Religion in the Early Eighteenth Century*, 94. See also C. Kirchberger, "Elizabeth Burnet," *Church Quarterly Review* 168 (1949): 42.

Poor who cannot reach to the price of a whole Bible."[45] In the eighteenth and nineteenth centuries especially, inexpensive pamphlets on liturgical topics also circulated widely, enabling literate women of all social classes access to the current state of theological controversies over worship.

Books and pamphlets were not the only printed material that helped women prepare for meaningful participation in Christian worship. Visual images have also been significant sources of instruction. Dorothy Coddington, a Roman Catholic laywoman writing in the Benedictine journal *Orate Fratres* in 1945, described the liturgical education of one little girl of her acquaintance. During Lent one year, the child spontaneously said to Coddington, "I received the Holy Ghost when I was baptized, and that's why we do things in Lent, because we die with Christ and rise with him." Coddington believes that the child's "very Pauline theology, which was far beyond what she had been taught in school," could be easily explained by the fact that

> she had been given, as a baby, one of Ade Bethune's lovely baptismal certificates, giving the facts of her baptism and quoting St. Paul. It had hung on the wall of her room and had been one of her treasured possessions. Each night when she was going to bed she insisted on her mother reading the certificate to her and answering, again and again, her questions about her baptism.[46]

During the nineteenth and early twentieth century, young women used more sentimental forms of religious iconography as models for their own devotional behavior, seeking to imitate the postures of the pious children depicted therein: eyes to heaven, hands meekly folded at their breasts in prayer.[47] These paintings, staged photographs, and lithographs became essential features of the décor of

---

45. Mary Clements, ed., *Correspondence and Minutes of the SPCK relating to Wales, 1699–1740* (Cardiff: University of Wales Press, 1952), 278.

46. Cited in K. Hughes, *How Firm a Foundation: Voices of the Early Liturgical Movement* (Chicago: Liturgy Training Publications, 1990), 73. "From the time they were very small, the children of this family had taken part in an annual ceremony of the renewal of their baptism, which included going through the entire ritual of baptism in the baptistry of their church. Moreover, the symbols used by Bethune — the water and the candle — were familiar to this child by constant use in the 'home liturgy'; holy water was in frequent use in the home, and she was accustomed to seeing the holy candle lit during the Saturday reading of the next day's gospel, because 'the gospel is Christ.'"

47. Occasionally, however, we find a woman who resists the power of these images. Sixteen-year-old Marie Bashkirtseff was a member of an aristocratic Russian family and the image of the cosmopolitan young lady of the nineteenth century. "At prayer in the church of St. Peter in Nice, with her chin resting on her lovely white hands, she rejected the temptation to ritualize femininity in angelic forms: 'I manage to make myself ugly as a form of penitence.'" Michela Del Giorgio, "The Catholic Model," in *History of Women in the West*, vol. 4: *Emerging Feminism from Revolution to World War*, ed. Genevieve Fraisse and Michelle Perrot (Cambridge, Mass.: Belknap Press of Harvard University Press, 1993), 186–87.

many children's bedrooms and exerted enormous power on young women's ideas of appropriate attitudes — both physical and mental — for Christian worship (see fig. 14). (Perhaps parents hope that such pious ornaments as the "Precious Moments" figurines will serve something of the same purpose for contemporary children.)[48]

These descriptions of Christian domestic life return us, however, to a point made earlier, that most liturgical instruction of women has been transmitted relationally, as a part of intimate associations between individuals in families, convents, religious societies, and churches: mothers teaching their children, abbesses teaching their novices, Christian elders teaching the newly baptized. Over and over again we find that even reading seems to be a basically social enterprise, with the content of books, including books of liturgical instruction, as a medium of exchange between and among women readers. The formation of women for meaningful participation in worship was itself both for the sake of a woman's own soul and for the sake of her relationships with the various communities of which she was a part.

Liturgical Propriety

Because of this close interplay between liturgical formation and social relationships, much of the material we have been describing was aimed at encouraging not only liturgical understanding and devout preparation, but also proper behavior of women in public worship. The fifteenth-century treatise *How the Good Wyfe Taught Her Doughter* is hardly unique in its concern that the daughter in question "behave meekly in church, bid her beads, observe holy days, and (in adulthood) to pay her tithes and give charity to the poor."[49] The numbers of books aimed specifically at women's liturgical propriety increased dramatically after the advent of printing in the fifteenth century, paralleling the rise in literacy among the general population. But even in more general books of manners, correct behavior in church was emphasized for the "well brought up" young woman. As the author of *How to Be a Lady: A Book for Girls, Containing Useful Hints on the Formation of Character* (1846)[50] tells his readers:

---

48. Assessment is yet to be made of the impact of the mass media on the formation of women for participation in worship, but surely the way in which women are formed by the worship that takes place on television and on the radio and in film deserves further exploration. See S. J. White, *Christian Worship and Technological Change* (Nashville: Abingdon, 1997), 178ff.

49. See Eileen Power, *Medieval English Nunneries* (Cambridge: Cambridge University Press, 1922), 312. The companion book to this is entitled *How the Good Wyfe Wold a Pylgremage* and was intended to instruct women pilgrims on the propriety of liturgical devotion "on the road."

50. Harvey Newcomb, *How to Be a Lady: A Book for Girls, Containing Useful Hints on the Formation of Character* (Boston: Gould and Lincoln, 1846).

On your way to the House of God, do not engage in any unnecessary conversation, especially that which is vain, light or trifling, to divert your mind, and unfit you for the worship of God. Do not stand about the doors of the meetinghouse, to salute your friends, or to converse with your young companions ... go directly to your seat, in a quiet, reverent manner; if any time intervenes before the commencement of public worship, do not spend it in gazing about the house, to observe the dress of different persons; but take the opportunity to compose your mind, to call in all vagrant thoughts, to get your heart impressed with a sense of God's presence, and to lift up the soul in silent prayer for his blessing.[51]

This author goes on to enumerate the various transgressions he has witnessed among young women in church, including whispering and laughing and reading books during the sermon ("this is not only very irreverent, but a gross violation of good breeding"), and gazing about during the singing or the prayers "as though they had nothing to do with the service." Such conduct, he concludes,

would be very unmannerly, if nobody were concerned but the minister; for it is treating him as though he were not worthy of your attention. But when it is considered that he speaks to you in the name of God, and that, in prayer, while you stand up with the congregation, you profess to join in the prayer; and while the hymn is sung, you profess to exercise the devout feeling which it expresses — when all these things are considered, such conduct as that I have described appears impious in a high degree.[52]

Until the mid-twentieth century, most manuals of etiquette continued to represent worship services as contexts for the public appraisal of feminine virtues, a situation that women were advised to exploit for the purposes of both matrimonial advantage and social advancement.

Dressing for Church

From the New Testament period onward, proper dress for women in church has also been the subject of considerable concern. Enforcement of dress restrictions was seen to be part of the control men needed to exercise in order that women's salvation might not be compromised. In addition, there seems to have been a constant temptation for some women to use the public occasion

---

51. Ibid., 71. Does this (male) author perhaps fail to appreciate the link between the maintenance of relationships and liturgical piety for women?

52. Ibid., 72.

of Christian worship to display their wealth and social standing by the way in which they adorned themselves. Both of these factors explain the regular attention given to matters of the proper dress and adornment of women worshipers not only in canonical legislation, but in devotional literature and books of etiquette as well.[53]

While the standards of dress for worship for ordinary laywomen tended to be enforced more by custom than by canon, head coverings were often required for certain liturgical occasions, and the courts (both civil and ecclesiastical) have sometimes stepped in where women's liturgical formation had failed to produce the "proper" behavior. In 1607, Catherine Capon of the district of Havering (near London) was reported to the consistory court for "refusing to come after the accostomed manner to give God thanks for her deliverance...in obstinate contempt of our minister and order." (In other words, she had presented herself at church for the Rite of Purification of Women after Childbirth without being properly veiled, contrary to the rubrics in the rite.) She claimed in response that she had indeed come to church "as an honest woman in her usual apparel but without a veil,"[54] yet she was found guilty and fined.[55]

Before long, however, social pressure (its own form of liturgical formation for women) would contribute to other difficulties over what women should wear on their heads in church. In the minutes of the vestry of the North Meeting House, Andover, Massachusetts, in 1758 we find the following notation: "Being put to a vote whether the parish Disapprove of the female sex setting with Hats on in the Meetinghouse, in time of divine service, as being indecent. It passed in the affirmative."[56] Within a hundred years, however, Sunday had become the premier occasion for women to display publicly their attainment of cultured refinement, and the wearing of hats became highly symbolic of that attainment. One nineteenth-century historian writes that "by the 1840s...little girls in one

---

53. See below, pp. 193–94. The most common concern in the early canonical literature seems to have been the matter of proper head covering for women generally, but their clothing and hair were also matters worthy of consideration. Consecrated virgins were to be "distinguished by their clothing, and their style of hair. They should learn especially to recite the psalms, to care for divine worship and to take notice of the time for singing the madrash [hymns]" (Canon 9 of the Nestorian Synod of Mar George I, 676. Migne, PG, 111, 191 (1960), 80). Here, it seems that clothing and hairstyle are viewed as being equally essential to the pursuit of holiness as the practice of prescribed liturgical devotions.

54. Marjorie Keniston McIntosh, A Community Transformed: The Manor and Liberty of Havering, 1500–1620 (Cambridge: Cambridge University Press, 1991), 44, n. 7.

55. During the previous two decades, fourteen women of the same district had been reported to the court for coming to church for purification without "a decent kerchief or veil." Ibid., 45.

56. Juliet Haines Moffard, And Firm Thine Ancient Vow: The History of North Parish Church of North Andover, 1645–1974 (North Andover, Mass.: Naiman, 1975), 94.

Methodist Sunday School, for example, not only learned about salvation, they also got a penny every time they wore their bonnets."[57]

We find the first clear evidence of "Sunday clothes" early in the fourth century, when they begin to be denounced as contributing to division within the Christian community, disturbing the solidarity and unity which was to find its visible expression in public worship. The wealthy — men and women alike — began to embroider their garments with scenes from the Gospels in order to "shine among the drab mass of their inferiors in spectacular Sunday clothes."[58] Increasingly as the centuries go on, household accounts books give evidence of the extra amounts of money spent on women's clothes and accessories for wearing to church,[59] and regularly women's diaries and letters indicate that the connection between what is worn to church and the experience of Christian worship is very close indeed (see fig. 15).

But equally regularly we find criticism of the attire women donned for worship services. Even in periods during which flamboyant male fashion was the norm, women are often singled out for unfavorable comment on the extravagance of the clothing they wore to church. In eighteenth-century France, for example, it was constantly stressed that women profaned churches by displaying themselves in unsuitable dress, seeking to attract admirers. As one male commentator complained:

> Today most women only come into the churches to see and be seen and to display their luxury, and make an ostentatious parade of their vanities.... One even sees some who are sufficiently dissolute to seek by their criminal glances and their indecent postures to draw from God those who had come with a sincere intention of participating in the sacrifice at the altar, and who thus deprive him of all kinds of victories.[60]

Women were also known to criticize their sisters for extravagance in dressing for church. Annie Wittenmyer, writing in 1871, speaks of earrings as an "evil

---

57. Kathryn T. Long, "Consecrated Respectability: Phoebe Palmer and the Refinement of American Methodism," in *Methodism and the Shaping of American Culture*, ed. N. Hatch and J. H. Wigger (Nashville: Kingswood, 2001), 283. She cites here John A. Roche, *The Life of Mrs. Sarah A. Lankford Palmer* (New York: George Hughes, 1898), 49.

58. P. Veyne, ed., *A History of Private Life*, vol. 1: *From Pagan Rome to Byzantium* (Cambridge, Mass.: Belknap Press of Harvard University Press, 1987), 275.

59. "This public character of private ritual accounts for the increasing expenditure on clothes. Even the poorest Italians in the Lorraine Basin were preoccupied with cutting a fine figure on Sundays." Michelle Perrot, ed., *A History of Private Life*, vol. 4, *From the Fires of Revolution to the Great War* (Cambridge, Mass.: Belknap Press of Harvard University Press, 1990), 136.

60. M. Lordelot, *Les Devoirs de la vie Domestique* (Brussels, 1707), 140–41, cited in Briggs, *Communities of Belief*, 250.

[which] has crept into the Church." But her concern is more for stewardship than for vanity:

> Thousands of women go to the communion table *with the money in their ears that ought to be in the missionary box, or educating some poor orphan child;* for there is enough treasure in the uncircumcised ears of the women of the Church, to send a corps of missionaries to every nation under the skies, and enough spent annually to sustain them in their work.... In truth they go to the Lord's table with the price of souls in their ears.

Vanity is also something of a concern for Wittenmyer. She continues:

> When we come into the Church, we take upon ourselves the vows of our holy Christianity, vows more solemn than any oath, in any earthly court. Before the Lord, and the great congregation, we renounce the devil and all his works — the vain pomp and glory of the world — and consecrate our souls and bodies a living sacrifice to God and accept publicly the Scriptures as the rule of our life and practice. But many, like Ananias and Sapphira, have *kept back part of the price,* and have stood before the altar to *perjure themselves by assuming vows that they did not intend to keep.*[61]

Gradually, however, Sunday finery became not only the mark of a woman's social standing, but of her devotion to God as well. From the mid-nineteenth century onward, in both America and Europe, style, taste, and manners began to assume religious significance, and so what women wore to church became a visible manifestation of their personal liturgical piety.[62]

During the 1960s, the notion of "Sunday best" began to fade, except in churches with predominately African, African American, and Afro-Caribbean congregations (see fig. 16). But in some circumstances it retains its old vigor. In the April 2, 2002, edition of the *New York Times*, under the heading "High church or low, all bow to the dress code," Ginia Bellafante interviews women as they come out of their churches on Easter Sunday. As she describes the situation:

> There are certainly houses of worship in New York where practitioners dress as if prayer were the leisure-time equivalent of going to a Rangers game.

---

61. Annie Wittenmyer, *Woman's Work for Jesus* (New York: Nelson and Phillips, 1871), 140.

62. See Richard L. Bushman, *The Refinement of America: Persons, Houses, Cities* (New York: Random House, 1993), chap. 10. Even the images of the saints seem to have been dressed to the height of fashion in some places. Lady Herbert, in her travels to France and Italy, was disturbed to see the "Blessed Virgin, decked out in gorgeous velvet robes, embroidered in gold, and covered with jewels, with lace pocket-handkerchiefs in the hand, and all the paraphernalia of a fine lady of the nineteenth century." Lady Herbert, *Impressions of Spain in 1866,* cited in Madeline Beard, *Faith and Fortune* (Leominster, U.K.: Gracewing, 1997), 111.

But more conspicuously, a sense of formality is still in place — a formality
of a particularly unpretentious sort little on view elsewhere in urban life.
For many women, there remains an unspoken code to church dressing, and
at no point in the year is that code in greater evidence than on Easter.

This dress code is as subtle as it is stable. As one parishioner of the Episcopal
Church of the Heavenly Rest on Fifth Avenue, New York City, describes it, "I
would not wear anything sleeveless to church, and I wouldn't wear pants. I might
go to dinner or luncheon without hosiery, but I always wear hose to church."[63]

Sometimes, however, women recognize that this kind of attention to propriety
can get in the way of true worship. At the first pentecostal meeting that revivalist
Aimee Semple McPherson attended as a young girl she was immediately struck
by the differences between the worship she observed there and the worship to
which she was accustomed:

> They seemed to be a very ordinary lot of people, none of the wealthy or
> well-known citizens of the town were there, and dressed as I was, with the
> flowers on my hat, a gold chain and locket, and rings on my fingers, I felt
> just a little bit above the status of those around me, and looked on with an
> amused air as they shouted, danced and prayed.[64]

She notices the local milkman in an ecstatic state, shaking from the power of the
Spirit, then falling to the floor praising God. "At all these things I giggled fool-
ishly, not understanding it and thinking it all very laughable. . . . There were no
announcements of oyster suppers or Christmas entertainments or sewing circles
made — no appeal for money. Not even a collection was taken." Suddenly, however, McPherson recognizes that it is precisely in the *lack* of attention to propriety
that the power of this form of worship lay: "It was just God, God from one end to
the other, and his words seemed to rain down upon me, and every one of them
hurt some particular part of my spirit and life until I could not tell where I hurt
the worst."[65]

---

63. Ginia Bellafante, "An Order of Worship: Bare Nothing but the Soul," *New York Times*, April 2,
2002, A22, cols. 1–4.

64. Aimee Semple McPherson, *This is That* (New York: Garland, 1985), 53.

65. Ibid. In the same way, Eliza Clitherall was very much distressed two centuries earlier that
"the vanity — dress & shew at the large church quenches devotion — and precludes the comforts
of sanctuary." Cited from the *Autobiography of Eliza Clitherall* in Elizabeth Fox-Genovese, "Religion
in the Lives of Slaveholding Women of the Antebellum South," in *That Gentle Strength: Historical
Perspectives on Women in Christianity*, ed. Lynda L. Coon, Katherine J. Haldane, and Elisabeth W.
Sommer (Charlottesville: University Press of Virginia, 1990), 224.

Liturgical Piety in Women's First-Person Writing

Women's intimate first-person writings provide a remarkable window onto their changing attitudes toward worship, their insights into the meaning and function of worship for their own lives and the lives of others, and the kinds of liturgical disciplines that were most important to them. We also see the ways in which women internalized the words and actions of the liturgy and used them in expression themselves. For many women, like the learned young Italian widow Vittoria Collona (1490–1547), the words of the liturgy are so familiar that they are used to express their deepest emotions and ideals. In one of her letters, Collona describes her absolute reliance on the remission of sin by faith through grace by quoting the Easter liturgy: "O felix culpa, quae tantum et talem meruit habere redemptorem!" [O happy fault, through whose great and unfathomable merit we have been granted redemption!][66]

The importance of the ongoing pattern of Christian common prayer in the lives is women in also evident in these writings. In the journal which Brattleboro, Vermont, resident Mary Palmer Tyler kept between 1821 and 1843,[67] she records rural social life in meticulous detail: callers, tea parties, cooking, visiting. But the worship services she attended in the Episcopal church at Guildford, two miles from her home, elicit her most effusive prose. Although she was able to make the trek only rarely, there she could experience "the happiness of again listening to the effusions of true Piety breathed in language Simple yet Elegant," resulting in what she describes as a hunger for grace, like the hunger of the fertile earth waiting for seed.[68] As one commentator says: "The solace Tyler found in faith, as well as the pleasure she took in the liturgy, dominated her presentation of herself. Social activities had their place in the routines of everyday life, but opportunities to praise God in the church of her first choice constituted life's grand occasions."[69]

On certain significant occasions this sense of the centrality of worship to women's lives comes through especially clearly. On May 4, 1861, Methodist Frances Willard made the following entry in her journal:

---

66. Kari E. Børresen, "Caritas Pirckheimer (1467–1532) et Vittoria Colonna (1490–1547)," *Women's Studies in the Christian and Islamic Traditions: Ancient, Medieval and Renaissance Foremothers* (Dordrecht: Kluwer, 1993), 327. This letter is probably addressed to the theologian Bernardino Occino. Collona is mentioned in the heresy trial of Carnescchi, executed as a heretic in 1567, and the letters between Pole and Vittoria make clear that she was deeply aware of the new theology in Germany and had very likely read Luther's commentaries on Galatians and Romans.

67. Vermont Historical Society, Montpelier, Document 49:1.

68. She says, "May the Infinite Being who saw and knows with what joy I receive this portion of the good deed, grant it may take root as in good ground well prepared, and spring up and bear fruit a hundredfold."

69. Catherine E. Kelly, *In the New England Fashion: Reshaping Women's Lives in the Nineteenth Century* (Ithaca, N.Y.: Cornell University Press, 1999), 169.

Tomorrow morning I expect to be baptized & received into "full connection" with the Church. Mr. Bibbins [the pastor of the Methodist Episcopal
Church Willard attended in Evanston, Illinois] will lay his hand upon my
forehead, & say the solemn words, "I baptize thee in the name of the Father, & of the Son & of the Holy Ghost...." O God! Make me better —
more worthy to call myself Thy child.... The vows I shall voluntarily make
tomorrow, may color my whole destiny. Help me to appreciate what I shall
promise then.[70]

She concludes this passage with the fervent prayer: "I have no wish so great... no
prayer so earnest, O! Father in Heaven, as that Thou shalt *'make me right.'*"[71]

Worship and Conversion

Very often, worship was the catalyst for the conversion of women: conversion
to the Christian faith, to a new depth of commitment, to one denominational
identity from another. Women's descriptions of the relationship between their
experience of Christian common prayer and their conversion are usually lyrical
and rhapsodic, providing us not only with information about the specific practices
they found meaningful, but also the affective impact of the liturgy as a whole. In
1674, for example, Agnes Beaumont describes what is clearly a mystical experience, received when she attended a service of the Lord's Supper in the company
of Puritan author and preacher John Bunyan:

> Oh, it was a feast of fat things to me! My soul was filled with consolation
> and I sat under His shadow with great delight and His fruit was pleasant to
> my taste when I was at the Lord's table.... I found such a return of prayer
> I was scarce able to bear up under it.... Oh I had such a sight of Jesus
> Christ that brake my heart to pieces... a sense of my sins and of His dying
> love made me love him and want to be with him: and truly it was infinite
> condescension in Him and I have often thought of His gracious goodness
> to me that Jesus Christ should so graciously visit my soul on that day.[72]

This particular conversion story would have momentous consequences. Upon her
return from that meeting, Agnes found that her anti-Puritan father had removed

---

70. Cited in Carolyn de Swarte Gifford, "'My Own Methodist Hive': Frances Willard's Faith
as Disclosed in Her Journal, 1855–1870," in *Spirituality and Social Responsibility: Vocational Vision of
Women in the United Methodist Tradition*, ed. R. Keller (Nashville: Abingdon, 1993), 93.
71. Ibid.
72. Cited in Gordon Rupp, "A Devotion of Rapture in English Puritanism," in *Reformation, Conformity, and Dissent: Essays in Honour of Geoffrey Nuttal*, ed. R. Buick Knox (London: Epworth,
1977), 129.

her belongings from the house. "The result was an angry confrontation in which her father fell dead with a seizure."[73] A suitor, jealous of Agnes's relationship with Bunyan, accused her of poisoning her father and she was put on trial. Agnes was acquitted, and she went on to be a famous preacher in her own right; her memoirs became a minor classic of Puritan literature.[74]

Sybilla Holland (1836–91), an English aristocrat and staunch member of the Church of England (her uncle had been dean of Canterbury Cathedral), is another woman whose conversion, to Roman Catholicism, can be traced to a service of Christian worship. While on the "Grand Tour" in Rome in 1889, she reached an irreversible turning point at a celebration of mass in St. Peter's Basilica. The experience left her with, as she says in a letter to her husband,

> a profound impression of the grandeur and force of the great unbroken Roman tradition; there is a savour of the antique pre-Christian ceremonial overlaid and sublimated by the medieval presentation of Christianity, and decorated by the pomp of the Renaissance — the imagination carried back 1800 years.[75]

In Bruges, she had a similar experience of the "dramatic *certainty* of Catholic worship." The "vast multitude" attending mass on Easter Day

> came crowding in hour after hour to the altars to be fed by the pale patient priests. A dense crowd [formed] in a side aisle, and it was the same at three other altars in the cathedral, and at all the other churches. Old, crippled people, young children, big boys and girls innumerable, rich and poor of all ages pressing steadily forward and streaming back with clasped hands and downcast eyes.[76]

The worship of the Calvinists, however, suffered by comparison. In Switzerland Lady Sybilla reports that "It seems there is no sort of sign of outward worship to be discovered in this country. . . . Anything more miserable than the afternoon service which we attended in the Staatliche Kirche of Montreaux cannot be imagined, a sort of service so much better suited to a white-washed meeting house."[77]

---

73. Ibid.

74. See G. B. Harrison, ed., *The Narrative of the Persecution of Agnes Beaumont, 1674* (London: Constable and Co., 1929).

75. Sibylla Holland to Francis Holland, November 12, 1889, in Mary Sibylla Lyall Holland, *Letters of Mary Sibylla Holland,* 3d ed., ed. Edward Holland (London: E. Arnold, 1907), 244.

76. Sibylla Holland to Agnes Bolton, April 10, 1870, in Sibylla Holland, *Additional Letters of Mary Sibylla Holland,* ed. Edward Holland (Edinburgh, 1899), 10.

77. Sibylla Holland to her son Bernard, April 20, 1880, in Holland, *Letters of Mary Sibylla Holland,* 65. Lady Sybilla thinks that she had begun this journey early. Her biographer notes: "As a young girl of fifteen she was staying at the home of her uncle, the Dean of Canterbury. She stole down to his

Similar experiences are recorded in the letters and diaries of many wealthy women of the period, whose travels brought them into contact with other forms of worship.[78] Many of them, like Lady Feilding, who traveled abroad with her husband the winter after their marriage in 1846, were warned of the dangers inherent in such "boundary crossing" by those who hitherto had had responsibility for their liturgical formation. Upon hearing the news that she would be touring France, Lady Feilding's domestic chaplain wrote to urge her "not to forget the doctrines of the reformed faith and be led astray by the temptations presented her by the Catholic liturgy."[79]

The conversion of others, particularly of close relations, was also important to women who deeply desired that their loved ones might share with them in the joys of Christian worship. In February 1815, Daniel Wadsworth, who had long supported the church financially, became a covenanted member of Hartford's First Church. His wife, Faith (Trumbull) Wadsworth, was overjoyed, and records in her journal, "Blessed be God for his unspeakable mercies. This day I have had the long wish'd for comfort of seeing my husband profess his faith in our Lord Jesus Christ, and join himself in full communion with the visible church in Hartford."[80] Three decades later in North Carolina, Catherine (Ruffin) Roulhac wrote to her to her husband Joseph of her deep desire that he join in Christian faith and worship with her:

> Oh! When shall my beloved husband bow with me round the altar and unite in partaking of the broken body and precious blood of our crucified

---

study one night when the house was asleep, took possession of the cathedral key, fearfully let herself into the dark, empty, and mysterious church, and passed almost the whole night prostrate before the altar." Mary Sibylla Holland, *Letters of Mary Sibylla Lyall Holland*, 78–79, cited in Clive Dewey, *Passing of Barchester* (London: Hambledon, 1991), 112.

78. A similar conversion story is told of Mabel Digby (1835–?), daughter of the last Baron Haversham, who became superior general of the Order of the Sacred Heart. On a visit to France with her mother, she was reluctantly persuaded by friends to enter a Roman Catholic church for the Benediction of the Blessed Sacrament. Once inside, however, Mabel sat defiantly with her arms folded while the other members of the congregation knelt in prayer. But as the monstrance was taken from its place, the bell rung and the Blessed Sacrament raised in Benediction, she "slipped from her seat to her knees and flung her arms across her breast with a clutch that gripped both shoulders. Her face seemed to be illuminated; her tearful eyes were fixed upon the Host until the triple blessing was complete. Then she sank crouching to the ground, whilst the last short psalm was intoned; she remained bent low and immovable. After a quarter of an hour she rose to her feet and took her sister's arm in the church porch. 'Geraldine, I am a Catholic. Jesus Christ has looked at me. I shall change no more.'" Madeline Beard, *Faith and Fortune* (Leominster, U.K.: Gracewing, 1997), 82.

79. Ibid., 100.

80. Faith Wadsworth, *Journal of Faith Trumbull Wadsworth*, February 5, 1815, Wadsworth Family Papers, Manuscripts and Archives, Yale University, cited in Gretchen Townsend Buggeln, "Elegance and Sensibility in the Calvinist Tradition: The First Congregational Church of Hartford Connecticut," in *Seeing beyond the Word: Visual Arts and the Calvinist Tradition*, ed. Paul Corby Finney (Grand Rapids, Mich.: Eerdmans, 1999), 434.

Redeemer? We hope to be meet partakers of his kingdom in Heaven, but how can we unless we use the means He has appointed to fit us for that kingdom, the affectionate and dying command of our Saviour was to "Do this in remembrance of me."?...Think of these things my dear husband put them not off to a more convenient season....There will never be a time more suitable....[81]

This correspondence shows not only Roulhac's need to share the most intimate aspects of her devotional life with her husband, but also the importance to her of the means of grace, and her profound sense that her companions around the altar table would also be her eternal companions in heaven.

Women also used their letters and diaries to work out the finer points of sacramental and liturgical doctrine for themselves and for others. For example, in 1875, at the beginning of what would become her full and final conversion to Roman Catholicism in 1889, Sibylla Holland wrote to her sister:

What do you understand by "Objective Presence in the Sacrament"? It surely means more than a special spiritual presence beyond that in the heart of the worthy receiver, which would be merely be subjective. Is this correct? And does our highest doctrine of the Sacrament differ so materially from that of God?[82]

Writing in Georgia, Grace Brown Ellmore uses her private diary to ponder similar kinds of theological questions. On July 24, 1863, the entry reads:

I have often heard the question, "What is the use of baptism and where is the good of the Lord's Supper?" And it does not surprise me that the answers are invariably vague and unsatisfactory to the irreligious. For the affect is so subtle, so purely spiritual, as to be wholly unexplainable in mere words, it must be felt to be wholly understood. And though felt in different degrees, and in different manner according to the temperament, intellect, and spiritual condition of the many individuals, [each recognizes] in it a common means of strength, a bond which unites them to each other and to God.[83]

---

81. Catherine Ruffin Roulhac to J. B. G. Roulhac, April 9, 1843, Ruffin-Roulhac-Hamilton Papers, Southern Historical Collection, Wilson Library, University of North Carolina, Chapel Hill, N.C. Cited in Richard Rankin, *Ambivalent Churchmen and Evangelical Churchwomen: The Religion of the Episcopal Elite in North Carolina, 1800–1860* (Columbia: University of South Carolina Press, 1993), 107.

82. Cited in Dewey, *The Passing of Barchester*, 110.

83. Weiner, *A Heritage of Woe*, 60.

This entry goes on for more than two pages as Ellmore attempts to clarify for herself (and for her unnamed interlocutors) what kind of change baptism and the Supper effects in the Christian believer.

Going Without

Given the importance to women of gathering with the Christian community for prayer, it is not surprising how often their private letters, journals, and diaries speak of the hardship they experience when they are deprived of the opportunity to attend church regularly. All kinds of women have been deprived of or denied access to Christian worship over the course of history: exiles and prisoners, slaves and settlers, immigrants, migrants, and the aged. Some of these have left us records of their response to this deprivation. Nancy Caldwell (1781–1865), for example, recalls in her *Memoirs* that there was no meeting for worship nor regular preaching in North Yarmouth, Maine, until 1795, when an itinerant preacher finally arrived. "I valued a meeting more than my necessary food," she says.[84] Women slaves had particular restrictions placed on their regular attendance at church services, required as they were to work at their masters' pleasure. One African American slave woman complained to Richard Boardman in 1769 that she deeply desired to hear the local Wesleyan preacher, but that her master prohibited her. "I told my Master I would do more work than ever I used to do," she says, "if he would but let me come; nay, I would do everything in my power to be a good servant."[85]

Sometimes women caught up in the theological controversies of their day were prohibited from participating in their accustomed forms of worship. In 1664, Angélique de Saint-Jean (1591–1661), the second abbess of the Paris convent of Port-Royal, was forced to leave her monastery by the bishop (supported by a cohort of archers) for failing to sign anti-Jansenist formularies, was moved out of the convent into "house arrest," and was deprived of the sacraments and the Divine Office. She recalls that during this time of exile she did all that she could to "make a church out of my prison":

> I chanted almost all of the office alone during those days at our usual hours.
> I also chanted the parts of the choir chants at the high Mass, when I knew
> them well, and at least the *Kyrie, Gloria, Credo, Sanctus,* and *Agnus Dei.*
> I followed in spirit all that the priest says in the sacrifice.... I even made

---

84. Nancy Caldwell, *Walking with God: Leaves from the Journal of Mrs. Nancy Caldwell*, ed. James O. Thompson (Keyser, W.Va.: For Private Distribution, 1886), 20–21.

85. Letter from Richard Boardman to John Wesley, November 4, 1769, cited in Brown, *Women in Mr. Wesley's Methodism*, 131.

the processions around my room, holding a cross in my hand and chanting what must be said in them. I did the same with holy water on Sundays, which I sprinkled all around my room, chanting *Asperges me*.[86]

In her own diary, one of Angélique's sisters, Agnes Arnaud, speaks of the spiritual pain that resulted from being deprived of the sacrament of penance during this time: "I was unable to escape the reproaches of my conscience which became my accuser and my judge."[87]

But occasionally we find women expressing concern about how their liturgical piety appeared to others. For example, Mary Perkins Ryan (b. 1912), a Roman Catholic laywoman, author, and lecturer on liturgical matters, reports having once been on a train reading the Office from her breviary. She paid little attention to the comings and goings of other passengers and the conductor:

But then in the door came a priest, and in one reflex action, I found I was sitting on the breviary and reading the Saturday Evening Post. I wondered for some time why I had done that; now I realize that it was because I was afraid the good father would think I was pious. There is nothing we are more afraid of.[88]

Other women report their deep distress at having failed to accomplish the liturgical disciplines they set for themselves. As Lord Egremont's (unnamed) sister was dying, she was deeply concerned that a previous illness had caused her to break the promise she had made when a young girl that she would always say her prayers on her knees. "She was so fatigued and ill she had not power to pray on her knees but did it as she lay in bed, which now in recollecting past matters [on her deathbed] was a scruple to her."[89]

---

86. Cited in F. E. Weaver, *The Evolution of the Reform of Port-Royal: From the Rule of Cîteaux to Jansenism* (Paris: Éditions Beauchesne, 1978), 141. See also Alexander Sedgwick, "The Nuns of Port-Royal: A Study of a Female Spirituality in Seventeenth-Century France," in *That Gentle Strength: Historical Perspectives on Women in Christianity*, ed. Lynda L. Coon, Katherine J. Haldane, and Elisabeth W. Sommer (Charlottesville: University Press of Virginia, 1990), 176–89.

87. Sedgwick, "The Nuns of Port-Royal," 181. Although all the nuns of Port-Royal who were deprived of the liturgy suffered greatly, they were wary of capitulating to the demands of the hierarchy — one of which was that the appointment of a confessor would be made by the bishop — simply to have the mass and office returned to them. "We benefit," Angelique writes, "from participation in the sacraments, the love and desire for which increases every day when we are deprived of them for a long time. Nevertheless, if they are restored to us, it might occasion perilous temptations, and if we were permitted to confess without a free choice of confessor, nothing could do us greater harm" (186).

88. Discussion at National Liturgical Week, 1940; cited in Hughes, *How Firm a Foundation*, 220.

89. Jacob, *Lay People and Religion in the Early Eighteenth Century*, 94.

Liturgical Visions

The liturgical lives of women are not simply to be assessed by looking at their physical liturgical participation and the interpretations they placed on it. The church's public worship has also figured prominently in the visionary and mystical lives of women. These visions fall into a number of categories, but many give women access to roles and modes of participation in the church's worship that they do not have in their ordinary lives. Some scholars[90] argue, for example, that increasing prohibition of the chalice to women in the thirteenth century can be correlated with increasing numbers of eucharistic visions by women in which they receive communion in a manner that circumvents clerical authority.[91] By the late Middle Ages, women would have had no direct experience of receiving the consecrated chalice, but over and over again this image of receiving the cup (often directly from the hand of Jesus) appears in their mystical visions. Ida of Léau was visited in a vision every Sunday by Jesus Christ, who offers her a chalice from his hand. She reports having "received more sweetness and savour" from her vision than she had ever obtained from the sacrament itself.[92] "Authoritative visions of this kind allowed women to bypass clerical control and claim access to the sacrament, albeit indirectly, in their own right."[93]

Sometimes these visions depict the woman receiving the chalice, but offering it to others. So, in Mechtild of Hackeborn's thirteen-century vision, she was given Christ's heart in the form of a beautifully chiseled cup at communion, and he commanded her to go and "offer to all the saints the drink of life from my heart."[94] At other times, women see visions of other women assisting at mass.

> After Juliana of Cornillon's death in 1258, a woman who had loved her saw the saint assisting Christ while he celebrated mass; the women approached the altar and received a beautiful and excellent chalice from the High Priest and his virgin assistant.... When a priest who had criticized Ida of Louvain was celebrating, she seems to have approached the altar and stood behind him, and it is said that in her ecstasy she "was robed in sacerdotal

---

90. Such as Caroline Bynum and Jo Spreadbury.
91. See Caroline Walker Bynum, *Holy Feast and Holy Fast: The Religious Significance of Food to Medieval Women* (Berkeley: University of California Press, 1987), 227–37, and J. Jungmann, *Mass of the Roman Rite* (New York: Benziger, 1951–55), 2:381–86, 412–14.
92. *Vita B. Ida Lewensis*, II:19–20.
93. Jo Spreadbury, "The Gender of the Church: The Female Image of Ecclesia in the Middle Ages," in *Gender and Christian Religion*, ed. R. W. Swanson (Cambridge: Boydell, 1998), 103.
94. *Sanctae Mechtildis virginis ordinis sancti Benedicti liber specialis gratiae* (Paris, 1877), 5–10.

vestments," as if she were a concelebrant, and she received the sacrament miraculously.[95]

Visionary women did not necessarily claim explicit sacerdotal authority from their mystical experiences. God does tell Hildegard of Bingen (1098–1179) that "those of the female sex should not approach the office of My altar."[96] (Later God goes on to say that a consecrated virgin, such as Hildegard herself, "has the priesthood and all the ministry of My altar in her Bridegroom, and with him possesses all its riches.") Sometimes women's visions serve to enhance what the priest experiences while saying mass.

> Diedala, a beguine, experienced a vision in which, one Christmas night, the Infant Jesus appeared and lay in her arms. She explained that she could not sufficiently wonder at this marvel unless her friend, a monk at Villers, could enjoy it also. So, miraculously, she was transported to the abbey and there presented the child to the monk who was saying mass.[97]

To have a vision during mass was often seen as clear confirmation of its authenticity, again without the necessity of adjudication by male clergy. According to Aelred of Rivaulx, describing the mystical piety of Ghilbertine nuns in the "Nun of Watton," when a member of the community died the sisters continued to offer prayers for her until they were assured of her salvation by seeing an apparition of the deceased nun standing at the altar during the prayer of consecration. In every case, the kind of union with Christ that is aspired to but rarely achieved in the sacrament itself occurred in the vision. Gertrude the Great (1256–c. 1302), who describes Jesus as "flesh of my flesh and bone of my bone," received the spiritual imprint of his wounds (the *stigmata*) and related it directly to receiving the cup from his hand: "By those wounds you healed me and gave me the cup of the nectar of love to drink."[98]

Liturgical visions could also be important in initiating or authorizing new worship and devotional practices. Loretta, Countess of Leicester, attributes devotion to the Five Joys of Mary to such a vision, traditionally said to have been experienced sometime in the late tenth century. According to the countess, a very

---

95. Spreadbury, "The Gender of the Church," 101–2, citing *Vita S. Julianae Corneliensi*, ii, 9, para. 54; ActaSS, April 1, 475, and *Vita Ida Louvensi*, iii, I, ActaSS, April 2, 183.

96. Vision 6, para 76, Hildegard, *Scivias* ii, trans. Columba Hart and Jane Bishop (New York: Paulist, 1990), 278.

97. Cited in Brenda L. Bolton, "Mulieres Sanctae," in *Sanctity and Secularity: The Church and the World*, ed. Derek Baker (Oxford: Blackwell, 1973), 94.

98. Gertrude, *The Herald of God's Loving-Kindness, Books One and Two*, trans. A. Barratt (Kalamazoo, Mich.: Cistercian Publications, 1991), ii, 4, para 3, 110, cited with explication in Spreadbury, "The Gender of the Church," 101.

devout woman lay dying while her dearest friend kept watch by her bedside. During her lifetime, the pious woman had been accustomed to divide the day into five parts, each devoted to a meditation on the Virgin Mary. After rising until breakfast time she meditated on the joy of Mary in the Annunciation; from breakfast until mid-morning on her joy at the conception; from mid-morning until early afternoon on her joy in the Resurrection of her Son; from early afternoon until supper on her joy at the Ascension, and from supper until she went to bed, on the joy that she had in her Assumption. While the friend was standing over the dying woman's bedside, she saw her smile five times, delightedly, after which she died. After her death, the woman appeared to her friend and explained why she had smiled. On her deathbed the Virgin had appeared to her five times in succession, exactly as she had been wont to imagine her in her daily meditations, and this had made her smile.[99]

The natural authority of this type of women's visionary experience has allowed all kinds of women to share in a degree of liturgical authority that has often been denied them in ordinary ecclesiastical situations. Narratives of these experiences were widely circulated, both orally and in writing, and have been very significant sources for the liturgical formation of other women.

Magic as Alternative Ritual

One of the most difficult lines to draw in any study of women's liturgical lives and the piety that has undergirded them is the line between Christian ritual and magic. From the earliest period of the history of the church to the present day, women's ritual behavior has regularly blurred or ignored the boundary between the two.[100] This is hardly surprising, given the constraints under which women

---

99. Maurice Powicke, "Loretta, Countess of Leicester," in *The Christian Life in the Middle Ages and Other Essays* (Oxford: Clarendon, 1997/1935), 167. The five joys are explicated in a liturgical anthem, "Gaude dei Genetrix," dating from the first part of the eleventh century.

100. Although magical practice had long existed in Europe alongside more properly Christian observance, both Catholic and Protestant Reformations identified witchcraft as a problem. The relationship between women and witchcraft is strong, and records show that most of those formally accused of witchcraft were women. In Essex, in the southwestern part of England, 91 percent of the 270 people accused of sorcery in the court of assizes between 1560 and 1680 were women; between the mid-fourteenth century and the end of the seventeenth century, 82 percent of those charged in the north of France were women; similar statistics are found in Germany, and in New England, where between 1647 and 1725, 79 percent of the 355 persons accused of witchcraft were women. Not all of this was the result of sex discrimination and persecution of the socially and legally weakest citizens. In many cases women were indeed the repositories of arcane knowledge, passed on orally from mother to daughter and neighbor to neighbor: knowledge about healing herbs and various predictive signs for the weather, crops, and the outcome of childbirth and illness, and a deeper understanding perhaps of the psychological power of ritual. The older and more experienced the woman in these things, the more likely she was to be accused. As Carol Karlsen has argued, most of those accused of witchcraft at Salem represented the possibility of female autonomy: widowed women who had inherited their

have been placed in their access to the ritual power centers of the Christian liturgy. Magic gives women access to supernatural power on their own terms and allows them to apply it to very practical necessities of immediate concern. It would be a mistake to consider magic the manifestation of illiterate lay culture as opposed to literate clerical culture. Not only does this ignore the culture the two factions *share* as participants in a common social structure, but it also overlooks the significant role parish clergy played as mediators between "elite" doctrine and practice (promulgated by bishops, councils, and popes) and the popular religion and practice of the laity. Although both clergy and laity alike have been concerned with "doctrine," the higher clergy have tended to seek consistency in doctrine, while the laity have been "more concerned with the practical expression of those truths as expressed in rituals."[101]

It is worth looking at magic in the present context of the formation of women's liturgical piety for several reasons. First, the process by which women are formed for ritual practice is sometimes clearer in the case of the transmission of the rituals of witchcraft than in the transmission of the rituals of the Christian liturgy, and we perhaps can make inferences from one to the other. In the fifteenth-century *Gospels of the Distaff,* for example, we find a group of "wise and prudent matrons" gathering to share, while spinning at their wheels, the various kinds of folk wisdom of women: how to tell the sex of an unborn child; how to ensure that a child will grow up to be virtuous; fortune telling; and the use of talismans, amulets, and charms for protection from harm. One by one, each woman presides over an evening's reading: "One of us would begin her reading and chapters in the presence of all who had gathered there so as to preserve the memory forever after."[102] (The only man allowed to attend the vigils is ordered to write down the "gospels.") It seems likely that the setting of the *Gospels* is modeled on a familiar scene in which more traditional kinds of liturgical piety and practice were shared among women in this manner over their spinning.

Yet another reason for attending to the question of magic here is that the involvement of women in magic provides evidence of their knowledge of other, officially sanctioned ritual forms. Trials, both ecclesiastical and civil, of women on charges of witchcraft have resulted in a great deal of recorded testimony, and because magical ritual has so often been intertwined with elements of the

---

husband's estate, single women with no dependents, as well as those who consorted with Native people and religious outsiders. Carol Karlsen, *Devil in the Shape of a Woman: Witchcraft in Colonial New England* (New York: Norton, 1987), 101ff.

101. Karen Louise Jolly, *Popular Religion in Late Saxon England: Elf Charms in Context* (Chapel Hill: University of North Carolina Press, 1996), 22.

102. Madelin Jeay, ed., *Les evangiles des quenouilles* (Montreal: Presses de l'Université de Montreal, 1985), 24.

authorized Christian liturgy, we can have some clear idea of the degree of women's familiarity with the official prayers and rites. So Isabel Mure, who was presented before the ecclesiastical court in 1528 for using rituals to divine the future, had quite obviously internalized the church's liturgy to a considerable degree. As the trial transcript tells us:

> she took fire and two young women with her and went to a running water and lit a wisp of straw and set it on the water and said thus, "Benedicite, see ye what I see. I see fire burn and the water run and the grass grow sea flow and night fevers and all other. God will," and after these words said fifteen paternosters, fifteen ave marias and three creeds.[103]

This blending of liturgical and magical elements into a single rite is not all that surprising. For most of Christian history, the formation and maintenance of magic as an alternative liturgical world for women has been a cooperative effort between clergy and laity. Not infrequently, we find the words of charms and exorcisms written in the margins of medieval liturgical texts, indicating that clergy needed ready access to these in addition to the official liturgical prayers. Abundant evidence exists that clergy blessed objects specifically for use in alternative rites, and exorcised sick animals, bedeviled persons, or haunted buildings. Beginning in the tenth century, charm remedies were collected and copied by Christian scribes, another indication that magic was a shared project of the practitioners of both popular and traditional religion, in a world "in which everything was alive with spiritual presences and the doors between heaven and earth were open all around."[104]

In the pre-Reformation period, women were acutely aware of the power of words in relation to objects and persons; in the church, the words had the ability to effect the transformation of bread and wine at the altar and water at baptism. A good example of mixing of supernatural agencies can be found in the eleventh-century *Leechbook*, which prescribes certain incantations for use when a disease of unknown cause affected horses.[105] The prescription instructs the priest to sing twelve masses over "dock seed and Scottish wax" before placing them, mixed in Holy Water, into the horse.

The most potent liturgical combination of act and words, therefore, was the recitation of the whole mass, in which the verbal power of the priest

---

103. Sharon L. Jansen, *Dangerous Talk and Strange Behavior: Women and Popular Resistance to the Reforms of Henry VIII* (New York: St. Martin's, 1996), 62.

104. Jolly, *Popular Religion in Late Saxon England*, 2.

105. This was commonly referred to as "elfshot."

ordained by the holy church opened the doorway through the natural elements to heavenly power. Masses said over the herbs in a remedy called down God's blessing on his natural creations (bread and wine for spiritual cure or the herb for physical cure) and served to drive out evil forces (worm, elf, or demon), just as the mass of exorcism did.[106]

Other evidence exists to support the idea that clergy colluded in the magical activities of women. When in 1582 Agnes Pinberry of Barnsely was brought up on charges of making potions, witnesses alleged that she had been "allowed to charm by the Bishop of Gloucester."[107] In Devonshire, sufferers from "fits" asked clergy for the church keys so that at midnight they could crawl under the communion table three times as a remedy for their illness.[108]

At the same time, women have used elements of the Christian liturgy as an antidote to magic they imagined was being used against them. In seventeenth-century France, "peasants who thought themselves threatened by witchcraft might use sacramentals, such as holy water, consecrated hosts, church candles, or objects blessed by the priest, as counter-magical agencies; often such techniques were advised by the *devins* [those with knowledge of the healing arts]."[109] Women have also circulated alternative, hybrid calendars, which conflated astrological almanacs and the liturgical year, each system transferring its inherent power to the other. These almanacs gave the reader the key astronomical events for the coming year and provided a prognostication based upon celestial movements, giving the best days for medical procedures, bathing, and travel, as well as all kinds of agricultural occupations. Their popularity continued unabated well into the late nineteenth century, and their use was supported by a large number of specialist consultants, who would clarify and make more precise the astrological calculations.[110]

Clearly, magical and religious belief and practice have never been mutually exclusive for women, and women have perennially sought out specialists in one form of ritual or the other to meet particular ritual and spiritual needs. Equally clearly, most scholars of the liturgy have never taken this aspect of women's ritual lives very seriously. As Karen Louise Jolly, a scholar of medieval books of incantations, writes, "These early medieval uses of the liturgy for "effective"

---

106. Jolly, *Popular Religion in Late Saxon England*, 122.
107. Ibid.
108. Anna Eliza Bray, *A Description of the Part of Devonshire Bordering on the Tamar and the Tavy*, 3 vols. (London, 1836), 1:330–32, 334; 2:291–92.
109. Briggs, *Communities of Belief*, 37.
110. Careful analysis has yet to be made of the degree to which contemporary Christian women also rely on astrology, to which astrological arcana are passed from one woman to another, and to which the liturgical year and the astrological calendar reinforce and interpret one another.

purposes were classified as magic by many modern scholars, especially liturgists, who shuddered at the degradation of a "pure" liturgy...."[111] She continues on to say that in the early medieval period, the gap between books of liturgical prayers and books of magical charms "was so small that they belong together as a single larger group of manuals for health and well-being along with penitentials."[112] (Objects also have partaken of this same blend of religious and magical piety: amulets were sometimes in the shape of tiny containers, filled with bits of the consecrated host, wax from the paschal candle, or holy oil to protect the bearer from harm.) In other words the combination of liturgical prayer and incantation, liturgical object and magical object was seen as more powerful than either one by itself, and women have felt entirely free to exploit that power whenever necessary.

The Shape of Women's Liturgical Piety

In these pages, we have begun to uncover certain key features of women's liturgical formation and liturgical piety. We have seen how groups of women, sharing concerns about their children, their health, their marriages, and their souls, have exchanged among themselves insights and processes that have proved useful in meeting these concerns. In some cases these insights and processes might be described as "women's folk wisdom" or magic, but it can probably be inferred that the exchange of women's wisdom in matters related to Christian worship happened in much the same way. Thus, the first quality of women's liturgical formation is that it is inherently utilitarian, and the second is that it is inherently social (see fig. 17).

Although overall women's liturgical piety cannot be described as "mystical," those women whose spirituality did have a mystical bent could circumvent constraints placed on their actual participation in worship by participation in numinous experiences of worship in which access to restricted roles and relationships was afforded them. Analysis of these visionary experiences helps us to understand the kinds of tensions inherent in women's liturgical piety, especially the tension between the desire to surrender completely to worship and the need to conform to social and ecclesiastical norms. Because they have an intrinsic authority, and because they are essentially antielitist, these mystical experiences have also been crucial to the liturgical formation of other women of all social strata.

---

111. Jolly, *Popular Religion in Late Saxon England*, 114. See F. E. Warren, *The Liturgy and Ritual of the Celtic Church* (Woodbridge: Boydell, 1987), for this position on "objectionable" additions to liturgical manuscripts, and C. E. Hohler, "Some Service Books of the Later Saxon Church," in *Tenth-Century Studies*, ed. David Parsons (London: Phillimore, 1975), 60–83.

112. Jolly, *Popular Religion in Late Saxon England*, 114.

Books have also played a part in the formation of women's liturgical piety, at least for literate women and their social circles. Although women have been generally less concerned with liturgical doctrine than with liturgical practice, books that reflect on the experience of worship, that prepare women for devout engagement with the authorized rites and prayers, and that allow women to integrate the worship they undertake in church with the worship they undertake in other settings have been enormously influential. In order to fill in the details of this picture, more complete records need to be compiled of the patterns of women's book ownership, the kinds of books owned by women, and how women have applied what they read in books to their liturgical lives. Women have also used their own writing to explore the depths of meaning of worship and to discover the links between liturgy and life; by ensuring that these writings are passed on to their daughters and granddaughters, they have contributed to the formation of future generations of women.

Finally, even in this brief outline of the formation and content of women's liturgical piety, one other quality shines through: women's liturgical piety is affective. In their diaries they have meditated on the consolation worship has given them and on the pain of separation from the worshiping community; in their conversion stories they have expressed the joy of finding a true liturgical "home"; in their letters to family members they have written of their deep sorrow that those they love most have not found the full measure of the grace to be experienced in Christian worship. All of these fundamental qualities — the affective, the social, the utilitarian, and in certain circumstances, the literate — combine to create a rich and detailed women's liturgical piety. Its formation, content, and application may be quite different from that of laymen and of the clergy. But it will be essential to appreciate and understand the role women's liturgical piety has played in the twenty centuries of the church's liturgical life if we are eventually to draw the full picture of the history of Christian worship.

Chapter Five

Going to Church on Sundays

Prior to leaving England, I had been for nearly twenty years a member of the Wesleyan Methodist Society, and consequently felt wishful, as soon as circumstances would allow, to join the religious body called Methodists in that country....   — Rebecca Burlend, 1831

Ever since New Testament times, going to church on Sundays has been the mainstay of Christian liturgical practice. In some cases, especially in the East, Sunday worship has been the only public gathering where men and women shared a single space; in other cases it was the only occasion in the week where women met and interacted with other women.[1] For women in very isolated circumstances — living on farms or in hermitages, for example — Sunday worship may have been the only occasion during the week when they assembled with other human beings. For some women, Sunday worship has not only been the only occasion on which women have gathered with other Christian believers, but also the only occasion on which they have said their prayers or heard the Scriptures read. For other women the Sunday service has been just one aspect of an overall pattern of life that included regular daily prayer, festal worship, and the pastoral rites. In either case, the experience of Sunday worship has been at the center of the liturgical experience of generation after generation of Christian women.

---

1. As we have seen (p. 155), while the sociability of gathering with others has been generally celebrated as an integral aspect of the experience of Sunday worship, occasionally it could cause something of a problem. In the years between 1218 and 1236, the minutes of one Bristol guild almost continually cautioned its members not to walk about in church during services "but to stand or kneel in the chancel as an example to other laity." Nicholas Orme, "Children in the Church," *Journal of Ecclesiastical History* 45, no. 4 (October 1994): 571. Five hundred years later things had not considerably improved. The London magazine *The Spectator* criticized people for "staring in church, and bowing and curtseying to one another during services and for giggling or arriving late. The *Guardian* commented adversely on the Earl of Nottingham's daughter for 'knotting' during the service at St. James's Picadilly and also criticized flirting and whispering in church." William M. Jacob, *Lay People and Religion in the Early Eighteenth Century* (Cambridge: Cambridge University Press, 1996), 65–66.

But what was that experience like for ordinary laywomen? We have seen[2] that women have exerted various kinds of influence over the shape and content of Christian worship, and very often this influence was felt most keenly in the Sunday service. Most women, however, have probably simply attended Sunday services year in and year out, without ever feeling as if they could shape the ecclesiastical proceedings to their own needs and desires. But this is not to suggest that the women we shall meet had no control over their own liturgical lives. In their preparations for worship, their interpretations of and responses to the various aspects of the Sunday service, and in some cases their refusal to connect with certain practices, many women actively took possession of their own worship experience. We attempt to draw here a picture of this more typical experience of ordinary Sunday churchgoing.

Church Attendance

It is tempting to imagine that before the encroachment of modern secularism every Christian woman attended church regularly, participating with pious attention and commitment in Sunday services and the pastoral rites. The especially devout perhaps also attended various weekday liturgies, preaching events, and revivals. We tend to picture these women seated reverently with their families, guiding their children and grandchildren through the intricacies of the prayers and rituals; we see rich and poor women forming one community of faith and worship and then returning to their homes for sedate entertainment throughout the rest of the day. But does the evidence bear this out? Were women habitually in church? Were rich and poor women in church in equal numbers and was their experience of Sunday worship the same? If they were not in church, what kept them away?

Certainly in most periods of Christian history women have made up the overwhelming majority of churchgoers. Statistics for a group of churches in antebellum North Carolina are not unusual: between January 1, 1855, and December 31, 1859, in the nine Episcopal parishes studied by Richard Rankin, new female communicants outnumbered male communicants by nearly three to one (268 women to 92 men).[3] (The ratio between all communicants in four of the churches studied was nearly five women for every man.) A safe conclusion is that in the West, the cultural expectation that women will be in church has been generally stronger

---

2. See below, pp. 81–119.
3. Richard Rankin, *Ambivalent Churchmen and Evangelical Churchwomen: The Religion of the Episcopal Elite in North Carolina, 1800–1860* (Columbia: University of South Carolina Press, 1993), 169.

in every period of Christian history than the expectation that men will be in church; this expectation has manifested itself in the preponderance of women over men in most congregations. But this statement is not the same as saying that the preponderance of women *in any given district* were in church; nor is it the same as saying that when women were in church, their motivations were always pious ones.

Of course, some women have indeed exemplified our idealized vision of devotion to church attendance. Every Sunday, Darcy, Lady Maxwell (1742–1810) is reported to have

> attended early morning and evening preaching at the Methodist Chapel. She also attended Morning Prayer, the sacrament and often the preaching as well at her parish church. Monday evening was the public prayer meeting at the chapel, usually followed by a band meeting. One or more classes met through the week. Thursday evening she led the class whose members were the preachers in the town and their wives.[4]

Obituaries and memorials are full of such descriptions of women with this kind of exceptional commitment to being at church for services of worship. Some women, such as Celia Fiennes (whom we shall meet again), traveled from church to church on a given Sunday, in order that they might be edified by different preachers. Writing from Truro on the Cornwall peninsula, Fiennes records that there were several good churches in the district, but that "I was hindered by raine on the Lords day . . . and so was forced to stay where I could hear but one Sermon at the [parish] Church."[5]

But questions remain about the degree to which diligent church attendance itself has necessarily been a mark of attentive participation. In a memorial sermon for Jane Ratcliffe in 1639, the preacher praised the deceased for her regular pres-

---

4. Earl Kent Brown, *Women of Mr. Wesley's Methodism* (New York and Toronto: Edwin Mellen Press, 1983), 127. See also Lady Darcy Brisbane Maxwell, *The Life of Darcy, Lady Maxwell of Pollock: Late of Edinburgh: Compiled from Her Voluminous Diary and Correspondence and from Other Authentic Documents*, 2 vols., ed. John Lancaster (New York: N. Bangs and T. Mason for the Methodist Episcopal Church, 1822).

5. Celia Fiennes, *The Illustrated Journeys of Celia Fiennes, 1685–1712*, ed. Christopher Morris (London: McDonald and Co., 1982), 203. Others were driven to church-hopping for reasons of their own spiritual distress. In the late eighteenth century, a woman referred to only as "Goody Bonner" sought the advice of a preacher-turned-physician in the neighborhood known for his ability to cure spiritual disorders. The woman was reported to have been anguished about her salvation, and the physician's notes on the case are illuminating: "For her sins she despaireth much. . . . A follower of sermons, threatened by the minister for leaving his sermons and going on to others. Will rise at the crying of the birds, saying that they cry out against her for her sins." Michael MacDonald, *Mystical Bedlam: Madness, Anxiety, and Healing in Seventeenth-Century England* (Cambridge: Cambridge University Press, 1981), 221.

ence at church services, and especially for "diligently listening with open ears and eyes (for she never slept in church as too many do use to do)."[6] Among sixteenth-century aristocrats at least, the prayers before the sermon seem to have been an opportunity for catching up on correspondence, as can be seen in a letter from Robert, Earl of Essex to Penelope Devoreaux. After describing at some length his current state of mind on various matters, he concludes his letter with the words: "The preacher is ready to begin and therefore he shall end this discourse though upon another text."[7]

The question of whether rich women have been more likely to attend church than their less well-off sisters is even more difficult to determine, because the percentages probably vary considerably among different periods and locations. Humbert of Rome's thirteenth-century advice manual for preachers gives us evidence from a period in which church attendance seems to have been very low among all classes of society. In a chapter on "The Poor," for example, he declares simply that "the poor rarely go to church, and rarely to sermons; so they know little of what pertains to their salvation."[8] But he goes on to say that the wealthy are hardly more faithful in their churchgoing. Women in large and busy Roman households are particularly susceptible to staying away from church: "This sort of *familia*, because of various occupations, is rarely accustomed to gather in church, unless perhaps on the great feasts, and then only for morning mass."[9] The diaries of aristocratic women in the centuries which follow indicate that, with certain notable exceptions, they indeed did not tend to be enthusiastic churchgoers. In the majority of cases, Sunday after Sunday goes by with no mention of Christian worship (except occasionally to say that the writer did not attend for one reason or another).[10]

But other women have gone to extraordinary lengths to attend Sunday services. When Catherine Cavender looked around the courthouse that served as a church for the scattered settlers of Hays, Kansas, in 1877, she observed that "some of those sunbrowned men and women and little children had driven miles

---

6. Nick Alldredge, "Loyalty and Identity in Chester Parishes, 1540–1640," in *Parish Church and People: Local Studies in Lay Religion, 1350–1750*, ed. Susan J. Wright (London: Hutchinson, 1988), 116.

7. Sylvia Freedman, *Poor Penelope: Lady Penelope Rich, an Elizabethan Woman* (Bourne End, U.K.: Kensal Press, 1983), 91.

8. Alexander Murray, "Piety and Impiety in Thirteenth-Century Italy," in *Popular Belief and Practice*, ed. G. J. Cuming and D. Baker (Cambridge: Cambridge University Press, 1972), 93. "The author will say much the same of magnates: 'men placed in high station are rarely accustomed to hear sermons.' This is corroborated by the preachers themselves. Giordano refers to people who, 'through negligence or presumption, do not attend the Eucharist, or make no attempt to fast in Lent.'"

9. Ibid.

10. See p. 219.

across the prairie to be there."[11] Celia Fiennes (1662–1741), who traveled around her native England in the years between 1685 and 1712, often records in her journal observations about the churches she attended, noting in at least one instance the extreme difficulty parishioners had in getting to church. At Truro in Cornwall, Fiennes walked a mile in the rain to the parish church, and reports that she had to travel over very difficult terrain, crisscrossed by fences and ditches:

> They are severall stones fixed across and so are like a grate or large steps over a ditch that is full of mudd or water, and over this just in the middle is a great stone fixed side wayes which is the stile to be clambered over; these I find are the fences and guards of their grounds one from another and indeed they are very troublesome and dangerous for strangers and children.[12]

But Fiennes was particularly impressed by her Cornish landlady, who, because of the pressures of work and a large family, was unable to attend church. She observed that the woman possessed "that pitch of soul, resignation to the will of God, and thankfulness that God enabled and owned her therein," to the extent that she had clearly "reached an attainment few reach that have greater advantages of learning and knowing the mind of God." She concludes, "This plainly led me to see that God himself teacheth soe as none teacheth like him, so he can discover himself to those immediately that have not the opportunity of seeing him in his sanctuary."[13]

With the rise of strict forms of Sabbatarianism, going to church on Sunday became understood as a necessary part of "remembering the Sabbath Day to keep it holy." In the American colonies, Blue Laws prohibited commerce and various forms of entertainment on Sundays so that citizens would not be distracted from going to church and other religious activities. Books for young women were filled with lurid cautionary tales of girls who failed to keep the Sabbath, and who instead engaged in such activities as "sail-boating" and "an excursion to Hoboken," and who suffered dreadful, and invariably fatal, consequences. Each of these diatribes

---

11. Joanna L. Stratton, *Pioneer Women: Voices from the Kansas Frontier* (New York: Simon and Schuster, 1981), 176.

12. Fiennes, *The Illustrated Journeys of Celia Fiennes*, 209. Sometimes the terrain was so difficult that in certain seasons, services had to be postponed or suspended. At the North Parish church in North Andover, Massachusetts, in 1740, the vestry "Voted that ye Sacrament be administered oftener in the summers and be omitted in the winter monthes by reason of the difficulty in attending it." Juliet Haines Moffard, *And Firm Thine Ancient Vow: The History of North Parish Church of North Andover, 1645–1974* (North Andover, Mass.: Naiman, 1975), 86.

13. Ibid., 210.

against failing to attend church and breaking the sanctity of Sunday rest ends with the warning: "GOD WILL NOT PROTECT THE SABBATH-BREAKER."[14]

Why Did Women Stay Away from Church?

Women have stayed away from church for a variety of reasons. Some undoubtedly have refrained from attending Sunday services because of their own indifference to religion. But many devout women, like Celia Fiennes's Cornish landlady, were kept from attending by various life circumstances. Some women who sincerely wished to go to church were impeded from doing so by unsympathetic husbands. Such was the situation of Mary Gore, a native of Birmingham, England, who had been converted by Primitive Methodist preaching in 1827 at the age of thirty-seven. Her husband had remained deeply opposed to Methodism, however, and often refused to let his wife back into the house after she had been to the chapel. On those occasions she had to "seek shelter elsewhere or spend the nights sleep in the open air." She persisted in her churchgoing perversity, and one day her husband threatened to cut her legs off with an axe if she went to the Methodist Sunday service again. "Then I will go upon my stumps!" Mary defiantly replied.[15]

In periods of extensive or rapid liturgical change, some women seem to have stayed away from church because their theological principles and the churches' new liturgical style did not correspond.[16] When Mary I (1516–1558) restored the Roman Catholic mass in churches that only a few years before had adopted the *Book of Common Prayer*, Dorothy Griffin and Anne Williamson were brought before the consistory court for failing to attend church. They defended their actions, saying that their "conscience was troubled" by the restoration of the mass.[17] Others seem to have stayed away because they did not approve of the preacher for the day. Once Darcy, Lady Maxwell "heard someone ask who was preaching at a given meeting, as if to suggest he would go only if the preacher sounded attractive. She remarked, 'It is no subject of inquiry, who is the Preacher; but [only] when is the time.' "[18] We think of "lack of relevance" as a modern excuse for staying away from church. But when the Lutheran Inspectors (successors to the episcopal Visitors) made their tour of the Protestant districts in Germany in the mid-sixteenth century, they complained that large numbers of people were

---

14. Harvey Newcomb, *How to Be a Lady: A Book for Girls, Containing Useful Hints on the Formation of Character* (Boston: Gould and Lincoln, 1846), 80–81.

15. Obituary, "Mary Gore," *Primitive Methodist Magazine* 31 (1850): 62.

16. See Eamon Duffy, *The Stripping of the Altars: Traditional Religion in England, 1400–1580* (New Haven: Yale University Press, 1992).

17. Susan Brigden, *London and the Reformation* (Oxford: Clarendon, 1989), 564.

18. Brown, *Women of Mr. Wesley's Methodism*, 127.

refusing to attend church. "When asked [by the Lutheran Inspectors] why they did not come to hear the pastors' Sunday sermons, they reportedly replied, 'the Turk and the Pope are not doing us any harm' — that is to say that they had no interest in the topics covered by the preachers who denounced the Roman pope and distant infidels. The themes of official propaganda were of no concern to the villagers."[19]

Often the pressures of work kept women away. Household servants, slaves, factory workers, market traders, and others were hindered from going to church by the demands of their employers or by the need to make a living wage. In the late seventeenth century, Joyce Worldly of Downton told the consistory court inquiring about her absence from church that she had not received the sacrament for three years because "her employment had not permitted her to do it."[20] In various English parishes in the mid-seventeenth century, the priest reported that between 50 and 80 percent of their flocks did not take Easter communion. "The extreme case seems to be a parish where only eighty out of seven hundred had taken communion, because the main occupation was that of flotteurs working the river-boats, which made Sunday work obligatory."[21] Apprentices were particularly vulnerable. One young girl testified "that her master had not taught her a trade, had pawned her clothes, had not taken her to church, and had 'lodged her with a most lewd and debauched woman.'"[22]

As pew rents became increasingly common, and the number of free seats in churches diminished, many working women had to choose between attending Sunday services and feeding their families. Some women did attempt to combine the demands of religion and employment, but the resulting exhaustion took its toll. On the Benjamin Montgomery plantation in Mississippi, complaints were regularly recorded that during revival time the slaves were unable to do the requisite amount of work. Montgomery's daughter Virginia lamented that her servants "were all broken down having to attend church every night."[23] As one

---

19. George Huppert, *After the Black Death: A Social History of Early Modern Europe* (Bloomington: Indiana University Press, 1986), 146.

20. Donald Splaeth, "Common Prayer? Popular Observance of the Anglican Liturgy in Restoration Wiltshire," in *Parish Church and People: Local Studies in Lay Religion, 1350–1750*, ed. Susan J. Wright (London: Hutchinson, 1988), 134.

21. Christopher Haigh, "Communion and Community: Exclusion from Communion in Post-Reformation England," *Journal of Ecclesiastical History* 51, no. 4 (October 2000): 732.

22. Steven R. Smith, "The London Apprentices as Seventeenth-Century Adolescents," in *Rebellion, Popular Protest and Social Order in Early Modern England*, ed. P. Slack (Cambridge: Cambridge University Press, 1983), 222.

23. William E. Montgomery, *Under Their Own Vine and Fig Tree: The African American Church in the South, 1865–1900* (Baton Rouge: Louisiana State University Press, 1993), 273. The author continues to say that, "On the David Barrow plantation in Georgia, August was revival time, and all work ceased as the people shifted their attention to worship and salvation. They slaughtered hogs,

commentator notes, revival times were difficult times for slaves and wage laborers alike in terms of their employment, and the need to attend the revival meeting could be "particularly troublesome in the cities, where domestic and other laborers were expected to be on the job on a regular basis and where employers complained most about disruptions and absenteeism."[24] In 1862, the young Englishwoman Catherine Hopley came to America to work as governess to the children of a wealthy family of Virginia Methodists. A faithful member of the Church of England, Hopley was dismayed to find that the nearest Episcopal church was twelve miles away, but she went along to the Methodist chapel with her employers. (She reports that she had initially mistaken the chapel for a barn, and was "surprised at entering to find a gallery for blacks and two doors, one for men and one for women.") The order of worship and sermon seemed "vulgar" to her, and she left the chapel determined that "the next Sabbath might be passed profitably in my own room, in the event having no other church to attend."[25]

Sanctions on women who stayed away from church varied by time and place. During the post-Reformation period, for example, women were regularly brought before the consistory court and required to explain why they had failed to attend Sunday services. Their answers to these charges vary, from scruples about the form of worship offered, to business that called them away on Sundays, to the need to care for children or elderly relatives. Usually those who were deemed by the court to have been absent without just cause were fined or made to perform certain penitential disciplines. When Martha Amee and the wife of Nicholas Moulder were presented before the Suffolk (Massachusetts) County Court in 1648, they were required to pay heavy fines for "neglecting the publique worship of God."[26] Sectarian women — Quakers, Mennonites, and others — were often tried not for heresy, but for failing to make an appearance at the parish church as required by law, and were not infrequently imprisoned and occasionally executed.[27]

---

lambs, and chickens to feed the body while the minister fed the soul with the Gospel of Christ, and 'for three or four days they do little else but preach, sing, and eat.' "

24. Ibid.

25. Richard Mullen, *Birds of Passage: Five Englishwomen in Search of America* (London: Duckworth, 1994), 181. This problem of the need to accommodate one's worship life to the demands of work was hardly new to the nineteenth century, however. Six centuries earlier, in his treatise *On the Teaching of Preachers*, Humbert of Rome observes that "Ladies' maids especially, were ill-placed for church-going. . . . Urged on by wicked masters, [they] omitted to go to church at all, ever, and violated feast-days into the bargain." Cited in Murray, "Piety and Impiety in Thirteenth-Century Italy," 93.

26. Carol Berkin and Leslie Horowitz, eds., *Women's Voices, Women's Lives: Documents in Early American History* (Boston: Northeastern University Press, 1998), 133.

27. To avoid these punishments, many English sectarian women observed what came to be called "occasional conformity," that is, the habit of attending their Church of England parish church only once a year at Easter in order to observe the letter (if not the spirit) of the law.

For women living under other temporal and geographical circumstances, sanctions for nonattendance could be more immediate. In the mid-nineteenth century, for example, Henry M. Tucker Jr., the owner of the Lichfield plantation in South Carolina ("whose faith in the Episcopal Church was said to be absolute"), "ensured the attendance of his slaves at services in the Lichfield chapel by having his overseer call the roll after service. Any slave missing who was not on the nurse's sick list for the day forfeited a weekly allowance of either bacon, sugar, molasses or tobacco."[28]

One wonders not only about the effect on such forced attendance on women, but also about the effect of such a captive congregation on Christian worship. Former slave Mariah Heywood gives us a hint about this. Interviewed for the oral history project of the Works Progress Administration (WPA) in the 1930s, Heywood reports that she and the other slaves were forced to go to the Presbyterian church near the plantation, whose pastor was in the employ of the owners. "Parson Glennie come once a month to Sunnyside. Parson Glennie read, sing, pray. Tell us obey Miss Minna."[29]

Sometimes women absented themselves from church in response to provocative actions of the clergy. Men and women alike stayed away from the parish church at Earl's Colne in Essex, where the rector, Ralph Josselin, refused to celebrate communion for nine years in the 1640s and early 1650s because he considered the vast majority of his congregation unregenerate. (When he finally reinstated the communion, he allowed only thirty-four persons to receive the sacrament.) This kind of suspension of the normal rites of the church was not as uncommon as one might suppose, especially in times of liturgical and theological turmoil. At Wilmslow, the parish accounts books record no expenditures for communion bread and wine from 1645 to 1650,[30] and at a meeting of ministers in 1653 the rector is reported to have argued that "suspension [of the Holy Commu-

---

28. Charles Joyner, *Down by the Riverside: A South Carolina Slave Community* (Urbana: University of Illinois Press, 1984), 22–23.

29. Cited in ibid., 155. In most periods, women slaves would have had no choice of which church to attend. "Sometimes the demands of their masters and mistresses gave slaves no choice of the church to attend. Rachel Bradley nearly always accompanied her mistress to church meetings and caught the spirit of evangelical revivalism as a result. 'Old missus used to go off to church and revivals and she's take me along,' she remembered. 'When they got to shoutin' I'd shout too.'" Montgomery, *Under Their Own Vine and Fig Tree*, 106. Of course for most of Christian history women and men alike would have had very little if any opportunity to choose the church they attended and its form of worship. "Choice" in churchgoing is a recent phenomenon, only really having meaning with the increase in popular access to the automobile in the late 1920s in North America (and later still in other parts of the world). In some rural settings, there is still very limited choice in where to attend church.

30. Although the pastor, John Berreton, did oversee the replacing of the altar with a communion table in 1644.

nion] would keep the Lord's Supper from pollution as well as excommunication [of particular individuals]."[31] Clergy have had other ways of making things difficult for their parishioners to participate. Mary Beckwith, who was brought before the consistory court in 1591 for failing to attend church at Easter, replied that when the minister, Mr. Wharton, examined her and her fellow parishioners for their worthiness to receive communion, "He asked them frivolous questions, as what should become of their bodies when they were in the ground, and whether all the world should be saved."[32]

Women settlers and travelers were often unable to find a church that suited their spiritual and liturgical needs. Rebecca Burlend, a Methodist who emigrated to America from England in 1831, was startled to find that the Methodist church nearest her new home was nothing like the one to which she was accustomed. "I attended a class meeting about two miles from our residence," she reports, "but the manner in which it was conducted was by no means congenial to my views and sentiments." The service began with the congregation standing.

> A sort of circle or ring was then immediately formed, with the whole assembly taking hold of hands, and capering about the house surprisingly. Their gesture could not be called dancing, and yet no term describes it better. This done, worship commenced with extempore prayer, not indeed in language or style the best selected, but with this I have nothing to do. I have no right to question the sincerity of the individual, and if his taste differed from mine, it is no proof it is wrong.[33]

In spite of this generous sentiment, however, Burlend admits that she found the entire service "exceedingly exceptionable," and vows never to return. "Finding in this mode of worship little that I could really respect," she says, "I resolved not long afterwards to absent myself from them altogether."[34]

---

31. Cited in Judith Maltby, *Prayer Book and People in Elizabethan and Stuart England* (Cambridge: Cambridge University Press, 1998), 214.

32. Christopher Haigh, "Communion and Community," 732.

33. Rebecca Burlend, *The Wesleyan Emigrants: A True Picture of Emigration: Or Fourteen Years in the Interior of North America; Being a Full and Impartial Account of the Various Difficulties and Ultimate Success of an English Family Who Emigrated from Barwick-in-Elmet, Near Leeds, in the Year 1831* (London, 1848 and Lakeside Classics, 1936), 146. She continues with her detailed and graphic description of this service: "All persons present being again seated, an individual started from his seat, exclaiming in a loud and frantic shriek, 'I feel it,' meaning what is commonly attested among them the power of God. His motions, which appeared half convulsive, were observed with animated joy by the rest, till he fell apparently stiff upon the floor, where he lay unmolested a short time, and then resumed his seat. Others were affected in a similar manner, only in some instances the power of speech was not suspended, as in this, by the vehemence of enthusiasm, I cannot give it a more moderate name."

34. Ibid., 147.

Children in Church

Determining whether children were regularly present in church is important for a study of women's liturgical history. Not only does it give us an indication of how soon young girls were exposed to the ordinary rhythm of the Christian liturgy, but also, given that women historically have been responsible for the care of young children, it can help us to determine the degree to which women's own churchgoing was affected by the presence or absence of their children in church (see fig. 18). Some women (like Catherine Cavender cited above) specifically mention the presence of children in services of Christian worship, but as a general rule children have been even more invisible than women to the historian.

In the early centuries, very young children do seem to have been regularly in church, and the problem of the disruption caused by infants was periodically addressed. St. Cyprian (c. 258) says that the churchgoer is to consider the noise of crying babies in church as a kind of prayer, and other preachers of this period interpreted it as a lament for the human condition. But such perennial attempts to soothe the frayed nerves of parishioners with theological and spiritual elucidations of children's noise seem not to have made a great deal of difference. Twelve centuries after Cyprian and his cohorts, an episcopal visitation in the diocese of Lincoln was informed that parishioners in Kimpton (Hertfordshire) were complaining that "infants for the most part laugh, cry, and call out in divine service,"[35] which they declared to be "provocative."

Other evidence, however, suggests that children may not invariably have been brought to church with their parents. Throughout the Middle Ages, we find women brought to court and charged with responsibility for the disastrous consequences that often resulted from leaving their babies at home alone while they attended church. The case of Edith le Taylour of Laycock, Wiltshire, is quite typical. In 1377 she was indicted for involuntary manslaughter in the death of her infant daughter, whom she had placed "in a cradle by the fire at prime where she went to mass — not anticipating that chickens would enter the house and set fire to the cradle with fatal results."[36] In a similar case in 1268, a two-year-old girl fell into a well and drowned while her parents were in church. In all of these cases, women attempted to argue that the fact that they left their child specifically in order to attend church services mitigated their guilt.

---

35. Hamilton Thompson, ed., *Visitation of the Diocese of Lincoln, 1517–1531* (Lincoln Records Society xxiii, 1940), 69. Cited in Orme, "Children in Church," 569. Sometimes it seems that children were taken to church for other purposes. "When two priests accompanied Margery Kempe to the church at Mintling near Kings Lynn in the fifteenth century, they 'took with them a child or two and they all went to the place together' — evidently the children acted as some sort of chaperone" (570).

36. Ibid.

It is perhaps also true that older children have decided themselves against churchgoing in favor of other Sunday entertainments, and there is some evidence that the sense that church was for the old and not for the young is not a recent phenomenon. This can be seen in an observation of the parish priest of Little Rollright in Oxfordshire in 1738 that young people were staying away from Sunday services when the eucharist was being celebrated: "The young ones above sixteen years old (notwithstanding all I can say in Church or Out) are resolved to think [the sacrament] belongs only to elderly people to receive it."[37]

The Sunday Service

Many women's first-person writings describe, in greater or lesser detail, the experience of going to church on Sunday. Leaving aside for a moment the inherent bias in the evidence from women's writing toward the well-born and literate that we discussed earlier,[38] these descriptions are a significant source of information about women's churchgoing. Many of these descriptions concentrate on the social aspect of Sunday worship: who was present, what people wore, what sort of personal interactions took place. Others attend to the preacher and the sermon, the prayers, the hymns, or the mode of celebration of the sacraments. We see this latter type of description in Catherine Cavender's memoirs, in which she gives details of a Sunday service in Hayes, Kansas, in 1877. "We sat on long hard benches," she says. "There was a little melodeon or small organ and a choir sang the morning hymn. The sermon, according to a little diary of mine, was from the 105th Psalm, 42, 43, and 44th verses. The theme was that the prairie might be made to blossom like the rose...."[39]

While such narratives can tell us a considerable amount about Sunday worship (in this case, that people sat in pews, that there was a melodeon to support the singing, a choir, and a sermon preached on a text from the Psalms), the problem is that these kinds of descriptions are very often repetitive, and only when something abnormal takes place do they come to life. Indeed in many cases it is only the *uncharacteristic* in worship that is reported at all. This has always been a serious problem for the historian of every period of the liturgy,[40] forcing a reconstruction of the experience of worship (in this case of women's experience of worship) from the odd rather than normal. That being said, however, if we are to believe our

---

37. Cited in Jacob, *Lay People and Religion in the Early Eighteenth Century,* 59.
38. See above, pp. 15 and 16.
39. Stratton, *Pioneer Women,* 175.
40. This is the reason for the frustration with such descriptions of Sunday worship as that of Justin Martyr (c. 100–c. 165), who periodically tells us that this or that element of worship was performed "in the usual manner," without any further explanation.

sources, the odd things reported by women diarists and letter writers really did take place in Sunday services.

Clearly not all Sunday services passed quietly; sometimes the main gathering for congregational worship was the occasion for serious disruption. In one of the many letters Lady Brilliana Harley wrote to her son, Edward, over a period of twenty years, she describes an incident at her parish church in 1642 at the beginning of the English Civil War. When one "Mr. David" came to preach from Hereford, invited by some parishioners with anti-royalist sympathies, his prayers caused a near riot.

> When he had ended his prayer before the sermon, which he was short in, because he was loth to tire them, 2 men went out of the church and cryed "pray God bless the kinge; this man dous not pray for the kinge"; upon which, before he read his text, he toold them that M[in]isters had that liberty, to pray before or after the sermon for the church and state; for all that, they went to the bells and range, and a great many went into the church-yard and cryed "roundheads," and some said "let us cast stones at him!" and he could not looke out of doors . . . but they cryed "roundhead." In the afternoon they would not let him preach; so he went to the cathedral. Thos that had any goodness weare much trubelled and weepe much. . . .[41]

The volatile combination of prayer and politics seems to have colored women's experience of Sunday worship in nearly every period of the church's history. In her *Reminiscences of My Life in Camp with the 33rd US Colored Troops . . .*, Suzie King Taylor's rare memoir of a free black southern woman, she describes an aborted service in Charleston just before the Civil War.

> Oh how those people prayed for freedom! I remember . . . a church meeting, and they were fervently singing this old hymn, — "Yes, we all shall be free, / Yes, we all shall be free, / Yes, we all shall be free, / When the Lord shall appear." — when the police came in and arrested all who were there, saying they were planning freedom, and sang "the Lord," in place of "Yankee" to blind anyone who might be listening.[42]

Sadly, the gathering of the Christian community for Sunday worship has always provided an opportunity for political violence, and this continues to affect

---

41. Thomas Taylor Lewis, ed., *Letters of Lady Brilliana Harley* (London: Camden Society, 1854), 329.

42. Suzie King Taylor, *Reminiscences of My Life in Camp with the 33rd US Colored Troops, Late 1st South Carolina Volunteers: A Black Women's Civil War Memoirs*, ed. Patricia Romero and Willie Lee Rose (Princeton, N.J.: Markus Weiner, 1988), 32.

women's experience of worship in places where civil disruption and the threat of terrorism are very real.

In some cases, however, divisions and disputes among members of the congregation have disturbed the sedate progress of Sunday services. Because of the intensified social interaction Sunday churchgoing has occasioned, ordinary difficulties between people have often made their way into the service. At the turn of the seventeenth century, a dispute over which of two women would have the honor of reading the lesson precipitated a wholesale brawl. When one of the combatants, Jane Clively, subsequently became ill, she accused the other woman of using witchcraft to cause her sickness. Clively, according to the testimony of the physician who examined her, "was desirous to read a chapter in the church; and a woman took away her book in the pew and turned her to a psalm to read, and she said she would have read a chapter, so presently took ill and fell sick. . . . The woman did it because she scorned she should have the upper place."[43]

Problems between clergy and parishioners have also played themselves out in the Sunday service. According to court testimony presented against Elizabeth Wilson, she had stormed out of the service at Aveley, Essex, on Easter Day 1608, shouting at the minister, "that he ever was and is a troublesome man, and that he makes the rest to say unto him the Lord's Prayer and the Belief [the Creed] for very fear, but she said he should never make her say them whilst he lived."[44]

Sometimes it was matters of doctrine that caused women to disrupt the Sunday service. On Christmas 1552, a teenaged boy stood at the front of the church while the curate was at the altar of the Church of St. Peter, Paul's Wharf (London), and imitated the priest's gestures. "When the curate, Mr. John Holland, expelled the child from church for 'profaning'. . . the boy's mother challenged him: 'My boy shall be here, and . . . he is more worthy to be here than thou, for thou canst not read, and thou art a very drunken and knave priest.' "[45] In the same period, some women routinely read the Bible aloud throughout the service, reportedly in order "to drown out the idolatry."[46] In 1630, when the rector of Holland Magna (Essex) preached on Adam and Eve making coats of fig leaves to cover their nakedness, the women of the congregation rose up and demanded to know where the primordial parents had gotten the needles and thread.

---

43. Report of the Reverend Richard Napier, who from 1597 to 1634 treated tens of thousands of patients for mental disorders. Cited in Macdonald, *Mystical Bedlam*, 109–10.

44. Haigh, "Communion and Community," 734.

45. Brigden, *London and the Reformation*, 442. There were other occasions for mockery of the Roman rite during the time of Mary. "At an Essex wedding, the bawdy ballad 'News out of London,' concerning the Mass and the Queen's 'mis-pronouncings' was sung" (600).

46. Ibid., 301.

Talking back to the clergy during sermons seems to have been quite common in some periods of the church's history. In Cuenca, Spain, in 1566, the bishop had to impose penalties on those who talked back to priests during their sermons. The proceedings of one Spanish synod insisted that priests "reprove" and "impose penances" on parishioners "who raise objections and have words with said priests and chaplains. And this is cause for much scandal, as it happens during high mass."[47] This kind of disruption seems to have been especially common when preachers were "rebuking or speaking ill of vices or sins of the people ... [who] stand up and reply to him and at times speak words that are rude, indecent, and unworthy of such a place."[48] Very occasionally, even more violent disturbances have resulted when parishioners have disagreed with the way in which clergy were conducting the service of Christian worship. In February 1985, for example, three people including a priest were shot to death in an Australian Roman Catholic parish church. The newspaper report stated that "the priest, Fr. John Rossiter, 64, was killed as he knelt at the altar after a mass for school children.... Witnesses said that before the mass a man had approached Father Rossiter and objected to the fact that 'Father was allowing the girls to do the reading at mass.'"[49]

At other times it has been the spiritual arousal of the worshipers themselves that has contributed to a certain degree of disorder. The following recorded exchange between an African American woman and her pastor husband gives us an idea of the spiritual and physical energy that has been released in some congregations.

REVEREND: Once I had to help pick up a woman that had the spirit and she hit me — "Wham!" — like that, so I couldn't help but holler out "Glory!"

HIS WIFE: But you never really hurt nobody if you got the spirit, no matter how much you shout.

REVEREND: I don't know about that. I grabbed my first wife one time when she was shoutin'. Then I didn't have no religion. That woman jerk me across every bench in church. I turnt her loose. I said I'll never grab that fool again.

HIS WIFE: That's cause you didn't have religion.[50]

---

47. *Constitutiones Sinodales*, Cuenca, 1566, 82r-v. Cited in William A. Christian Jr., *Local Religion in Sixteenth-Century Spain* (Princeton, N.J.: Princeton University Press, 1981), 166.

48. Another Spanish synod complained that "the laity are in such firm control that they order the priests around as if they were day laborers." *Constitutiones Sinodales*, Burgos, 1575, 237, cited in Christian, *Local Religion*, 167.

49. "Three Killed in Church," *Sydney Morning Herald*, February 9, 1985, 17.

50. Cited in Mechal Sobel, *Trabelin' On: The Slave Journey to an Afro-Baptist Faith* (Princeton, N.J.: Princeton University Press, 1988), 139.

"His wife" goes on to describe a friend who, whenever she is moved by the Spirit, runs up and down the aisles of the church and laughs. "And Lord, she'll run up and down the aisle till she feel satisfied, just laughin' hard as she can. Diggy-diggy-diggity-dig!"[51]

But generally, and especially once Victorian ideals of propriety had begun to infuse the conduct of Christian worship in the mid-nineteenth century, the Sunday service increasingly came to be an occasion when a heightened degree of formality and decorum prevailed. Indeed, the Sunday service in many places has developed and retained its own set of social conventions that may no longer apply to life outside the doors of the church. In the Tidewater, North Carolina, Missionary Baptist Church, for example, even today "men greet newcomers with a handshake during the Prelude. This is the only time in Tidewater when men shake hands and is formally designated 'the right hand of fellowship.' Women do not shake hands at this time."[52] Because of the innate conservatism of Christian worship, these conventions — which may have once prevailed in Tidewater society generally but have now passed into oblivion — continue to live on in the church. In many places, however, the prevailing culture has regularly intruded into the Sunday service. As eighteen-year-old Cinda Howard wrote to her sister Dorothy in the spring of 1868 from Bright Star (Hopkins County), Texas:

> I went to church last Sunday a week with a young man that had a pistol buckled around him. I thought of what I said before I left Mississippi, that if a young man had to go to church with firearms he could not go with me. But in such a place as that I think they are perfectly justified in carrying them. He knew his life was in danger.[53]

Although many women through the centuries have expressed their deep appreciation of the Sunday service, others have been known to be highly critical. Often this criticism is occasioned by changes in the normal pattern of common prayer, or by attending services away from home which are conducted in a manner unfamiliar to them.[54] Several women travelers, for example, describe the

---

51. Ibid., 140. In another place we find similar behavior. "It took some good ones to hold [Aunt Kate] down when she got started. Anytime Uncle Link [the Preacher] or any other preacher *touched along the path she had traveled* she would jump and holler. . . . The old ones in them times walked over benches and boxes with their eyes fixed on heaven. God was in the midst of them" (145).

52. John Forrest, *Lord I'm Coming Home: Everyday Aesthetics in Tidewater North Carolina* (Ithaca, N.Y.: Cornell University Press, 1988), 130.

53. Dorothy Howard, *Dorothy's World: Childhood in Sabine Bottom, 1902–1910* (Englewood Cliffs, N.J.: Prentice Hall, 1977), 44.

54. Although the views on the matter of worship of some European women travelers to America depended more on their "reading, their friends, and their prejudices" than on firsthand knowledge, many visited churches out of curiosity and reported what they saw. R. Mullen, *Birds of Passage: Five Englishwomen in Search of America* (London: Duckworth, 1994), 52.

uncertainty of Sunday services at sea. In 1862, young Catherine Hopley wrote a series of travel articles for *The Sunday Home: A Family Magazine* (published by the Religious Tract Society), including one entitled "Two Sabbaths on the Atlantic"[55] about Sunday services on shipboard during her first crossing to America. Other voyagers have reported on these services as well. On one occasion, English Dissenters and American Protestants became enraged at having to put up with the ship's captain reading the service of Morning Prayer from the *Book of Common Prayer*, with one woman declaring that it was a case of "English impertinence which ought to be steadfastly resisted by all Americans."[56] But the captain did not lead the service that Hopley observed; indeed, she was startled to see an American passenger push himself forward to lead Sunday worship. He seemed to have had a fixation on the number seven, she says, and "much of the service revolved around this magic number."[57]

This kind of disapproval of the conduct of worship is quite common in women's first-person writing. The travel journals of the redoubtable Isabella Bird (1831–1904) certainly exemplify this. An English clergyman's daughter and the product of a rather stern evangelical Anglican upbringing, Bird was prescribed travel as a cure for her chronic complaints of aches and pains, insomnia, and lethargy, and her first trip, to the United States, resulted in the publication of her travel journal *A Lady's Life in the Rocky Mountains* and *Aspects of Religious Life in the United States of America*.[58] Her complaints about Sunday services range from the haphazard mode of addressing the deity to the theological content of the prayers to the rigid Sabbatarianism of the parishioners. The following description of a service in Colorado is typical:

> [Mr.] Chalmers "wales" a psalm, in every sense of the word wail, to the most doleful of dismal tunes; they read a chapter round, and he prays. If his prayer has something of the tone of the imprecatory psalms, he has high authority in his favor; and if there be a tinge of Pharasaic thanksgiving, it is hardly surprising that he is grateful that he is not as other men are when he contemplates the godlessness of the region. Sunday was a dreadful day. The family kept the Commandment literally, and did no work.[59]

---

55. Catherine Hopley, "Two Sabbaths on the Atlantic," *The Sunday Home: A Family Magazine* 9 (November 8, 1862): 14–15.

56. Mullen, *Birds of Passage*, 173.

57. Ibid., 181.

58. These were followed by further travel journals, which give us some idea of the curiosity and courage of this remarkable woman traveler: *Six Months in the Sandwich Islands; An Englishwoman in America; Korea and Her Neighbors; The Grand Cheronese;* and *Unbeaten Tracks in Japan*.

59. Isabella L. Bird, *A Lady's Life in the Rocky Mountains* (Norman: University of Oklahoma Press, 1960), 48–49.

One Sunday morning at the turn of the eighteenth century, Celia Fiennes attended a Quaker meeting in Scarborough, during which she heard, perhaps for the first time in her life, women speak in a service of public worship: "but it seem'd such confusion and so incoherent that it very much moved my compassion and pitty to see their delusion and ignorance."[60] But Fiennes's objection is not solely on the grounds of the lack of order and decorum. She has a liturgical-theological point to make as well. She continues, "I observ'd their prayers were all made on the first person single, tho before the body of the people, it seems to allow not of ones being the mouth of the rest in prayer to God tho' it be in the publick meetings...."[61]

Eucharist

Even though for many Christian communities the main Sunday service has been only one occasion on which the eucharist (or Lord's Supper) has been celebrated; and even though for many Christian communities the eucharist has not been celebrated every Sunday; and even though when the eucharist *was* celebrated regularly on a Sunday in any given place, women might not have received communion with any regularity, the association between Sunday worship and Lord's Supper is an ancient and persistent one. With a few notable exceptions,[62] however, the traditional study of the history of the eucharist is a very typical example of the failure to attend to the *experience* of the liturgy in favor of the *texts* of the liturgy.

As we have seen,[63] many women came to the Sunday service having prepared themselves for devout participation in the eucharist. But that preparation would have taken different forms among different communities at different times. For some women, it would have entailed confession of their sin privately to a priest; for others an examination of conscience guided by their "class" or "band," or by their minister in private; for still others, a period of fasting or meditation would have been undertaken. Many early manuals for confessors require lay people to abstain from intercourse for three days before receiving communion (although there is little evidence for the degree to which laypeople adhered to this prohibition).[64] For

---

60. Fiennes, *The Illustrated Journeys of Celia Fiennes*, 101.

61. Ibid.

62. Duffy's *The Stripping of the Altars* is perhaps the best recent example of the attempt to study the reform of the eucharistic liturgy from the perspective of those being reformed rather than from the perspective of those doing the reforming.

63. See above, pp. 130–33.

64. The *Penitential* of Theodore [c. 750] is one example of this prohibition. *Theodore Penitential* II, XII, 1–2, in A. W. Haddam and W. Stubbs, *Councils and Ecclesiastical Documents Relating to Great Britain and Ireland* (Oxford: Clarendon, 1869–78), iii, 199.

Darcy, Lady Maxwell (whose devout attention to worship we have seen before), each Friday before the Sunday communion "was a special day of abstinence and renewal of dedication to God. She normally undertook a review of the week on that day and made a list of the blessings she had enjoyed."[65] Some women brought devotional aids with them into the service: books or rosary beads.[66] An Italian visitor to England in 1500 reports seeing, "the women carrying long rosaries in their hands, and those who can read taking the Office of Our Lady with them, and with some companion reciting it in the church verse by verse, in a low voice, after the manner of churchmen."[67]

Probably the most common form of preparation for communion has been some form of confession of sin, accompanied by penitential disciplines imposed or suggested by the confessor, class meeting, or family member. Not only have penitential disciplines been a prerequisite to worthy communion for many Christian women, for some it became an integral part of the Sunday liturgy itself. In England, both before and after the Reformation, a woman guilty of some sin against the good order of the church (such as failing to be churched or to have her baby baptized) might be ordered "to proceed before the Sunday procession, clad in a white sheet, barefoot and bareheaded, carrying a lighted candle" which she would present, kneeling at the high altar, to the celebrant.[68] Sometimes such a person was required to name aloud the fault of which she was guilty, and to ask the gathered congregation to forgive her. In 1544, Dionese Constable of London, having admitted that her over-familiarity with a neighbor was open to misinterpretation, stood before her fellow parishioners to read the following formal confession: "Neighbours, whereas I have offended God and commonwealth, in that you have had me in suspicion of ill living with George Wakefield, I cry God for mercy, and am sorry for it; and I pray you be in love and charity with me."[69]

---

65. Brown, *Women of Mr. Wesley's Methodism*, 127.

66. A rosary is a string of counters, either beads or knots, to be touched or moved along the string one by one so that one can repeat a given prayer a prescribed number of times without losing count. A primer printed in 1545 gives instruction for women in church: "And such among the people as have books, and can read, may read them quietly and softly to themselves: and such as cannot read, let them quietly and attentively give audience in the time of said prayers."

67. *A Relation, or Rather a True Account, of the Island of England . . . about the Year 1500*, ed. C. A. Sneyd (Camden Society, Old series, 37, 1847), 23 (cited in S. Brigden, *London and the Reformation*, 16).

68. Brigden, *London and the Reformation*, 148. (This form of public penance was only rarely used by the end of the sixteenth century in England.) "People who refused to appear or to accept the authority of the court were excommunicated, first in writing and eventually barred from any apparent involvement with the church or — in theory — the other parishioners." A similar pattern is found in the district of Havering, near London, in which women involved in serious offenses were made to stand bareheaded and barefooted in the church during the Sunday service, wearing only a white sheet. See Marjorie Keniston McIntosh, *A Community Transformed: The Manor and Liberty of Havering, 1500–1620* (Cambridge: Cambridge University Press, 1991), 242ff.

69. McIntosh, *A Community Transformed*, 243.

In Norfolk in the same period we have evidence of a more elaborate ritual of public penance at the Sunday eucharist. As in other places, the offender was made to "stand penitently in the Middle Alley, before the Minister's Seat or Pulpit," barefooted and dressed in a white sheet. In this case she would also have a white rod in her hand and a piece of paper pinned over the breast on which was written details of the sin committed:

> "and then and there in such Sort to continue during the whole Time of Divine Service and Sermon, and at the End of the Same, before the Congregation is dismissed, and the Blessing given, shall upon [his or her] Knees make ... humble Confession, repeating every Word after the Minister with an audible Voice." Finally the penitent was required to beseech the congregation to join with him or her in the words of the Lord's Prayer.[70]

For those accused of serious sin, this sort of public liturgical act was not only a prerequisite to receiving communion, but sometimes for participation in any of the other rites of the church. (When Samuel Wesley was rector at Epworth, he refused to marry a woman until she had done penance for giving birth to an illegitimate child several years before.[71]) The importance of confession was underscored not only by canon law, ecclesiastical practice, and social convention, but by pious legend as well. In one story widely circulated around Germany and the Low Countries, St. Elizabeth of Thuringia (d. 1231) encounters a beggar woman who is resistant to go to confession, saying she would like to be allowed to sleep instead. "The sainted Elizabeth thrashed her with switches until the recalcitrant woman finally went."[72]

Public penance as a prerequisite to communion was intended to act as a public acknowledgment that an offense had occurred which had broken not only the individual's bond with God, but the bond of mutual charity that existed within the local community. The social implications of sin and repentance often found their way into the Sunday eucharist.

> Joanna Carpenter challenged Margaret Chambers at Mass in St. Michael Queenhithe in 1529. As Margaret knelt at the altar, preparing to receive the host, Joanna took her by the arm, insisting, "I pray you, let me speak a word with you, for you have need to ask my forgiveness before you receive your rights."[73]

---

70. Norfolk Record Office, ANF/10/3, cited in Jacob, *Lay People and Religion in the Early Eighteenth Century*, 147.

71. Jacob, *Lay People and Religion in the Early Eighteenth Century*, 153–54.

72. Walter Nigg, ed., *Die heilige Elizabeth von Thüringen* (Dusseldorf, 1963), 79.

73. Brigden, *London and the Reformation*, 20.

Clearly Carpenter believed that Chambers was unworthy to receive communion until she had reconciled their differences. More important, she took it upon herself to stand between Chambers and the eucharist, rather than leaving it to the parish priest. At more than one parish church after the Reformation, stocks were erected outside the church door, "a constant reminder of the limits of behaviour."[74]

The practice of insisting that individuals make public confession of their sin in church during the Sunday service of Holy Communion was carried to America with the Puritans, where it seems to have lasted into the eighteenth century. In order to gain admission to communion in one New England Congregational church, a prospective member had to testify to a transforming religious experience; the testimony of Sarah Fiske of Massachusetts is one such confession. The evidence of her need for conversion seems to have consisted largely of her failure to be a dutiful wife ("her carriage towards her husband in accounting him an enemy and...saying he loved another woman better than his wife"), and her unwillingness to accept the reproof of the congregation ("that she still justifies herself and such like").[75] But at last she repented of these faults, and on November 11, 1645, she declared to the church that she "saw that she was in a worse condition than any toad &c. Soon after the Lord spake to her (as twere a voice)...whereupon she examined herself and found that it rested with God thus she had walked so unevenly...." Upon her confession, the congregation voted that Fiske should "upon the Lord's day next make a public acknowledgement of her miscarriages." It was moved that she show her assent to the church confession of faith. Three weeks later, on December 5, 1645, "In the close of the day Brother Phineas Fiske's wife called and made her confession, particularly of the evil by her speeches of her husband and against the church and the pastor. It was voted satisfactorily. The covenant was administered to the wife of Brother Phineas Fiske."[76]

By the last quarter of the eighteenth century, public distaste for this kind of public ritual of penitence was growing in the British Isles and Europe, as well as in North America. Its decline was hastened by social mobility, industrialization, and urbanization, all of which made people unwilling to expose themselves to public humiliation for intimate transgressions in front of comparative strangers.[77]

74. Claire S. Schen, "Women and the London Parishes, 1500–1620," in *The Parish in English Life, 1400–1600*, ed. Katherine L. French, Gary Gibbs, and Beat A. Kümin (Manchester: Manchester University Press, 1997), 263.

75. Carol Berkin and Leslie Horowitz, eds., *Women's Voices, Women's Lives: Documents in Early American History* (Boston: Northeastern University Press, 1998), 148.

76. Cited in ibid., 148–49.

77. Stewart Brown, "No More 'Standing in the Session': Gender and the End of Corporate Discipline in the Church of Scotland, c. 1890–1930," in *Gender and Christian Religion*, ed. R. N. Swanson (Woodbridge, U.K.: Boydell, 1998), 448.

Increasingly throughout the nineteenth century, public penance seems to have been used almost exclusively in cases of extramarital sex, and tended to focus on women who became pregnant out of wedlock. ("Men were seen to be simply acting according to their natures, and little effort was placed on discovering the identity of the father."[78]) Although it lasted longest in rural areas, by 1900 public confession at the main Sunday service had disappeared virtually everywhere, "to be replaced by a more private and less judgmental form of pastoral care, which reflected changes in society and an awareness of new attitudes to gender and sexuality."[79]

But there was another option for confession in preparation for receiving communion. Many women have confessed their sin in private, either to a priest or in a personal examination of conscience. Because of the inviolability of the seal of the confessional, and the relative scarcity of women's spiritual autobiographies, the history of private ("auricular") confession has few archives and can probably never be written. Some priests have been willing to be severely punished rather than divulge the confessions of their parishioners. In the mid-1650s, a Lady Waller records the violence inflicted on a priest attempting to maintain the seal of the confessional: "Douglas Wagner of St. Paul's Brighton was physically assaulted in the street for refusing to reveal in court what had passed between him and one of his penitents, Constance Kent, accused of murdering her stepbrother."[80] Despite the expectation that priests would not reveal the content of women's confessions, there was still considerable concern that private confession would disrupt both family life and the social order more generally, especially if a wife were to tell the priest something hidden from her husband.[81]

Traditionally, the sign of reconciliation and restoration with the Christian community after due penitence was the kiss of peace, which from ancient times was the ritual preamble to the prayers at the altar table. In its earliest manifestation,

---

78. Cited in Berkin and Horowitz, *Women's Voices, Women's Lives*, 456.

79. Brown, *Women of Mr. Wesley's Methodism*, 448.

80. E. W. Harcourt, ed., *Harcourt Papers*, "Lady Waller's Journal," 1650s (Oxford, n.d.), 180–90. Private confession to a priest had other risks for parishioners, however. Béatrice de Planissoles, a French noblewoman, reports what transpired when she went to make her confession in August 1320: "I went to the church of Montaillou to confess my sins. While I was there, I went to the curé who was hearing confessions behind the altar of Saint Mary. When I knelt in front of him, he kissed me and said there was no woman in the world he loved as much as me. Dumfounded, I left without confessing." Cited in Christiane Klapisch-Zuber, ed., *A History of Women in the West*, vol. 2: *Silences of the Middle Ages* (Cambridge, Mass.: Belknap Press of Harvard University Press, 1992), 487. The potential for this kind of abuse is confirmed by the warnings in numerous penitential manuals, in which both confessors and penitents were warned repeatedly not to look upon or touch one another.

81. Sometimes those parishioners who did not feel their guilt assuaged by confession before the Easter communion asked the priest to beat their upturned palms with willow branches called "disciplining rods."

the peace was exchanged by members of the Christian community equally (lead-ing to charges of promiscuity against Christian women), and then increasingly men with men and women with women. But from about the year 1000 in the Roman liturgy, the kiss of peace began to be shared in hierarchical order: "in-stead of being exchanged at random between neighbors, it passed from the priest through the clerks to the higher ranks of the laity, and on down through the scale of status."[82] Soon after (certainly by the thirteenth century) actual kissing began to decline. One medieval Russian manual of etiquette gives us a hint of some of the difficulties it raised. "If you kiss someone in Christ's name," the anony-mous author advises, "you should kiss him or her holding your breath, without sputtering. Remember human weakness: we disdain the uncouth spirit of garlic, intoxication, sickness, and all such odors."[83]

The mutual exchange of a kiss was replaced, in England at least, by a wooden board known as the pax or pax-board, which was passed around and kissed by the members of the congregation in turn. But of course this produced its own difficulties, and "there are numerous literary references to the ceremony in late-medieval literature ... [which] refer to quarrels among the congregation about the order in which the pax was to be kissed."[84] Ellen Morgan, a parishioner at the church of St. Anne and St. Agnes in London, was certainly not the only woman to refuse to kiss the pax board altogether because the order in which it was passed was offensive to her.[85] But the physical kiss seems to have survived for some occasions. In London at the turn of the seventeenth century, Gertrude Crockhay, fearing that her fault would lead to perdition, was advised by her parish priest to "confess her fault to the congregation that 'she be received into their fellowship again.' Like Christians of the apostles' time, they saluted one another 'with a holy kiss.' "[86] And in her vivid description of the final Sunday service of the camp-meeting revival at Sabine Bottom, Texas, in the first decade of the twentieth century, Dorothy Howard tells us that a ritual remnant of the kiss of peace was the climax, when "the families of the shouters went forward to hug and kiss their repentant kin while the preacher lined out the song 'Amazing Grace.' "[87]

---

82. John Bossy, "Blood and Baptism: Kinship Community and Christianity in Western Europe from the Fourteenth to the Seventeenth Centuries," in *Sanctity and Secularity: The Church and the World*, ed. Derek Baker (Oxford: Blackwell, 1973), 141. On the kiss of peace, see also J. Jungmann, *Mass of the Roman Rite* (New York: Benziger, 1951–55), 2:325ff.; Maynard Smith, *Pre-Reformation England* (New York: Russel & Russel, 1963), 96ff.; and Johan Huizinga, *Waning of the Middle Ages* (Garden City, N.Y.: Doubleday, 1954), 37.

83. Cited in Carolyn Johnston Pouncy, *The Domostroi: Rules for Russian Households in the Time of Ivan the Terrible* (Ithaca, N.Y.: Cornell University Press, 1994), 67–68.

84. Brigden, *London and the Reformation*, 364–66.

85. Ibid., 365.

86. Ibid., 602.

87. Howard, *Dorothy's World*, 281–83.

In the years since the Second Vatican Council (1962–65), attempts at the restoration of the ancient kiss of peace as a ritual preamble to communion have been widespread in Protestant and Roman Catholic churches alike. A number of women who have been active in the promotion of the liturgical movement and its principles have emphasized the peace as an important link between the liturgy and social justice and reconciliation.[88] (At the same time, however, anecdotal evidence suggests that women have also been vocal opponents of the inclusion of the peace in services of Christian worship, often voicing their concern about the disruption it causes in the orderly progress of the Sunday service.)

Communion

Because of the intimate association between the communion bread and wine and the presence of Jesus Christ (however that association is conceived), and because women's "purity" has so often been an issue for those who have traditionally controlled access to the sacrament, women's relationship to the partaking of communion has been a quite complex one, and never as straightforward for women as it has been for men. In early Merovingian times, for example, the consecrated bread was routinely placed in the hands of each communicant at mass regardless of gender. But the sixth-century Council of Auxerre stipulated that when a woman received the body of Christ, she must wrap her hand in her dress, as though some trace of impurity, having to do with menstruation, attached to her flesh. To receive communion is also to declare oneself in solidarity with the Christian community, which has meant that the ordinary stresses and strains of community life have commonly found their way into women's experience of participation in the Lord's Supper (see fig. 19).

The importance of communion to women can be seen in the degree of responsibility they have always taken for seeing to it that all the necessary appurtenances were provided and the place made ready for the celebration. In the early Christian house churches, for example, women heads of households often served as the host for the gathering, overseeing the preparations for the eucharistic meal, and in many periods of the church's life the bread used at communion was baked by women, either householders or nuns. The financial outlay for eucharistic bread and wine could be considerable in an ordinary parish, and women's monetary contributions often made communion possible. Sometimes the process for collecting money was integrated into the communion service itself. At the North Parish (Congregational Church), Andover, Massachusetts, in the mid-eighteenth

---

88. See pp. 114–17.

century, "communicants annually contributed 'their severall proportions of money for the providing for the Lord's Supper, said contributions to be made on a Sacrament Day, each communicant to put his money in a piece of paper with his name written on it.' "[89] ("Poor widdoes" were exempted from this fee.)

In most churches, these preparations for communion were seen as a natural extension of women's domestic housekeeping duties. The parallels can be seen clearly in this description of women's duties at the Baptist Church in Tidewater, North Carolina:

> A standing committee of women is responsible for preparing the basic accouterments of the [communion] service, glasses, dishes, and table linen as well as the bread and "wine." Before the service begins the women of the committee lay the communion table with a clean white linen cloth. In the center they place a silver jug and goblet, to one side four silver plates containing small cubes of white bread and to the other side four trays of small glasses filled with grape juice. Then they cover everything with white linen napkins.[90]

Women often were concerned that the church have at its disposal all the necessary items for a suitably dignified celebration of communion, in much the same way that they were concerned that their households have everything necessary for polite entertaining. In 1672, the Dorchester (Massachusetts) Church recorded its "thanks to Mrs Thatcher of Boston for her gift to ye Church wch was a Silver Cupp for ye Sacrament & a greene Cushin for ye Desk." Sometimes the boundary between the domestic and the ecclesiastical tableware was rather thin. In the same congregation "in 1692, Widow Capen returned to the church the sacramental tableware she had kept as Deacon's wife, which included '4 flagons; 3 silvar Bools 3 silvar Beakers; 4 pewter cups 1 pewter pint pot; 4 pewter platters, 3 small table clothes; 2 baskets; 2 bottels.' "[91]

But some women could also be responsible for the failure of communion to take place at all in the orbit over which they had influence. In her diary for March 27, 1619, Lady Anne Clifford reports that "in the morning I sent for Mr. Rand [her domestic chaplain] and told him that I found myself not fit to receive the Communion" at Easter, ordering that it should be postponed for the entire household until the Sunday of Pentecost. On Easter Day, however, she says

89. Moffard, *And Firm Thine Ancient Vow,* 88.

90. Forrest, *Lord I'm Coming Home,* 151.

91. Amanda Porterfield, *Female Piety in Puritan New England: The Emergence of Religious Humanism* (Oxford: Oxford University Press, 1992), 132.

that she "began to repent that I had caused the Communion to be put off."[92] But by then, of course, it was too late for the huge numbers of her staff who had had to go without. Disruption of the eucharist could also occur over the maintenance of social hierarchies among women parishioners. In 1598, at a celebration of the Lord's Supper in a Reformed church in the town of Ganges in the Cévennes mountains,

> a spectacular fracas erupted as the congregation, the men followed by the women, moved in measured procession toward the communion table. The community's most prominent noblewomen became engaged in a fierce shoving match, each trying to elbow her way ahead of the other and, presumably, establish superiority of social position. It was a battle for precedence, fought here in sacramental circumstances, between the leading families.[93]

Violent dissent leading to the disruption of communion could also be the result of doctrinal differences between clergy and laywomen. When Edward Underhill, a priest of the Reformed spirit, decided to remove the pyx from the altar at Stratford le Bow in 1551, the wife of Justice Tawe and other women of the parish attacked him, and, in his words before the consistory court, "conspired to have murdered me."[94]

But most often, women have approached communion in good faith, finding in the act of receiving nourishment for their growth in spiritual maturity and godliness. The experience of Mary Ames in the mid-eighteenth century is not uncommon. In the spring of 1763, Mary's sister Rebecca Fish (1739–66) was taken ill, and as she was recovering she "grew in her conviction of God's beneficent grace." As a result, Fish committed herself to making a public profession of her faith at the Easter communion. In April, Mary writes to Rebecca telling her that at the Easter service in her own church, "I remember'd you, dear sister at the Lord's Table and pleas'd myself with the thought that it was likely you were that day making a publick profession and performing your vows that you made in your distress."[95]

---

92. D. J. H. Clifford, ed., *The Diaries of Lady Anne Clifford* (Stroud: Alan Sutton, 1990), 70.

93. Raymond A. Mentzer Jr., "The Reformed Churches of France and the Visual Arts," in *Seeing beyond the Word: Visual Arts and the Calvinist Tradition*, ed. Paul Corby Finney (Grand Rapids, Mich.: Eerdmans, 1999), 214. The author concludes that, "In the minds of many, these religious formalities, to include the order of reception for the Lord's Supper or seating patterns at worship, announced and sustained an overall social order."

94. Brigden, *London and the Reformation*, 431.

95. Mary Ames, *From a New England Woman's Diary in Dixie* (Springfield, Mass.: Plimpton Press, 1906), 46.

Women's eucharistic piety also led them to question the communion practices they witnessed in other places which seemed to violate the true spirit of the occasion. When the remarkable Nancy Prince (1799–c. 1856), a black woman who left a detailed record of her world travels in the early nineteenth century, was in Jamaica, she became concerned that communion was adding a serious financial burden to poor members of the congregation. She reports that the parishioners attended class meetings each week, where they paid three pence apiece (a total of twelve shillings a year), "besides the sums they pay once a month at communion, after service in the morning."

> On these occasions the minister retires, and the deacons examine the people, to ascertain if each one has brought a ticket; if not, they cannot commune; after this the minister returns and performs the ceremony, then they give their money and depart. The churches are very large, holding from four to six thousand; many bring wood and other presents...as a token of their attachment; where there are so many communicants, these presents, and the money exacted, greatly enrich these establishments.[96]

But sometimes the eucharistic worship women observe away from home makes their accustomed services seem pale by comparison, as we can see in another description of a Jamaican communion service, this time from Mary Ann Hutchins, who became deeply involved in the struggle for emancipation in Jamaica in the 1830s. In one of her journal entries Hutchins recalls, "I was much pleased at one of the Sabbaths I was in at Montego Bay, to see a Chapel pretty well filled with communicants, and instead of two — *fourteen bottles of wine* were used at the Sacrament. Oh! when in my dear native land will a scene like this be witnessed?"[97]

Sometimes ministers' wives have taken it upon themselves to see that communion went smoothly in the congregations in which their husbands pastored. One anonymous nineteenth-century clergy spouse suggests to her counterparts in other churches that they can do a great deal to encourage the proper attitude toward communion. "A tender word of appreciation from the pastor's wife, her word of inquiry or regret when one is absent, can do much to make the service

---

96. Nancy Prince, *A Black Woman's Journey through Russia and Jamaica: The Narrative of Nancy Prince* (New York: Markus Wiener, 1990), 75–76.

97. T. Middelditch, *The Youthful Female Missionary: A Memoir of Mary Ann Hutchins, Wife of the Rev. John Hutchins, Baptist Missionary, Savanna-la-Mar, Jamaica; and Daughter of the Rev. T. Middelditch of Ipswich, compiled chiefly from her own correspondence by her Father* (London: G. Whiteman and Hamilton Adams, 1840), 99, 104. See Catherine Hall, *White, Male, and Middle-Class: Explorations in Feminism and History* (New York: Routledge, 1992), 128–29. "Later, after witnessing her husband's first baptism, Hutchins wrote to her mother describing the scene: 'a song of praise, a fervent prayer, and then nine of *our* — yes *your* black brethren and sisters buried in the stream.'"

what it should be — a solemn spiritual feast for the soul."[98] She continues in a more practical vein:

> If the pastor or his people wish to see the bread broken, a finger bowl and napkin should be included in the service, and the pastor must not fail to use it. It can be done so quietly and naturally that the act will scarcely be noticed. The one who prepares the bread should cut it into small squares so that it will come apart easily. The most beautiful and impressive way to serve the bread is for each one to wait until all are served. Then let the pastor, with the bread in his hand, say "Eat ye all of it." We have not seen the individual communion cups, but we should think where they are used, it would add to the service to repeat, "Drink ye all of it." We believe most emphatically in the unfermented wine, or in the fermented with the ferment taken out. We used it in one church, and it was universally liked. We now use the unfermented and no reformed drunkard is tempted with it.[99]

But she concludes this rather prosaic set of instructions with a rich description of the relation between what takes place in church on Sunday morning at communion with the eschatological banquet. In her mind she sees the table surrounded by "the pastor earnest and true, the seven deacons, 'unspotted from the world, visiting the widow and the fatherless in their affliction,' the great rank and file of faithful ones, who think no denial is too great to come to the church to 'show the Lord's death till he come.'" At this table even the lowly clergy spouse will find a place when there "shall be that last great supper where we, his honored guests, shall see him in person. The deacons' and pastors' wives who are faithful here will not be forgotten."[100]

In September 1992 a group of women met in Geneva for a few days to share their memories of the ecumenical movement and their hopes for its future. They did not work with documents, but kept a record of their conversations, which were collected by ecumenist Pauline Webb, one of the members of the consultation. Many of the participants in Geneva spoke of the deep impact on the act of communion, and on its meaning to them, which had come with the first women presiders.

> One described how a woman pastor she met did not, as the traditional male practice is, serve herself first but, like a mother feeding her family, gave food

---

98. "One of Them," *What a Pastor's Wife Can Do* (Philadelphia: American Baptist Publication Society, 1893), 60.

99. Ibid., 62–63.

100. Ibid., 63.

and drink to everyone else before she took any for herself. Another spoke
of how much more personal the service seemed to become as the minister
spoke to each one directly, naming them as she gave them the elements.

These steps taken by women pastors toward a more "domestic" and "celebratory"
table fellowship were common experiences across cultures. Webb continues, "We
were told of Asian women bringing their babies and feeding them with some of
the communion bread, of a three-year-old bringing her playmates and asking to
be allowed to come to the party...."[101]

Communion Refused

Excommunication has always been an option within the Christian church. In the
early centuries of the church's life, the barring of a person from communion (and
hence from fellowship with other Christians) was a serious matter indeed, since
if a person was out of relationship with the Christian community, she was out of
relationship with God, placing her eternal destiny in peril. Hence, excommunication was reserved for occasions of very serious sin — such as murder, adultery, or
apostasy — and restoration was only effected after a long, rigorous, and uncertain
process of penitence. Gradually, as schism and heresy begin to be the principal
concerns of church authorities, the focus of excommunication widened to include
those who persisted in heterodox views about the fundamentals of Christian belief. In all periods of the church, however, the refusal to allow a person to receive
communion has been a powerful weapon in the keeping of good order, especially
in times of rapid theological and liturgical change.

We can see how this practice affected women by a closer look at excommunication in the period just before and after the English Reformation. This period
is illuminating for a number of reasons. First, women from all social classes were
deeply involved in the various theological, political, and liturgical controversies
of the day, and literate women wrote of their experience of dissent. The words
and actions of troublesome women were also recorded by parish clergy and in the
records of court cases brought against them. Although the political and social
implications of heresy in this period were quite sharply defined, the wide diversity
of other motivations for excommunication (and women's responses to it) is also
exemplified.

Although we usually think of excommunication principally as a weapon in
the war against heresy, in the case of women in the post-Reformation period at

---

101. Pauline Webb, *She Flies Beyond: Memories and Hopes of Women in the Ecumenical Movement*
(Geneva: WCC, 1993), 61.

least, excommunication was more likely to be used as a way of controlling errant behavior, and it seems to have been quite commonly employed. As late as 1743, for example, women were refused communion in twenty-six different churches, most for violation of prevailing social and moral codes. The stated reasons included adultery, fornication, "violent suspicion of fornication," having a bastard child, perjury in a lawsuit, unlawful wedlock, "causing variance," drunkenness, "long absence from church," "a scandalous petition against the incumbent" and "for leaving another church."[102] Clergy were also concerned, of course, that the women in their churches knew at least the rudiments of Christian doctrine as a prerequisite to receiving communion—at the very least that she could recite by heart the creed and Lord's Prayer, the Ten Commandments, and (for many) the catechism. Some women could or would not do this.

> It was reported in 1608 that Margaret Jones of Barking was never allowed communion because "she understood not," and in 1609 Elizabeth Hills of Widford was barred "since by reason of her ignorance she is not fit." The curate of Stow Maries did his best with Anne Sammes in 1617: when she could not repeat the answers he recited for her from the catechism, he concluded "she was so ignorant that I durst not admit her."[103]

Other women contested clerical challenges to their doctrine. When Jane Carter knelt to take communion on Easter Day, her minister demanded that she first recite the creed. "If others do, I will," she said. But the minister persisted, "If you will not say your Belief I pray you avoid the place."[104] Many women were never admitted to communion at all on account of ignorance. In London by 1699 there were a number of people "aged between twenty-five and thirty who had been unable or unwilling to acquire basic knowledge of the faith, who were therefore not being admitted to take their first communion."[105]

Other women were refused for being at variance with their neighbors, and as the time for communion drew near, clergy encouraged people to reconcile their differences, sometimes with the assistance of the warring parties' neighbors and friends. Many of these efforts were probably successful, as in the case of the parish in Kent in 1564 in which, as the Sunday appointed for communion approached,

---

102. *Archbishop Herring's Visitation Returns*, 1743, ed. S. L. Ollard and P. C. Walker (York: Yorkshire Archeological Record Series, 1928–30), 71.

103. Haigh, "Communion and Community," 733.

104. Ibid., 737.

105. Robin Briggs, *Communities of Belief: Cultural and Social Tensions in Early Modern France* (Oxford: Clarendon, 1995), 313. Some women resisted being examined for their knowledge of doctrine. "Ranulf Catlin tried to examine his parishioners at Great Wenham, Suffolk, but they refused and he had to back down" (Haigh, "Communion and Community," 729).

the churchwardens and principal parishioners, "minding to end all controversies between Warner's wife and Wooten's wife," brought the two women
together and persuaded them to be "at unity and concord and each to forgive [the] other": Wooten's wife shortly afterwards received communion
"as a Christian woman ought to do...with divers other parishioners...
declaring thereby her reconciliation."[106]

But the extant evidence tends to indicate that the failures outnumbered the
successes in these endeavors. In another parish on the Sunday after Easter 1603,

> between morning service and communion, Roger Hill of Pewsey, Wiltshire,
> got into an altercation with Joan Monday: "Goodwife Monday, remember
> yourself and how you have used me, do not think to go to the place (viz. to
> the said communion), and to take communion and take God by the hand,
> and forsake God and go to the devil." The minister advised Monday to
> abstain from communion, and she went away — but during the service she
> returned to challenge Anne Pike, accusing her of being the cause of her
> trouble with Hill.[107]

In another case, Elizabeth Buckeridge called her neighbor Alice Hickes "a lying
drab" at communion on Palm Sunday 1581 at South Stoke in Oxfordshire. "Alice
replied 'I will know what drab's tricks you know by me, and therefore you shall
not receive on this day.' Elizabeth was indeed refused communion, though the
vicar said later it was because she had not given in her name beforehand."

Men were sometimes so outraged by the behavior of women neighbors that
they effectively excommunicated themselves in response. In 1580 George Allison
of Coggleshall refused to take communion and complained that Mary Webb had
been admitted by the minister: "He had been as good to have received a dog to
the communion, and said further in derision that it was a worthy communion
he warranted in respect of the said Mary Webb's receiving."[108] But despite the
occasional involvement of men in the process of excommunication, historian
Christopher Haigh concludes his study of the social history of exclusion from
communion in this period by noting that "unsurprisingly, the rows which led to
exclusion were often between women...."[109]

---

106. Martin J. Ingram, "From Reformation to Toleration: Popular Religious Cultures in England,
1540–1690," in *Popular Culture in England, c. 1500–1850*, ed. Tim Harris (New York: St. Martin's,
1994), 117–18.
107. Haigh, "Communion and Community," 731.
108. Cited in ibid., 730–31.
109. Ibid. At Townsey in Oxfordshire in 1590, Margaret Adams and Agnes Long argued when
Margaret accused Agnes's husband of cheating the landlord. When communion day arrived, Agnes
was outraged to see Margaret present herself at the Easter communion, even though she had informed

Women were often refused communion for difficulties with their parish clergy. When the parishioners of St. Botolph, Aldersgate, reported their minister to the bishop for living with a woman, the errant clergyman declared them all excommunicate until they asked for forgiveness from him and from his mistress. From the pulpit on the Sunday of communion he reviled them, saying, "Ye be accursed and I pronounce you accursed!"[110] Ephraim Udall, rector of St. Augustine's Watling Street, London, "was adamantly against people receiving [communion] in their pews, claiming that there was a real danger of spilling wine on communicants' heads, as well as it being unseemly for clergy to scramble over women and maids wile attempting to communicate them."[111] The worthiness of clergy to minister the eucharist was of special concern to women. At her trial in Aldermanbury in 1510, Lollard Elizabeth Sampson declared that "I would not give my dogs that bread that some priests doth minister at the altar when they be not in a clean life, and also said that thyself could make as good bread as that was and that it was not the body of Our Lord, for it is but bread, for God cannot be both in Heaven and on earth."[112] In a similar trial eight years later, Sampson was again charged with refusing the communion bread administered by priests "where they be not in clean life."[113]

So what did those who were rejected do? Some tried to push their way in, or argued for their "rights." Others who were excluded for being at enmity with their neighbors attempted to make peace. "In 1583 Anne Bradbury was the only parishioner not to take Easter Communion at Wicken Bonhunt, Essex: she told the court 'there is a controversy between me and Mr. Swynho, the parson there, and that he hath very greatly misused her, so that she cannot, with quiet conscience receive communion before there be a reconciliation.'"[114] They did effect a reconciliation, and she was admitted to communion thereafter. Many excluded from communion at their own church went to other parishes but could be brought before the consistory court for failure to attend their own parish church. But

---

the priest of Margaret's slander. "This is the woman that offended me!" Agnes shouted, and Margaret was refused communion (732).

110. Brigden, *London and the Reformation*, 150.

111. Ephraim Udall, *Communion Comlinesse* (London, 1641), 4–5, cited in Brigden, *London and the Reformation*, 97.

112. Cited in ibid., 91. The Mass was not only ridiculed while it was taking place. "In May, 1539 a group of neighbors, both men and women, were out drinking in a London tavern when one of them said, 'Let us make our reckoning that we may go to church and hear our High Mass.' 'Tarry,' said Giles Harrison, and taking the bread he lifted it over his head, and bowing over a cup of wine he made the sign of the cross, and raising the cup, asked 'Have ye not heard Mass now?'" (Brigden, *London and the Reformation*, 402). At the same time, Lollard women were making other attacks on traditional practices of the church. Alice Cowper declared that pilgrimages are good for nothing save to make the clergy rich (93).

113. Ibid., 66.

114. Ralph Houlbrooke, "Women's Social Life," *Continuity and Change* 1 (1986): 183.

many, perhaps, followed the example of the wife of Richard Lee, whose minister at St. Ebbes in Oxford in 1593 was highly selective in his distribution of communion, passing over certain parishioners as they knelt at the communion rail. When he came to the Lees, the minister "bid this examinate and his wife rise and go away from the table." But they refused to go and "were left waiting for four hours (they claimed), until they gave up and went home."[115] As was the case here, exclusion from communion was particularly offensive to parishioners when the minister had already taken their communion offerings.

Whatever the outcome of excommunication for the individual parishioner, it does seem clear that women were keenly aware of who was and who was not receiving communion. In 1521, one women was charged with defaming another by alleging that, "Thou art an heretic for thou tookest not thy rights at Easter."[116] Women were equally ready to complain when someone was admitted when he or she was deemed to be unworthy. In various places, women complained that their minister admitted those to communion "that be above twenty years old which cannot say the catechism."[117] The patterns of exclusion that begin to emerge in this period of the church's history for which we have considerable evidence may well apply to many other eras and geographical locations as well, and awaits the work of patient historians to reveal them. Suffice it to say, the experience of being denied communion was, until relatively recently, an integral part of both the liturgical and the social lives of women.

The Rites of Christian Initiation

To place the question of women's experience of the rites of Christian initiation here in the context of a discussion of Sunday morning worship is not to say that baptism, the laying on of hands (often called Confirmation), and the first reception of communion would invariably have been associated with the main Sunday service in all times and places. In many periods of the church's history, baptism has been carried out in private, either at the church before the main service or on a convenient weekday, or at home. At other times, baptism or confirmation would have been the natural consequence of a revival meeting or preaching series. All too often, Christian initiation has also been a component of the kind of forced conversions that took place after the conquest of a people.[118]

---

115. Haigh, "Communion and Community," 736–37.
116. Brigden, *London and the Reformation,* 152.
117. Haigh, "Communion and Community," 737.
118. The graphic depiction of the conversion of the "conquered infidels" by the crusader army depicted in *The Song of Roland* comes to mind.

There is also considerable evidence that the rites of initiation have sometimes been conducted in a perfunctory and haphazard manner. One sixteenth-century description speaks of a rather careless Confirmation ceremony:

> the Bishop examined us not at all in one article of faith; but in a churchyard, in haste we were set in a rank, and he passed hastily over us, laying his hands on our head, and saying a few words, which neither I nor any that I spoke with, understood, so hastily were they uttered, and a very short prayer recited, and there was an end.[119]

For many generations of Christian women, though, as well as for the church more generally, the rites of Christian initiation have been taken more seriously, and the day on which Christians gather together to celebrate the resurrection has been understood to be the most appropriate context for the occasion in which new Christians are drawn into the resurrection life by water and the spirit. As a result, the association between the rites of Christian initiation and Sunday worship has tended to be seen as an intimate and necessary one.

Unfortunately, however, women's first-person writings about baptism are extremely rare. This is so for a number of reasons. First, for most of the church's history, the practice of infant baptism has prevailed, and as a result women cannot describe their memories of their own baptisms. Women in communities that did baptize believers — Baptists and Anabaptists, for example — historically have tended to be literate in much smaller numbers than their Reformed and Anglican and Roman Catholic sisters. Among the latter group, as we shall see, women were rarely present at the public baptisms of their children, and by the time larger numbers of adults were being baptized in these churches, the tradition of spiritual autobiography had declined. Occasionally, Roman Catholic mothers and godmothers describe the confirmations and the rites surrounding the first communion of their daughters, but because those occasions have usually been conducted for children at about the age of seven, once again, detailed first-person writings of the event are scarce. Some Protestant women relate their experience of their confirmations and of the first time they gathered with the community for the Supper, but again, with little concrete detail. Of course, women have observed the baptisms and confirmations of others, and occasionally we find nonpolemical writings about the participation of women in these rites. But very often these descriptions are lacking in any real warmth or substance. The observations of Barbara Leigh Bodichon of a baptism in an African American church in Mississippi are typical:

---

119. Richard Baxter, cited in Paul Elmer More and Frank Leslie Cross, *Anglicanism: The Thought and Practice of the Church of England* (London: SPCK, 1935), 450.

"After the sermon four babies and four or five adults were baptized. Two of the babies were very white, two mulattoes. One baby was as white as any white baby I ever saw — blue eyes and flaxen hair. Then we all sang 'Passing Away,' and I went out and the Sunday School began."[120]

But there is another, perhaps more significant, reason that women seem to be more elusive in the history of baptism than in the history of other aspects of the church's liturgical life. For much of the church's history, perhaps from the third to the eighteenth centuries (and much later in some places), baptism was "men's business." Baptism was the premier occasion when ties of fealty and kinship were publicly displayed, and paraded (quite literally) before the community. For all but the very poorest family, in the choice of godparents and those invited to the ceremony, in the purchase of gifts (both to participants from the family and to the child from participants), and in the elaborateness of the procession to and from the church or baptistery,[121] a family declared its standing in the community, and as the first public presentation of a child, baptism was a celebration of a family's future. The baptismal kinship network was an important social structure in its own right, protected by the civil and ecclesiastical prohibitions on marriage within the prohibited degrees of affinity, which included one's godparents.[122] Spiritual kinship was, in most cases, seen as the equivalent of blood kinship in terms of its demands of loyalty and commitment, and in periods in which power was held or lost depending on the fidelity one could command, baptism allowed the head of a family to extend his power base in the choice of godparents for his children.[123]

---

120. Barbara Leigh Smith Bodichon, *An American Diary 1857–8,* ed. Joseph W. Reed Jr. (London: Routledge and Kegan Paul, 1972), 83.

121. In some places, baptism has also been traditionally accompanied by certain folk rituals, which were thought to ensure a secure future for the child. Those that were observed at Massaic in Auvergne in rural France at the beginning of the nineteenth century were probably not uncommon: "The children of the village followed the procession after a baptism, raising a terrible racket with hammers and rattles in order to make sure the child would not grow up deaf and dumb and, in the case of a girl, that she would have a pleasant speaking and singing voice." Jacques Gélis, "The Child: From Anonymity to Individuality," in *A History of Private Life,* vol. 3: *Passions of the Renaissance,* ed. Roger Chartier (Cambridge, Mass.: Belknap Press of Harvard University Press, 1989), 312.

122. Hence the periodic attempts to impose limitations on the numbers of godparents chosen, in order to decrease the likelihood that one would unwittingly marry a member of one's spiritual kinship network. Again, these prohibitions were largely ignored, and there is evidence that some children of noble families had as many as twelve godparents. Children were most often named after the godparent of the same sex, hence the small number of given names in the medieval period. It was not unusual that children were chosen as godparents. This traditional practice was first approved by the Council of Soissons in 1403.

123. A contemporary depiction of the force of these spiritual kinship ties can be seen in the relationships of obligation depicted in Mario Puzo's *The Godfather.* In one dramatic scene in the film version of this novel, in which a baptism becomes the occasion for the men of the family to settle old scores by murdering their enemies, the understanding of baptism as "men's business" is graphically displayed. Certainly godparents had religious functions as well. The Sarum Missal charged godfathers and godmothers "that ye lerne or see it lerned the Pater Noster, the Ave Maria, the Creed, after the law of all holy church and in all goodly haste to be confirmed of my lord of the diocese or his

We can see the intense investment of men in baptism when we consider the response to the periodic attempts by various authorities to control the expense of baptisms. In April 1473, for example, "the government of Florence put a ceiling on the sumptuousness of display exhibited during the baptismal ceremony. The previous month the government had also set limits on the amount of money on the celebratory dinner after a baptism."[124] The church, too, made an effort to curtail the amount spent on the baptismal ceremony but, in Florence at least, men rose up in protest saying that such restrictions represented "an attack on the right of the good families of Florence to display their honor."[125] The money spent for baptism was understood to be an investment in a family's future, and accounts books show that a child's baptism was one of the more expensive occasions in a family's economic life. As a result, civil and ecclesiastical injunctions in this matter seem to have been routinely ignored.[126]

This strong link between baptism and male power, money, and honor — this sense that it is "men's business" — has meant that women's investment in baptism has been (until fairly recently) relatively low. Indeed, those baptismal practices that would seem to concern women directly, such as the prohibition on baptizing women while they are having their menstrual period, seem to go unchallenged. Certainly canon law does not dwell on such matters at any length, which seems to indicate that noncompliance by women is not a particular problem. But perhaps another example makes the case of women's lack of involvement more clearly.

Although in the earliest centuries of the church's life, baptisms were generally performed once a year at the Easter Vigil, by the fourth century things began to change. The association of baptism with the forgiveness of sin (and later so-called "original sin") solidified, and as the anxiety rose that a child might die unbaptized, baptism of infants *quam primam* ("as soon as possible") came to be the canonical and social norm. As a result, everything possible was done to ensure that children were baptized immediately, no matter what the day of the week or season. As was

---

depute." And John de Burgh in his influential handbook for clergy *Pupilla oculi* (1385) assigned the duty of teaching children to godparents. These understandings that godparents were in some measure responsible for the religious training of their godchildren persisted well into the nineteenth century in some places.

124. Louis Hass, *The Renaissance Man and His Children: Childbirth and Early Childhood in Florence, 1300–1600* (New York: St. Martin's, 1998), 69. There are similar statutes in many of the Italian city-states during the Renaissance period.

125. Ibid.

126. There are additional reasons for saying that baptism has been largely understood to be "men's business." For instance, it is men who have tended to be concerned with the "gate-keeping functions" of the liturgy, discerning who is deemed to be "inside" and who is deemed to be "outside" of the church, which came with the increasing Latinization of the Christianity from the fourth century onwards. In the Reformation period, similar debates with the Anabaptists about the boundaries of the church and the nature of inclusion were conducted.

suggested above, the result was that throughout the Middle Ages and well into the Reformation period, very few women would have seen the baptisms of their own children, unless the rite was conducted at home.[127] Even if new mothers had not been confined to bed (which they probably would have been), they would not yet have undergone the Rites of Purification, a service in church conducted forty days after the birth, which served as a prerequisite for rejoining the worshiping community. The typical pattern was that the baby was washed and dressed for baptism by the midwife, the father sent word to the godparents and the parish priest to meet them at the church. The midwife (or the godmother if she had been present at the birth) carried the baby to church, sometimes as a part of an elaborate procession, and the baptism was carried out. After this, a dinner was customary, at least among the gentry.

One would have thought that the importance of seeing one's own children baptized would have led large numbers of women to protest their exclusion from the rite, but little evidence survives to indicate that they did. Occasionally, especially when women were active participants in dissenting or sectarian movements, we do find them using the baptisms of their children to make a point of their rejection of the religious status quo. (Many of the attempts to curtail the practice of baptism by midwives indeed came from the fear that this was a mechanism by which women could avoid having clergy who did not share their theological or ecclesiastical convictions baptize their children.) But for the most part, women do not seem to have considered baptism to be of sufficient personal concern to challenge the prevailing baptismal practice, and there is certainly no baptismal equivalent of Lady Mildmay's medieval treatise, "Admonitions for the Lord's Table."

In some periods of the church's history, of course, women's investment in baptism is slightly higher, and if we follow the evidence they have left behind we can see where their interest lies. For very powerful women, who actively participated in the regimes of their male relatives, the baptisms of their children were often of interest for the same reasons they were of interest to men, and they commonly became the scenes of other, more political, ceremonial events. Early in the year 401, for example, Bishop Porphyry of Gaza went to Constantinople to

---

127. Until the seventeenth century, the norm would have been baptism in the church or baptistery (if it was a separate building as in places like Pisa and Florence). It was generally only in the case of very sickly babies that baptism at home was practiced. Later, pressures to baptize children at home were strong in some places, especially among the well-to-do. In 1717, the minister at Burnstow in Surrey reported, "The parishes are extremely large in this neighbourhood and a custom has prevailed (but not of very long standing) to baptise everybodies' children at home, and the ministers hereabouts use the form of publick baptism on such occasions ... I have been used a little rudely sometimes for not complying with them in that particular, as some of my neighbours do." W. R. Ward, ed., *Parson and Parish in Eighteenth Century Surrey; Replies to Bishops' Visitations*, Surrey Record Society, 34 (1994), 153, cited in Jacob, *Lay People and Religion in the Early Eighteenth Century*, 73, 74.

seek permission from the Emperor Arcadius Augustus to destroy a popular temple of Zeus in his neighborhood. In an audience with the pregnant Empress Eudoxia, a staunch supporter of the eradication of paganism from the district, he promised her a male child in return for her intercession with the emperor. But because the inhabitants were generally docile and paid their taxes, the emperor withheld his permission. Even so, Eudoxia did give birth to a boy, who would be Theodosius II, and from that point on his mother contrived to have her way in the matter of the detestable pagan shrines. The child's baptism on the Feast of the Epiphany (January 6), 402, gave her the opportunity she sought.

> As the imperial cortege left the church, Porphyry and his associates, instructed by the empress, brought a petition to the infant Theodosius and the man who bore him. Demanding silence, the bearer, who was in on the charade, raised the child's head with his hand and proclaimed: "His majesty ordains that whatever is in this petition shall be granted." Those who observed prostrated themselves in wonder and congratulated Arcadius for his son's precocity.... Arcadius soon discovered that his son had granted Porphyry's requests, but acquiesced because "the lady empress nagged him incessantly."[128]

Although this powerful woman's experience of the baptism of her child is clearly atypical, it does give a sense of the way in which the political, social, and ecclesiastical intertwined in a noble household, and it underscores the link between baptism and power.

Ordinary women did occasionally raise their voices in the matter of baptism. Given that Christian baptism has been in so many periods of the church's history such a highly charged public occasion, in which the display of social rank often took precedence over the spiritual and theological import of the rite, that those women who did become serious about the religious significance of baptism would focus on the connection between baptism and propriety is not surprising. In 1871, for example, Annie Wittenmyer witnessed a baptism in which a young woman presented herself as a candidate "arrayed in all the extravagance of the prevailing fashion." After describing the woman's multilayered dress, her necklaces, earrings, bracelets, and rings, she turns her concern to her coiffure:

---

128. Kenneth G. Holum, *Theodosian Empresses: Women and Imperial Dominion in Late-Antiquity* (Berkeley: University of California Press, 1982), 54–55. "Porphyry took the order to be a blanket approval of the destruction of all pagan Temples, and on the ruins of the Temple of Marnas, he built a great Christian basilica as a visible sign of his gratitude to Eudoxia. She funded the project lavishly, and donated thirty-two marble columns for the interior, although she did not live to see the church's completion."

But the most complex and showy part of her costume she carried upon her head. Although her neck was slender and her head small, an immense chignon displayed its well-rounded proportions; over and around this excrescence of fashion, a mass of curls and frizzes spread themselves in every direction; mingling freely with the flowers and ribbons of an elaborately trimmed hat, the crowning glory of the whole, on the pinnacle of which a full-blown rose and a full-grown butterfly rested in quiet beauty.[129]

When the vows had been made and the baptismal water was about to be applied, Wittenmyer's concern is intensified. When the women candidates removed their hats, she writes,

> I saw, to my dismay, that the immense excrescence in the young lady's head covered the entire scalp, leaving no room for the application of water after the usual mode. "What will the minister do?" I questioned, mentally. "Will he baptize that excrescence of fashion, or will he baptize the woman?" And if he applies the water to that mass of frizzed hair, belonging, may be, to someone under the sod, will that be a valid baptism — will not that, rather, be *a baptism for the dead than the living?* It was a moment of intense interest to all, when the minister stood before her, for it was very manifest that he did not see his way out of the difficulty at once.

But the minister seems to have overcome the problem:

> However, after a moment or two of perplexity, with one hand he raised her head, *and with the other he applied the water to her face.* And now I ask, *Can any one in the immediate violation of the obligations of the Church, and without any purpose to live new lives, take these solemn vows without moral perjury?*... We ought to blush with shame, when we see the vanities and sins that now despoil the Church, and make it a show-room of fashion.[130]

Annie Wittenmyer's personal investment in the process of baptism is clearly very high, as is her understanding of the theological import of the rite. But baptism takes up only a very small percentage of her attention in her comprehensive book on women's religious duties, and her concern is shared by only a few other women in mainline churches.

---

129. Annie Wittenmyer, *Women's Work for Jesus* (New York: Nelson and Phillips, 1871), 128.
130. Ibid., 129–30.

In her book *What a Pastor's Wife Can Do*,[131] an anonymous woman (styled "One of Them") speaks of the contribution a clergy wife can make in the baptism of women parishioners.

> The pastor's wife may often suggest improvements in these methods [of baptism].... A baptism loses much of its beauty and solemnity because those who are to be baptized are not told beforehand what they are expected to do.... A warm-hearted, intelligent sympathetic patience will accomplish much. If it is in her heart, let her whisper to those who are to be baptized: "Do not look around the room or seem to see anyone in the audience; look straight forward until you close your eyes; then, with a prayer in your heart that God will so help you to honor him that someone else will be led to Christ in baptism, commit your way to him, and remember that I am praying for you."[132]

Like Annie Wittenmyer twenty years earlier, this woman gives real evidence of an essential seriousness about baptism. But interestingly, unlike her treatment of communion which we saw earlier, the context within which this discussion is set is a larger discussion about the wife's ability to further her husband's ministerial career. "The way in which a pastor administers the ordinances will very largely affect his success," she says. So, once again, baptism is essentially about the enhancement of male authority and prestige.[133]

Although baptism has not traditionally been at the center of women's liturgical concern, more recently, with the heightened attention to baptismal spirituality in the churches — the sense that it is in baptism that our Christian vocation is inaugurated — women have been more ready to reflect on their experience of the rites of Christian Initiation. For many women, the images and rituals of baptism have been an enormously powerful source of spiritual nourishment. But women (perhaps precisely because they have traditionally sat a bit more lightly to the process) also have been ready and able to transfer baptismal imagery and ritual to other situations of personal and communal renewal. At the 1992 meeting of women who had been involved in the ecumenical movement discussed above, Aiko Carter from Korea described a "peace walk" made by a number of women to the battlefield at Okinawa where many Koreans had been killed. Stones gathered in Korea had been brought to Okinawa to make a monument to commemorate the dead, and Carter tells of the spontaneous ceremony that took place there

---

131. Philadelphia: American Baptist Publication Society, 1893.

132. "One of Them," *What a Pastor's Wife Can Do*, 59–60.

133. Compare this with the combination of pastoral theology and lyrical prose she uses to describe Holy Communion, which we saw above, pp. 182–83.

when the women gathered, as she put it, "to listen to the stones": "One of the Korean women stood by the stones weeping. It was like keeping vigil in the Garden of Gethsemane. She then gathered her tears in her hands and baptized the others with them, sharing her pain and bidding them: 'Go forth into the world in peace.' "[134]

Certainly, women have always been subject to the rites and the disciplines of baptism in equal numbers to men, but their active interest in both the practice and the theology of baptism has been, in general, surprisingly low. More evidence about their concern with baptism is likely to come to light. An unpublished series of remarkable letters written between 1880 and 1883 from Ellinwood, Kansas, from Charlotte M. McDowell to her brother Amos, who had recently become a member of the Christian Church (Disciples of Christ), is one small example.[135] Although we only have Charlotte's half of the correspondence, these siblings were clearly engaged in a vigorous theological and liturgical debate about the biblical evidence for infant baptism, the necessity of baptism by immersion, the question of baptismal regeneration, and other weighty topics. Charlotte's argument is carried out at a very high level of theological sophistication, but she never once in this exchange of letters refers to her own baptism or to that of anyone else of her acquaintance.

Confirmation and First Communion

Women have expressed slightly more concern with the processes of confirmation and the first occasion for receiving communion, although still very few examples exist of first-person reminiscence of these rites, or reflection on their meaning by the candidates themselves, largely because for most of Christian history they would have occurred at a young age. (Although certainly older women have been confirmed and communicated for the first time in every period.[136]) Sometimes

---

134. Webb, *She Flies Beyond*, 56–57. Webb reports that at the conclusion of this story, "Having told us the story, it was typical of an Asian woman that she wanted to share with us a gift too. Aiko sent around the table to each one of us a tiny paper dove, and for a moment we paused from our talking to ponder in our hearts on the pain of women the world over who are left weeping after the wars of men."

135. The originals of these letters are in the possession of one of the descendants of the McDowell family, Hattie Kingsley of Beaumont, Texas. I express my gratitude to my colleague Professor Mark G. Toulouse for lending me his photocopies of this correspondence.

136. This sometimes happened among paedo-baptists in previous generations. In 1701, for example, a woman of sixty was reported to have been confirmed. Susan J. Wright, "Catechism, Confirmation and Communion," in *Parish Church and People: Local Studies in Lay Religion, 1350–1750*, ed. Susan. J. Wright (London: Hutchinson, 1988), 215. With more and more adults presenting themselves for the rites of initiation, this will surely become less uncommon in those churches that normally baptize babies. In the Believers' churches, of course, first communion following baptism as an adult is the norm.

women observers, either the mothers of the candidates or ordinary parishioners, comment on these occasions and give us some sense of the ways and means of women's participation in the rites.

Confirmations have not always been solemn occasions. In the mid-eighteenth century, one woman reports that "the noise, the tumult, and the indecency with which young people crowded into the chancel, looked more like the diversions of a bear garden than the solemn performance of an apostolic office."[137] In 1883, Sibylla Holland writes to her daughter, Agnes, and describes a confirmation service in Canterbury Cathedral that similarly went disastrously wrong. She reports that when she arrived at the church for the Sunday service, a crowd of people was already "pushing, struggling, and jostling together trying to get into the choir." The archdeacon was attempting to keep order, telling the people that if they would only sit down there were sufficient places reserved for them in the nave.

> "There ain't no seats," was the rude rejoinder, and they pushed forward so, I thought the little archdeacon would have been crushed! Papa [the rector], very tall, stern, and commanding, tried to make way for the candidates who followed his procession, looking rather alarmed and saying, "Stand back, you *must* stand back, it is no use, you cannot get into the choir." The vergers and beadles, scarlet with heat and anger, stood helpless by the gates.[138]

Clearly these disruptions of good order made a profound impression on this Victorian matron. (Indeed, one of her stated reasons for her later attraction to the Roman Catholic Church was its "dignity and order.")

Other women were less troubled by a bit of chaos at confirmation, seeing it as a sign of spiritual vigor. In a letter to a friend, a member of the wealthy DeRosset family of North Carolina describes in vivid detail the revivals there in 1857–58 and their impact on the Episcopal Church of St. James in Wilmington.

> Oh we had such a glorious time last night darling Kate — So much enthusiasm and solemnity in the Church — the aisles filled with the candidates for confirmation. To see elderly men kneeling in the aisles — not room for them at the altar — is a sight never before witnessed in our Church — the hearts of all the congregation seemed overflowing.[139]

---

137. Cited in Norman Sykes, *Church and State in England in the XVIIIth Century* (Cambridge: Cambridge University Press, 1934), 218.

138. Sibylla Holland to Agnes Holland, June 8, 1883, in Clive Dewey, *Passing of Barchester* (London: Hambledon, 1991), 66–67.

139. Mrs. A. J. DeRosset to Katie Meares, April 11, 1858, DeRosset Family Papers, South Carolina Historical Commission.

But again, this is one of only a handful of women's first-person descriptions of confirmation; their paucity seems to indicate that women are generally less invested in the rite than they are in other aspects of the church's liturgical life. (There is, for example, virtually no mention of confirmation in any of the several extant diaries of medieval women, except very occasional statements that so-and-so was confirmed.)

There is evidence that the first reception of Holy Communion is of greater consequence to women, especially as it began to take on the function of a rite-of-passage for young girls. Beginning in the mid-nineteenth century, Roman Catholics increasingly began to restyle and reinterpret the rite to prefigure marriage, with all the accompanying accoutrements. Young girls began to be dressed in miniature versions of bridal wear (boys in black suits) for their first communion, and to receive presents worthy of a wedding: jewels, watches, and other elegant accessories (see fig. 20). A reception usually followed, culminating with the cutting of a cake very much like a wedding cake. "Feminine life in its first period unfolds between two white veils," wrote the Comtesse de Gence in 1910, "the veil of the first communion and the nuptial veil."[140] In response to the increasing pressure to turn the rite into an occasion for ostentatious display, in 1910 the Vatican attempted to lower the age of first communion from early puberty to the age at which children first had a rudimentary knowledge of the doctrines of the faith, or around seven years of age.[141] But while churches and parishioners complied with the Vatican directive, first communion was simply transformed from a rite of passage from adolescence to adulthood into a rite of passage from childhood to adolescence, and the paraliturgical trappings remained the same. A girl's first communion "was not only the first conscious stage of spiritual life, but an entire socio-sentimental existence."[142]

The deep significance of this rite for young girls can be seen in the diary of twelve-year-old Parisian Elisabeth Arrighi, which is headed on January 1, 1879, "The Year of my First Communion." In preparation for receiving communion for the first time on May 15 at the Church of Saint-Germain-des-Pres, she made a three-day retreat with her parish priest and the rest of her catechism class, and on May 14 she went to confession and "repented of teasing her little sister."

---

140. The Contessa was the author of the most influential Italian religious manual of the early 1900s. See Michela Del Giorgio, "The Catholic Model," in *History of Women in the West*, vol. 4: *Emerging Feminism from Revolution to World War*, ed. Genevieve Fraisse and Michelle Perrot (Cambridge, Mass.: Belknap Press of Harvard University Press, 1993), 186.

141. This is contained in a pronouncement by Pius X, *Quam singulari Christus Amore*, which also authorized private communion.

142. Del Giorgio, "The Catholic Model," 186.

She recounts the details of the service in great detail, the hymns, the organ music, and the intensity of the prayers. Of the moment when she went to the altar to receive communion, she says: "I heard God speaking to my soul, saying to me over and over: 'I am yours, you possess me.'...Oh! I shall remember the emotion I felt at that moment for the rest of my life."[143]

For many a little girl, of course, the veil worn at her first communion prefigured not her wedding veil but the veil she would take in a formal religious profession as a nun, and bridal imagery was employed there as well to elucidate the meaning of the commitment that was being made.

Women's Sundays

Any attempt to track the ways and means of women's worship on Sundays is a profound challenge, with a number of nearly insurmountable obstacles. For every period of the church's history, descriptions of the "ordinary" are less common than descriptions of the "extraordinary," and for some periods virtually no first-person material exists at all about the ordinary pattern of common prayer on Sunday. It is safe to say that women's experience of ordinary Sunday worship in the first ten centuries or so of Christianity is largely a blank page that remains to be filled in.[144] So, rather than try to build an elaborate edifice of bricks made of very little straw, it has seemed wiser to wait until more construction material is available, but this approach has biased this particular chapter more emphatically toward our more recent liturgical past.

A second obstacle to drawing a complete picture of the ordinary churchgoing experience of women is that Sunday worship has always been a particularly complex blend, made up of diverse forms of rite, symbol, prayer, song, and social interaction, and women have engaged with these elements in various ways. Rituals that have been an invariable part of some women's experience of Sunday, such as the eucharist and the peace, have not been central to others, and occasionally

---

143. Cited in Perrot, *A History of Private Life*, 4:326. On May 10, 1879, a few days before she received communion for the first time, young Elisabeth writes of her desire that her father should receive communion with her on the day.

144. There is perhaps some first-person evidence embedded within one woman's fourth-century travel diary, but the diary largely consists of the author's observations of the special case of festal worship in Jerusalem rather than her normal Sunday experience in Spain. Intertwined within another woman's advice to her son about worship may be some sense of her own Sunday pattern in the ninth century, but her principal concern centers around ensuring that her boy's behavior (including his religious behavior) is such that it upholds the family honor.

a rite of considerable value to a small group will have almost no part in the liturgical life of the mainstream.[145] In addition, the "character" of worship, always a difficult thing to pin down, changes for women depending on the circumstances in which they find themselves, and we sometimes can only identify this character in periods of liturgical and ecclesial upheaval. In many of the Protestant churches, for example, the character of the Sunday service undoubtedly changed when women began to lead worship and to preside at the sacraments, and when imagery arising from women's experience of the relationship with God began to influence the language of the liturgy. All of this has meant that we have had to be content here with talking more about the trajectories and trends in women's Sunday worship; a more detailed tracking of these subtle differences will have to be left for a longer study.

But another, and perhaps a more serious, obstacle arises in our attempts to draw an accurate and detailed picture of women's worship on Sundays. Although women's commitment to Sunday churchgoing has generally been high, and although women have found in Sunday worship nourishment for the living of the Christian life, it is more often in the cloister, the bedroom, the street, and the shrine that women have been able to shape the liturgical experience to their particular needs and hopes. Inside the church the shape of their liturgical experience has been largely in the hands of others. This fact explains why their observations and accounts of their Sunday worship have a distinctly different quality, as well as why we have far more evidence from women about their *preparations* for making their communion than about the *act* of receiving itself, and about their attempts to organize the peace rather than about the act of exchanging the peace. Finding women in ordinary Sunday services has been difficult because it has not always been easy for women to find themselves in Sunday worship.

---

145. One such example is the practice of footwashing in many of the Believers' churches, which we have not had the occasion to consider here.

CHAPTER SIX

WOMEN, WORSHIP, AND THE CHRISTIAN HOUSEHOLD

Under the east window of our dining room we have a flower-bed. We call it our memory-bed because Clyde's first wife had it made and kept pansies growing there. We poured the water from my little lost boy's last bath onto the memory-bed. I kept pansies growing in one side of the bed in memory of her who loved them. In the other, I plant sweet alyssum in memory of my baby. —Letter, Elinore Pruitt Stewart, October 25, 1912[1]

Throughout Christian history, the household has been a significant sphere of liturgical activity for women, not subordinate to the church but linked to it in a relationship of mutual interdependence. In the home women have learned and practiced the prayers and rituals of the liturgy; there they have taught these to their children, and there they have faithfully kept the church's feasts and fasts. Other women have drawn their households into the patterns of the church's public prayer by establishing domestic chapels and erecting shrines to their patron saints. On occasion, women have superintended the baptisms of their children in the home, as well as family weddings, the rituals with the dying, and the burial of their dead.

Among certain women — especially the economically and socially disadvantaged, whose distrust of institutionalized Christianity ("where they rarely had any voice"[2]) has been quite high — the rituals of domestic religion have usurped or undermined the church's authorized rites. Those women who have been caught up in various forms of religious dissent have used their homes as havens from the perceived depravities of the liturgical status quo, organizing and superintending meetings for worship in their kitchens and sitting rooms. Other women's houses have been the center for their practice of witchcraft, either as a replacement for — or more usually, as an adjunct to — the worship of the church. Some women have

---

1. Elinore Pruitt Stewart, *Letters of a Woman Homesteader* (Boston: Houghton Mifflin, 1914), 160.
2. See Lillian Lewis Shiman, *Women and Leadership in Nineteenth-Century England* (New York: St. Martin's, 1992), 31.

felt that their ordinary domestic lives created insurmountable impediments to their spiritual and liturgical aspirations, women like the mystic Angela de Foligno (b. 1309), who prefaces the account of her visions with a thanksgiving prayer to God for causing her mother, husband, and children to be carried off by the plague so that she could devote herself entirely to God's service. But for most women, the liturgies of kitchen and parlor and bedchamber have intertwined meaning-fully with the liturgies of church and chapel to create an overall liturgical pattern of great richness and texture.

The Changing Character of Domestic Space

Most of us tend to think of our houses as "private space," as opposed to the "public spaces" outside of the house. But this idea is relatively recent, and for most of Christian history the notion that one's dwelling place is an isolated, self-contained domain would have seemed very odd indeed.[3] At the very least, previous generations of our forebears have generally not been able to afford to have their domestic sphere isolated,[4] because the family economy depended on work done in and around the house by the members of the household, which usually included not only the mother and father and their minor children, but very often older unmarried offspring, brothers and sisters of the parents, possibly their elderly parents and grandparents, and their servants, apprentices, and other workers. Among the wealthy this definition of "household" might have been ex-tended even further, as various "poor relations" and hangers-on gathered around the house in order to take advantage of the economic success of the family. In the houses of the poor, in some cases even the distinction between inside and outside breaks down, as chickens, pigs, dogs, and sheep (perhaps the family's only assets) have wandered in and out of the house freely.

But increasingly, in some places by the early seventeenth century and in the West more generally by the mid-1800s, work and home began to be separated, at least among the increasingly prosperous middle class. We see this sense of home described in Alfred, Lord Tennyson's (1809–92) late Victorian poem, *The Princess:*

---

3. For a good discussion of the problems inherent in attempts to make sharp dichotomies between public and private in the early American situation, see Karen Hansen, *A Very Social Time: Crafting Community in Antebellum New England* (Berkeley: University of California Press, 1994), 5–7.

4. As one historian of domestic life asserts, until relatively recently "there were no frontiers between business life and private life. These activities tended to go on in the same living/working area. The household was the center of both domestic activity and mercantile activity." Catherine Hall, *White, Male, and Middle-Class: Explorations in Feminism and History* (New York: Routledge, 1992), 48.

> Man for the field and woman for the hearth;
> Man for the sword and woman for the needle she;
> Man with the head and women with the heart;
> Man to command and woman to obey;
> All else confusion.

As this verse suggests, as the domestic space becomes increasingly "private space," housework and child rearing are increasingly defined as exclusively "women's work" (at least for families in which women could afford to stay at home while their husbands went out to engage in salaried employment), "and increasingly low on the scale of importance, except as a context for the husband's well-being."[5] But as the separation of men's (public) work and women's (domestic) work became increasingly hardened, the oversight of the family's religious life and piety began to be seen more exclusively as a part of women's domestic responsibility. So William Wilberforce, writing in 1797, could argue as follows:

> When the husband should return to his family, worn and harassed by his worldly cares or professional labours, the wife, habitually preserving a warmer and more unimpaired spirit of devotion than is perhaps consistent with being immersed in the bustle of life, might revive his languid piety.... This is women's noble office.[6]

Women become, for Wilberforce and others of his generation, a sort of domestic priesthood, "the medium of our intercourse with the heavenly world, the faithful repositories of the religious principle...."[7] Ironically, however, at about this same time stronger assertions of male headship over the domestic sphere began to be made. "Every family when directed as it should be, has a sacred character," another essayist of the period says about the role of men in the home, "in as much as the head of it acts the part of both the prophet and the priest of the household, in instructing them in the knowledge, and leading them in the worship of God; and at the same time, he discharges the duty of king, by supporting a system of order, subordination and discipline."[8]

---

5. Ibid. Hall continues on to say that this situation did not necessarily apply to all women equally. "Again, poor women had to work and thus kept some of their equality longer; but as wealth increased, women would be relegated to the home, and servants took over what generally useful work there was to do to keep the household running."

6. William Wilberforce, *A Practical View of the Professing Christians in the Higher and Middle Classes in this Country Contrasted with Real Christianity* (London, 1797; Peabody, Mass.: Hendrickson, 1966), 453.

7. Ibid.

8. John Angell James, *The Family Monitor, or a Help to Domestic Happiness* (London, 1828), 17.

Because we are inheritors, to one degree or another, of these complex (and sometimes contradictory) attitudes toward the nature of the domestic house and the character of the space it encloses, we are surprised when we read descriptions from times when other paradigms prevailed. A story from the great revival in 1630 at Shotts in Scotland is one such description. The revival had been so successful that it was decided to carry it over an extra day, and one of those attending, a Lady Culross, was lodged in the house of one of the local gentry for the night. In the morning, reported one of the preachers, the family and its guests dispersed into their respective rooms for their private devotions.

Lady Culross went into her bed in the large room she had been given and drew the curtains [around the bed] that she might set herself to prayer. William Rigg of Atherone [another of the preachers], coming into the room, hearing her have a great motion [of the Holy Spirit] upon her, although she spoke not out, he desired her to speak out [loud], saying that there was none in the room but him and her women, as at that time there was no other. She did so, and the door opened, the room filled full. She continued in prayer, with wonderful assistance, for three hours time.[9]

That a woman's private devotions in her bedroom could so easily become a public occasion is not the detail that the reporter finds worthy of comment here, but rather the sheer power of the prayer that had been activated in the revival. Still other, even more intimate, activities have been open to public scrutiny as well. Certainly by about the year 700 and continuing on for at least another seven centuries, women were often present to witness a newly married couple in bed.[10]

The changing character of domestic space and of the relationships between its inhabitants necessarily colors our interpretation of the liturgical activity that has taken place there, and of the role of women in that activity. If the house has at times been considered a "public space," then has not household worship been, in some sense, "public" as well? If at times women have been viewed as priestly mediators of their husbands' spiritual aspirations, then do women not exercise a measure of that same sacerdotal authority over the domestic prayer they superintend in their homes? To fail to keep these questions in mind as we attempt to understand the importance of the house as a ritual setting for women

---

9. David Patrick Thomson, ed., *Women of the Scottish Reformation: Their Contribution to the Protestant Cause* (Crieff, Perthshire, Scotland: Book Department, St. Ninian's, 1975), 39.

10. In the thirteenth century, Lambert of Ardres tells the story of a woman who is about to consummate her marriage to a knight, but they are interrupted by a member of the court of a powerful neighbor, who demands from her a sum of money as a sort of tax for having married out of her rank. See Georges Duby, *A History of Private Life*, vol. 2: *Revelations of the Medieval World* (Cambridge, Mass.: Belknap Press of Harvard University Press, 1988), 133.

would be to miss (or worse, to misinterpret) this fundamental aspect of women's liturgical lives.

Women and the Liturgical Catechesis of the Household

Although definitions of "family" have changed over time, the persistent importance of the family to the establishment and maintenance of the Christian faith is indisputable. Many theologians have considered the Christian household to be "the church in microcosm," in which women play an essential role in maintaining patterns of worshipful living, and in encouraging of husbands, children, parents and siblings toward deeper engagement with the Christian life. Indeed, the Christian home has been a crucible for the whole process of Christian evangelization, as one scholar of the early period says:

> For every monk, fiery preacher, or zealous priest we need to imagine women in their domain, which included the family and daily religious practice. The influence of women in the spiritual life of the home has been overshadowed by the public conversion events emphasized in the narratives, but in fact the transformation of everyday rituals was probably accomplished largely by women.[11]

Women's concern for making the ritual connections between home and church made the life of the family a significant sphere for both conversion and liturgical catechesis, and many missionaries have understood that "if a new religion were truly to convert a people, it would have to penetrate to the level of the home, the locus of the most deeply rooted religious practices."[12] Christian history is filled with notable examples of the powerful influence of women over the worship lives of their families: Monica's influence over Augustine, Helen's influence over Constantine, Ethelberga's influence over Edwin. But ordinary women had precisely the same kind of influence, even if the political impact was not as great. The tribute to Margaret Corbet (d. 1656) for her role in the religious and liturgical education of her household could well be applied to millions of other women:

> Look upon her in Relations, as a Wife, a Mother, and Mistress, and you shall see she was mindefull of her duty to God in them all: Her great care and endeavour was to set up God in her Family; in order whereunto she

---

11. Karen Louise Jolly, *Popular Religion in Late Saxon England: Elf Charms in Context* (Chapel Hill: University of North Carolina Press, 1996), 43.
12. Ibid., 44.

bestowed great pains in *Catechising* of her children, and other near Relations committed unto her charge.[13]

Even during periods when the subordination of women to men was being emphasized in public discourse, both religious and political, women have clearly provided leadership in promoting liturgical piety and practice in their families. The Paston correspondence offers a unique window onto the private and public life of a fifteenth-century family, and in one letter from Margaret Paston to her husband, who is away on business, we can see her own sense of responsibility for her husband's liturgical life. She writes, "I pray you hear mass, and other services that you are bound to hear, with a devout heart, and I hope verily that you shall speedily conclude all your matters, by the grace of God. Trust verily in God and love him and serve him and he will not deceive you."[14]

Women clearly have understood their husbands' worship practices to be matters of their deep concern, and over and over again their letters, journals, and diaries give evidence that women have little hesitation in exercising their influence to keep their male partners on the liturgical "straight and narrow." But even more widespread is evidence of women's concern for the liturgical lives of their children and, in some cases, servants, who were in most instances the primary objects of training in the ways and means of Christian worship.

The Liturgical Training of Children

In the earliest centuries of the church, the education of children in the doctrine, ethics, and rituals of the faith was taken for granted as an aspect of Christian parenthood. Although we have numerous letters and treatises from this early period on the subject of the proper form and content of instruction for children, written by such theological heavyweights as Chrysostom, Jerome, and Augustine, these do not include first-person writing from women about their role as teachers of their children in the patterns of Christian common prayer. But since some of these writings of men are designed as responses to women's letters and queries, we can certainly reconstruct their concern with this matter. In 403 C.E., for example, a Roman aristocrat named Laeta has evidently written to Jerome asking his advice on how she should undertake the Christian upbringing of her infant daughter, Paula. In his response, Jerome encourages Laeta to pursue what can only be described as a form of postbaptismal catechesis. "[Paula] ought to

---

13. Samuel Clarke, *Life and Death of Mrs. Margaret Corbet, who dyed Anno Christi, 1656* (London, 1662), 15.

14. James Gairdner, ed., *The Paston Letters, 1422–1590*, 4 vols. (Westminster: A. Constable, 1900), 122 (my transliteration).

learn in what army it is that she is enrolled as a recruit and what Captain it is under whose banner she is called to serve." Women's silence on the question of the liturgical formation of their children lasts for over eight hundred years. No evidence survives to dispute the sentiments expressed by the sixteenth-century reformer Johann Bugenhagen: that, as Christian parents, mothers are to be considered "bishops in their own houses," charged with instructing "the children and servants as simply as they can" in such traditional liturgical matters as "the decalogue, the Creed, the Lord's Prayer, the sacrament and prayers at table."[15]

The earliest, and perhaps the most poignant, of women's descriptions of a mother's role in the Christian liturgical formation of her children is the remarkable *Handbook for William* written in the middle of the ninth century by a Frankish noblewoman named Dhuoda.[16] Begun in 841 c.e. and sent to her son William two years later, the *Handbook* was written during a period of intense social and economic instability in the kingdom caused by the power struggle among the three grandsons of Charlemagne for the right to occupy his throne. The youngest of the three (Charles the Bald) eventually triumphed, but Dhuoda's husband had backed one of the elder grandsons, and his allegiance to the new king was suddenly suspect. As a pledge of loyalty to the victor, he sent their fourteen-year-old son William and his infant brother to live at court. Throughout the *Handbook* we sense Dhuoda's longing for her absent sons and her deep desire that William might learn to serve God faithfully in a world where the epitome of Frankish aristocratic behavior consisted of, in the words of J. M. Wallace-Hadrill, "cutting throats and endowing churches."

With a keen sense that the training of children in the ways and means of Christian worship is a mother's responsibility, even when they are separated, Dhuoda encourages William to adopt a quasi-monastic pattern of prayer, psalmody, confession, charity, and moral discipline. After urging respect for the clergy, she tells her son to "offer them your true confession as best you know how — in privacy, with sighings and with tears. As the learned authors say, true confession liberates the soul from death, and prevents it from going to hell. Do not hesitate, I urge you, to entrust your mind and body to the hands of priests."[17] He is to pray for the clergy, for the nobility in general, for his own lord (Charles the Bald), for his father, and for enemies, travelers, the sick, needy, and those suffering trials. "Read the prayers for Holy Friday, the day of our Lord's Passion, and there you

---

15. "Hamburg Church Ordinance," 1525, in *Creeds of Christendom*, ed. Philip Schaff (Grand Rapids, Mich.: Baker, 1983), 1:296–98.

16. Dhuoda, *Handbook for William: A Carolingian Woman's Counsel for Her Son*, trans. Carol Neel (Washington, D.C.: Catholic University of America Press, 1991).

17. Ibid., 42.

will find how you must pray for all people."[18] She also directs her son to say the seven Hours of the Divine Office, and gives him advice on which psalms to say on various occasions.[19]

Dhuoda is expressing a concern shared by Christian women in all centuries for ensuring that their children participate meaningfully in the official liturgies of the church. Seven centuries later, in the fifteenth-century household manual *How the Good Wyfe Taught her Doughter*, the mother is to see to it that her child "behaves meekly in church, bids her beads, observes holy days, and (in adulthood) pays her tithes and gives charity to the poor."[20] A hundred years later, literate Russian women could consult the various manuals for household management (called the *domestroi*) on this matter of the proper liturgical formation of their children. Because the *domestroi* were principally concerned with encouraging Russian aristocratic families to adopt the manners and fashions of the West, which were beginning to take root in the reign of Ivan IV (usually known as "the Terrible," 1530–84), much of this advice represents a creative blend of piety and decorum. Mothers are told to instruct their children to

> take the bread carefully from the priest's spoon into your mouth. Do not snap it up with your lips, but take it in your hand and touch it to your chest like a Christian. Eat the communion bread and any holy food carefully. Do not drop the crumbs on the floor, nor chew the communion bread with your teeth as though it were ordinary bread.... You should not drink just any liquid with the bread; you may sip water or add dill to consecrated wine or eat it by itself, but use nothing else.[21]

Sometimes women simply exposed their children to their own devotional life, in the expectation that both their liturgical piety and their liturgical practice would be absorbed. The example of Lady Denbigh, a Roman Catholic convert from the Church of England, gives a sense of this type of "osmotic" education for children in the ways and means of worship.

> After their prayers, the children — by now three sons and four daughters — sat on stools at their mother's dressing table sewing or crocheting for the

---

18. Ibid., 84–85.

19. "The singing of the Psalms, when it is done with the heart's concentration, prepares for our omnipotent God a way to enter in, infusing those who intently meditate with the mystery of prophesy or the grace of compunction. Whence it is written, 'The sacrifice of praise shall glorify me.'" Ibid., 29.

20. There is a companion text, *How the Good Wyfe Wold a Pylgremage*.

21. Carolyn Johnston Pouncy, ed. and trans., *The Domostroi: Rules for Russian Households in the Time of Ivan the Terrible* (Ithaca, N.Y.: Cornell University Press, 1994), 67. Although the *domestroi* are written anonymously, they were likely written by a priest, Sil'vestr, whose name is generally associated with the texts.

poor. The maid dressed Lady Denbigh's hair while she read to her children the lives of the saints. Holy Mass was at 8:30 and on Sundays the Gospel lesson was learnt by heart. . . . For [visitors] it was . . . wonderful to be in the midst of a family whose activities and life were centered round the presence of the Blessed Sacrament. The cheer, the peace of the house came from the chapel.[22]

In many households, this liturgical formation was shared among the several adult women who formed the domestic unit. Mary Elizabeth Lucy tells of her upbringing in Warwickshire in the first quarter of the nineteenth century and describes the religious influence of strong women in her household: grandmother, mother, elder sister, nurse, and governess. "After Grand Mama's death, my own darling Mama taught everything," she wrote, "and heard me say my prayers."[23] As a schoolgirl, Lucy was in the habit of reading the morning psalms with her mother downstairs and the evening ones upstairs in the company of her sister under the supervision of her governess (see fig. 21).

Clearly Lucy's pattern was guided by the rites in the *Book of Common Prayer*, which was quite usual in English households where the women could read. In his famous biography of Samuel Johnson, James Boswell relates a story about the young Johnson and his mother:

Mrs. Johnson one morning put the common prayer-book in his hands, pointed to the collect for the day, and said "Sam, you must get this by heart." She went upstairs leaving him to study it: But by the time she had reached the second floor, she heard him following her. "What's the matter?" said she. "I can say it," he replied; and repeated it distinctly, though he could not have read it more than twice.[24]

Women used various kinds of liturgical books for the instruction of their children, for instruction not only in worship, but also in reading and the Christian virtues. From the preface to Katharina Zell's hymnal (1534–35), we have some sense not only of the importance of hymn singing in the ideal Reformed household, but also of the role of liturgical books in the devotional life of families and the development of doctrine. Children are to be taught to sing these simple hymns, and to understand that when they do,

22. Madeline Beard, *Faith and Fortune* (Leominster, U.K.: Gracewing, 1997), 72–73.

23. A. Fairfax-Lucy, *Mistress of Charlecote: The Memoirs of Mary Elizabeth Lucy* (London: Gollancz, 1983), 16–17.

24. J. Boswell, *Life of Samuel Johnson* (Harmondsworth: Penguin, 1986), 36.

they please God much better than any priest, monk, or nun in their incomprehensible choir song, as they lifted up some foolish devotion of useless lullaby to the organ. A poor mother would so gladly sleep, but at midnight she must rock the wailing baby, sing it a song about godly things. That is called, and it is, the right lullaby (provided it is done in faith) that pleases God, and not the organ or organist.[25]

Women's concern with their children's formation in the patterns of Christian common prayer was perhaps more important in communities that did not routinely use liturgical books, because such teaching patterns of "true worship" were seen as part of an overall domestic strategy for the renewal of church and society. Beginning in the 1620s the numbers of "mothers' advice books" multiplied, and in many ways replaced service books and hymnals in the domestic liturgical education of those of more independent ecclesiological inclinations. One such manual was Dorothy Leigh's *The Mother's Blessing* (1621), which remained in print for nearly fifty years through fifteen editions. In a chapter titled "The Preeminence of Private Prayer," Leigh suggests that in times of oppression the necessity of forms of prayer learned at home was especially acute, serving as an indispensable source of spiritual fortitude to those on the front lines of religious dissent. The chief virtue of these prayers, Leigh says, is that they can never be taken away:

> Some have had their Bibles taken away, that they could not reade. Preachers have been banished, that they could not heare: they have beene separated from company, that they could not have publike prayer, yet private prayer went with them: thereby they talked with God, and made all their miseries knowne unto him, and craved his assistance in all their troubles. And this is the greatest comfort that all good Christians have, that no man can barre them from private conference with God. Then take heed you doe not barre your selves from it, since none else can doe it, and you know not what neede you shall have of it in the houre of death.[26]

Clearly many Puritan women took this to heart. Lucy Hutchinson, wife of a Puritan commander in the Civil War, describes her mother's role as "the care of the worship and service of God both in her soul and in her house, and the education of her children."[27]

25. Preface, cited in Elsie A. McKee, *Reforming Popular Piety in Sixteenth-Century Strasbourg: Katharina Schütz Zell and Her Hymnbook*, Studies in Reformed Theology and History 2, no. 4 (Princeton, N.J.: Princeton Theological Seminary, 1994), 40.

26. Dorothy Leigh, *The Mother's Blessing, or The Godly Counsel of a Gentlewoman, Not Long Deceased, Left Behinde Her for Her Children* (London: E. Coates, 1667), 201.

27. Lucy Hutchinson, *Memoirs of the Life of Colonel Hutchinson* (London: Oxford University Press, 1973), 25–28.

Women have also considered forms of interior decoration as contributions to the liturgical education of their children. In a 1470 household manual, Dominican Giovani Dominici encourages the bourgeoisie mother to

> incline her son toward religion by keeping him occupied around a domestic altar, which he should decorate, illuminate, and serve like a real acolyte. The child should even learn to mimic the priest in front of the altar — after observing him in church — by ringing a bell, singing, saying mass, and preaching.... [The author] also had suggestions for decorating the altar at which the child was to officiate.[28]

The rise of what has been called "devout domesticity" among Protestants in the mid-nineteenth century saw the increase in religious decorative arts for the home (cross-stitched mottoes, reproductions of da Vinci's *Last Supper*, and neo-Gothic ornaments, for example), and these functioned both as statements about the piety of the household and as teaching tools for children. In the same period, settings for the acts of devotion of wealthy Roman Catholic girls also became more elaborate, and even very little children were encouraged to erect small Marian shrines in their bedrooms for their personal use.[29] In 1910, the pontifical decree *Quam singulari Christus Amore* authorized private communion, and women in wealthy households often set up and furnished a family altar for that purpose, at which they taught their children the patterns of eucharistic devotion. But rich and poor alike shared the sense that somehow religious articles in the home could inoculate one's children from the uncertainties of the world outside. The famous bank robber Willie Sutton, born in Brooklyn's Irishtown in 1901, recalls that his mother "filled the house with religious paintings and artifacts and was always stuffing rosary beads and religious medals into our pockets."[30] (Clearly in this case, the "inoculation" was not wholly successful.)

Because women have understood Christian worship as more than simply the formal rites that took place within the four walls of the church building, many

---

28. Cited in Christiane Klapisch-Zuber, *Women, Family, and Ritual in Renaissance Italy* (Chicago: University of Chicago Press, 1987), 321. Savonarola is described as having busied himself as a child "setting up little altars and [engaging in] other devotions of the same sort." (G. F. Pico della Mirandola, *Vita R. Hieronimi Savonarolae* [Paris, 1674], 6, cited in Christiane Klapisch-Zuber, *Women, Family and Ritual in Renaissance Italy*, 322.)

29. In her *Journal*, Caroline Brame describes her childhood bedroom in Paris as having "a little oratory" for her personal use. C. Brame, *Journal Intime*, ed. M. Perrot and G. Ribeill (Paris: Montalba, 1985), 21.

30. Cited in Hugh McCleod, "The 'Golden Age' of New York City Catholicism," in *Revival and Religion since 1700: Essays for John Walsh*, ed. Jane Garnett and Colin Matthew (London: Hambledon, 1993), 258.

were concerned with forming their children for participation in these "extramural" forms of worship as well. The widowed mother in Chaucer's *The Prioress's Tale* takes her seven-year-old son with her on the pilgrimage to Canterbury, and teaches him to say the "Ave Maria," and to kneel and repeat it in front of each statue of the virgin Mary they encounter along the route. Six hundred years later, much the same method of instruction is illustrated in *Pictures for Sunshine*, a book of moral guidance for children published by the Religious Tract Society in 1892. Under one depiction of a little girl and her mother standing together by a gravesite is the caption: "Baby's gone back to God, and her little body lies under the turf in the churchyard, where mother and Mary come on summer evenings, and think of and talk to the darling child, who is no longer with them, but whom they look forward to meet by-and-by in a better world."[31] For many women in isolated situations, where there was no local church, the establishment of a worship space outside the home for themselves and their children was a highly significant process. Jerrine Stewart remembers that when she was growing up in Wyoming, her mother Elinore used to lead her out into a grove of pine trees behind their house to worship. "There was no better church than pines or mountains. God was in every garden," Elinore told Jerrine.[32]

Until the advent of modern methods of birth control, most married women spent the majority of their lives either pregnant, recovering from childbirth, or nursing an infant (that is if they were fortunate enough to survive multiple births).[33] Childhood was short for our Christian forbears, with the early marriage of girls and outside work for boys being economic necessities for many families. Sadly, all too often these children died before reaching the age of majority, so great numbers of women never had the opportunity to see the mature liturgical

---

31. *Pictures for Sunshine*.

32. Elizabeth Fuller Ferris, "Foreword," in Elinore Pruitt Stewart, *Letters on an Elk Hunt* (Lincoln: University of Nebraska Press, 1979), xii.

33. The case of Martha Gibbins, wife of a Birmingham button manufacturer, is not in the least unusual. Having married at the age of twenty in 1778, she gave birth to her first child early the next year. In the next eighteen years this child was followed by sixteen others, thirteen of whom survived. In the year 1800, Gibbins "had an infant of one, a toddler of two, a little boy of four, one of seven, one of eight, and one of nine, in addition to the five boys and girls in their teens and the three who were yet to come. The responsibilities involved were unending" (Hall, *White, Male, and Middle-Class*, 183). While this picture is generally accurate for many places and times, not all married women would have had very small children at home. Among the medieval well-to-do, the use of wet nurses was common. A manual from about 1370 advises families to "visit [children put out to nurse] often, so as to see how they are, and if they are not well, to change them on the spot to another nurse," but often the first hint that the child was not well was when the bailiff came knocking at the door to say that the child had died. In Florence, for example, in the years between 1300 and 1530, 17.4 percent of children put out to nurse died in their care, most often by sickness, but also as a result of being suffocated when the nurse or her mate rolled on the child in their sleep. See "Blood Parents and Milk Parents: Wet Nursing in Florence, 1300–1530," in *Women, Family, and Ritual in Renaissance Italy*, ed. Klapisch-Zuber, 132–64.

lives of those they had nurtured. Although both family size and infant mortality began to decline in the 1860s, at least among middle- and upper-class women, and although schools, "confirmation classes," and Sunday schools gradually began to take over the liturgical education of many Christian children, women have continued to prepare their children for meaningful participation in both world and church by providing active instruction, role models, and rich visual and devotional environments.[34]

The Liturgical Catechesis of Servants

For women of means, responsibility for guidance and spiritual nurture in the household has often extended to all those over whom she had oversight, including apprentices and servants. "To have children and servants is Thy blessing, O Lord," says an English primer of 1553, "but not to order them according to Thy will deserveth Thy dreadful curse."[35] In his *Life and Death of Mrs. Margaret Corbet, who dyed Anno Christi, 1656*,[36] Samuel Clarke encourages his readers to see Corbet as an example of pious attention to those in her employ:

> Much pains she took in Catechizing and instructing her servants, especially before they were to receive the Sacrament of the Lord's Supper. She used to examine them of the Sermons they heard, and she customarily read over those Sermon Notes to them which she had taken at Church, so that they might be the better prepared to give an account thereof to her Husband.[37]

Up to the second half of the eighteenth century, women generally organized the working days of their staff in order to accommodate daily prayers in the house. The biographer of Elizabeth, Lady Hastings tells us that she

---

34. Occasionally, however, we find children responsible for the liturgical catechesis of their parents. Such a case was that of Phoebe Bartless, "one of the most famous converts in evangelical literature," who was a member of Jonathan Edwards's Northampton (Massachusetts) congregation, who was "exceedingly importunate" in calling her parents and siblings to their duty to attend church services faithfully. See Patricia J. Tracy, *Jonathan Edwards, Pastor: Religion and Society in Eighteenth-Century Northampton* (New York: Hill and Wang, 1979), 117.

35. Cited in Hall, *White, Male, and Middle-Class*, 53.

36. This is included as one of Clarke's *Lives of Ten Eminent Divines* (1662), which contains sixteen biographies, four of which — those of Jane Ratcliffe, Margaret Ducke, Elizabeth Wilkinson, and Margaret Corbet — were of women.

37. Cited in Suzanne Trill, Kate Chedgzoy, and Melanie Osborne, eds. *Lay by Your Needles, Ladies, Take the Pen: Writing Women in England, 1500–1700* (London: Arnold, 1997), 214. On their return from church on Sundays, the mistresses of large and complex households such as this would gather the household together to rehearse the text and content of the sermon. See William M. Jacob, *Lay People and Religion in the Early Eighteenth Century* (Cambridge: Cambridge University Press, 1996), 103.

assembled her household "or such of them as could be spared," four times a day to join in prayer and Bible reading from the Church's service. These prayers were either conducted by the vicar, who acted as her chaplain, or one of the senior servants. Devotional works were also read aloud for those preparing to receive communion.[38]

So high was the expectation that women would train their servants to participate fully in Christian worship that they often came under fire for failing in this duty. "That the singing in our Presbyterian congregations is dismal has already been proclaimed far and wide," the editor of the *English Presbyterian Messenger* laments in 1850.[39] "It is not enough that a dozen or twenty men and women volunteer into the singing-pew for the two or three meetings on the Sabbath. We want every person with a singing voice trained to take his or her part either in the singing pew or elsewhere." So what is the solution to this problem? "Domestic training" is needed, the author argues, particularly of servants; and for this the mistress of the house is to be responsible.

> If our servants were so aided, we should do so much to improve the public singing of praise.... Contrive, then, that when the children assemble, and the family practice takes place, Betty and Jane, as well as the governess, may be there and get their fifteen minutes' practice. There ought to be no more difficulty about this than there is about getting them to take part in our family prayers.

But this will have more far-reaching effects still, with "Betty" and "Jane" — that is, the servants of lowest rank — reaping innumerable social benefits in the future. "Look a little further ahead," the author says to his women readers:

> Ten years afterward Betty is a wife and mother. She has not forgot her singing lessons. She has persuaded Harry to buy a modulator and she has taught him and little Jack and Lizzy to take their parts in many a song. If you are passing the door, you will be delighted to hear how you have contributed to make one home a happy one, among the many miserable ones; how the father got a taste for home enjoyments, rather than for the beer-shop. You need not fear to enter the house and find Betty with a blackened eye. You will meet with a beaming welcome. Will you not have your reward?[40]

---

38. C. E. Medhurst, *Life and Work of Lady Elizabeth Hastings* (Leeds: Richard Jackson, 1914), 59.
39. *English Presbyterian Messenger,* no. 145, "new series," 6.
40. Ibid., 7.

The extent to which the sort of domestic scene envisioned by the editor of the *English Presbyterian Messenger* actually occurred needs further investigation, as do the details of the liturgical lives of the "Bettys" and "Janes" in well-to-do households. But we can certainly conclude from the evidence we have that, until relatively recently, the complex household functioned as both a center of worship in its own right and as a school for training in the forms of worship that took place in church, not only for the family, but for their domestic staff as well.

Women's Domestic Worship

In the apocryphal Acts of Peter, fidelity to Christ is exemplified by two women "in the lodging-house of the Bithynians and four who could no longer go out of the house; and being thus confined they devoted themselves to prayer day and night."[41] But necessity was only one of women's many motivations for engaging in domestic worship; others included the desire for liturgical autonomy and to provide models for their children and servants, to have immediate access to God in times of deepest distress, and to make their household a "lamp set on a lampstand" in the neighborhood. Varied, too, were the settings of women's domestic prayer. Some women set up elaborate private chapels, furnished with all the necessary liturgical paraphernalia and decorated as elaborately as any church. Others had to make do with a corner of their bedroom or a bench in their garden. But whatever the motivation and the environment, women's domestic prayer was an integral part of the total liturgical experience of women and their households.

From a very early period, women were encouraged to draw their families into their domestic liturgical lives, as Tertullian (c. 160–c. 225) suggests in his advice to wives: "Let the two sing psalms and hymns and incite each other to see who can sing better to God."[42] Slightly later, John Chrysostom (c. 347–407) also tells women to sing liturgical hymns and psalms at home, "not only while weaving and doing other work, but especially at table" before and after eating, where they should "erect a fortress of psalms, so to speak, against [the Devil]," and when leaving the table "to sing holy hymns to God."[43] Women's own writings give evidence that their private devotions were not only for the sake of their own souls, but as an example to their households. As Lady Grace Mildmay (daughter

---

41. Acts of Peter 2:4.

42. Tertullian is arguing against the intermarriage of Christian and unbelievers. "What shall her husband sing to her and she to him? No doubt she will hear something from the stage." Tertullian, *Ad uxorem* 2, 5 (I, 692).

43. *Homilia in Ps. 41* (Quasten, PG 55, 157), 130.

of Sir Walter Mildmay, a Puritan and secretary to Queen Elizabeth I and founder of Emmanuel College, Cambridge), writes:

> A private household of family (which may resemble a whole common-wealth), consisting of the master and mistress, the husband and the wife, children and servants, all of one mind in love, fear, and obedience, being all well-chosen, instructed and governed with true judgment, that the house may be called a house of God. But if the master and mistress and the family be careless of their own duties to God and one towards another and in the education of their children, . . . there is nothing to be looked for but confusion.[44]

Although Lady Mildmay conceives this pattern of domestic prayer and piety to be the joint responsibility of husband and wife together, many women have been called upon to superintend the domestic religion of the whole household without the support of their mates. On the day that her husband left for service in the Revolutionary War, Mary Fish Stillman (1736–1818) chose Psalm 91 for the psalm at family evening prayers ("Thou shalt not be afraid for the terror by night; nor for the arrow that flieth by day; Nor for the pestilence that walketh in darkness; nor the destruction that wasteth at noonday . . . ; There shall no evil befall thee; neither shall any plague come nigh thy dwelling"). Mary's biographer tells us that "when the last 'Amen' was done, Stillman rode away." He would not return alive.[45]

In the East, wealthy women had begun to build private chapels in their houses at least by the fourth century, and to furnish their bedchambers with various devotional items: small portable icons, reliquaries, and other liturgical parapher-nalia.[46] In the West, the numbers of private Books of Hours, portable altars, statuary, and relics owned by the laity steadily increased as we move into the Middle Ages, indicating to some observers "a general movement in religious feel-ing, towards a more intimate and personal relationship with God, perhaps in the face of preoccupation with death and concern with the afterlife, especially escape

---

44. Mildmay, pt. 2, folio 843. See also Linda Pollock, *With Faith and Physic: The Life of a Tudor Gentlewoman, Lady Grace Mildmay, 1552–1620* (New York: St. Martin's, 1993), 46–47. Lady Mild-may's own household prayers are recorded in her diary under the heading "Spiritual Meditations" and include prayers of illumination, prayers for preservation (that she might be received into "the society of the godly"), confessions of faith, prayers for sanctification, and prayers in preparation for death. "The corner reserved for icons in Orthodox homes then and now is prefigured in the illustrations in the Madrid manuscript of Scylizes, which shows Theodora, wife of Theophilus, the last iconoclastic emperor, secretly worshiping holy images arrayed in a secret closet in her apartment." Robert Taft, "Women at Church in Byzantium: Where, When — and Why?" *Dumbarton Oaks Papers* 52 (1998): 34.

45. Marilyn Westerkamp, *Women and Religion in Early America, 1600–1850: The Puritan and Evangelical Traditions* (New York: Routledge, 1999).

46. Paul Veyne, ed. *A History of Private Life*, vol. 1: *From Pagan Rome to Byzantium* (Cambridge, Mass.: Belknap Press of Harvard University Press, 1987), 576.

from purgatory, so prevalent in Europe during and after the plague years."[47] Later still, inventories and wills show portable altars as a common feature of the bed-rooms of wealthy women, even though most women seemed to have chosen the Daily Office over mass as their preferred pattern of domestic prayer. The liturgi-cal habits of Cicely, Duchess of York (mother of Edward IV and Richard III) are probably quite common. Her biographer tells us that, "When she rose at seven in the morning...her chaplain was ready to say Matins of the day and Matins from the Little Office of Our Lady with her, followed by various other services throughout the day."[48] And Lady Mildmay, whom we met earlier, followed a sim-ilar daily regime, augmented by extensive readings from scripture. "I did read a chapter in the books of Moses and another in one of the Prophets," she tells us, "one chapter in one of the Gospels and another in the Epistles to the end of the Revelation and the whole Psalms appointed for the day, ending and beginning again and so proceeded in course."[49]

As we have seen,[50] women who established chantries in their houses had a great deal of control over their domestic prayer, even though church authorities tended to be concerned that chantry chapels would remove wealthy parishioners from their parish churches and granted licenses with various stipulations attached. One household was granted a chantry only for the lifetime of the grantee's mother, who was ill and was unable to attend church, and another license required the household staff to attend church in the village whenever the family was not in residence. Yet another wealthy woman was granted the right to establish a chantry in her home as long as she accompanied her family to the parish church on the "four major feast days."[51] With the growth in the early Middle Ages of masses for special intentions (primarily for the repose of the souls of the dead), however, the independence of chantries grew and women found themselves the employers of many clergy, and authority over the rites practiced in their chapels.[52] Many adapted the liturgical calendar to the devotional needs of the household (which

---

47. R. G. Mertes and K. A. Mertes, "The Household as a Religious Community," in *People, Politics and Community in the Later Middle Ages*, ed. Joel Rosenthal and Colin Richmond (Gloucester, U.K.: Alan Sutton, and New York: St. Martin's, 1987), 123.

48. "Devotional Life of Cicely, Duchess of York, Mother of Edward IV and Richard III," in *Orders and Rules of the House of Princess Cecill, Mother of King Edward IV, A Collection of Ordinances and Regulations for the Government of the Royal Household* (London: Society of Antiquaries, 1790), 37–39.

49. Mildmay, folio 45, in Pollock, *With Faith and Physic*, 34. See Ann M. Hutchinson, "Devotional Reading in the Monastery and in the Household," in *De Cella in Seculum: Religious and Secular Life and Devotion in Late Medieval England*, ed. Michael G. Sargeant (Cambridge: Brewer, 1989).

50. See above, pp. 61–63.

51. See Emma Mason, "The Role of the English Parishioner, 1100–1500," *Journal of Ecclesiastical History* 27 (1976): 22.

52. See Mertes and Mertes, "The Household as a Religious Community," 131.

in the case of some noble families could include well over a hundred people), and stipulated the pattern of daily and weekly services.[53]

The idea of the domestic chapel did not end with the Middle Ages, however. In her grand Italianate palazzo, "Fenway Court" in Boston, the wealthy socialite Isabella Stewart Gardner (1840–1925) built an elaborate chapel in neo-Gothic design with a stained-glass window chosen by Henry Adams over the altar. Her friend, the Australian singer Nellie Melba, describes the combination of theater and religion that Gardner superintended: "We all gather," Melba says, "[and] Mrs. Gardner lights a taper. Very slowly she walks down the gallery in silence, while we wait…and then we see her gravely light two little candles in front of an altar at the far end."[54] She did not hire a personal chaplain, but various local clergy served the chapel for special occasions.[55] Mrs. Gardner had a breadth of religious interest, however, and she also erected a Buddhist temple in her house, which she used as meditation space. When her friendship with poet-artist Okakura Kazuko deepened, she established the tea ceremony and a pattern of Shinto rites at Fenway Court as well. Each year on the anniversary of her death, the (Anglican) Cowley Fathers hold a service of Holy Communion in her chapel, as stipulated by her will.

We saw earlier that after the Reformation many ordinary women regularly used the church's official service books in the liturgical formation of their children. The diary of Catherine Livingston Garrettson, the famous Methodist preacher and evangelist (and wife of fellow preacher Freeborn Garrettson) shows one of the ways in which such books were used in women's own domestic liturgy. As she reports on Sunday, October 13, 1787:

> I arose early with a heart full of expectation, came down to breakfast, took a cup of tea and then retired to my room, bolted the door, and opening my prayer-book (for we had then only preaching once in three weeks) I read over the Church Service in my knees with clasped hands and uplifted eyes, I prayed. "By Thine agony and bloody sweat: by thy cross and passion: by Thy glorious resurrection and ascension: by the coming of the Holy Ghost."[56]

---

53. The accounts books from Lady Margaret Beaufort's household show that the candle consumption continued during her absences from the house, indicating that services went on even without her. Ibid. See also K. L. Wood-Legh, *Perpetual Chantries in Britain* (Cambridge: Cambridge University Press, 1965).

54. Douglass Shand-Tucci, *The Art of Scandal: The Life and Times of Isabella Stewart Gardner* (San Francisco: HarperCollins, 1997), 249.

55. For example, the (Episcopal) Church of the Advent had no midnight service on Christmas Eve, so she had the rector come to Fenway Court to hold one in her private chapel for herself and her friends. After her death the service was introduced at the Advent.

56. Catherine Garrettson, *Autobiography* (1817); see Document 1, Rosemary Skinner Keller, ed., *Spirituality and Social Responsibility: Vocational Vision of Women in the United Methodist Tradition*

But even when women were illiterate, or for some other reason did not use service books in their devotions, over and over again liturgical phrases appear in their domestic prayer, giving credence to the idea that they "followed the view . . . that the Church was a fellowship of prayer which extended beyond public worship into their household and private devotions. Even if they merely heard prayers read by the clergy when they attended the public worship of the church, those prayers became part of their own vocabulary."[57] Surely, evidence from many women leads to the conclusion that liturgical prayer and devotional prayer form a seamless whole in their lives. The diary of Lady Margaret Hoby is particularly clear on this matter:

> The Lordes Day: 5 [April 1601] Having praied I brake my fast and then went to the church wher havinge hard the sermon and received the Lordes Supper I returned home and privatly gave thanks the rest of the day after the afternone sermon I spent in readinge singing praing and hearing repeticions.
>
> The Lordes day 22 [March 1601] this day was ranie so that I Could noe durst goe abroad but exersised in the house with prainge and reading and singing Psa[lmes] and Conferinge in the after none Came Mr. Fuller from Mr. Edgertons sermon and he delivered unto us some of what her had delivered after I praied and supped and so when to bed.[58]

But the ritual formulae women used (or failed to use) in times of stress could also have serious repercussions. Helen Stark of Perth, the only woman martyr of the Scottish Reformation, was charged with several offenses that took place within her own home and was subsequently executed. The first charge against her was that, while in the agony of childbirth, "she did not call on the name of the Virgin Mary for help, as tradition and custom required, insisting instead in calling on the name of God the Father."[59] The mother of four, Stark made her final testimony from the scaffold on January 25, 1544, with her infant child nursing at her breast.

(Nashville: Abingdon, 1993), 33–34. Garrettson goes on to describe the dramatic consequences of this meditation: "Scarce had I pronounced those words, when I was received and made unspeakably happy. A song of praise and thanksgiving was put in my mouth — my sins were pardoned, my state was changed; my soul was happy. In a transport of joy, I sprang from [my] knees, and happening to see myself as I passed the looking glass I could not but look with surprise at the change in my countenance. . . . All things were become new."

57. Jacob, *Lay People and Religion in the Early Eighteenth Century*, 95.

58. Dorothy M. Meads, ed. *Diary of Lady Margaret Hoby, 1599–1605* (London: Routledge, 1930), p. 186.

59. David P. Thomson, *Women in the Scottish Church* (Skinnergate, Perth: Munro and Scott, 1975), 15. The second charge against Stark was that she had been heard to declare that had she lived in the time of the virgin, God might well have called upon one such as herself to be the mother of Christ, there being no intrinsic merit in Mary, but the choice and exaltation being simply of God's free and unmerited mercy.

Feasting and Fasting

Although women have been largely responsible for maintaining the cycle of liturgical feasts and fasts within the household, their motivations have been complex and multifaceted. Some, of course, have been driven by a deep sense of pious obligation, but for many women, exercising control over foods eaten and not eaten in their households was a means by which they, in Caroline Walker Bynum's words, "controlled their social and religious circumstances quite directly and effectively."[60] Over and over again in women's writing, the keeping of the feast is among the most important aspects of their domestic religion, remembered and claimed by women as their own peculiar domain (see fig. 22). Nellie Gross, who went to the Kansas frontier with her family in the 1870s, remembers the Christmases of her childhood fondly, even though the family was poor. But the men of the family never factor in her descriptions. "Grandma did some handwork out of pretty flannel scraps . . . ," she says, "[and] made little flannel mittens and bound them with wool braids . . . and mother always shared with her neighbors, especially did the little folks enjoy the bread and jam (corn bread usually)." She concludes her reminiscences by saying, "That was real Xmas (sic)."[61] So important was the liturgical calendar to women, through the late fifteenth century certainly and probably much later, that women tend to orient themselves to the Christian year as their primary way of dating events. "A Monday between Michaelmas and Martinmas," "somewhere after St. John Baptist," "Lent (because we were eating fish)," "the Tuesday of Easter Week last" was the closest that most women acting as witnesses to the late-fourteenth-century court cases studied by Dorothy Owen could come to identifying the month or season at which a particular event occurred.[62] Dhuoda, whose motherly advice for her son we have seen earlier, ends her *Handbook for William* with the inscription:

> This little book was begun in the second year after the death of Louis, the late emperor, two days before the Kalends of December, on the feast of St. Andrew, at the beginning of the holy season of the Lord's Advent. With God's help it was finished four days before the Nones of February, the feast

---

60. Caroline Walker Bynum, *Holy Feast and Holy Fast: The Religious Significance of Food to Medieval Women* (Berkeley: University of California Press, 1987), 220.

61. Joanna L. Stratton, *Pioneer Women: Voices from the Kansas Frontier* (New York: Simon and Schuster, 1981), 153.

62. Dorothy M. Owen, "White Annys and Others," in *Medieval Women*, ed. Derek Baker (Oxford: Basil Blackwell, 1978), 336. In addition, other liturgical events provided benchmarks for dating: "about the time Agnes's mother was churched," "just after my third boy was baptized" and "in the same summer we buried John."

of the Purification of the holy and glorious Mary, always virgin, under the favorable reign of Christ and in the hope for a God-given king.[63]

Part of the reason for this deep penetration of the liturgical year into women's consciousness was that their domestic superintendence of the cycle of liturgical feasts and fasts occupied a considerable amount of their time and attention. Evidence in the journals and accounts books of women shows the complex calculations necessary to the administration of the cycle of feast and fast. Not only was there a pattern of weekly abstinence during most of Christian history (usually Fridays at least, but in many places Wednesday as well), but weekly feasting on Sundays in varying degrees of elaborateness according to the season ("as attested to by the increased provision of food on that day in the accounts" in the late-Middle Ages[64]). Indeed, the domestic "Sunday dinner" tradition may be among the most persistent and ubiquitous of all Christian religious rituals.

In a letter to her absent husband, Lady Margaret Paston describes the provisions she is making for keeping a meatless Lent in about the year 1440: "As for herring, I have bought a horseload for four shillings, five pence. I can get no eel yet; as for beverages, there is promised me some."[65] Of course the specific details of feasting and fasting have been widely variable according to the time, place, and religious community. Particular foods eaten or prohibited, practices engaged in, dress and preparation rituals have all marked out religious, cultural, and ethnic identities. Such details have been particularly important in times of social and religious transition, as the bearers of the cultural character of families and communities over great distances of time and space. The maintenance of these practices has been almost exclusively the responsibility of women. In the Polish diaspora, for example, women in Poland would send their families who had emigrated to other parts of the world large oblong loaves of "Christmas bread," which were carefully preserved until the festal dinner on Christmas Eve, when it was shared among the members of the family, each of whom made three wishes as they broke off a piece. Similar stories can be told about the role of women in the cycles of feasting and fasting of the Italian, Irish, Spanish, Czech, and German diasporas as well.

But the liturgical calendar affected women's lives in other ways, because throughout much of Christian history it had implications for their sexual activity as well as their culinary obligations. From about the eleventh century onwards,

---

63. Dhuoda, *Handbook for William*, 106.
64. Mertes and Mertes, "The Household as Community," 131. "Often these included unusual or exotic foods, herons or swan, boars, and increased quantities of wine."
65. Gairdner, ed., *Paston Letters*, n. 149.

women were encouraged to abstain from intercourse on Sundays and other major feast days (and their respective vigils), throughout Lent, around the time of receiving communion, and in the time between childbirth and churching.[66] (In other words, in a year that a woman gave birth she would theoretically be restricted for nearly two hundred days.) Penitential texts, manuals for confessors, and religious tracts routinely included detailed instructions for regulating intimate relations according to the Christian year, including cautionary tales with lurid details of the dire consequences of lapses in discipline.[67] In a late fourteenth century book of advice for householders, for example, a "Brother Cerubino" advises husbands to encourage their wives' liturgical devotion. He says, "If your wife wants to receive communion three or four or ten times each year, help her along, comfort her, do this favor for the service of God. . . . Leave her alone at least three days before and three days after communion; in this way you will share in the good she is doing."[68] The degree to which women followed these admonitions is uncertain, but the anxiety it seemed to create in church authorities seems to indicate widespread noncompliance. Attention to "liturgical abstinence" was not high on the agenda of the Reformers, but continued to be expected of Roman Catholic and Orthodox women until at least the middle of the twentieth century, at least on certain days in the liturgical year.

Although for many women Sunday has meant the added work of preparing the main festal meal, for strict Sabbatarians, among whom the abstention from work on Sundays has been rigorously enforced, women have particularly welcomed the opportunity to "rest from the heavy household tasks like soap-making and candle-making." "All work ceased from 3:00 on Saturday afternoon until 9:00 pm Sunday," an eighteenth-century Congregational Church history recalls.

> Beds were not even made, and men were not permitted to shave. Cooking for the Sabbath had to be done a day ahead since "the smell of food cooking was an abomination to the nostrils of the Lord." The only travel allowed

---

66. In Russia women were to abstain from intercourse not only on Sundays, feast days, and during Lent, but in addition all Wednesdays and Fridays, and feasts of the virgin. See Pouncy, *The Domostroi*, 87–88.

67. Usually, this involved the offspring of a child conceived during a prohibited time. According to Caesarius of Arles (Sermon 44.7), a child conceived on a Sunday or during Lent, for example, might be epileptic or leprous. In the sixteenth century a woman from Bury St. Edmunds who gave birth to a crippled, blind, and mute son, admitted before the consistory court that she had conceived him on a Sunday.

68. Cited in Rudolf M. Bell,. "Telling Her Sins: Male Confessors and Female Penitents in Catholic Reformation Italy," in *That Gentle Strength: Historical Perspectives on Women in Christianity*, ed. Lynda L. Coon, Katherine J. Haldane, and Elisabeth W. Sommer (Charlottesville: University Press of Virginia, 1990), 119–48, 121.

was to and from the meeting house. It was not even permissible to kiss one's children goodnight, for this day belonged exclusively to the Lord.[69]

Some women have surely found the strictures of Sabbath-keeping onerous, because whatever work was not done on Sundays would simply have to be done during the week; some women found the rules excessively dour and solemn for their lively natures. (In about 1850, English tourist Frances [Fanny] Wright reports hearing a young man in New England say that "it would have been better to have picked someone's pocket on a Saturday night than to have smiled on a Sunday."[70]) Others, however, found the break in the normal rhythm of the week delightful. "No one need talk to me of 'Puritan' Sundays — long and tedious," wrote Kathleen Elspeth Oliver about Sundays on the Kansas frontier at the end of the nineteenth century:

> ...It was a day quite different from other days — a superior day — a day full of delightfully "different" things. In lieu of play, the long drive to town, church and Sunday School and a picnic lunch eaten in the wagon on the way home were compensating pleasures. In the afternoon Mother read to us in her beautiful intelligent voice....Father read too from the Bible — the solemn things from the Prophets and Proverbs and from Revelations....Mother read us the brighter things — the Psalms.[71]

Wherever life has been hard, Sunday rest has been appreciated by women. As Lydia Mitchell reports, meetings for worship on Sundays at her Kansas home "were social as well as religious and were the only break from the hard toil of the empire building, home making pioneers, except an occasional quilting, sheep-shearing or sorghum-making gathering."[72] With the relaxation of the Sunday Blue Laws in the last half of the twentieth century, the character of women's Sundays has changed considerably, although more recently women have also been at the forefront of various political movements aimed at restoring legislation to restrict Sunday trade and entertainment, such as the "Keep Sunday Special" campaign in the United Kingdom.

Women sectarians have also defied the prescribed feasts and fasts of the church in order to make a public stand against the liturgical status quo. They have feasted

---

69. Juliet Haines Moffard, *And Firm Thine Ancient Vow: The History of North Parish Church of North Andover, 1645–1974* (North Andover, Mass.: Naiman, 1975), 27.

70. Richard Mullen, *Birds of Passage: Five Englishwomen in Search of America* (London: Duckworth, 1994), 52.

71. Stratton, *Pioneer Women*, 183.

72. Ibid., 210.

when they should have been fasting, and vice versa, "to criticize powerful secular or religious authorities," and "to claim for themselves ... reforming roles."[73]
Sixteenth-century Lollard Margery Baxter openly cooked bacon on the fire during
Lent, and broke the Friday fast stating publicly that "it is better to eat Thursday's leftover meats of Friday than to go to the market for fish."[74] Ailie Erskine
Scott, who found herself in a theological dispute with her minister-husband and
his church, was evidently "in the habit of spinning on the fast days appointed by
the Gateshaw church to show her disrespect for them."[75] But not every woman
who broke the fast did so for purely religious reasons. In March 1557 the wife
of Peter Bartly was imprisoned for breaking the Lenten fast, but she defended
herself saying that all they had done was to eat a cockerel that they had found
on a dunghill; "they be very poor folks and did eat it of very necessity and not
out of contempt."[76]

House Meetings

Although now generally associated with various Christian renewal and sectarian
movements ("house churches"), the domestic house was almost surely the earliest setting for Christian common prayer. In the first generation after the death of
Jesus, the heads of wealthy households generally hosted the local Christian community, and when the head of a particular household was a woman, she surely
functioned in this role.[77] There is some evidence, too, that when the church began
to occupy specially designated church buildings before the turn of the fourth century, women who had been in the habit of providing hospitality in their houses
simply turned those houses over to the church for use exclusively as a place of
worship.[78] Women sectarians of later periods have often self-consciously related
their own domestic religious gatherings to these earliest house meetings.[79]

73. Caroline Walker Bynum, "Women Mystics and Eucharistic Devotion in the Thirteenth Century," in *Fragmentation and Redemption: Essays on Gender and the Human Body in Medieval Religion,* ed.
Caroline Bynum (New York: Zone Books, 1992), 220.
74. Cited in Margaret Aston, *Lollards and Reformers: Images and Literacy in Late Medieval Religion*
(London: Hambledon, 1984), 93.
75. Thomson, ed., *Women of the Scottish Church,* 133.
76. Susan Brigden, *London and the Reformation* (Oxford: Clarendon, 1989), 622.
77. See David L. Balch and Carolyn Oseik, *Families in the New Testament World: Households and
House Churches* (Louisville: Westminster John Knox Press, 1997).
78. In Acts 17:4 we read that "not a few of the leading women" became converts, which has led
many scholars to assume that these were wealthy heads of households. See A. J. Marshall, "Roman
Women and the Provinces," *Ancient Society* 6 (1975): 108–27.
79. In the presence of persecution, sectarian women sometimes related their meetings to the
gatherings of the frightened followers of Jesus just after his death. When the seventeenth-century
Puritan leader Rose Hickman, for example, received into her house "well disposed Christians," she
noted that "we did table [take communion] together in a chamber, keeping the doors shut for fear

Because the workings of the household have generally been under women's control, their role in these domestic forms of religion has been a prominent one. "They made their homes available to the classes and other groups and gave hospitality to itinerant preachers, dependent on their generosity for daily bread and a bed at night. A warm kitchen was a good meeting place for neighbors, and a simple meal would suffice."[80] Many readers may characterize the meetings that Susannah Wesley (1669–1742) held in her kitchen in the rectory at Epworth as her own contribution to the spiritual nourishment of her husband Samuel's congregation while he was away from the parish. She argues with him for their necessity in a letter dated February 6, 1712:

> ...though the superior charge of the souls contained in [the parish] lies upon you...yet in your absence I cannot but look upon every soul you leave under my care as a talent committed to me under a trust by the great Lord of all the families, both in heaven and on earth....I cannot conceive why any should reflect upon you because your wife endeavours to draw people to church.[81]

That Church of England renewal movement which became Methodism built upon this memory of Susannah Wesley's kitchen gatherings, establishing a network of "classes" and "bands" (derived from similar groups among the Moravians) that met in private houses for prayer, testimony, mutual encouragement, examination of conscience and, periodically, the Love Feast.

Long before the Wesleyan revival, domestic dwellings had been used as liturgical spaces by many other sectarian and renewal groups. For Waldensians, Ranters, Wycliffites, and a multitude of smaller religious sects the house allowed both freedom of liturgical expression and security from persecution. The thirteenth-century Guglielmite sect, for example, which believed that only with the advent of this female church would worldwide salvation be possible, is charged in the Inquisition records with allowing women to distribute "blessed hosts" at meetings in private houses, within which the group seems to have established a full-fledged sanctuary with its own symbolic program.

---

of the promoters, as we read in the Gospel the disciples of Christ did for the Jews." Rose Hickman, "Recollections of Rose Hickman," *Bulletin of the Institute of Historical Research*, ed. M. Dowling and J. Shakespeare, 4 (1982): 97–102.

80. Shiman, *Women and Leadership*, 31.

81. C. Wallace, ed. *Susannah Wesley: The Complete Writings* (Oxford: Oxford University Press, 1997), 79; see also C. Wallace, "Susannah Wesley's Spirituality: The Freedom of a Christian Woman," *Methodist History* 33 (1983–84): 138–73. Mary Bosanquet (1739–1815), wife of John Fletcher, held similar services in her kitchen.

Emblazoned on a banner above [an] altar was a picture representing the Trinity with Guglielma and, presumably Christ, releasing captives from prison. On the altar itself was placed the liquid which remained after the washing of Guglielma's dead body and this water was used as chrism to anoint the sick....[82]

Although sectarian groups that encouraged women's leadership commonly (and quite naturally) gravitated to the kitchen and parlor for their services of worship, others who found themselves outside of the bounds of authorized religious practice also met in domestic settings for common prayer. Indeed, many sectarian groups owe their very existence to the willingness of women to provide a safe and intimate setting for worship. In the early decades of the seventeenth century, for example, the hospitality of women provided the principal sustenance for the Puritan movement in England. "Acting in their capacities as housewives and mothers," one historian of the period argues, "women organized their homes as religious centers and saw to it that all members of their household were taught Puritan principles. Without the action of these women within their traditional roles, the Puritan sect would not have flourished."[83] (The same can be said, of course, about the importance of women to the contemporary *comunidades de base*, which have precipitated an unprecedented renewal of Christian faith and life in Latin America.)

Not all women who opened their homes to worship were sectarians; women who found themselves in isolated circumstances often welcomed local Christians into their homes out of their need both for communal prayer and for contact with their neighbors. Lydia Murphy, whom we met earlier, remembers that soon after their arrival in Shawnee, Kansas, their home "became the center of the social and religious life of the community."

Arrangements were made for services every two weeks at our house. Saturday afternoon and evening was the day selected. Irrespective of former religious affiliations, the new settlers came bringing all the family. Sister Ella was given the duty of keeping the babies as quiet as possible. Brother Emmett entertained the young children with games in the yard.... What fervent Amens arose during the sermon! The walls of the house fairly shook with the Methodist hymns "lined" by Douglas MacDougall, who lost his life in the war.[84]

---

82. Stephen E. Wessley, "The Thirteenth-Century Guglielmites: Salvation through Women," in *Medieval Women*, ed. Derek Baker (Oxford: Basil Blackwell, 1978), 289.

83. Shiman, *Women and Leadership*, 15.

84. Stratton, *Pioneer Woman*, 132–33.

Here we can see that the domestic environment is not merely a "setting" for worship for women, but is the context for an entire set of sensitivities to family, to the liturgical needs of various generations, and to the essential bonds among members of the community, even though some may be separated by death. This sensitivity is what has given the house meeting its vitality and strength, and the role of women in establishing and maintaining these forms of domestic worship cannot be overestimated.

Baptisms and Weddings

As we saw earlier,[85] women's concern with Christian initiation rites was not high for most periods of Christian history. But under some circumstances, women retained control over the baptism of their children as a domestic ritual. While baptism in church has always been the practical and theological norm, with the spread of infant baptism beginning in the fourth century (and, somewhat later, with increasing anxiety that infants might die unbaptized), very sickly babies began to be baptized at home. The role of the midwife in this process was crucial, because once the child was born her responsibility would have been to prepare the infant for baptism by tying off the umbilical cord and bathing the newborn in oil or warm water. Although it was expected that clergy would be called to baptize an infant who was too frail to leave the house, in many cases — if the myriad attempts to curtail the practice are anything to go on — the midwife herself would perform the rite. (If the mother died before the baby was delivered, midwives were encouraged to cut her open and extract and baptize the baby.) Usually, midwife baptisms were a routine matter, and parents were simply asked by church officials to attest to the fact that their child had indeed been baptized using water and the proper formula. Sometimes, however, baptism by midwives at home became a form of religious protest. After the Reformation, for example, increased opposition arose to midwife baptism because there was some (probably well-founded) suspicion that Catholic mothers were having midwives baptize their babies, sick or healthy, in order to avoid baptism by Protestant clergy.

Although essentially a domestic rite during at least the first thirteen centuries of the church, marriage was, as historian George Duby points out, "a serious matter and therefore a male affair."[86] The only thing needed from the bride was her consent before and during the wedding and her willingness to consummate the marriage afterwards. But by the nineteenth century, especially in the New

---

85. See above, pp. 189–92.
86. Georges Duby, *Love and Marriage in the Middle Ages*, trans. J. Dunnett (Cambridge: Cambridge University Press, 1994), 46.

World, the notion that brides might have a significant part to play in nuptial rituals had become quite well established, and we begin at last to find women's first-person accounts of the role of weddings in both their domestic liturgical life and in their wider religious experience. Indeed, they have by this time even begun to exercise some degree of control over the rites, as we can see from Carrie Adell Strahorn's description of the preparations for her own wedding, which took place in Northern Illinois immediately before her emigration to Wyoming in 1877.

> It was really funny last night to hear him [her fiancee] tell Rev. Hutchinson, the minister, that the bride-to-be wanted the word "obey" left out of the ceremony because there is Woman's Suffrage in Wyoming, and suggest, "If you don't want to leave it out entirely, just put it in my part, for I've been running wild so long I just want to be obliged to obey somebody."[87]

Domestic weddings in this period were formal occasions, even in the homes of those of slender means. Jessie Hill Rowland, whose father was a minister on the Kansas frontier in the 1870s, remembers accompanying him to a wedding held in a poor family's house, which consisted of a single room dug two feet below ground level, with only a bed, a table, a bench, and two chairs (one without a seat) for furnishings, as well as a stove and a motto hung over the door that read "God Bless our Home." When the Rowland family arrived, the mother of the bride was at the stove, preparing the wedding feast, but she stopped long enough to greet her guests "with all the dignity of the first lady of the land ... ":

> A sheet had been stretched across one corner of the room. The bride and groom were stationed behind this, evidently under the impression it would not be proper to appear until time for the ceremony, but they were in such close quarters and the sheet was so short it put one in minds of an ostrich when it tries to hide by sticking its head in the sand. ... [After the wedding], all sat down to the wedding supper. The sheet that had been hung across the corner of the room was taken down and spread over the table for a cloth.[88]

For this very poor family, much of the month's food rations had obviously gone into the festal meal for this wedding, which, Rowland reports, "consisted of ground

---

87. Carrie Adell Strahorn, *Fifteen Thousand Miles by Stage: A Woman's Unique Experience during Thirty Years of Path Finding and Pioneering from the Missouri to the Pacific and from Alaska to Mexico* (New York: Knickerbocker Press, 1911; reprint: Lincoln: University of Nebraska Press, 1988), 8.
88. Stratton, *Pioneer Women*, 135–36.

dried carrots with seven different kinds of sauce, all made of plums put up different ways, bread, butter and fried pork."[89]

The symbolic power of being married at home has not been lost on women and their families. In a 1983 interview for an oral history project of the National Extension Homemakers Council, Arkansas native Essie Simmons, then aged eighty-one, remembers a conversation with her father-in-law at her own wedding:

> We got married at four o'clock on Sunday afternoon, October 16, 1921. Jim had four nieces and they had gone out and found autumn leaves and flowers, and decorated the whole house. The women of the family had cooked a wonderful wedding supper, and they had invited the family. Jim's father said to me after the marriage ceremony, "Jim was married on the exact same spot he was born." He was born February 22 when the house was so cold they moved Ma Simmons' bed near the fire.... And that was my wedding.[90]

Various other domestic rituals were a part of many weddings, some of which can be traced back to pre-Christian times. Many of these are designed to ensure fertility, long life, or protection from harm for the couple, and vary widely by geographical region. The "jumping of the broom," which many scholars believe was an African custom transported to the New World with the forced diaspora of African people in the eighteenth and nineteenth centuries, is described by Tempie Herndon, who recalls her wedding before the Civil War, which was held "on de front porch of de Big House" at an "alter Mis' Betsy done fixed":

> Everybody come stand round to watch. Marse George hold de broom about a foot high off de floor. De one dat jump over it backwards, and never touch handle, gwine boss de house. If both of dem jump over without touchin' it, dey won't gwine be no bossin', dey just gwine be congenial. I jumped first, and you ought to seed me. I sailed right over dat broom stick same as a cricket. But when Exter jump de broom...his feets was so big...dat dey got all tangled up in dat broom.[91]

---

89. Ibid.

90. Eleanor Arnold, ed., *Voices of American Homemakers: An Oral History Project of the National Extension Homemakers Council* (Columbus, Ohio: NEHC, 1985), 89.

91. Tempie Herndon, in *Life under the "Peculiar Institution": Selections from the Slave Narrative Collection*, ed. Norman R. Yetman (New York: Holt, Rinehart and Winston, 1970), 164. She continues to say, "Dat de prettiest altar I ever seed. Back against the rose vine dat was full of red roses, Mis' Betsy done put tables filled with flowers, and white candles. She done spread down a bed sheet, sure 'nough a linen sheet, for us to stand on, and dey was a white pillow to kneel down on."

(The sad reality for this couple, as it was with so many slave couples, was sep-aration by their respective owners.[92] Herndon concludes her narrative by saying that, "After the weddin' we went down to de cabin Mis' Betsy done all dressed up, but Exter couldn's stay no longer den dat night 'cause he belonged to Marse Snipes Durham and he had to go back home.")

Women and the Rituals of the Deathbed

Many of us in the industrialized West easily forget that for most of Christian history dying and death have been domestic events that took place at home rather than clinical events that occurred in places such as hospitals.[93] The rituals around the deathbed have been some of the most significant and well-attested of all domestic rituals, recorded in innumerable memoirs, obituaries, and in the *vitae* of the saints, serving as testimonies to the life of faith and as preparations for the life to come for the dying person. Historically, however, dying has been not only a domestic event, but a public event as well: Christian men and women have most often died as they were born, in a room full of people, and the rituals of dying and death have often been a ritual event of the dying person's whole social network, with each person playing a designated part in the drama. Philippe Ariès has described the premodern deathbed liturgy as "a public ceremony organized and presided over by the dying individual and following a standard protocol."[94] We can see this in the scene at the deathbed of St. Melania the Younger (c. 383–438):

> When the distinguished women of the city learned of her imminent death, they all came, and she, having seen them for a short while, at last said: "Lo, the heavens are opening, and I see an ineffable light and a suspended crown." And she departed with these words. Then there broke forth great

---

92. Because of the potential for slave marriages to be terminated by the terms of their ownership or by sale to a distant owner, many churches debated the appropriateness of their involvement in slave weddings. On the one hand, the church had an interest in supporting stable relationships among slaves (as well as regulating sexuality), but on the other they were anxious about the church's involvement in marriages that were likely to be interrupted. In 1858, the all-Black Wood River [Baptist] Association came to this solution: "QUERY — if a slave man is married to a slave woman, and should they be separated by the master . . . and marry another, is he or she guilty of bigamy? RESOLVED, That we believe the marriage of slaves to be morally binding, yet we do not believe it to be legal. We would, however, caution the churches to look well into the matter before they act." Cited in Mechal Sobel, *Trabelin' On: The Slave Journey to an Afro-Baptist Faith* (Princeton, N.J.: Princeton University Press, 1988), 178. Sometimes the vows in slave weddings were changed from "Until death us do part" to "Until death *or distance* us do part."

93. Not until the 1930s, with the United States taking the lead, did people begin to die in hospitals. Now between 80 percent and 90 percent of people die in the West in hospitals.

94. Philippe Ariès, *Essais sur de la Mort en Occident du Moyen age a nos Jours* (Paris: Seuil, 1975), 19.

weeping and wailing, raised by both her husband and the women. When the lament quieted down, they prepared the funeral bath.[95]

The narrative of the last moments of Alice Grisby in 1538 gives us another example of the public nature of the process, as well as a sense of the deep religious significance it held for the participants. As she lay on her bed in her house in Aldermanbury, Grisby's priest and women friends sat anxiously around her, "imploring her to 'look upon the sacrament,' 'to remember the passion of Christ' ":

> They "knocked her upon the breast," and pleaded, "What, will you die like a hell hound and a beast, not remembering your Maker?" At the last, Alice did "knock herself upon the breast," and looked up at the sacrament, and "so continued until the extreme pains of death." So she died a good Catholic. The relief of her friends and neighbours about her way of dying (*ars moriendi*) says much about the collective anxiety of the community for the Christian life of its members.[96]

The sheer numbers of such deathbed scenes in literature from the fourth century onwards, in which women play a critical role as ritual actors, attests to their symbolic and emotional significance for women. The final conversations with the dying — and the details of gifts given, hymns sung, psalms and other Bible verses recited, and gestures made — have been reported in obituaries and memorial volumes, and the pious biographies of the saints, usually in stylized form, serving to heighten certain ritual expectations among literate women of all social classes. As one commentator says, in all of these cases, "death was structured around female rituals with close friends assuming major roles at this time."[97] Little girls learned at a very young age the importance of these deathbed rituals and were expected to play their own part. In an mid-nineteenth-century illustration from a book of cautionary tales for young people, a small girl stands by the bedside of a young woman. The caption reads, "Charlotte is very ill, and has sent for her little cousin to give her a parting gift, for she thinks she may never see her again; and Susie promises to value it, and to remember Charlotte's teaching and be a good girl, and learn not to be afraid to die; but hope to meet her in heaven."[98]

---

95. Cited in Sharon E. J. Gerstel, "Painted Sources for Female Piety in Medieval Byzantium," *Dumbarton Oaks Papers* 52 (1998): 101.

96. Brigden, *London and the Reformation*, 22–23.

97. Jane Tibbetts Schulenbourg, *Forgetful of Their Sex: Female Sanctity and Society, ca. 500–1100* (Chicago: University of Chicago Press, 1998), 359.

98. *Pictures for Sunshine.*

Sometimes, of course, the official rituals of the church have intertwined with the domestic rituals of sickness and dying. Those who were morbidly ill might be brought communion, and the preparation for death has also at times involved calling for clergy to anoint the dying person and to receive his or her confession. But this was never an invariable practice. In post-Revolution France, for example, the clergy were suspected of using the occasion of a death to "use their spiritual leverage over the dying to exact promises of financial gifts. . . ." The parishioners of Douce in Maine-et-Loire, for example, wrote (May 20, 1831) to the prefect that their abbé Martin had been heard to say at the deathbed of a woman parishioner, "Give, give, you owe nothing to your children!"[99] But even when perfectly appropriate clerical activities at the deathbed did take place, it would be a serious mistake to interpret them as understood to be somehow more potent than or superior to the liturgy of death presided over by women as a part of their care of those they love. For Christians who have died at home (in other words, the vast majority of all Christians), the responsibility for ensuring that all of the rituals of death — including those administered by the clergy — were rendered with dignity and care has historically been the responsibility of women as a part of their overall domestic responsibility.

As we move into the nineteenth century, the "beautiful death" came to be understood to have certain essential components, and was choreographed to fit the dramatic conventions of a given period and community. Published obituaries gave the stylized "beautiful death" both a wider audience and a high degree of authority; in the *Arminian Magazine* from 1804 to 1821, for example, the obituary column in which these deathbed scenes were detailed was entitled "The Grace of God Manifested." As one historian says:

> Deaths of family members became worshipful events, with the dying person
> recapitulating her or his "religious history" and hopes for heaven, as rela-
> tives and friends took turns reading the Bible, praying, and singing the dying

---

99. Thomas A. Kselman, *Death and the Afterlife in Modern France* (Princeton, N.J.: Princeton University Press, 1993), 99. This was certainly an understandable fear, because clergy had the power to withhold the sacraments of anointing, penance, and communion from the dying, thus opening the way for the "spiritual blackmail" of parishioners who might otherwise be reluctant to share their estates with the church. This was also the motivation for legislation at various times that prevented the clergy from drawing up and witnessing wills. In England, however, the practice was common; indeed the Order for the Visitation of the Sick in the *Book of Common Prayer* (1662) enjoins the priest to encourage the sick person to draw up a will (which the clergy often wrote for him or her), and some seventeenth- and eighteenth-century editions included a preamble for this purpose. So, it is not surprising that one of the witnesses for the will of Anne Ashby, a wealthy widow who died at the end of February 1515, was her parish priest in Rickmansworth, Thomas Cotton, who wrote the document with his own hand. He was also a beneficiary, being left Anne Ashby's beads of "white ambre gawdid with silver and gylt and corall." See Margaret Aston, *Faith and Fire: Popular and Unpopular Religion, 1350–1600* (London: Hambledon, 1993), 246.

one's best-loved hymns. [Frances] Willard's journal is punctuated throughout with detailed descriptions of many such worshipful events shortly after they happened or of fond, nostalgic reminiscences of them long after they had occurred.[100]

Eighteenth-century newspapers in the American colonies frequently carried accounts of the final hours of local inhabitants, together with last words from the dying person alerting others about the spiritual perils of dying unprepared. "The Declaration, Dying Warning and Advice of Rebekah Chamblitt" (Boston, 1733) represents a common type. As she lay dying, Chamblitt is said to have made the following confession to the friends gathered at her bedside:

> My mispence of precious Sabbaths lies as a heavy burden upon me; that when I might have gone to the House of God, I have been indifferent, and suffer's a small matter to keep me from it. What would I now give, had I better improv'd the Lord's Day! I tell you, verily, your lost Sabbaths will sit heavy upon you, when you come into the near prospect of Death and Eternity.[101]

Many women in this period carefully choreographed the "beautiful death" not only for their friends and their relatives, but for themselves as well. When Eugénie la Ferronay was dying in Naples in the 1830s, she ensured that she would be surrounded with roses and orange trees, and she sang for her friends, "as gay as a bird, brilliant like a ray of sunshine." With her family gathered around, she declared, "Oh...how beautiful life is! What then will heaven be? Is *death worth more than all that?*"[102] Such deathbed vignettes could be found not only in the pages of pious tracts and religious magazines, but also in more secular publications and on the stage; women of all social classes and religious persuasions did their best to imitate the scenes described (see fig. 23).[103]

One example of the kind of deathbed scene that was envisioned by the Victorian Christian can be seen in the description of the death of "Mrs. Simpson,"

---

100. Carolyn de Swarte Gifford, "'My Own Methodist Hive': Frances Willard's Faith as Disclosed in Her Journal, 1855–1870," in *Spirituality and Social Responsibility: Vocational Vision of Women in the United Methodist Tradition*, ed. R. Keller (Nashville: Abingdon, 1993), 85.

101. Cited in Carol Berkin and Leslie Horowitz, eds., *Women's Voices, Women's Lives: Documents in Early American History* (Boston: Northeastern University Press, 1998), 150.

102. Michela Del Giorgio, "The Catholic Model," in *History of Women in the West*, vol. 4: *Emerging Feminism from Revolution to World War*, ed. Genevieve Fraisse and Michelle Perrot (Cambridge, Mass.: Belknap Press of Harvard University Press, 1993), 197.

103. See Maurice J. Quinlan, *Victorian Prelude: A History of English Manners 1700–1830* (Hamden, Conn.: Archon Books, 1965), 194–95.

reported by her friend Julia Foote (1823–1900), the first African Methodist Episcopal Church Zion preacher and evangelist, and the first woman to be ordained
deacon (and only the second woman to be ordained elder) in that denomination.
"As the morning dawned," Foote recalls:

> Mrs. Simpson sank into a quiet slumber, which lasted several hours. She
> awoke singing: "How happy are they who their Savior obey, / And have laid
> up their treasure above." She was comparatively free from pain for several
> days, though very weak. She talked to all who came to see her of salvation
> free and full. Her last morning on earth came. She was peaceful and serene,
> with a heavenly smile upon her countenance. She asked me to pray, which
> I did with streaming eyes and quivering voice. She then asked us to sing the
> hymn, "O For a thousand tongues to sing/My great Redeemer's praise." She
> sang with us in a much stronger voice than she had used for many days. As
> we reached the last verse, she raised herself up in bed, clapped her hands
> and cried: "He sets the prisoner free! Glory! Glory! I am free! They have
> come for me!" She pointed toward the east. Her mother asked her who had
> come. She said, "Don't you see the chariots and horses? Glory! Glory to the
> blood!" She dropped back upon her pillow, and was gone. She had stepped
> aboard the chariot, which we could not see, but we felt the fire.[104]

Although this is a written account, the huge number of such descriptions handed
on by word of mouth must also be taken into account in calculating their power.
To "die well," to choreograph your own death and the deaths of others, to play
your part in the rituals at the bedside of the dying: all of this was women's liturgical
work, played out on the domestic stage. But all too soon, the rites of death moved
out "into the open" as a part of the church's formal burial rites.

The Rituals of Burial

Before the rituals of death moved into the larger public sphere, women traditionally undertook further forms of domestic liturgy involving the preparation of
the body for burial. In the very earliest descriptions of women's roles after the
death of a Christian — that is, from the third century — we find them laying out,
washing, and dressing the corpse. If the deceased was a newborn infant, then the
midwife or godmother (if she had been present at the birth) would perform these

---

104. Julia Foote, *A Brand Plucked from the Fire: An Autobiographical Sketch by Mrs. Julia Foote*
(Cleveland: W. F. Schneider, 1879), 195.

tasks; otherwise it would be the female head of household or a "senior friend."[105] In his *Life of Macrina* (c. 327–79), Gregory of Nyssa complains that a rather self-important woman called Lampadion, the leader of a group of deaconesses, was bustling around after his sister Macrina's death, claiming that she "knew Macrina's wishes about burial exactly."[106] She seems to have "dismissed with great finality his mild suggestion that to put finer clothing on Macrina's body as a last respectful office before burial would not go amiss. She took charge of the body and the preparations for burial and the behavior of the sisters at the ceremony."[107] When Melania the Younger died, her sisters dressed her in the clothes of other saints, both male and female, since they thought that "it was fitting that she should be buried in the garments of those whose virtues she had acquired while she was alive."[108] Fourteen hundred years later, the role of female friends in a death had hardly changed, as we can see from Dorothy Howard's memories of the deaths of five neighbor children in a fire in East Texas at the turn of the twentieth century. While her own father, the father of the children, and other male friends went off to the sawmill to prepare the five small coffins, Dorothy's mother "washed and ironed Little Brother's baby dress and a white dimity (I had outgrown) to take with her to Mrs. Hughey's, where she, Mrs. Hughey, and Mrs. Irwin were to wash and dress the five little children for their coffins."[109]

Some women became acknowledged specialists in performing the rituals of birth and death, as is seen in this description:

> Mademoiselle Neau of Doue-la-Fontaine in Anjou, who practiced as a burial expert (ensevelisseuse) in the early twentieth century, described placing the dead in their shrouds "as if they were babies," a comparison that has also struck some contemporary ethnographers. In the Nievre it was not uncommon for the same woman to be both the midwife (accoucheuse) and the ensevelisseuse. On both occasions women specialists watched over the critical passage in the life of the individual and the family, affirming their entry into a new stage of existence and a new relationship with each other.[110]

---

105. A remnant of this activity in the contemporary West might be the task of choosing the clothes in which the deceased will be buried.

106. Gregory of Nyssa, *Life of Saint Macrina*, ed. Kevin Corrigan (Toronto: Peregrina, 1987), 114.

107. Gillian Cloke, *"The Female Man of God": Women and Spiritual Power in the Patristic Age, A.D. 350–450* (London: Routledge, 1995), 208.

108. This according to her friend and biographer Gerontius, writing about 452. Elizabeth A. Clark, *The Life of Melania the Younger: Introduction, Translation, and Commentary* (New York and Toronto: Edwin Mellen Press, 1984), 81–82.

109. Dorothy Howard, *Dorothy's World: Childhood in Sabine Bottom, 1902–1910* (Englewood Cliffs, N.J.: Prentice Hall, 1977), 75.

110. Kselman, *Death and the Afterlife in Modern France*, 51.

Once a body had been washed and dressed, whether in ordinary clothes or in a shroud,[111] women would ensure that it was properly "laid out," which almost since the beginning of Christian history has meant placing it in a traditional position with the hands folded across the breast and eyes shut. Often, the preparations having been made, neighbors and friends would make a formal farewell visit (see fig. 24). In nineteenth-century France, the rituals of this formal visit became gradually more elaborate:

> After the body had been washed and clothed, it was displayed on the bed, and neighbors would pass by for a final visit and farewell. In the course of the century it became increasingly common to place rosaries, crucifixes, and other pious objects in the hands of the deceased. A table next to the bed held a burning candle and a pitcher of holy water, which the guests would sprinkle on the dead with a branch of laurel or a palm preserved from Palm Sunday....[112]

Women have also acted as celebrants of the rituals of lamentation. In the earliest centuries of Christian history, women were clearly understood to be the community mourners,[113] as is attested by their almost invariable presence in the iconography found in the parts of churches where funeral rites took place. "By placing images of women on the walls of the narthex and in other funerary contexts within the church," one historian of early Christian art opines, "the donor guaranteed continuous intercessory protection through the female saints who participated in the ongoing lamentation over the deceased."[114] Women in this early period also remained in physical contact with the body through the burial, and later at the exhumation of bones.

But women's oversight of the domestic rituals of death would eventually come to an end, at least in the industrialized West. Indeed, the most far-reaching change in the role of women in all of domestic liturgy has been the rise in the professionalization of death from the eighteenth century onwards: "In a long Victorian perspective, the bereaved family steadily lost the help of relatives, neighbors, and

---

111. Among some Christians, the shroud replaced ordinary clothing as burial dress, and women were also responsible for placing the body in its shroud for burial. The power of the economics of death can be seen in this question of shrouds. In England, woolen shrouds were required by law in 1678 as an incentive to the wool trade, with a five-pound penalty imposed for noncompliance. Those in the upper classes were willing to accept this fine in order that they might be laid out in a linen shroud. See Julian Litten, "The Funeral Trade in Hanoverian England, 1714–1760," in *The Changing Face of Death: Historical Accounts of Death and Disposal*, ed. Peter C. Jupp and Glennys Howarth (New York: St. Martin's, 1997), 49.

112. Ibid.

113. The rituals of grieving have most often involved cutting off the hair, the wearing of a black veil, and among the wealthy an elaborate arched crown to attach it.

114. Gerstel, "Painted Sources for Female Piety in Medieval Byzantium," 110.

clergy, and accepted the proffered and additional service of other entrepreneurial groups, including funeral directors, drapers, memorial masons, cemetery staff, and later, medical professionals."[115] The transfer of domestic rituals from the hands of women into the hands of male "death experts" (morticians and their staff) marks a significant deterioration in women's liturgical lives. "The desire of undertakers to utilise their newly acquired 'scientific' techniques, combined with the realisation that the body was fast becoming the key to funeral rituals, meant that they were keen to take custody of the corpse."[116] Once the corpse was handed over to undertakers, and later when the body of the dying person was handed over to the hospitals, the rituals of death and dying largely passed from women's control. The deep sense that the rituals surrounding death were by their nature women's rituals can be seen in the various complaints expressed about the new funeral industry. In her *Reflections on the Present Condition of the Female Sex* (1798), Priscilla Wakefield makes the following recommendation: "Every undertaker should employ women for the express purpose of supplying the female dead with those things which are requisite. How shocking the idea of our persons being exposed, even after death, to the observation of a parcel of undertaker's men."[117] (Although this admonition was not generally followed, the undertaker's wife usually was responsible for making shrouds at least for the next fifty years.)

We tend to think that even if there is no equality in life, at least there is equality in death, but this is hardly the case when we look at Christian burial. Like the story of marriage, the story of the burial of the dead is really multiple stories, one that follows the rich and another that follows the poor, one that follows men and another that follows women. Just as they were responsible for the rituals of dying, until the rise of the modern funeral industry, women were almost solely responsible for the significant rituals that took place before and after the interment (and, in some communities, only rarely attended the burial itself). Because these rituals held a high degree of religious and social significance, the experience of the rich and that of the poor diverged from the moment the person was pronounced dead.[118] Indeed, we already begin to see the differences

---

115. Peter C. Jupp, "Enon Chapel: No Way for the Dead," in *The Changing Face of Death: Historical Accounts of Death and Disposal*, ed. Peter C. Jupp and Glennys Howarth (New York: St. Martin's, 1997), 102.

116. Glennys Howarth, "Professionalising the Funeral Industry in England, 1700–1900," in *The Changing Face of Death*, ed. Jupp and Howarth, 124.

117. Priscilla Wakefield, *Reflections on the Present Condition of the Female Sex* (London: J. Johnson, 1798), 165.

118. Perhaps the one time that the experience of burial for rich and poor was equalized was in time of plague. During times of cholera epidemic, interments were particularly horrible, with hasty burials, coffins containing lime, and shrouds dipped in tar. See S. J. White, *Christian Worship and Technological Change* (Nashville: Abingdon, 1997), 29–34.

between rich and poor in the rituals at the bedside. For example, until the late nineteenth century, throughout Western Europe certainly and other places more occasionally, the extended family and close friends gathered at the bedside for a final farewell, summoned by the "passing bell," rung from the church tower once for each year of the dying person's age. Because there was a fee for this activity in most parishes, poorer families would have foregone the luxury, relying instead on the more demotic ritual of "pious gossip." Such differences between rich and poor only increase as we draw progressively nearer to putting the body into the ground.

For the rich, a burial and its associated events would have likely been the single largest expense of a given year. Like weddings, funerals were occasions for public display of a family's wealth and prestige, and were often very well-attended. Most usually, the single largest expenditure was for food and drink for guests after the funeral. The accounts ledger of Lady Gieselle Baillie (1692–1733), a Scottish noblewoman, gives some sense of the costs involved:

	1698 Expenses of my mother's funeral			
	To her dead linen	£60		
	To her coffin	£76		
	To charge her lying in the church	£29		
	For breaking the ground	£14	10s	
	To the bathells	£7	5s	
	For the morcloth [shroud]	£11	12s	
	To the bell man	£2	8s	
	To the poor	£6		
	For coach and hearse	£2		
	For the man that drove the hearse	£2		
But also				
	For plumcake and biscuits	£54		
	For writing letters and paper		14s	
	For drink money to the surgeon's man		7s	8d
	A Total of	£263	56s	8d[119]

The elaborate preparations of the rich to bury their dead often took considerable time, and in some cases the burial occurred several months after the death, during which time the body would be embalmed and encased in a lead-lined coffin, or in an earlier period, disemboweled and boiled.[120] For the poor, things have

---

119. Robert Scott Montcrief, ed., *Household Book of Lady Gieselle Baillie, 1692–1733* (Edinburgh: Edinburgh University/Scottish History Society, 1911), 79.

120. Peter Jupp and Glennys Howarth, eds., *The Changing Face of Death: Historical Accounts of Death and Disposal* (New York: St. Martin's, 1997), 158. Queen Eleanor was prepared for her postmortem journey from Nottinghamshire to London in 1290 by the Ghilbertine nuns just south of Lincoln.

been quite different. Before the rise of the modern funeral industry, a coffin would have been considered an undue luxury, and poor people would either have done without a coffin altogether, burying their dead in a simple shroud, or would have used a reusable communal coffin to carry the body from home to church and from church to grave. Certainly the idea of putting perfectly good clothing into the ground to decay would have seemed to the poor a needless extravagance. Delay was expensive and in many periods seen to be dangerous (both spiritually and hygienically) without expensive embalming procedures, and so the poor woman would have been buried much sooner after death than the rich woman.

But on the whole, while women have a great deal to say about the domestic rituals of dying and its immediate aftermath, when it comes to the actual burial of the dead, women grow silent. When the guilds were in operation, women retained some control over the rites of burial, but with the Reformation, the dissolution of fraternities and the sanctions placed on "superstitious devotions," and the restrictions on funeral and burial extravagance, "women's participation in the life of the parish had to be re-negotiated."[121] Often, these renegotiations resulted in women losing their role in the rites of burial. In some periods of Christian history, women have not been included among those who gathered at the gravesite. Funerals in the Reformed traditions in the sixteenth, seventeenth, and eighteenth centuries, for example, traditionally would have been male-only occasions; there is some suggestion that women were excluded from the funerals of the very wealthy in Georgian England.[122] In all periods, many women would have been kept home from funerals because of the need to tend small children, as Dorothy Howard recalls in her memoirs that only her father attended the burial of the neighbor children killed in the fire: "The next morning Papa dressed up

---

After her organs were removed and the cavity washed in vinegar and filled with salt and spices, she was wrapped in cere-cloth (cloth impregnated with wax) and then dressed in her regalia. The evisceration of the body of a saint had another purpose, of course; the internal organs could be divided among various sites for veneration. But in some instances it was not only the rich who practiced a delay between one ritual of death and another. Among some communities of slaves in the American South, a delay, sometimes by weeks or months, between burial and funeral often took place. "Mary Wright of Gracey, Kentucky later recalled that on at least one plantation where she resided, funeral services were held annually on the fourth Sunday in August. On that day, probably at the conclusion of the regular worship services, 'all the colored folks would take a basket dinner ter de church en each family dat had buried a nigger would pay der preacher te preach the sermon foh dat darkie dat died.'" At first this seems to have been a matter of expediency in rural areas where preachers were scarce; but later it came to be a matter of custom, even in the cities, among slaves and former slaves. William E. Montgomery, *Under Their Own Vine and Fig Tree: The African American Church in the South, 1865–1900* (Baton Rouge: Louisiana State University Press, 1993), 297.

121. Claire S. Schen, "Women and the London Parishes, 1500–1620," in *The Parish in English Life, 1400–1600,* ed. Katherine L. French, Gary Gibbs, and Beat A. Kümin (Manchester: Manchester University Press, 1997), 257.

122. No one would have attended such an elegant funeral without an explicit invitation, but no invitation cards for women survive, leading some to conclude that they were never issued.

and, alone, drove off in the buggy to the funeral. Mama and the children stood on the front gallery to watch the procession go by."[123] On the whole, we can say that women have not given the actual burial of their dead the same kind of ritual weight as the other kinds of domestic rituals of death over which they had more direct control.

But of course some women have been responsible not only for the rituals immediately before and immediately after the death of a friend or family member, but for their burial as well. Women in remote locations and very poor women generally have had to make do when it came to burial. Indeed, one of the reasons that the domestic rituals of death have been so important to women could indeed be that the rituals of the church on this occasion have sometimes been so uncertain. On the American, Australian, and Canadian frontiers, where many women buried child after child and some buried all of their children, women often found themselves without clergy to oversee the burial and had to rely on their own liturgical resources (see fig. 25). In a letter home dated 1874, one settler on the Western frontier of the United States poignantly describes the death and burial of her young son. Holding her baby as he takes his last breath, Elinore Stewart details the process of dressing his body and preparing it for interment. She then arranges for the making of the coffin:

> Clyde is a carpenter, so I wanted him to make the little coffin. He did it every bit, and I lined and padded it. Not that we couldn't afford to buy one or that our neighbors were not all that was kind and willing; but because it was a sad pleasure to do everything for our little first-born boy. As there had been no physician to help, so there was no minister to comfort, and I could not bear to let our baby leave the world without leaving any message to a community that sadly needed it. His little message to us had been love, so I selected a chapter from John and we had a funeral service, at which all our neighbors for thirty miles around were present.[124]

Indeed, this may perhaps be the most common kind of experience Christian women have had in the burial of their dead: tending to the sick person until the end, washing and dressing the body, arranging for a suitable box and burial dress, and seeing to it that the proper words are said over the body.[125] Some women

---

123. Howard, Dorothy's World, 75.

124. Stewart, Letters of a Woman Homesteader, 190–91.

125. Other women have lived in fear of the long-term consequences of failing to perform the proper rituals of death and burial. Some women believed that their behavior at a burial and attention to the rituals of mourning had serious spiritual consequences. Former slave Jesse Collins was proud to report that when her husband died, she had given him a "fine funeral," after which she went into deep mourning; she wore continually a "long widow's veil" and went every day to visit the cemetery,

had further ritual obligations still. In 1877, one young woman living on the high plains who took on the care of many young brothers and sisters after her mother's death told a friend, "Why, I've been saving up for a tombstone [for my mother] for twelve years, but I gave to help Pa once and awhile, and I sometimes think I will never get enough money saved. It's kind of hard on three dollars a week."[126]

"and cry all day by his grave." But this seems not to have been sufficient honor for the deceased. Collins continues on to say, "But his spirit started to haunt me somethin' terrible. I had chickens and every night he'd come back wearin' a white apron and shoo my chickens. Every mornin' some of 'em would be dead.... Then I got mad and I quit goin' to the cemetery and I took off my widow's veil. I put black pepper 'round the sills of all my doors. That stopped him." Cited in Sobel, *Trabelin' On*, 47.

126. Jerrine Stewart, Letter to "Mrs. Coney," Burnt Fork, Wyoming, July 8, 1914. Stewart, *Letters on an Elk Hunt*, 71.

CHAPTER SEVEN

WOMEN AND
THE LITURGICAL ARTS

We sat on long hard benches. There was a little melodeon or small organ and a choir sang the morning hymn.... From the little organ came a short prelude, and a woman's voice, clear and sweet with deep cello notes, pealed out in sacred melody. —Cordelia McDowell, diary entry, 1877[1]

The liturgical life of the Christian church is not constructed solely of words in sequence, but of an interaction of sight and sound that combine to create a rich tapestry of visual and auditory associations. The liturgical arts — music, painting, architecture, sculpture, textiles — have always provided an avenue for women both to express their deepest sense of intimate religious encounter and to contribute to the worship experience of the wider church. Women have used the arts as a mode of theological expression and a mode of intensified participation in worship. The adornment of church buildings in various ways and the production of sacred sound has been important to every generation of Christian women, and even in circumstances in which they were restricted in the exercise of the whole range of artistic ministries, their creative impulses still managed to find expression in the context of worship.

In this chapter we look at two forms of women's liturgical art: sacred sound (music) and sacred objects (visual art, including church architecture). Little attempt is made to distinguish "high art" from "popular art" because, in the case of women certainly, the underlying motivation was the same for each. (Indeed, this discussion is probably weighted more heavily toward the latter, because the majority of women's artistic activity in and for worship has been undertaken by nonprofessional and untrained women artists.) Whatever form their artistic contributions have taken, however, women have almost invariably interpreted them

---

1. Joanna L. Stratton, *Pioneer Women: Voices from the Kansas Frontier* (New York: Simon and Schuster, 1981), 176.

as liturgical ministries of real significance, and in some situations, participation in the liturgical arts has been the most active liturgical ministry available to women.

Singing in Church

When we first begin to hear women's voices in the liturgy we hear them singing. Although we have little evidence of women as a distinct category of liturgical singers in the first two centuries of the church, we do hear over and over again that the whole congregation sings in worship "as with one mouth."[2] But soon, women do begin to be identified as having particular roles in the corporate singing of the congregation. In his Easter Hymns (c. 350), Ephraim the Syrian (c. 306–73) rejoices that "Again, O Lord, the recesses of our ears are filled/with the musical strains of the virgins . . . ," and he goes on to speak of the gathered community weaving a "magnificent crown" for the Risen Lord, each participant in the Easter liturgy adding a specific strand:

The bishop weaves into it his biblical exegesis as his flowers;
The presbyters their martyr stories,
   the deacons their lections, the young men their alleluias, the boys their
      psalms, the virgins their madrâshe [strophic hymns],
the rulers their achievements,
the lay people their virtues,
   Blessed is the one who has multiplied victories for us.[3]

---

2. Johannes Quasten, *Music and Worship in Pagan and Christian Antiquity* (Washington, D.C.: National Association of Pastoral Musicians, 1983), 77.

3. Many references to this women's hymn singing are found in this early period. The Canons of the Nestorian Synod describe the work and dress of consecrated virgins, who "should learn especially to recite the psalms, to care for divine worship and to take notice of the time for singing the madrash [hymns]." Canon 9 of the Nestorian Synod of Mar George I, 676, cited in ibid., 80. But by the time of Chrysostom, women's singing seems to have declined. "Shall I name still another treasure chest that has been robbed of its original beauty?" he laments to his congregation at Constantinople. "In times past all came together and sang the psalms as a community. This we no longer do. Formerly there was one heart and one soul in everyone, but today we can no longer perceive such harmony of soul and everywhere there is much discord." Homily 36 in Epist. I Corinthios (PG 61, 313). Was this simply general congregational apathy? Or was it because already there was a debate about the appropriateness of women's singing? Ambrose, Chrysostom's contemporary, in his commentary on Paul's injunction that women were to "keep silent" in the churches, says: "The Apostle commands women to be silent in church, but they may sing the psalms; it is fitting for every age and for both sexes." Enarratio in Ps. 1 (PL 14, 925). But at about the same time, we find an injunction against women's singing in the writing of Alexandria, Isidore of Pelusium (d. 438): "The apostles of the Lord, who wanted to put an end to idle talk in the churches, and who were our instructors in good behavior, wisely permitted women to sing psalms there. But as every divine teaching has been turned into its opposite, so this, too, had become an occasion of sin and laxity for the majority of the people. They do not feel compunction in hearing the divine hymns, but rather misuse the sweetness of melody to arouse passion, thinking it is no better than the songs of the stage. Thus it is necessary — if we

In the second half of the fourth century, the feisty and curious pilgrim traveler Egeria describes women's liturgical singing in Jerusalem, where she sees convents of nuns attached to the holy sites singing the psalms. As she reports that

> Every day before cockcrow all the gates of the Anastasis are opened and all the monks and virgins, or as they say here, the *monozantes* and *parthenae*, descend — not merely they but lay people, men and women, as well. . . . And from that hour until the break of day hymns and psalms are sung in alternate chant, and so too are the antiphons. And after each hymn, a prayer is said.[4]

In some places, women's liturgical singing became a particularly important weapon in the fight against heresy. When the disciples of the philosopher Bardasanes and his son Harmonius were disputing with Ephraem the Syrian, they gathered a great following with choirs of women (and of boys as well), who sang heterodox hymns in meetings and on the streets. But Ephraem fought back and established his own women's choirs, who went about the streets singing the hymns he had composed expressing a more orthodox theology.[5]

Some of these liturgical choirs of women singers seem to have been led by women. In some churches, consecrated virgins served as cantors,[6] and at the monastery of Arnisa in Pontus, a woman deacon called Lampadion "directed the choir of virgins, each with the rank of deacon."[7] Theodoret of Cyrus mentions in his *Church History* a woman named Publia, who also "had a choir of virgins who were praiseworthy for their lifelong virginity. . . ."

> At the time when the Emperor [Julian] died they sang more loudly than usual, for they considered the evildoer contemptible and ridiculous. They sang those songs most often which mocked the weakness of idols, and they said with David, "The idols of the pagans are silver and gold, the works

---

would seek what is pleasing to God and do that which is of public benefit — that we stop these women . . . from singing in church . . ." (Epistle I: 90; PG 78, 244–45).

4. G. E. Gingrass, *Egeria: Diary of a Pilgrimage* (New York: Newman Press, 1970), 12–15. Much of the liturgical singing Egeria witnesses, however, is done by choirs of boys.

5. An anonymous writer of the period describes the occasions: "When the holy Ephraem saw how they were all being torn away by the singing . . . he himself founded choirs of consecrated virgins, taught them the hymns and responses whose wonderful contents celebrated the birth of Christ, his baptism, fasting, suffering, resurrection, and ascension, as well as the martyrs and the dead. He had these virgins come to the church on the feasts of the Lord and on those of the martyrs, as they did on Sundays. He himself was in their midst as their father and the citharist of the Holy Spirit, and he taught them music and the laws of song." From the anthology of Assemani, *Bibliotheca Orientalis I* (Rome, 1720), 47–48.

6. The Arabic version of the *Canons of the Apostles* enumerates the participants in worship. Women are listed as being lectors, cantors, deacons, subdeacons. Canon 52 of the *Canons* directs children to the ambo, where the woman lector exercises her office. Quasten, *Music and Worship in Pagan and Christian Antiquity*, 81.

7. Gregory of Nyssa, *Vita Sanctae Macrinae* (PG 46, 988).

of human hands. Those who make them are like them, and so are all who trust in them."[8]

This kind of women's singing at funerals and gravesites is hardly unusual; as we have seen, ritual mourning has always been among their most common liturgical functions, and the central role of women singers at funerals is often noted in contemporary descriptions and injunctions. In the Canons of Mar George I (676), nuns are instructed "on the day of burial [to] sing the *madrâshe* while following the coffin, and on the memorial days they shall recite the *madrâshe*."[9] Gregory of Nyssa recalls the crowd of women who attended the funeral procession of his sister Macrina, and who began to weave lamentations into their singing of the psalms, "for she had been much loved for her works of charity."[10]

As we move into the fifth century, the prohibitions against women's liturgical singing in congregations increase, and these usually cite the Pauline injunction about women "keeping silence"; information about women's actual singing roles begins to evaporate at about the same time. But then also, groups of pious women were beginning to live together in community, in the first instance attached to cathedral churches and elected and ordained for special service to the church. Traditionally called "canonesses," these women had responsibility for daily prayer in cathedrals, for singing the appointed psalms, canticles, and responses. But gradually the canonesses were turned out of their cathedrals by male canons, and forced to live and worship separately under an existing rule, such as that of St. Benedict.[11] But in at least one case, cathedral canonesses managed to retain their ancient liturgical role, including their responsibility for singing the office and the mass in the cathedral church. At the Abbey Church of St. Waudru, which functioned as the cathedral in Mons, Belgium, canonesses sang the musical settings of the services until the eighteenth century, despite numerous attempts on the part of the male canons to eject them.[12] In the twelfth century, when the count of Hainault took over the right to appoint clergy to the cathedral, he sought to replace all the canonesses with male canons. One morning when the canonesses arrived at the church, they found the door closed, and the canons inside had already begun chanting the mass.

---

8. Cited in Quasten, *Music and Worship in Pagan and Christian Antiquity*, 81.
9. Ibid., 164.
10. *De Vita Macrinae* (PG 46, 992).
11. Joan Morris, *The Lady Was a Bishop: The Hidden History of Women with Clerical Ordination and the Jurisdiction of Bishops* (London: Macmillan, 1973), 11.
12. See L. Deviller, *Chatres du Chapitre de Sainte Waudru se Mons*, 2 vols. (Brussels: Archives de Hainault; Mons: Archives de l'Etat, 1884–1906).

But they mistakenly were singing the Common of Martyrs instead of the Proper of Saint Vincent, which was correct on that day. The canonesses forthwith from outside the church intoned the correct chant. The Count thereupon changed his mind and sided with the women, for he realized that they were more precise in maintaining the liturgical regulations. He turned out the canons and permitted the canonesses to take their place.[13]

In other places, however, the cathedral canonesses were successfully ejected, as was the case in the twelfth century in Milan when the group of women serving the church of St. Dei Genetrix was forced to become a contemplative order rather than continuing in service to the church.

Evidence of the singing of communities of women in religious orders is more readily available. Sometimes the nuns seem to have conducted their own sung services, such as at Kecharitomene, an Orthodox convent near Constantinople, where the abbess led the singing of the seven Daily Offices and the nuns sang the hymns or tropes at mass.[14] Some of these monastic communities are quite remarkable in their encouragement of women's choral song. The convent of Las Huelgas in Spain is one that was particularly renowned for its music and for its trained choir of girl singers. By the time of Abbess Berenguela (1241–88), there were one hundred nuns in the choir and forty girls in training. The high quality of their singing is evident in some of the musical manuscripts that were a part of the convent library, many of these dating from the thirteenth century. As one musicologist writes:

> The very complicated polyphonic motets and sequences show that the mon-astery must have had a very highly trained choir in order to sing such musical compositions. The motets in the codex cover the widest possible repertory of the most ancient tunes and give evidence of contract with schools of music in many different countries, such as the schools at Notre-Dame, Paris and Montpelier in France, besides those in Germany and other parts of Spain.[15]

It is difficult to believe that this choir was unique to Las Huelgas, and similar choirs must have served the liturgical needs of convents all over Europe during

---

13. "In the *Annals of Hainault* by Jacques de Guise there is a miniature illuminating the way the clergy, who attempted to eject the canonesses from their choir stalls in the Collegiate and Parish Church of Saint Waudru, were themselves ejected." Morris, *The Lady Was a Bishop*, 11.

14. Alice Mary Talbot, "Women's Space in Byzantine Monasteries," *Dumbarton Oaks Papers* 52 (1998): 125.

15. Morris, *The Lady Was a Bishop*, 91. This is the *Codex Musical* de Las Huelgas, which was copied from an earlier manuscript transcribed by Maria Gonzalez de Aguero about 1325.

this period. But unfortunately, the presence of such choirs of women in convents tells us nothing about what ordinary laywomen might have been singing (if anything) in their parish churches. By the fifteenth century certainly, and probably much earlier, choirs of men and boys had taken over the singing in the cathedrals and minster churches,[16] and if any liturgical singing was left to the congregation (that is, to laymen or women) in other places, we have little evidence of it until the sixteenth century.

Clearly, however, women's liturgical singing took place in other places than churches: at home, at cemeteries and shrines, and in processions. We see this in the enormous range and variety of folk music with religious themes, and in the records of what seems to be the residue of ancient choral music practices. Such is the case recorded in southwest Wales in the sixteenth century, where at Christmas the men and women of the village "come over to Church at about Cock crowing [2 am] and bring either candles or torches with them, which they set to burn, everyone, one or more upon the Grave of his departed Friend, and there set themselves to sing Halsmyod [responsorial psalms] and continue so to welcome the approaching Festival till Prayer time."[17] This ritual of women's graveyard singing very likely predates the coming of Christianity to Wales, and interweaves practices from the old winter solstice rites into the celebration of Christmas. The important thing here, however, is that even if women's congregational singing had likely disappeared from the ordinary worship in churches by about the eighth century in the West, it survived in the other kinds of settings in which women's liturgical lives unfolded.

A rise in vernacular hymnody seems to have occurred in the late Middle Ages in some places, but it was left to the continental reformers to restore congregational hymnody and psalmody to a central place in worship and thereby to return women's singing to the normal church service. The writers of hymns and metrical psalms envisioned multiple uses for their compositions: in family worship and private meditation, as teaching tools, and as expressions of faith for singing at the sickbed and deathbed. In church, women soon joined with men to form choirs that sang psalms, hymns, and anthems in church. John Byng, a self-described "connoisseur of church music" who traveled from church to church in the early eighteenth century recording his perceptions of the music he heard,

---

16. Indeed, in the Anglican family of churches, the prohibition of women in cathedral choirs was reinvigorated with the Oxford Movement in the nineteenth century, both in England and America. The cathedral choir of St. John the Divine in New York City was said to be the only Anglican cathedral choir regularly to include women and girls, which it has done since 1975.

17. Erasmus Saunders, *A View of the State of Religion in the Diocese of St. David's* (St. David's, 1721; reprinted Cardiff: University of Wales Press, 1949), 35.

describes both choir and congregational singing involving women.[18] At Folkingham in Lincolnshire, for example, Byng mentions not only the "numerous and
decent congregation," but also "a singing loft crowded" with singers, among whom
was one lady in a blue silk bonnet, "who sung notably."

For nearly three centuries, Protestant Christians understood choral singing as
a ministry in which women had a full and indispensable part. In early America, mixed choirs of men and women are common in churches from at least the
first quarter of the eighteenth century, and perhaps earlier, and many congregations established "singing schools" in order to ensure high-quality music. But
in the mid-nineteenth century, with the attempts on the part of the Ecclesiolo-
gists and Tractarians in England to return to medieval patterns of worship and
church architecture, the presence of women in choirs was discouraged among
congregations in the Church of England that were influenced by these movements. Even African American Episcopalians, which had traditionally taken a
more egalitarian view of music leadership, were affected by this trend, but the
resulting limitation of women choristers in black Anglican churches seems to
have been of shorter duration than among their white counterparts. One historian of the African American Episcopal Church experience states that, "By
the 1890s, we know for certain that women had been [re-]admitted to church
choirs. At St. Matthew's (Detroit) where women were admitted to the choir
in 1892, they were not allowed in the choir stalls but had to occupy the
front pews."[19]

In churches without the resources for a choir, women often took it upon themselves to "get the singing going" (see fig. 26). Lillian Van Natta Smith recalled
that at the turn of the twentieth century in the small community of Wilmington
(Kansas) an abandoned log cabin served the neighborhood as both schoolhouse
and church.

> All the neighbors gathered there on the Sabbath for Sunday School and
> church. Mother had a good voice, so had my Father and they were chosen
> to start all the songs. We had no musical instrument of any kind, just an old
> style tuning fork owned by L. W. Bush, a teacher of music. He would strike
> the tone, and all begin to sing. I remember how happy they all seemed.[20]

---

18. John Byng, *The Torrington Diaries, Containing Tours through England and Wales of the Honourable John Byng, 1781–1794*, 4 vols. (London: Eyre & Spottiswoode, 1934–38), 1:177.
19. Irene V. Jackson, "Music among Blacks in the Episcopal Church," in Irene Jackson, *More Than Dancing: Essays on Afro-American Music and Musicians* (Westport, Conn.: Greenwood, 1985), 108–25.
20. Stratton, *Pioneer Women*, 173.

Mary Ellicott Arnold and Mabel Reed, who spent sixteen months in the Klamath River area of northern California in 1908–9, describe the worship services they led among the Karok Indians and others of their near neighbors.[21] Arnold tells of the uncertain opening minutes of each service, just after the congregation has settled in: "At this point, Mabel is usually called in. She not only guides the tottering voices of the Indians, she guides my tottering voice as well.... We sing the same verse over eight or ten times, the sound rising in volume and intensity. Then we stop, draw a long breath, and get ready for the next carol. 'Peautiful song,' Jim remarks gravely."[22]

Music could be problematic in these small congregations (just as it could be in larger congregations), as women often report in their diaries and journals. Recalling her time in Cheyenne, Wyoming, as a young bride, Carrie Strahorn recalls an incident in 1877 when she happened to board a train for Nebraska in which the bishop of the diocese was also traveling. "There were nearly as many churches in Cheyenne in '77 as there are now [1925], but I hope there is less rivalry. The divine head, Rector Thomkins, of the Episcopalian diocese, was so angry that I preferred to sing in another choir than his, that he rode in the same Pullman car in a section opposite my own all the way to Omaha without seeing me."[23] Other women report that those wishing to disrupt worship services that they found offensive often used music to do so. Alice Curwen, the leader of the Quakers in Oyster Bay, New York, in the last quarter of the seventeenth century, reported having trouble with Ranters interrupting her meetings with "Roaring, Singing, and Dancing."[24] Women themselves used hymn singing as a form of protest. Ardent Sabbatarians allied themselves with temperance women to urge Sunday closings of saloons; often they held prayer meetings in front of the saloons on Sunday mornings, at which "hymns were sung and portions of the Scripture read."[25]

Women who had strong views on the matter of singing in church could not only influence the music of their congregation, but could use their religious song to influence the wider musical establishment. In the first quarter of the twentieth

---

21. See appendix 4.

22. Mary Ellicott Arnold and Mabel Reed, *In the Land of the Grasshopper Song: Two Women in the Klamath River Indian Country in 1908–09* (Lincoln: University of Nebraska Press, 1980), 173.

23. Carrie Adell Strahorn, *Fifteen Thousand Miles by Stage: A Woman's Unique Experience during Thirty Years of Path Finding and Pioneering from the Missouri to the Pacific and from Alaska to Mexico* (New York: Knickerbocker Press, 1911; reprint: Lincoln: University of Nebraska Press, 1988), 15.

24. David S. Lovejoy, *Religious Enthusiasm in the New World: Heresy to Revolution* (Cambridge, Mass.: Harvard University Press, 1985), 141.

25. Lillian Lewis Sutton, "'Changes Are Dangerous': Women and Temperance in Victorian England," in *Religion in the Lives of English Women, 1760–1930,* ed. Gail Malmgreen (Bloomington: Indiana University Press, 1986), 206.

century, virtually all black churches except the Pentecostalists rejected Gospel music as too "worldly," largely "because of its demonstrative delivery style and instrumental accompaniment, which closely [paralleled] that of Black secular music."[26] Blues and Gospel singer Mahalia Jackson (1911–72) writes of her initial experiences singing Gospel music in church: "In those days the big colored churches didn't want me and they didn't let me in. I had to make it my business to pick little basement-hall congregations and store-front churches and get their respect that way. When they began to see the crowds I drew, the big churches began to sit up and take notice."[27] At the age of seventeen, Jackson remembers being publicly denounced from the pulpit of a church in which she wished to sing. "O Shame! This shouting, and bouncing, and clapping [is] unseemly in church," the minister is reported to have said. But Jackson held her ground, replying to the preacher:

> I am serving God! You read the Bible — you see right there in Psalm 47: "O clap your hands, all ye people; shout to the Lord with the voice of a trumpet." I'm doing what the Bible tells me to do.... How can you sing Amazing Grace? How can you sing prayerfully of heaven and earth and all God's wonders without using your hands? I want my hands...my feet,...my whole body to say all that is in me. I say, "Don't let the devil steal the beat from the Lord!" The Lord doesn't like for us to act dead.[28]

The drawing power of women's singing was not lost on women evangelists, who have often used their own singing as a key element in their ministries. Amanda Smith (1837–1915), one of the early African American women circuit riders, remembers that in the early days of her revival work, "I used to sing a great deal, and somehow the Lord always blessed my singing."[29] She recalls a particular Sunday afternoon camp meeting in Ossining, New York, where a deacon called upon her to stand up on a stump so that people could hear her sing. She obliged, and soon a crowd of about four hundred persons had gathered around. After she sang several songs, the deacon said, "Sister Smith, suppose you tell the people your experience, how the Lord converted you." At that point, Smith recalls, "the

---

26. Lawrence Levine, *Black Culture and Black Consciousness* (New York: Oxford University Press, 1977), 183.

27. Cited in ibid.

28. Melonee V. Burnim, "The Black Gospel Music Tradition: A Complex of Ideology, Aesthetic, and Behavior," in *More than Dancing*, ed. Jackson, 152.

29. Amanda Smith, *An Autobiography: The Story of the Lord's Dealings with Mrs. Amanda Smith, the Coloured Evangelist* (Chicago: Meyer and Brother, Publishers, 1893), 194.

power of the Spirit" fell upon her, "and many of the people wept, and seemed deeply moved and interested."[30]

Even in Christian communities in which the Pauline injunction that women "keep silence" in church is taken very seriously, singing is generally exempt from the rule. In many of these traditions, congregational singing is not only the sole form of participation allowed to women, but the sole form of any kind of congregational participation in the entire service. This is certainly the case among Primitive Baptists in Appalachia, for example (in which, as one woman put it when asked about women's roles in worship, "they did not have a 'role'... and that's all there is to that!"[31]). In many Primitive Baptist congregations, women not only sing the hymns, but also feel free to request hymns from the song leader during that part of the service devoted to singing, and in this way they "direct the course of a meeting that is otherwise led by men."[32] The hymn choices these women make are taken from a fairly narrow repertoire, and there is little attempt to match the hymn to the occasion or to the church year; songs are sung repeatedly in different situations in order to reinforce congregational identity. ("We are the people who sing these hymns.")

> Singing, then, becomes a powerful provoker of memories, and women become participants in the process of activating memory when they request songs. Certain hymns, they know, will evoke particular images and emotions. One woman said, "they were singing 'O how happy are they' when I joined the church, and I always associate that song...with the day I joined the church." Others remember certain friends or family members when they sing particular songs. Memories may be personal or collective, or some combination...but insofar as they are associated with the church they serve the whole group as a bond.[33]

Congregational singing and song leading has always been a significant, and highly meaningful, form of liturgical participation for women. In almost every Christian congregation throughout the world, even those in which women have

---

30. Ibid., 174–75.

31. Beverley Bush Patterson, *The Sound of the Dove: Singing in Appalachian Primitive Baptist Churches* (Urbana: University of Illinois Press, 1996), 61.

32. Ibid. This method of choosing hymns is quite common in Independent and Free Church traditions. In North Parish Church (Andover, Massachusetts), "The congregation tries to participate by singing hymns, most of which contain terrible poetry, some of which profess a theology we no longer accept. This dilemma was solved by 'congregation's choice,' permitting people to select the hymns they wish to sing, a practice which had become an informal Sunday morning tradition the past few years." Juliet Haines Moffard, *And Firm Thine Ancient Vow: The History of North Parish Church of North Andover, 1645–1974* (North Andover, Mass.: Naiman, 1975), 279.

33. Ibid., 192–93.

no other voice in worship, the contributions of women cantors, choristers, soloists, as well as all those who add their voices to congregational song, have shaped and guided the sacred sound of the liturgy.

Women Hymn Writers

In all likelihood, women began writing hymns very early in Christian history as a part of their own desire to express their faith in sacred poetry. Sadly, however, none of these early works survive (or none that survive have been definitively attributed to women), nor are there any contemporary references to their existence.[34] It seems indisputable that many women in religious orders have composed hymns for use by their sisters in the convent chapel. Perhaps the most widely known of these is Hildegard of Bingen (d. 1179), but she is by no means unique, nor even the most accomplished of these women hymn writers. In some religious traditions, the hymns of significant women leaders have carried much of the weight of the sung theology of the whole community. This was certainly the function of the hymns of Mother Ann Lee (1736–84) for the United Society of Believers in Christ's Second Appearing (commonly called the "Shakers").

The first important woman hymn writer of the continental Reformation was Katharina Schütz Zell (1497?–1562), along with her husband Matthew, was involved in the reformation of Strasbourg. Vernacular hymns set to popular tunes had been increasingly popular throughout northern Europe in the quarter-century before the Reformation, but these often reflected a theology that was unacceptable to the reformers on such topics as the eucharist, the saints, and the virgin Mary. In her hymnal, *Von Christo Jhesu Lobgsäng* (Strasbourg, 1534/35), Zell sought to replace these undesirable hymns with more edifying texts, and to set them to "religious" tunes rather than secular tunes. As she said:

> Since, however, now so many scandalous songs are sung by men and women
> and also by children throughout the world . . . it seemed to me a very good
> and useful thing to . . . convey the whole business of Christ and our salvation
> in song, so that people may thus, enthusiastically and with clear voices, be
> exhorted to their salvation, and the devil with his songs may not have any
> place in them.[35]

---

34. The earliest extant piece of Christian music, both notation and text, is scribbled on the back of an invoice for grain, and dated from somewhere in the last quarter of the third century.

35. Cited in Elsie A. McKee, *Reforming Popular Piety in Sixteenth-Century Strasbourg: Katharina Schütz Zell and Her Hymnbook*, Studies in Reformed Theology and History 2, no. 4 (Princeton, N.J.: Princeton Theological Seminary, 1994), 28–29.

Based on a 1531 hymnal by Michael Weisse, an elder of the Bohemian Brethren, Zell's hymnbook contains 159 hymns and was produced in four small volumes in order that they might be affordable for families as both a hymnal and a teaching tool. In the foreword to her hymnal,[36] she says, "Indeed, I ought much rather to call it a teaching, prayer, and praise book rather than a songbook, although the little word 'song' is well and properly spoken, for the greatest praise of God is expressed in song...."[37]

Hymnody has been described as both "sectless" (in other words, one would be hard pressed to identify and define a specifically Anglican, Presbyterian, or Baptist hymnody) and "sexless" (it is equally difficult to tell if any given hymn was written by a man or a woman).[38] But women hymnodists have returned to certain themes again and again. One of these themes is the death of children, which was an all-too-common fact of life for women in the premodern period (see fig. 27). In her own hymnal, Katharina Schütz Zell includes such a hymn, in which she undoubtedly expresses her own sense of bereavement at the loss of two children in infancy, as well as offering a Christian perspective on untimely death. (Zell describes it as a "hymn of comfort, [telling us] how the death of children is bearable, and not much to be bewailed."[39]) Mrs. Felicia Hemans, née Browne (1794–1835), was perhaps the preeminent expositor of hymns on the death of children, with innumerable poignant verses to her credit which generally follow a theme similar to this "Funeral Hymn" for a baby boy:

> Woods unknown receive him,
> Midst the mighty wild;
> Yet with God we leave him,
> Blessed, blessed child!
> And our tears gush o'er his lovely dust,
> Mournfully, yet still with hearts of trust.[40]

Some of these hymns on death in childhood are written for children themselves. Jane Taylor (1783–1824) and her elder sister Ann Taylor Gilbert (1782–1866)

---

36. The "foreword" to Zell's hymnal is found in ibid., appendix 1, 65–67.

37. Cited in ibid, 26. Zell concludes the foreword, saying: "But so that you may not complain: 'So we may never sing! Must we become like sticks and stones?' Therefore now sing these songs, which express so admirably God's love towards us, and exhort us so faithfully not to neglect the salvation offered to us" (30).

38. Samuel Rogal, *Sisters of Sacred Song: A Selected Listing of Women Hymnodists in Great Britain and America* (New York: Garland, 1981), xi–xii.

39. McKee, *Reforming Popular Piety in Sixteenth-Century Strasbourg*, 56.

40. "Funeral Hymn," in Felicia Dorothea Browne Hemans, *Poems* (Edinburgh and London, 1849), 581.

came from a prominent Independent family, in which hymn singing was encouraged and frequently employed in private and family devotion. The sisters produced
many hymns for children, including *Hymns for Infant Minds* (1808) and *Original
Hymns for Sunday Schools* (1812), all of which encourage children to cultivate
the virtues of cheerfulness, industry, duty, gratitude, and honesty. In her hymn
"Against Anger and Impatience," Jane Taylor uses the inevitibility of death to
give force to her central message: "These hands and feet and busy head, / Shall
waste and crumble quite away; / But though your body shall be dead, / There is
a part which can't decay."[41]

But it is not only the death of children that seems to occupy the minds of
women hymn writers; a body of sacred song also arises out of what one hymnol-
ogist describes as a "culture of the women invalid." As we move further into the
Victorian period, one social commentator observes,

> melancholy and dark thoughts of death overtook women hymnwriters. A
> plaintive piety, a vague romantic melancholy, crept like mildew over much
> of women's hymnwriting, and the numbers of fainting hearts, distressed
> souls, drooping spirits, feeble voices and invalids in "low and languid" states,
> given over to "moaning and sick sighs," increased alarmingly.[42]

These hymns were not only for use in church; in the sickroom, at the deathbed,
and among despondent insomniacs they often found the most fertile spiritual
ground. The woman who perhaps best represents this kind of tragic woman hymn
writer was also the most distinguished woman hymnodist of the eighteenth century, the Baptist Anne Steele (1717–78), "hailed by historians as the 'mother' of
English women hymn writers."[43] Steele was the daughter of a Baptist minister in
Broughton, Hampshire, and was frail and sickly all her life. She was only three
when her mother died, and her father quickly remarried a woman who was intensely jealous of her new husband's affection for his young daughter and who
made the little girl's life a misery. But at the age of twenty, Steele fell in love and
was soon engaged to be married; on the afternoon before the wedding, however,
her fiancée was drowned. Steele never would leave home, living with her father
and hostile stepmother until they died more than twenty years later. A recent

---

41. Ann Taylor, *Hymns for Infant Minds* (London, 1808), 24. The work of the Taylor sisters found
a wide audience, not only in England, but in the United States as well; their hymnals went through
many editions in the nineteenth century, and many of the individual hymns found their way into
denominational hymnals throughout the world.
42. Margaret Maison, "'Thine, Only Thine!': Women Hymn Writers in Britain, 1760–1835,"
in *Religion in the Lives of English Women, 1760–1930,* ed. Gail Malmgreen (Bloomington: Indiana
University Press, 1986), 23.
43. Ibid, 14.

biographer says of Anne Steele that "outward tranquility concealed depths of pain, frustration, and suffering as she progressed along her 'pathway of affliction' to God."[44] In 1760, two volumes of her hymns were published,[45] and they reflect her longing for a warm and intimate relationship with Jesus, which is often described in the language of a lover yearning for the object of her affection. ("Too oft, alas, my passions rove, / In search of meaner charms; / Trifles unworthy of my love / Divide me from thy arms."[46]) Widely imitated by her women hymn-writing contemporaries, Steele's emphasis on great consolation as afforded by the Scriptures, prayer, pious meditation on the crucifixion, and the healing effects on the wounded heart of love for Jesus linked the worship of the gathered congregation with the worship of the wandering soul in a web of affective imagery.[47]

The flood of women's hymn writing in the nineteenth century was unleashed by a number of factors: the rise of evangelical revivalism which encouraged pious introspection, the Romantic movement with its attention to the grand themes of love and death, increasing literacy and educational opportunities for women, and the pietism which marked some denominations with a reflective spirituality that demanded self-expression. Many women were also caught up in the economics of hymn writing in a boom time for the industry. (One of Fanny Crosby's contracts with a publisher called for three songs per week throughout the year. This goes some way to explaining how this remarkable blind poet could produce more than three thousand hymns in her lifetime.[48]) These women have left us some of the best-loved and most moving Christian hymns for congregational worship, including "O Perfect Love" (Dorothy Gurney, 1883); "Take My Life and Let It Be" (Frances Ridley Havergal, 1874); "Just As I Am, Without One Plea" (Charlotte Elliott, 1836); "All Things Bright and Beautiful" and "Jesus Calls Us O'er the Tumult" (Cecil Frances Humphreys Alexander, 1848 and 1852); "I Know That My Redeemer Lives" (Alice Mannington, 1863). These women who wrote hymns for congregational singing and private use in this period are from a wide denominational spectrum — they are Baptists and Roman Catholics[49] and Lutherans,

---

44. Ibid.

45. *Poems on Subjects Chiefly Devotional*, 2 vols. (London, 1760).

46. "Jesus the Best Beloved," in ibid., 1:163.

47. Anne Steele, *The Hymns of Anne Steele* (London: Gospel Standard Baptist Trust, 1967). *Julian's Dictionary of Hymnology* lists seventy-five of Steele's hymns still in use in the 1890s, and a paperback edition of the hymns appeared in 1967 to mark the 250th anniversary of her death. For a good index to women hymn writers in English, see Rogal, *Sisters of Sacred Song.*

48. See Bernard Ruffin, *Fanny Crosby* (Philadelphia: United Church Press, 1976), and Fanny J. Crosby, *Memories of Eighty Years* (Boston: James H. Earle, 1906).

49. The number of Roman Catholic women hymn writers is admittedly small, and many of these have been largely ignored. One such is Sister Mary Austin [nee Mary Ryan] (c. 1790–1827), one of the several Ryan sisters who came to the United States from Ireland at the turn of the nineteenth century as founding members of the Ursuline convent in Charlestown, Massachusetts. Sister Mary

Presbyterians and Anglicans and Unitarians, but their contributions to Christian hymnody were received across denominational lines. One historian argues that women's hymn writing of this period is not only important for women's contributions to the churches' liturgical life, but is "a significant breakthrough in women's writing [more generally]. Often they wrote as women to women, about women's concerns and difficulties, their pains and problems, their hopes and aspirations. They wrote too as laywomen and not as theologians...."[50]

Many of these women not only wrote hymns, but also reflected on the hymn writing process. Frances Ridley Havergal (1836–79), author of at least twelve hundred hymns, gives a sense of the experience of divine inspiration.

> I can never set myself to write verse. I believe my King suggests a thought and whispers a musical line or two, and then I look up and thank Him delightedly, and go on with it.... The Master had not put a chest of poetic gold into my possession and said, "Now use it as you like!" But He keeps the gold, and gives it me piece by piece just when He will and as much as He will, and no more.[51]

Other women had still more ecstatic experiences of hymnic inspiration. Baptist prophet Anna Trapnell recounts her spiritual experiences in three volumes published in 1654. Having gone with a "Mr. Powell" to London, she waited for him in an antechamber while he attended a political meeting. Suddenly she was "seized upon" by a strange power and was "carried forth in a Spirit of Prayer and Singing." She was taken to bed and lay there for twelve days, uttering prayers and spiritual songs day and night to people who crowded into her little room. For the last eight days, her songs and prayers were written down by a friend and were printed the following month as *The Cry of a Stone.* ("Her utterances consist of prayers couched in highly emotional language, alternating with ecstatic hymns in common metre."[52]) It is clear that many women hymn writers feel strongly the weight of their calling. In her autobiography, the astonishingly prolific Fanny Crosby says

---

Austin was a noted hymn writer in her day, and her hymns were not only sung in her own convent chapel, but also in the cathedral church of the diocese of Boston as well.

50. Maison, "Thine, Only Thine!" 36–37.

51. Frances Ridley Havergal, *Letters of the Late Frances Ridley Havergal* (Edinburgh: Morrison and Gibb, 1885), 143. For a convenient collection of Havergal's hymns, see *The Poems and Hymns of Christ's Sweet Singer, Frances Ridley Havergal*, selected by Tracy Bly (New Canaan, Conn.: Keats Publishing, 1977).

52. Owen C. Watkins, *Puritan Experience* (London: Routledge & Kegan Paul, 1972), 92. (Watkins's appendix has a list of seventeenth- and eighteenth-century Puritan, Baptist, and Quaker spiritual autobiographies.) See also Anna Trapnell, *Strange and Wonderful Newes from Whitehall, or, The Mighty Visions Proceeding from Mistris Anna Trapnel...* (London: Robert Sale, 1654).

simply, "At times the burden of inspiration is so heavy that the author himself cannot find words beautiful enough or thoughts deep enough, for its expression."[53]

Of course, the piety and faithfulness of many women also served as the inspiration for male hymn writers. The young John Wesley was deeply affected by the patient trust of the Moravians he met on the long sea voyage to Georgia, and during this journey he translated into English thirty-three German hymns from the Herrnhut hymnal (1735) and the Freylinghausen hymnbook. Fully one-third of the hymns Wesley chose for the proto-Methodist societies in America were those of Moravian hymn writers Anna Döber (1713–39) and Maria Magdalena Böhmer (167?–1743). John Newton, probably most famous for the hymn "Amazing Grace," was also inspired by the power of women's faith. In February 1774, when he was serving as a curate at Olney, one of his most supportive parishioners, Betty Abraham, died suddenly and Newton composed a funeral hymn for her, describing her as a "Mother in our Israel ... exceedingly useful, especially to the lambs of our flock." The publication of his *Olney Hymns* in 1779 made this, and other hymns inspired by the Christian piety of women, available to a wide public.[54]

The "bright succession" of women hymn writers continues to this day, and compositions (both texts and tunes) by this new generation of women are found in virtually every contemporary denominational hymnal and hymn collection. Many have become famous not only for their own hymns, but for their advocacy of congregational song as the foundational music ministry of the church. The full story of women's hymnody has yet to be written, but it surely needs to include the names of such twenty-first-century teacher-composers as Jane Parker Huber, Jane Marshall, Carol Doran, Ruth Duck, and Shirley Erena Murray, to name only a very few. These women are exploring the boundaries of both theological imagery and sacred sound, and partake of the ecumenical spirit of the age, which gives their hymns a wide and diverse utility.

Transcribers and Collectors

The Christian hymn tradition has been handed on not only by congregations and individual singers, but also by those who collected, transcribed, and documented hymns that might have otherwise been lost. The awareness that congregational song was a treasure of the church that needed preservation was late in coming, but once it was established, sometime in the late nineteenth century with the

---

53. Crosby, *Memories of Eighty Years*, 187.

54. D. Bruce Hindmarsh, *John Newton and the English Evangelical Tradition: Between the Conversions of the Wesleys and Wilberforce* (Oxford: Clarendon, 1996), 203.

rise of Romanticism and its concern with the revitalization of the past, women were at the forefront of the preservation process. The most remarkable of these women were those who collected and transcribed the slave songs and Negro spirituals, which after the end of the Civil War were threatened with extinction as African American communities were dispersed. Among the earliest of these were the women who were involved in the Port-Royal experiment, designed by abolitionists to prepare former slaves for life as free men and women. One of these was Charlotte Forten Grimké, a Black teacher from the North, who was keenly aware of the place of hymnody in maintaining religious identity and the serious consequences that would befall any community that lost its native hymnic voice. Having made a tour of Black churches in the South, Grimké says that she and her colleagues saw "crowds of freedmen singing not their own beautiful hymns, I am sorry to say; I so fear that these will be superseded by ours, which are poor in comparison, and which they do not sing well at all."[55] These more "scientific" women observers and collectors were preceded by innumerable ordinary women travelers who, because they were unimpeded by the kinds of strong institutional identities that tended to constrain their husbands and brothers, often were willing and able to penetrate alien worship services and to record with both accuracy and passion what they saw and heard.

Lucy McKim (1842–77) was the only practicing musician among the collectors of slave songs in the South Carolina Sea Islands, a Union enclave, during the Civil War, having accompanied her father there in June 1862. Although she only remained there for three weeks, she was deeply impressed with the songs of the freedmen, and notated them. On her return to her home in Philadelphia, McKim tried unsuccessfully to bring them to public notice. In 1865 she married Wendell Phillips Garrison, literary editor of *The Nation*, who assisted her in gathering the first comprehensive collection of slave songs, in collaboration with William Francis Allen and Charles Pickard Ware. The resulting book, *Slave Songs of the United States* (1867), is described as "a seminal work of lasting importance, still the best-known source of slave music."[56] In the 1930s, the Works Progress Administration (WPA) sent many women out into the field to record the memories of the dying generation of those who remembered life before the abolition of slavery, further contributing to the preservation of traditional church music. At about the same time, Ruth Denson Edwards, one of the prominent Denson family of Sacred Harp

---

55. *The Journal of Charlotte L. Forten*, ed. Ray Allen Billington (New York: Dryden Press, 1953), 183.

56. Dena J. Epstein, "Garrison, Lucy McKim," *New Grove Dictionary of Music and Musicians* (London: Grove, 2001), 6:114, and Dena J. Epstein, "Lucy McKim Garrison, American Musician," *Bulletin of the New York Public Library* 67 (1963): 529–46.

singers, was recording and transcribing the shape-note singing of the American South and Appalachia, which resulted in the three volumes of *The Original Sacred Harp* ("Denson Revision") published in 1936 under the auspices of the Sacred Harp Publishing Company.[57] (She was also on the editorial committee for the 1967 and 1971 editions of the Sacred Harp collection.[58])

But the person who perhaps best understood the power of the memory and tradition in the African American churches was the daughter of a wealthy New York family. Mary White Ovington (1865–1951) was an early leader of the Civil Rights movement, a founding member of the NAACP, a leader of the antilynching campaign, and a friend of W. E. B. Du Bois and James Weldon Johnson. She spent thirty years traveling, lecturing, and writing about the unequal treatment accorded African Americans in the United States, and she uses her descriptions of church services, and especially singing in church services, to prick the consciences of her audiences on the issue of civil rights. In a Black congregation in Alabama, for example, she hears the people singing with "the sorrow of the slaves."[59] But it was in Calhoun, Georgia, that she felt that she had "heard the spirituals for the first time."

> At Calhoun I heard them as they were originally sung, primitive music, great group singing. It was disappearing even then, but ... where the hymn-book and the book of popular songs had not penetrated, folk singing still existed.... They sang at Calhoun the way their fathers and mothers must have sung, always in harmony, but always unexpected. I used to hear that on San Juan Hill, but not the extraordinary harmonies that accompanied it. They sang with the sorrow of the slave. Again I heard, "Bye an' bye, bye an' bye/I's gwine ter lay down did heaby load." A hopeless sorrow that lingered in this generation.[60]

---

57. Denson's father and uncles had been influential in the publication of the James edition of *Sacred Harp Music* (1911) — which Ruth Denson expands in her 1936 edition — and many of the songs were composed and arranged by the early members of the Denson family.

58. Buell E. Cobb, *The Sacred Harp: A Tradition and Its Music* (Athens: University of Georgia Press, 1978), 111–13. The Sacred Harp tradition of congregational song was not only maintained by collections such as these, but also by the annual Sacred Harp conventions. The Sunday service at these conventions is an interesting liturgical event in its own right. One of the distinguishing features of this service was the "memorial lesson." "This is a period set aside, usually on Sunday before the dinner hour, to memorialize the singers or 'lovers of Sacred Harp Music' from the area who have died during the past year. This part of the session is a sober contrast to the spirited quality of the singing.... Two or three singers, selected by the families of the deceased or appointed by the singing officers, lead a commemorative 'lesson' and often eulogize their friends or comment on the implications of the mortality of the singers — the mortality, by extension, of Sacred Harp singing as well."

59. Mary White Ovington, *The Walls Came Tumbling Down* (New York: Harcourt, Brace, 1947), 71.

60. Ibid., 71–72.

But for Ovington, African American church singing was not only a window onto the sorrows of life under segregation; the whole approach to worship in Black congregations had much to teach white worshipers whose own liturgical freedom had gradually been eroded by concern for "propriety." She makes this point in a description of a service at Union Baptist Church, an African American congregation on San Juan Hill in New York City:

> No Billy Sunday had to stride up and down our platform, arousing religious emotion. It was close to the surface and the Negro sang and cried Amen, not droning his responses, but in a lusty voice. Civilization loves decorum and is forever putting things before our eyes and ears while demanding that we give no answering word. It laughs at the worker who sings at his task. I think a psychiatrist would find something to say in favor of our shouting in church — gone now, moved to Harlem. And if the congregation were the sheep in this Baptist pasture, they aspired to be definitely parted from the goats who make their noise in unsavory retreats.[61]

This connection between "hearing" and "understanding" is characteristic of many women observers of church music. In the previous century, Frederika Bremer, the extraordinary Swedish woman traveler who visited camp meeting revivals and African American churches in the south in the 1870s, puts it most simply when she says of the church music of former slaves that "one must see these people singing if one is rightly to understand their life."[62]

Patrons and Commissioners

Many women have used their financial resources and personal power to enhance the music of the church. Even though many of these women were motivated more by the desire to enhance their own prestige and ensure their safe passage into eternity than the desire to enrich the church's liturgical life, the result was a very real contribution to church music (see fig. 28). In the early centuries of Christian history, women who endowed churches undoubtedly would have included the money needed for trained singers. Many of these women have simply left instructions in their wills for specific music to be performed at their death. In 1513, for example, widow Jane Stokker, a prominent parishioner at St. Mary, Rickmansworth, left the church innumerable liturgical furnishings (among which were a silver cross for the altar and a stained-glass window for the south aisle)

---

61. Ibid., 40–41.
62. Cited in Mechal Sobel, *Trabelin' On: The Slave Journey to an Afro-Baptist Faith* (Princeton, N.J.: Princeton University Press, 1988), 153.

in her will, along with detailed instructions for her entombment and the sung services that should be performed. She left the sum of nine marks per year for "a discreet priest to be hired . . . to sing for two years at the altar of St. Katherine for the Stokkers and all Christian souls."[63] Women also paid for ceremonies on the octave of their deaths (in other words, on the eighth day following), and on the anniversaries, and in a few cases they established choirs of singers in order that their wishes be carried out. In 1482, for example, Mary of Burgundy gave to the Church of Our Lady in Bruges "an annual endowment of £108 to augment the livings of the Master of Choristers and the organist, and to increase the number of choristers by four. In return, two Masses were performed daily for her soul, one a Lady Mass and the other a Requiem."[64]

Sometimes women commissioned compositions that would become important elements in the church music repertoire. In about the year 1484, Ariadene, wife of Donaes de Moor, a wealthy fur merchant in Bruges, endowed polyphonic masses to be sung annually on the feast day of her name saint, St. Adrian, and that of her husband, St. Donatian, in the parish church of St. James, Bruges. One musicologist argues persuasively that it may well have been for Ariadene that Jakob Obrecht was commissioned to compose his Mass *De Sancto Donatiano*.[65] In many cases wealthy women employed composers to serve in their household chapels, and much of the music produced for these settings found its way into the church's wider choral repertoire. So, for example, Lady Margaret Beaufort's choirmaster Thomas Farthing (?–1521) was enormously important to the development of English church music and left many compositions that were written under her patronage.[66] Sometimes women have banded together into guilds and societies in order to provide for music for the church. The Guild of Our Lady, which was concerned with worship in the parish church in Bergen op Zoom, the Netherlands, in the late fifteenth century,

> sponsored the choir for some 433 extra services per year, on probably all of which polyphony was used; 364 observances of the "Lof" (a service of praise and intercession to the Virgin); 52 weekly Lady Masses, and the

---

63. "The executors and discreet of the parish were to hire 'an honest preest which can syng in the quere and also can doo such thynges as are convenient to a discrete preest to doo.'" Margaret Aston, *Faith and Fire: Popular and Unpopular Religion, 1350–1600* (London: Hambledon, 1993), 245.

64. Roger Bowers, "Aristocratic and Popular Piety in the Patronage of Music," in *The Church and the Arts*, ed. Diana Wood (Oxford: Basil Blackwell, 1992), 218.

65. See Reinhold Strohm, *Music in Late Medieval Bruges* (Cambridge: Clarendon, 1985), 61–62, and Bowers, "Autocratic and Popular Piety in the Patronage of Music in the Fifteenth-Century Nederlands," 221.

66. R. G. Mertes and K. A. Mertes, "The Household as a Religious Community," in *People, Politics, and Community in the Later Middle Ages*, ed. Joel Rosenthal and Colin Richmond (Gloucester, U.K.: Alan Sutton, and New York: St. Martin's, 1987), 130.

six principal Marian High Masses. The guild also provided music-books for these occasions, and paid extra stipends for widely-acclaimed soloists to join the choir for specific services.[67]

This guild also seems to have hired composers, including Jakob Obrecht and Johannes Ghiselen (alias Verbonet), to provide musical settings, motets, and especially Marian hymns for these services. Among Obrecht's twenty-nine surviving masses, five early works are based on Marian hymns, and may well have been commissioned by the Guild of Our Lady.[68] Women of means who had established chantry chapels in their houses had even more control of the liturgical music in these settings, and we find clear indications of their explicit instructions for those in their employ. Sometime around the year 1380, Isabella de Friskenny stipulated that her chaplain should be "sufficiently trained in church music and grammar."[69] In very large houses, a choir would also have been available for every service in the chapel.[70]

The influence of women patrons on church music continues to this day. Women still leave money in their wills for hymnals and choir music, and still commission (or encourage the commissioning of) hymns and anthems for use in their churches. The contributions (of both energy and money) of women to organ-building projects, the establishment of bell choirs, and, more recently, the provision of resources for various forms of electronic music cannot be overestimated. Not only do these gifts enhance the liturgical life of a given congregation, they have often played a part in the establishment of trends in church music that soon more widely took on a life of their own.

Teachers and Commentators

So important has music been in the liturgical lives of women that they often were deeply concerned with teaching the various arts of sacred song to others

67. Bowers, "Aristocratic and Popular Piety in the Patronage of Music in the Fifteenth-Century Nederlands," 210.

68. Ibid., 212. This pattern was duplicated all over Europe in the fourteenth, fifteenth, and early sixteenth centuries, with varying degrees of elaborateness. In the Church of Our Lady in Antwerp, for example, there was "a complete weekly cycle of fraternity masses, sponsored by the laity, attended by the singers of the choir, duly rewarded for their services" (217). For these masses, as well as for the daily "Lof," a great deal of polyphonic music must have been composed, although none that survives can be directly connected with Antwerp (216).

69. K. L. Wood-Legh, *Perpetual Chantries in Britain* (Cambridge: Cambridge University Press, 1965), 185.

70. C. L. Kingford, ed., *The Stonor Letters and Papers, 1290–1483* (London: Camden Society, 1900).

and commenting on trends in church music. Sometimes this was done formally, with formal musicological qualifications for the task; at other times (and perhaps more commonly) the work of teaching liturgical music was done as an amateur. For example, innumerable parish records mention that "the minister's wife had a special gift for music,"[71] and then go on to describe her work directing children's choirs, playing the organ, or organizing "hymn-sings." This kind of quiet influence in the teaching ministry of the church is of immeasurable significance. At the same time, however, other women were more widely influential still through their teaching, and some shaped whole movements in liturgical music.

Two of these women teachers worked as a team: Justine Ward (1879–1975) and Mother Georgia Stevens (1871–1946), cofounders of the Pius X Institute of Liturgical Music and codirectors of the institute for several years. In 1903, Pius X issued a *motu proprio* that encouraged the restoration of Gregorian chant; Justine Ward was deeply influenced by the vision presented in that document. In articles for Roman Catholic periodicals, Ward argued for the positive effects of chant on Christian spiritual development and for the inherent inferiority of the current romantic, polyphonic church music. Having developed a simple method (ever after called the "Ward Method") of teaching chant to children, she joined with Mother Georgia Stevens, R.S.C.J., to found an institute for the promotion of Gregorian chant at Manhattanville College of the Sacred Heart, with the stated goal of preparing teachers to teach children to chant in order for them to participate actively in the liturgy. When the enthusiasm for Gregorian chant as the key to lay participation in worship died in the years leading up to the Second Vatican Council, and it became clear to Ward that chant was not destined to be a part of the church's immediate musical future, "Ward's world collapsed. In her anguish she wrote: 'They want to lower the prayer of the church to mud level in order to attract the most ignorant people.'" To the end of her life, Justine Ward was convinced of the central role of Gregorian chant in the life of the Catholic liturgy, and that the church had missed an opportunity for genuine renewal. Just before her death, she summed up her wholehearted commitment to chant: "If chant is not there to make me pray, let the cantors be silent. If chant is not there to appease my inner anxiety, let the cantors leave. If chant is not as valuable as the silence it breaks, let me go back to silence."[72]

---

71. Such is the description of the wife of the minister of North Parish Church in Andover, Massachusetts, at the turn of the twentieth century. While he is known by name (William Stanley Nichols), his wife, whose contributions to church music in the parish seems to have been considerable, is simply referred to as "the minister's wife." Moffard, *And Form Thine Ancient Vow,* 247.

72. Cited in Kathleen Hughes, *How Firm a Foundation: Voices of the Early Liturgical Movement* (Chicago: Liturgy Training Publications, 1990), 256.

The liturgical change that was a feature of all of the mainline churches after about 1965 caused many women this kind of anguish. Some were dismayed by the loss of traditional hymns, and particularly the recasting of old hymns into modern language. In a 1990 essay by Margaret A. Doody, professor of literature at the University of Notre Dame, she wrote of the "wholesale and merciless revision" of liturgical language, and especially the language of hymns, because it denies the integrity of the religious experiences of the authors, and presents congregations with "tinkered and adulterated goods."[73] Other women commentators on contemporary church music adopt a more sardonic tone. In the January–February 1987 issue of the short-lived satirical magazine *The Christian Challenge*, journalist Kathleen Reeves lampoons the current gender-inclusive revision of traditional hymns with her own parody of "Immortal, Invisible, God Only Wise":

> We've thrown out the cliches of Sin and of Grace
> We have modern concepts to put in their place.
> How naïve our fathers (and mothers as well)
> To live with such notions as "Heaven" and "Hell."
>
> Alas, poor foreparents, unable to see
> That the Holy Spirit is surely a "She."
> They wallowed in doctrines, absurd, unalloyed,
> Not knowing theology started with Freud.
>
> Ah now, we're enlightened, we understand all!
> No longer accepting catchwords like "the Fall."
> Thou'rt made in our image, oh help us to see
> 'Tis not being "with it" that keeps us from Thee.[74]

This hymn, says Reeves, would best be sung by "The Cathedral Choir of All Sexes at St. Zeitgeist's Within the Walls."

The history of women and liturgical music is particularly difficult to uncover. Although many women have contributed to the musical life of their churches in multiple ways — as patrons, commentators, composers, singers, instrumentalists, and choir directors — most left only trace evidence of their contributions, and the work of so many others has been falsely attributed to men. As a result, for every period of Christian history much of the record remains to be compiled, and many questions left to be answered. It seems, however, that there was no time in which the women's singing voices were silenced, and no time in which their

73. "Changing What We Sing," in *The State of the Language*, ed. Christopher Ricks and Leonard Michaels (Berkeley: University of California Press, 1990), 336.
74. K. Reeves, "Hymn," *The Christian Challenge* (January–February 1987), 33.

devotional poetry was not set to music for the sake of the common prayer of the Christian community. Indeed, the vast numbers of women liturgical musicians and hymn writers, and even the opponents of change, have not only shaped the sacred sound of congregations at worship, but have understood their work as a part of the theological formation of the Christian people for deeper participation in the mission of God in the world.

Women and the Liturgical Arts

If an "artist" is someone who uses material to create objects and environments that mediate beauty and meaning, most liturgical artists in the history of Christian worship have been ordinary women parishioners. They have embroidered textiles and decorated altars, they have arranged flowers and painted murals around the baptismal font. Because of the ephemeral nature of these art forms, most of their work has vanished, but to the extent that it has contributed to the texture of the liturgical life of every congregation, it has shaped the liturgical history of the church as a whole and must not be overlooked in our rush to honor more "notable" women artists (see fig. 29). The principal form of women's liturgical art has probably always been the decoration of the church for worship. This picture of women's work in a North Carolina church can probably be applied over a wide range of situations throughout the history of the church:

> The sanctuary is decorated each Sunday by women on a rotational basis, the assignment being given by a standing committee. Decoration usually consists of a flower arrangement on the communion table and conforms with the seasons: bulbs in spring, dried and everlasting flowers in fall. On special occasions decoration may be . . . more elaborate. At Easter, for example, the windows and choir loft are filled with Easter lilies and spring bulbs. Also some women commemorate the anniversary of the death of a relative with elaborate floral displays.[75]

As we can see, in this church — whose preaching and prayers would not be likely to follow the Christian calendar — it is left to women's decorative artistry to tie this church to the larger rhythms of the church year. In those churches that do follow a liturgical calendar, women's decorative schemes help to reinforce visually the message of the lessons and prayers for the season. In late-nineteenth-century England,

---

75. John Forrest, *Lord I'm Coming Home: Everyday Aesthetics in Tidewater North Carolina* (Ithaca, N.Y.: Cornell University Press, 1988), 124.

Laura Petre and her sister-in-law Lady Julia Howard made it their job to "adorn the altar of Repose...with the costliest exotics from Costessy Hall," while at the other end of the social spectrum, Margaret Hallahan built a Sepulchre at Coventry, "with very poor materials," before which "people watched with unwearied ardour."[76]

Liturgical street processions, in which images of the saints or the eucharistic bread were carried, were further occasions for the artistry of women parishioners who produced the banners, special vestments for the statuary, and uniforms for the members of pious confraternities.

As important as these ordinary women have been to the worship settings of local churches, a number of highly skilled women artists have also contributed to the liturgical environment. Some of these women were multitalented, and among the most remarkable of these was Catarina dei Vigri (1413–63), abbess of the convent of Corpus Domini, Bologna. Born in Ferrara to an educated and well-to-do family, Catarina grew up at court and soon became a celebrated artist, musician, and illuminator, as well as a noted patron of musicians and artists. When a local heiress was caught in a violent dispute with the community of women that had been established in a house she was left in a will, over which rule of life they would adopt, the young Catarina, then only eighteen, intervened. The heiress was ejected from the house in 1432, and Catarina became its abbess, placing the women under the Rule of St. Clare. Putting her artistic, musical, and architectural talents to work, Catarina supervised the necessary renovations to the house, and soon her hymns were being sung by the convent choir in the chapel decorated with her paintings.[77]

Women architects have designed a number of historically important churches, and have revised the plans of others. Mère Angélique, founder of the Paris convent of Port-Royal, supervised the building of her chapel, and "a comparison of the architect's original sketches with pictures of the completed structure reveals the measures taken by Mère Angélique to modify [architect Antoine] Le Pautre's plans for a little baroque...gem in order to make it a Cistercian abbey church."[78] Because Port-Royal was modeled on the Cistercian pattern, Mère Angélique radically simplified the original design, removing most of the unnecessary ornamental detail.

---

76. Susan O'Brien, "Making Catholic Spaces: Women, Décor, and Devotion in the English Catholic Church, 1840–1900," in *The Church and the Arts*, ed. Diana Wood (Oxford: Basil Blackwell, 1992), 460.

77. Laura M. Ragg, *The Women Artists of Bologna* (London: Methuen and Co., 1907), 38–46. Catarina also wrote a series of Latin sermons for her nuns at Corpus Domini.

78. F. Ellen Weaver, *The Evolution of the Reform of Port-Royal: From the Rule of Cîteaux to Jansenism* (Paris: Éditions Beauchesne, 1978), 89.

Poverty was of such importance in the spirituality of Port-Royal that the idea penetrated all the art it commissioned.... She had all ornamentation suppressed and to the great ox-eye window preferred a vertical window with a more modest ox-eye over it. Similarly, she had the design of the roof simplified. Finally she suppressed, she very much suppressed; no ballustrated steps nor vases of flame over the lateral porches; and on the interior, no decoration of the cupola, nor statues in the niches between the columns. The taste for poverty thus opened the door to sobriety.[79]

Other women made thorough renovations of existing buildings to suit new liturgical needs. The Duchess of Leeds bought the ruined bishop's palace at Mayfield, Sussex, and gave it to Cornelia Connelly and her Society of the Holy Child Jesus in 1863, on the condition that it be restored. Connelly hired the notable expositor of the Gothic Revival Edward Welby Pugin as architect and began raising funds for restoration. Once the Synod Hall had been turned into a church, Connelly was solely responsible for its furnishing and decoration, and she herself did paintings of "Our Lady of Sorrows" and "St. Ignatius" and at least one set of Stations of the Cross.

Convents and convent churches, of which Mayfield was one of the most spectacular and public examples, gave many Catholic women, both lay and religious, the opportunity to exercise aesthetic and devotional preferences, and thereby to play an active part in the transformation of the English Catholic Church during the middle decades of the nineteenth century.[80]

Some women are reported to have had supernatural assistance in their architectural endeavors. The revelation to found a religious order (and the rules for that order) came to the future St. Bridget (c. 1303–73) during a period of residence at the court of her kinsman, Magnus Erikson, king of Norway and Sweden, in 1346. St. Bridget was given a detailed plan of the churches of her foundation, including at Syon Abbey, in which both the community of men and the community of women worshiped, including its exact measurements.[81]

---

79. Bernard Dorival, "Le Jansénisme et l'Art Français," *Bulletin de la Societé de Amis de Port Royal* (1952): 13–14. Cited in Weaver, *The Evolution of the Reform of Port-Royal*, 89–90.

80. S. O'Brien, "Making Catholic Spaces," 458.

81. Julia B. Holloway, *St. Bride and Her Book: St. Birgitta's Revelations*, translated from Middle English (Cambridge: Boydell, 2000), 120–24; see also *Regula S. Salvator* (Rules of Saint Saviour), cap xii, xxi, xxv and Revel. I: 18, III, IX, 28, 29, 31, 34, 38. See also *The Bridgettine Breviary of Syon Abbey* (Worcester: Henry Bradshaw Society, 1963). She was also given in a vision by Christ that his angel would dictate to her the lessons to be read by the sisters at Matins throughout each week. "The twenty-one long lessons are collectively entitled 'Sermo Angelicus,' and the story of their communication to Bridget, who day by day awaited the angel in her chamber pen in hand,

Textile Artists

The oldest extant example of embroidery is from the eleventh century, but clearly the provision of ecclesiastical textiles has been a part of women's artistic work for the church from very early times. In the early period of Christian history, textiles were considered to have potent power and could be used as weapons in the war against invisible enemies who would be repelled by the Christian symbols appliquéd or woven into the fabric. For the original wearer, these decorative motifs "were not just ornaments, but also guarantees of his or her own well-being and safety."[82] This kind of protective function of textiles was more important in liturgical vestments, because the wearer was closer to the holy mysteries and would have been considered to be in even more danger from supernatural malice than ordinary Christians.[83]

The textile arts for the church were undertaken by all kinds of women: women and consecrated virgins in the early period, nuns in convents, ordinary women, aristocrats, and professional embroiderers later on. From the late thirteenth to the mid-fifteenth centuries, Beguines commonly supported themselves by sewing and embroidering ecclesiastical textiles, including not only vestments but altar frontals, veils, funeral palls, alms bags, and decorative hangings as well.[84] Like much of women's work, women's textile artistry for the church was often poorly paid. If a patron wished to donate elaborate vestments to the church, he or she would likely set up an independent embroidery workshop, which might employ several dozen professional embroiderers and apprentices. So, while Henry III paid £220 (the equivalent of $100,000) for a bejeweled and embroidered altar frontal, the four women who did the work over a period of three years received only £36 for their labor. In some cities there were "embroidery dynasties" such as the Heyroun family, and records show that Johanna Heyroun supplied a set of black vestments in 1327–28 for use in Edward III's chapel to celebrate the Office of the Dead (almost certainly for the funeral service of his murdered father Edward II).

Many women embroiderers have not been professionals, however, but women of means who saw their work as a part of their pious duty to the church. (Queen

was related by Alfonso de Vadaterra (d. 1388) in his Prologus in Sermonem Angelicus de Eccellentia Virginis Mariae ... " *Bridgettine Breviary* (Worcester: Henry Bradshaw Society, 1934), xxvii.

82. Henry Maguire, "Garments Pleasing to God: The Significance of Domestic Textile Design in the Early Byzantine Period," *Dumbarton Oaks Papers* 44 (1990): 215.

83. Ibid., 220.

84. "The manufacture of ecclesiastical vestments and fine tapestries was often a specialty of women's communities in various parts of Europe. Many beguinages supported themselves by working in the lowlier processes of the great cloth industry of Flemish and other Northern towns." Mary Martin McLaughlin, "Looking for Medieval Women: An Interim Report on the Project 'Women's Religious Life and Communities, 500–1600 A.D.,'" in *Monastic Studies: The Continuity of Tradition*, ed. Judith Loades (Bangor, Wales: Headstart, 1991), 274.

Eleanor, for example, embroidered the orphereys on the copes in the Church of St. Thomas, Hereford.[85]) Many vestments were the product of embroidery workshops set up in convents, which are among the best documented of all medieval textiles. The Syon Cope, for example, gets its name from Syon Abbey in Middlesex where it was housed in the sixteenth century. Worked somewhere between 1300 and 1320 by nuns in East Anglia for an unknown priest called "Peter," the cope is covered with embroidered scenes from the life of Christ and the virgin framed in architectural panels, with heraldic shields and hierarchies of angels around the edges of the panels. The Syon Cope is stitched with silver and gold thread and shows evidence that the convent's manuscript illuminators were involved in the design. It was saved from Reformation iconoclasts by the Bridgettines of Syon, who took it out of the country when they were exiled by Elizabeth I. They returned with the cope to England in 1810, and the Victoria and Albert Museum bought it in 1864.

The importance of textiles in the lives of women generally can be seen in the large numbers of women whose concern for the church was expressed in donations of cloth. Sometimes this took the form of clothing the donor had worn in her lifetime; at other times she directed that altar cloths, paraments, and other fabrics necessary for the conduct of Christian worship be made. Quite often women donors were very specific (more specific than their male counterparts) in stipulating the details of these fabrics. For example, in 1523, Joan Thurcross, a parishioner at the Church of St. Mary, Hull, left money in her will for a black velvet pall to be made especially to cover the hearse owned by the church. She dictated that an image of the Holy Trinity was to be wrought in gold on the cloth, and a dead man in a winding sheet was to be depicted lying before the Trinity; at the sides there were to be four angels, in gold and needlework, with candlesticks in their hands as though they were giving reverence to the Trinity, and at the feet of the dead man was to be written "For a Memorial."[86] But probably more typical were women like Mary Goose, a single woman of St. Gregory, Norfolk, who died in 1695, and who simply "out of her pious devotion [did] give to this church a crimson velvet Pulpit cloth and a Cushion and a border for the desk of the same."[87]

With the Reformation, great numbers of vestments were destroyed, the jewels removed, and the gold and silver thread reused. The few that escaped this

85. R. N. Swanson, "Liturgy as Theatre: The Props," in *The Church and the Arts,* ed. Diana Wood (Oxford: Basil Blackwell, 1992), 250.

86. Peter Heath, "Piety in the Late Middle Ages," in *The Church, Politics, and Patronage in the Fifteenth Century,* ed. Barrie Dobson (Gloucester, U.K.: Sutton, 1984), 218.

87. William M. Jacob, *Lay People and Religion in the Early Eighteenth Century* (Cambridge: Cambridge University Press, 1996), 197.

fate were lost in the next wave of iconoclasm which came with the rise of Puritanism in the mid-seventeenth century. Very occasionally a ceremonial vestment was made in this period, such as the cope made for Charles I's visit to Durham Cathedral in 1633, but on the whole, the art of ecclesiastical embroidery was lost. More recently, with the revival of the church crafts that began with the Tractarians in England, but which was consolidated in the 1930s with the attempts by Percy Dearmer, J. N. Comper, and others to "re-Anglicize" the liturgy and its environment,[88] women took up the task of the recovery of ancient techniques and patterns of ecclesiastical embroidery. Women, such as Janet Eeles, were founding members of the Wareham Guild, committed to teaching craft and design methods for the liturgy. Eeles was also the head of the Royal School of Needlework and made many of the hangings and altar cloths proposed by Percy Dearmer.[89] More recently, the extraordinary contemporary ecclesiastical textiles and designs by Beryl Dean (b. 1921), teacher, writer, and embroiderer, have found their way into European churches that sought to renew their liturgical settings after the devastation caused by the Second World War.[90]

Although these kinds of elaborate textile programs for churches guided and worked by women deserve a great deal of attention as one of the most important contributions of women artists to the liturgical life of the church, most church vestments have historically been produced on a small scale by ordinary women parishioners. In many periods, the activity of sewing and embroidering were seen as perfectly acceptable female activities and thus encouraged by husbands, fathers, and male clergy. Beginning in the nineteenth century, Protestant women joined together in sewing circles and Roman Catholic women in pious confraternities (such as the Children of Mary and the Rosary Guild) "and, like many other Victorian women, they spent a good deal of their time sewing as they listened to edifying readings or talks."[91] When the need arises, women continue, in groups or as individuals, to provide textiles for the church. The needlepoint on the pontifical sedilla at the Cathedral of St. John the Divine (New York) was worked and given in the 1970s by Mrs. William Warner Hoppin, and in the same period the needlepoint kneelers were produced by women who formed a guild for the purpose.

Not all women have the leisure nor the financial security to engage in this more "social" form of textile artistry. Some women have simply been concerned with

---

88. See Percy Dearmer, *Linen Ornaments of the Church* (London: Mowbray, 1930).

89. See Brian Taylor, "Church Art and Church Discipline Round about 1939," in *Church and the Arts,* ed. Wood, 489–98.

90. See Beryl Dean, *Ecclesiastical Embroidery* (London: Batsford, 1958), and *Church Needlework* (London: Batsford, 1961).

91. O'Brien, "Making Catholic Spaces," 462.

providing the most dignified textiles possible in limited circumstances. Vodhana Voros, a Czech nun who served as a missionary teacher in Papua New Guinea for nearly thirty years in the middle of the twentieth century, describes the rather trying conditions she withstood during this time; from her narrative we get the sense of how those with meager resources in all periods of the church's life must have solved the problem of providing liturgical textiles. "For almost ten years," Voros says, "I didn't have a table, only a bed, and I'd sit on a box. After school I came home exhausted. The priests had no vestments. We had to make their vestments, raincoats and all sorts of things they needed."[92]

Scribes and Illuminators

The production of liturgical books for use in Christian worship was not only a practical necessity, but also an opportunity to make beautiful objects "to the greater glory of God." When we think of an illuminated manuscript, we tend to think of a monk hunched over his desk in his monastery. But, as one historian says, "it is time to make room for another mental image: that of generations and generations of nuns, silently transcribing, collating, miniating, composing."[93] The earliest of these women book designers, scribes, and illuminators were indeed likely to have been women living in community, who saw the book arts as their special contribution to the worship of the church. For many of these women, work in the convent scriptorium was not only an artistic process, but a devotional exercise as well. Margherita d'Este entered the convent of Corpus Christi in Ferrara in 1427, and began there a remarkable output of illuminated ecclesiastical manuscripts. The story is told of her transcribing and illuminating a breviary: "She wrote her breviary, moistened with spirituality even in its decoration . . . and often it was necessary to take it away from in front of her, because she would have ruined it with the abundant tears she shed from her piteous eyes. . . ."[94] The expert work of the women scribes at Chelles has been known for some time,[95] and most scholars credit the nuns at Corbie with a large number of manuscripts

---

92. Chilla Bulbeck, *Australian Women in Papua New Guinea: Colonial Passages 1920–1960* (Cambridge: Cambridge University Press, 1992), 78.

93. Chiara Frugoni, "The Imagined Woman," in *Women, Family, and Ritual in Renaissance Italy*, ed. Christiane Klapisch-Zuber (Chicago: University of Chicago Press, 1987), 410.

94. Cited in Jeryldene Wood, *Women, Art and Spirituality* (Cambridge: Cambridge University Press, 1966), 138.

95. Bernhard Bischoff, "Die Kölner Nonnenhansschriften und sas Skriptorium von Chelles," in Bischoff, *Karolingische und ottonische Kunst: Werden, Wesen, Wirkung*, 395–411. Reprinted in Bischoff, *Mittelalterliche Studien* (Stuttgart: Hiersemann, 1966), 1:16–34.

copied in the clear and beautiful "a-b script."[96] Some of these books were commissioned by churches in the district around the convent, others were for use in the convent chapel itself. Caesaria, sister of Caesarius of Arles, required her nuns to make "fine copies" of manuscripts (probably meaning illuminated), and wanted clear and legible copies for distribution to the sisters.[97] But others worked independently or in city scriptoria which were supported by noble families in order that their donations of liturgical books to churches might be done under their direct supervision. (Christine de Pisan, although primarily known as a writer in her own right, supported herself and her large family by working as a copyist in such a city scriptorium. Several extant portraits of her working are found in illuminated manuscripts.) Sometimes secular copyists would work for convents that did not have their own scriptoria.

These women scribes and illuminators were involved in the production of many different kinds of liturgical books — Bibles, gospel books, missals, and sacramentaries, for example — and often they would specialize in one particular aspect of the process or in a particular type of book. In 1279, Allegra, the wife of a man named Ivano, promised the Carmelites near Paris that she would copy out an entire Bible, and in Cologne in about the same period, the widow Tula was employed as a professional *rubeatrix* (copier of rubrics).[98] But others seem to have been adept at all aspects of book production. A late twelfth-century homiliary (collection of sermons) from a monastery in the middle Rhine region contains a veiled woman encapsulated within an initial letter D (for "Dominus"). "Its caption reads: *Guda, peccatrix mulier, scripsit et pinxit hunc librum*" (Guda, sinful woman, wrote and illustrated this book). One hand grips the curved belly of the letter, the other is raised in the gesture of a witness who confirms the truth of the statement.[99] A description in the biography of Ida of Léau, a thirteenth-century copyist, could well be applied to all these women: "At all times were all her faculties engaged in writing, carefully copying books for the Church, correcting a fairly

96. See Rosamond McKitterick, "Frauen and Schriftlichkeit im Frühmittlealter," in *Weibliche Lebensgestaltung im fruhen Mittlealter,* ed. Hans Werner Goetz (Cologne: Böhlau, 1991). In these convent scriptoria, "The 'chauntres' was responsible for 'alle the bokes ... that longe to diuynr seruyse, chapter and freytour' and for ascertaining that 'they be corrected, and made of one acorde' though this latter stipulation suggests that it was mainly the service books that were her responsibility...." Ann M. Hutchinson, "Devotional Reading in the Monastery and in the Household," in *De Cella in Seculum: Religious and Secular Life and Devotion in Late Medieval England,* ed. Michael G. Sargeant (Cambridge: Brewer, 1989), 217–18.

97. See Gillian Clark, *Women in Late Antiquity: Pagan and Christian Life-Styles* (Oxford: Clarendon, 1993), 137–38.

98. For images of these women working, see Christiane Klapisch-Zuber, *Women, Family, and Ritual in Renaissance Italy* (Chicago: University of Chicago Press, 1987), 401, plate 42.

99. Frugoni, "The Imagined Woman," 415, illus. 53. This illumination is especially interesting because it is one of the oldest signed self-portraits of a woman, certainly the oldest self-portrait of a woman artist.

large manuscript of weekday lessons for Matins; her name has been placed on numerous other manuscripts copied most diligently."[100] When printing replaced hand-lettering for liturgical books, convents continued to create beautiful texts for use in Christian worship. In the late fifteenth century, the nuns at San Jacopo di Ripoli in Florence, which had had a flourishing scriptoria, embraced the new technology and became equally famous for their printing.

Sculptors and Painters

Although there has been some research into the contributions of women sculptors and painters to the liturgical environment, much more remains to be done. Bolognese sculptor Properzia de Rossi (c. 1490–1530) is one about whom we do know something, because payments for her work on the Church of San Petronio in Bologna are recorded in the ledgers of the church. In 1524, a papal legate invited her to decorate the canopy of the high altar in the church he had recently restored outside the gate of San Stefano. "She undertook this commission and created a beautiful confection of intertwined foliage, birds and fruit which still wreaths the altar in the church of Santa Maria del Baraccano, Bologna."[101] Her reputation established, de Rossi was invited to compete for the decoration of the new church of San Petronio to be built in Bologna to rival the church of Santa Maria del Fiore in Florence. She died before the building was finished, but not before she had completed a portion of the work on the west front, a number of figures, and at least two full sculpted images (one of the visit of the Queen of Sheba to Solomon, and another of Joseph and Potiphar's wife). Other women sculptors have worked in more manageable materials than stone. In Spain there is a large and elaborate silver crucifix with figures in relief attributed to the sixteenth-century goldsmith and sculptor Sancia Guidosalvi.

Contemporary women sculptors (and indeed women artists in general) sometimes feel constrained by a commission for a "church piece," fearing that they will be forced to produce work in a more conventional style than they usually employ. But with sensitive and adventurous clients, some women artists have broken through this anxiety and have produced for liturgical settings sculptures that stretch the boundaries of Christian imagery. "Christa," the crucifix by English sculptor Edwina Sandys, distinguished by the obviously female corpus hanging on it, was unveiled at the Cathedral of St. John the Divine on Maundy Thursday, 1984. An enormous amount of controversy ensued, and the sculpture was moved

---

100. *De Ida Lewensi virgine*, in *Acta Sanctorum* (XIII:113), cited in Frugoni, "The Imagined Woman," 414.

101. See Ragg, *The Women Artists of Bologna*, 132–33.

to a less accessible place in the church, partly for its own protection. A smaller piece, based on Sandys's original, was part of a processional cross carried in Manchester Cathedral in October 1993, in the presence of the bishop. (One strenuous objector described the occasion as "an indication of the growing acceptance of the feminist perspective in theology and worship."[102]) A less "radical" approach to a sculpted crucifix was taken by Cornelia van Aukin Chapin, who produced the corpus on the Great Cross over the High Altar at St. John the Divine.

Because painting has traditionally been seen as a more "feminine" art than sculpture, the number of women painters who have contributed to the enhancement of the liturgical environment is larger by comparison with the number of sculptors (see fig. 30). Most of these women, however, worked on a small scale, and their paintings have tended to be for private, rather than public, use. It is also true that the majority of paintings by women found in churches have been by amateur, rather than professionally employed, artists and are often given the label "folk," "vernacular," or "regional" art. While we may dismiss copies of Sallman's "Head of Christ" and da Vinci's "Last Supper" which adorn the walls of innumerable country churches as being "not really art," they are clearly expressions of women's artistic impulses and create a very particular historical and devotional associations within the worship environment. But professional women artists have also worked to adorn the interiors of Christian churches, some of whom have produced work of lasting value.

There seems to have been an increase in professional women painters during the Renaissance, many of whom worked for the church during a period in which a great deal of energy and money was being put into the building and decoration of churches. Three or four of these women deserve mention. Barbara Longhi, born in Ravenna in 1552, was taught by her father Luca Longhi, and with him worked on altarpieces for local churches. Soon, however, she graduated to production of her own work, painting both the "Cappucini Altarpiece" (named for the patron who financed it) and "The Healing of St. Agatha," as well as panel paintings of the virgin and child for the cathedral church in Ravenna. At the same time in Bologna, Lavinia Fontana served as a court painter for the papal court of Pope Gregory XIII, and worked on commissions for churches from the 1580s until she died in 1614. In 1603 the pope asked her to paint the altarpiece portraying the stoning of St. Stephen for one of the papal chapels. She also painted a very large (ten feet by six feet) piece for the Church of the Holy Trinity, "The Birth

---

102. He continues his report in a polemical tone: "The hymn 'I Vow to Thee My Country' was re-written for the occasion as 'I Vow to Thee My Sisters'... and ended 'and God she'll stand among us and join our victory song.'" Barry Spurr, *The Word in the Desert: Anglican and Roman Catholic Reactions to Liturgical Reform* (Cambridge: Lutterworth, 1995), 147.

of the Virgin," and another for the Church of Santa Maria della Pieta of the multiplication of the loaves and fishes. In Santa Maria del Baraccano (a church in which sculptor Properzia de Rossi also worked), there is a portrait of the Holy Family by Lavinia. Some women not only painted for churches, but were founders of groups of women ecclesiastical painters. Plaitilla Nelli (1523–88) was abbess of the convent of Santa Caterina de Siena in Florence, where she taught four of her sisters to paint, and Elisabetta Sirani (b. 1638) started an atelier in which a number of Bolognese women painters were trained and which produced a large number of paintings for churches.[103] This extraordinarily rich tradition of Italian women painters persisted until the first half of the eighteenth century, and the last of these women, Giulia Lama (1681–1747), left three surviving altar pieces in and around Venice.[104]

For various complex reasons, women artists are not well represented in the Protestant traditions in the two centuries after the Reformation. So, for example, although there are nearly two hundred painters, architects, engravers, goldsmiths, and sculptors indexed in a recent volume dedicated to the visual arts in the churches of the Reformed tradition,[105] not one of these is a woman. The notion that when it comes to the knowledge of God, the ear is less easily led astray than the eye is surely responsible, in part, for a reticence about the visual arts as a medium for religious expression. Added to this was the strong sense that women's domestic lives were a viable form of religious vocation, in which their artistic impulses could be employed for the edification of their families and the expression of their own devotional aspirations. But much more research is needed to flesh out the story of Protestant women painters, sculptors, and practitioners of the other liturgical arts from the sixteenth century onwards.

While women liturgical artists have contributed a great deal to the enhancement of the environment for worship in many local churches, there is perhaps a more significant way in which women have played a part in the various liturgical arts and crafts that needs to be mentioned. A visit to any ordinary Christian church in any ordinary town quickly reveals the contributions to the environment for worship of women patrons and benefactors. Plaques bearing the names of women donors are found on altar tables, fonts, pulpits, paintings, and altarware. Women have given their parish churches vestments and chalices, hymnals and other liturgical books, and stained glass windows. Many wealthy women have

---

103. It is said that Sirani was poisoned by a jealous rival painter, Lucia Tolomelli.
104. These are "Virgin and Child with Saints" (Santa Maria Formosa, 1722), "Crucifixion" (San Vitale, Venice, 1730), and "Assumption of the Virgin" (parish church of Malmocco, 1739).
105. See Paul Corby Finney, ed., *Seeing beyond the Word: Visual Arts in the Calvinist Tradition* (Grand Rapids, Mich.: Eerdmans, 1999), 535–38.

given money for elaborate decorative schemes for their churches, and the church was for so long able to be a "patron of the arts" because of the monetary gifts of women and their stipulations for the use of those gifts. So, when in the fourteenth century Isabel Despenser directed that an effigy of herself be set up on both sides of her monument "all naked with her hair cast backward," while at the sides were to be sculpted "poor men and women in their poor array with their heads in their hands" (presumably consumed by grief over her death), she was encouraging the creative work of sculptors as well as altering the liturgical environment.[106]

Although it may be quite difficult to assess the actual impact of the multitude of these innumerable small contributions to the history of the liturgical arts, gifts of liturgical art have given women yet another avenue for artistic influence on the church that should not be overlooked. There have indeed been certain serious constraints on women's artistic expression, but the power of the arts in the human religious quest is such that women have, in the words of historian Anne Higonet, always found "diverse and multiple detours around the artistic domains forbidden to them."[107]

---

106. Andrew Martindale, "Patrons and Minders," in *The Church and the Arts*, ed. Diana Wood (Oxford: Basil Blackwell, 1992), 170.

107. Anne Higonet, "Images," in *History of Women in the West*, vol. 4: *Emerging Feminism from Revolution to World War*, ed. Genevieve Fraisse and Michelle Perrot (Cambridge, Mass.: Belknap Press of Harvard University Press, 1993), 177.

Conclusion

Knowing Their Place

Brother Hammock asked me if I would supply them some salt-rising bread to use in the Communion services. Of course, I was glad to do what I could in religious work and I readily agreed to provide the bread. But they did not get to have Communion services the next day. It came down the biggest rain I ever saw in my life. Lubbock did not have any drainage system and water stood everywhere. When we got up the next morning and looked down at the house where the preachers were camped, we knew that they could not get out and cook their breakfast on a camp fire, so I hurried and fixed a basket of hot food for them....

—Mrs. J. B. Mobley, Lubbock, Texas, recorded December 28, 1936[1]

This book began with a number of presuppositions. First, we presumed that liturgical texts, rubrics, and learned commentaries on the church's common prayer should not be confused with Christian worship itself. Such documents may be road maps to worship, or shadows of worship, or models for worship, but they must never be equated with the genuine act of the gathered community saying their prayers and singing and ritualizing their faith. In some cases, liturgical texts may be quite accurate maps of the geography of worship; in other cases, they simply represent the pious aspirations of their authors or the efforts of ecclesiastical authorities to control the spiritual and ritual impulses of believers. We can see this most easily when we consider the prohibitions on liturgical behavior found in rubrics and canonical legislation, which for a very long time we believed gave us a clear and unambiguous indication of liturgical behavior: "If the rubric says people were not to stand during such-and-such a prayer, then surely people were not standing." Of course, some worshipers may indeed have remained seated. But almost invariably when we find a statute that tells people not to stand during such-and-such a prayer (or not to run up and down in church, or not to neglect the baptism of their children), we can assume that this is precisely what many

---

1. Federal Writers' Project, "American Life Histories," recorded by Ivey G. Warren, Library of Congress, Works Progress Administration Collection.

of them were doing. There are two sides to every official text: the text itself and its silhouette, and often in looking at the silhouette of the text we gain a more accurate sense of the reality of public worship.

The second presupposition was that there are various kinds of histories: "official" histories and "unofficial" histories, "elite" histories and "nonelite" histories, "macrohistories" and "microhistories." Each of these kinds of history requires different methods, different sources, and different modes of analysis, and although the truth claims of one type of history may be pitted against the truth claims of another, only by blending these various kinds of history can we arrive at some accurate sense of shape of the historical narrative. A *History of Women in Christian Worship* is a first attempt at an "unofficial, nonelite, microhistory" of Christian worship, with women's liturgical experience as the initial point of entry. The book is grounded in a firm belief that the processes of history are to be explained not only by attention to high-level power politics or privileged ideologies, but also by subtle changes in popular taste, values, and attitudes. We have presumed that the engine of liturgical processes is driven both from above and below.

We have tried in this process to listen to the quieter voices of liturgical history and to those voices that have been ignored. We have tried to imagine what the experience of women at worship must have been, and how worship affected other aspects of women's lives. We have begun to suggest the multitude of locations, both the mainstreams and the backwaters, where the stories of women's liturgical experience can be found. But much, much more is yet to be done. In an effort to attend more seriously to the worship lives of women in congregations, we have paid less attention to the worship lives of women in religious orders. For seventeen centuries, women living in community have been enormously creative in their approach to the construction of their own liturgical worlds, and in certain crucial periods, women have been the engine for liturgical change on a wide scale. In addition, very influential women have tended to fade into the background in favor of their more ordinary sisters; any larger study needs to take a closer look at how royalty, saints, abbesses, and scholars have influenced the course of liturgical history. The lives of women missionaries are all too often overlooked (although recent research by Lavinia Byrne and others is beginning to remedy that), and much more attention must be given to the liturgical aspects of the work of evangelization. How were women's interpretations of worship formed? How did these interpretations differ from those of their fathers, brothers, and sons? Although we did spend some time on the various liturgical arts, including music, we only skimmed the surface of this critical area of women's involvement in worship. There is surely a vast amount of information to be gathered on those art forms we have discussed here, and others (such as dance) should be treated. Some periods of Christian history are seriously underrepresented here, and complexities of attempting to put together the jigsaw puzzle that is early Christian history need to be tackled. Clearly, the material here is biased toward the West and the North, and in a fully realized history of women at worship, the South and East will receive equal treatment. As Mrs. Mobley's simple description of her contribution to the worship life of turn-of the-century Lubbock, Texas (quoted above), demonstrates, a vast amount of previously collected oral history is still to be examined for information about women's worship lives. Finally, longer narratives, such as that of "The Field Matrons" (appendix 4) and "The Peasants" (appendix 5), must be collected over a wider range of historical periods and analyzed for their significance to the history of Christian worship.

Is such an ambitious program possible? Can we compile a complete "history of women at worship"? I hope so. But if this hope is to become a reality, a number of preconditions must be met. This kind of project will never be accomplished by a single person working alone in her study, but by a whole network of people, working collaboratively across disciplinary boundaries. Although we who are specialists in Christian worship may take the lead, we will need to spend a great deal of time talking to social scientists and folklorists, learning the methodologies of oral historians and statisticians, and asking economists, musicologists, philosophers of science, and human geographers how they organize and interpret their data. Students of Christian worship, those of us who make a living at it and those who do not, will need to draw ordinary congregations into the task, and to encourage them to gather and record the history of women at worship in each place.

But even if no such grand scheme is ever undertaken, I hope in developing the preceding chapters several results have been realized. First, it seems clear that despite all of the efforts to silence them and to mask their presence, women are neither silent nor invisible in the history of Christian worship, if we only know where to listen and look. The narrative of their participation in Christian common prayer may not fit neatly into the traditional categories of liturgical historiography, and, indeed, the narrative itself may point out certain critical inadequacies in those categories. But to see women worshipers as historical actors in their own right, rather than simply as those "acted upon" by others, is to move closer to completing an accurate picture of the history of Christian worship. Many readers may have been surprised at the large number of forthright and courageous women who have not been willing to let their worship lives be dictated for them, and who have gone to such extraordinary lengths to meet their own ritual needs. Others might have been amazed at women's willingness to redefine the terms of their liturgical participation, and their ability to find their own meaning in rites largely defined by men. That having been said, however, the history of women at worship is not an unambiguously heroic one: there is as much pettiness and silliness here as anywhere in ecclesiastical historiography, and in the end, readers need to draw their own conclusions about the meaning of this work for the current living reality of women in the churches.

Have women generally "known their place" in Christian worship? The answers to that question are as ambiguous as the question itself. In one sense they certainly have not. Over and over again they have revealed themselves to be wonderfully obstinate and unmanageable when it has come to keeping within the parameters of prescribed roles and practices. Despite all the efforts to control their liturgical behavior, women have been ready and able to find new modes of liturgical self-expression and alternative sources of ritual nurture, and to use their creativity to refashion and reinterpret existing rites as wellsprings of Christian hope. In another sense, however, women have known their place: They have known that to stand before God in worship is to claim a place in the life of faith and the mission of God. They have known that their place in worship is a place of honor, not to be given or taken away by other human beings, but bestowed by God to all God's people, men and women alike. In both knowing and not knowing their place, women have created an intricate mosaic of religious act, thought, and meaning. In other words, they have created Christian history.

Women and "Churching"

The practice of setting a woman apart and enforcing abstinence from the normal religious and social activities for a fixed period of time following childbirth is common to many traditions. Often, a rite was conducted to mark the end of this period of purification. In Leviticus 12:1–6, women were declared "ceremonially unclean" (i.e., ineligible to participate in temple sacrifices) for forty days after giving birth to a son and eighty days after giving birth to a daughter. The mother was then to go to the temple bringing both a lamb (as a burnt offering) and a turtledove (as a sin offering), which the priest would offer "to make atonement on her behalf." From as early as the fifth century onward, we begin to find evidence of this kind of practice in the Christian church,[1] but official rites for the readmission of new mothers into Christian fellowship are not found in liturgical books until about the eleventh century. This is not to say that the liturgical and theological appropriateness of rites of purification after childbirth (which from at least the fourteenth century were commonly called "churching" in English) was not a matter of discussion. We get some hint of the debate in twelfth-century Ireland in an 1198 letter to the Archbishop of Armagh from Pope Innocent III, who advocated that women immediately enter the church after childbirth, arguing that the gospel superseded the requirements of the old law. But, the pope continued, "The Archbishop should not deny women access to the church if they desired to give thanks, for otherwise they would appear to be penalized for their labor pains, as if for a fault. However, women who desired to wait out of reverence were also praiseworthy for their devotion."[2]

To classify churching simply as another example of male attempts to marginalize women and to ritualize their loathing and suspicion of women's natural bodily functions is to ignore several facts. First, churching was enormously popular

---

1. In the year 460, for example, the Emperor Leo prohibited women from taking communion within forty days of her delivery, but in the case of emergency to join the eucharistic fellowship was not to be considered a grave sin.

2. Cited in Constance M. Rousseau, "Gender Difference and Indifference in the Writings of Pope Innocent III," in *Gender and Christian Religion*, ed. R. N. Swanson (Woodbridge, U.K.: Boydell, 1998), 108. Gregory the Great gave similar advice. See also Waltar von Arx, "The Churching of Women after Childbirth: History and Significance," *Concilium* 112 (1979): 63–72.

among women, and even when clergy attempted to stamp it out, women resisted mightily. It is not surprising that women naturally responded to a ritual that took so seriously their experience of the "liminal," of having stood at the boundary between life and death in childbirth; churching was a significant rite of passage for new mothers. For most periods of Christian history, the high rate of mortality for women in childbirth made the thanksgiving element of the rite "more immediate for women than for the male clerics who both defended and degraded the ceremony."[3] The period of social exclusion after childbirth, which in some cultures could last up to two hundred days, also served as a way of protecting women from the rigors of work, especially in rural, agricultural societies where their labor was most easily exploited. Although, as we shall see, women dissenters used their resistance to churching as a form of liturgical protest, this was a part of the larger protest against all official rites of the church rather than a direct attack on churching, which did not in itself tend to pose a serious theological difficulty, even for women dissenters. Churching was also supported by a whole range of folk beliefs (e.g., a women did not regain her strength except by being churched, the food she cooked would not be as nutritional for her family, unchurched women were likely to bring plague or infestations of rats to their neighborhoods[4]) that gave it additional authority among women. This combination of folk wisdom and ecclesial sanction led to the belief among many women that they would be denied a Christian burial if they died between childbirth and churching.[5]

We can see the popularity of this rite among women in an example from the diocese of Lincoln in the mid-seventeenth century, when objections to the rite among Puritan clergy were at their height.

> The wife of Richard Ravens of Elstow, Bedfordshire was presented in the archdeacon's court for having "churched herself." Upon the failure of the priest to appear at the time appointed for her thanksgiving, she read the first part of the service from the *Book of Common Prayer* (presumably Psalm 121) "openlie" in the church and considered herself quite satisfactorily churched, for she went home and apparently did not seek out the incumbent in order to go through the service again with him.[6]

---

3. Judith Maltby, *Prayer Book and People in Elizabethan and Stuart England* (Cambridge: Cambridge University Press, 1998), 64.

4. Anne O'Connor, "Listening to Tradition," in *Personally Speaking*, ed. Liz Steiner-Scott (New York: Attic Press, 1985), 36.

5. See Keith Thomas, *Religion and the Decline of Magic* (New York: Oxford University Press, 1997), 38–39.

6. Maltby, *Prayer Book and People in Elizabethan and Stuart England*, 63. This incident is also recounted by David Cressy (*Birth, Marriage, and Death: Ritual, Religion, and the Life-Cycle in Tudor and Stuart England* [Oxford: Oxford University Press, 1997], 214–15), although there is some confusion

Mrs. Ravens was dismissed with a warning, but soon after her minister, Mr. Bird, was cited by the court for neglect of pastoral duty, including not only his failure to church Ravens, but also for failing entirely to hold a Sunday service on at least one occasion. Whether Mr. Bird's failure to church Mrs. Ravens was a form of godly protest on his part, or whether it was simple neglect is difficult to say, but in any case, as historian Judith Maltby puts it, "Either way . . . a laywoman who was able to read was determined to have the comfort of the lawful liturgy."[7] It is interesting to note that in the various questions posed by bishops in their annual visitations of the churches in their dioceses, they are much more likely to ask about the priest's diligence in performing churchings than to ask about women parishioners' diligence in coming to be churched.[8]

Other women who were unsatisfied with the seriousness with which their pastors took the rituals of churching made alternative arrangements. "Henry Machymn described the alderman's wife in 1560 who preserved the neighborly and celebratory function of churching by organizing her own ceremony, with a dinner to follow, since her priest would perform the service only at six in the morning, if it was to be held in the church."[9] Some women seem to have made the rite of churching into a more fashionable occasion. In the early eighteenth century, one man reported that when his wife was churched after their son was born, "she was carried [to the church] in a Sedan" wearing an elaborate veil, with several women in attendance."[10] But most women were so anxious to be churched properly that they were willing to resort to quite extreme means to see that it was done. At Selsey, Sussex, a dispute between the women of the parish and their minister, Thomas Kent, occupied the courts for several years in the 1630s. The women charged that Kent, "rode off, leaving women waiting to

about the name of the accused. (Cressy calls her "the wife of Richard Claw."). Cressy's chapter "Purification, Thanksgiving, and the Churching of Women," pp. 197–229, is an invaluable resource for this subject.

7. Ibid., 64.

8. So, for example, in John Cosin's visitation for 1576 (*John Cosin's Visitation Articles*, chapter 11), we find the following query and answer: "Touching the Churching of Women: 'Doth your Minister duly observe the order and forme prescribed in churching of women after childbirth? Is the same done publikely and reverently in the Church, the woman coming in that decent and grave attire which hath bin accustomed, and the Minister attending in his surplice, causing her to kneel neere the place where God's Table standeth, and to make her thanksgiving and her off'ring, as is prescribed?' "

9. Claire S. Schen, "Women and the London Parishes, 1500–1620," in *The Parish in English Life, 1400–1600,* Katherine L. French, Gary Gibbs, and Beat A. Kümin (Manchester: Manchester University Press, 1997), 252.

10. William M. Jacob, *Lay People and Religion in the Early Eighteenth Century* (Cambridge: Cambridge University Press, 1996), 74. See also Gail Gibson, "Churching as Women's Theater," in *Bodies and Disciplines: Intersections of Literature and History in Fifteenth-Century England,* ed. B. A. Hanawalt and D. Wallace (Minneapolis: University of Minnesota Press, 1996), 139–54. The wearing of a veil for churching persisted after the Reformation, but there was a debate about whether it was required or simply a matter of local custom.

be churched."[11] Humphrey Wildblood, a minister of Puritan sensibilities in the diocese of Peterborough, "was confronted by a group of angry women who demanded to be churched after childbirth [when] the godly Wildblood refused to hold the service."[12] Even those women who were cited in the consistory courts for failure to adhere to the ritual of churching seem to have been guilty only of failing to follow certain technical conventions. Catherine Capon was reported to the consistory court in 1607 for "refusing to come after the accustomed manner to give God thanks for her deliverance . . . in obstinate contempt for our minister and order." She claimed in her defense that she had indeed come to be churched "as an honest woman in her usual apparel but without a veil."[13]

The churching of women after childbirth is one of the very small number of rites of the church which center on women as the primary focus of liturgical attention. But the others — queen-making (coronation) rites, the enrollment and veiling of widows, the vows taken by women entering the consecrated life, and the consecration of an abbess — tend to be for very exceptional women under very exceptional circumstances rather than for women of the more ordinary sort under ordinary circumstances. While it may be astonishing to modern women that churching was so enormously meaningful to their sisters in previous generations, its power lay in its ability to function as the closest thing to a rite of passage for most women. It tapped into their deep anxieties about pregnancy and motherhood, and their sense of relief that they had safely navigated the journey through childbirth. Even though the traditional churching service was infused with the language of penitence and purification, these more "negative" aspects of the rite did not seem to hinder women from finding deep meaning and satisfaction in being churched. (Indeed, when one thinks of the pain of childbirth undiminished by anesthetic, it would not be so surprising if women felt as if they had been through inchoate experiences of penitence and purification that demanded ritualization in church.) Although by the nineteenth century, the marriage rite had begun to take over some of the functions of churching as the preeminent rite of passage for women, the ambiguities, extravagances, and family tensions that are so often a part of weddings make it unlikely that the wedding will ever carry the religious force that churching did for Christian women of the past.

---

11. Anthony Fletcher, "Factionalism in the Countryside," in *The Church in Town and Countryside*, Studies in Church History 16 (Oxford: Blackwell, 1979), 293. See also William Coster, "Purity, Profanity, and Puritanism: The Churching of Women, 1500–1700," in *Women in the Church*, ed. W. J. Shiels and Diana Wood, Studies in Church History 27 (Oxford: Blackwell, 1990), 357–87.

12. Maltby, *Prayer Book and People*, 63.

13. Marjorie Keniston McIntosh, *A Community Transformed: The Manor and Liberty of Havering, 1500–1620* (Cambridge: Cambridge University Press, 1991), 45–46. McIntosh continues, "Between 1589 and 1607, thirteen women from Hornchurch and one from Romford were reported to the Archdeacon's court for refusing to be churched or for coming 'without a decent kerchief or veil.'"

Appendix Two

Women as Patrons
and Benefactors

From the very beginnings of the Christian church, women benefactors and patrons have made significant contributions to the enhancement of common worship. In 1 Timothy 5, a "real" widow is described as chaste, honorable, and "given to good works," which is code for "was a benefactor" to the church,[1] and inscriptions from as early as 43 C.E. extol women for their generosity in giving. Some women have given money for the purchase of liturgical accessories; some have given vessels, vestments, and altar furnishings; others have supported the building of churches or chapels that reflected their own liturgical inclinations. When, for example, in a period of ceremonial austerity Lady Alice Dudley chose to give to the Church of St. Giles in the Fields in the 1630s "a rich green velvet cloth" for the back of the altar, with the letters "IHS" embroidered in gold, "very handsome rails to guard the altar of the Lord's table from profane abuses," and communion plate "of all sorts in silver and gilt, for that sacred use, which is as large and rich as any in city and suburbs," she is making a clear statement that her own preference for a Laudian approach to worship be undertaken in the church.[2] Some women used their wills as attempts to reach out from the grave to control the worship of the congregations of which they had been a part. Anne Ashby, a wealthy widow who died at the end of February 1515, wished to be buried "within the pasissh chirch of Rykmersworth afore the ymage of saint Kateryn in the new Ile of siad chirch." In her will, she directed her executors to spend five pounds on a pyx of silver and gilt and two pounds on a pair of silver cruets, all of which were "to remayne to the church of Rykmersworth for ever."[3]

---

1. See Bruce W. Winter, *Seek the Welfare of the City: Christians as Benefactors and Citizens* (Grand Rapids, Mich.: Eerdmans, 1994), 93.
2. All these articles except the plate were sold during the Civil War when they were regarded as hopelessly "superstitious and popish." R. Boreman, *A Mirror of Christianity and a Miracle of Charity, or True and Exact Narrative of the Life and Death of the most Virtuous Lady, Alice, Duchess of Dudley* (London, 1699), 22–24.
3. Margaret Aston, *Faith and Fire: Popular and Unpopular Religion, 1350–1600* (London: Hambledon, 1993), 246.

Some women's donations were more immediately self-serving. In 1405 Alice Styllyngfleet provided thirty-two pounds of wax for torches to surround her hearse in her own funeral procession, and in 1438 the Widow Gregg arranged for no fewer than eighteen torches to burn about her body during her exequies.[4] But the motivations of most women in making donations of worship material (or money to provide such materials) to their parish churches can only be guessed at. In many cases, women seem to be using their bequests in order to continue to be part of the worshiping community after their deaths. When Margaret Sale died in 1527, she stipulated that candles burn in perpetuity before "the images she had honoured in her life: before Our Lady, St. Katherine, St. Anne, St. Sythe," in the church of St. Margaret Pattens, and also "before Our Blessed Lady at Barking, and St. Gabriel at St. Gabriel Fenchurch."[5] Sometimes the liturgical items left by women reflect their simple need to feel they will not be forgotten by their congregation, and in many cases, inscriptions on liturgical paraphernalia have made it clear to future generations of worshipers who the donor was. When Katherine of Valois (1401–37) , daughter of King Charles VI of France and widow of King Henry V of England, gave vestments to her parish church, she ordered that each piece be embroidered in gold with a large letter "K" surmounted by a crown.[6] But for many generations of Christian women, who have accepted what one historian has called the "gift-exchange economy of salvation,"[7] a donation of liturgical accouterments to the church was a part of their preparation for eternal life. We can see this perhaps most clearly in the bequests women have made to underwrite prayers to be said for the repose of their souls. Dame Thomasyn Percivale "provided for sick householders to say prayers for her in their own homes, and for her corpse's attendants to sit, stand, or kneel, depending on their physical abilities. She hired more poor householders, and 'such of them as can' to say selected prayers"[8] after her death. Such attempts by women to combine their perceived obligations to the liturgy and to charity in their bequests is not uncommon.

Sometimes women benefactors used their money to direct the larger worship lives of congregations according to their own particular liturgical sensitivities.

---

4. Peter Heath, "Urban Piety in the Later Middle Ages: The Evidence from Hull Wills," in *The Church, Politics and Patronage in the Fifteenth Century*, ed. Barrie Dobson (Gloucester, U.K.: Sutton, 1984), 217.

5. Susan Brigden, *London and the Reformation* (Oxford: Clarendon, 1989), 9.

6. See R. N. Swanson, "Liturgy as Theatre: The Props," in *The Church and the Arts*, ed. Diana Wood (Oxford: Basil Blackwell, 1992), 249.

7. Ibid.

8. Clare S. Schen, "Women and the London Parishes, 1500–1620," in *The Parish in English Life, 1400–1600*, ed. Katherine L. French, Gary Gibbs, Beat A. Kümin (Manchester: Manchester University Press, 1997), 255, 257.

Lady Maxwell, an associate of John Wesley and a Methodist, was executor for the estate of her friend Lady Glenorchy (d. 1786), who was influenced by the Countess of Huntingdon's more Calvinist form of Methodism. Glenorchy had founded and endowed many churches and chapels, and Lady Maxwell "faced problems with building upkeep, procuring ministers, paying bills, reconciling members, resisting the demands of the blood relatives of Lady Glenorchy, and strong local prejudice against forms of worship divergent from those of the Church of England or the Kirk." One of the most problematic of the churches under her care was Hope Chapel, which Maxwell seems to have governed with an iron hand. In a letter to Alexander Mather, she makes her wishes clear: "Hope Chapel will use the prayer book services. It will not be under the governance of the Bishop. They will hire a 'church minister... truly alive to God,' i.e., an evangelical. Services will be on Sunday only. The communion will be open only to those with a ticket. The pulpit will be open to worthy preachers what ever their denomination."[9]

Occasionally whole liturgical movements came under women's patronage. The nineteenth-century Oxford ("Tractarian") and Cambridge Movements, which aimed at the restoration of richer liturgical ceremonial to the worship of the British churches, have usually been portrayed by historians as essentially clerical-ist and thus male, but the first great supporter of both movements in Scotland was a woman, Cecil Kerr Chetwynd, widow of the Seventh Marquis of Lothian. She would become "one of the leading Scottish Tractarians during the 1840s until her conversion to Roman Catholicism in 1851."[10] Lady Lothian built and endowed the neo-Gothic Church of St. John, Jedburgh, designed under her close supervision by a member of the Cambridge Camden Society and the first Episco-pal church to be built to Camden Society principles, with a stone font and altar. Tractarian leaders were present at its consecration, held on August 15, 1844, which was itself a showcase for Tractarian liturgical ideals. "The incumbent in-toned Matins with the choir chanting the responses and the psalm, in what has been reckoned as the first choral service in Scotland since the Revolution. There

---

9. Letter from Lady Maxwell to Mather, June 24, 1791, cited in E. K. Brown, *Women of Mr. Wes-ley's Methodism* (New York and Toronto: Edwin Mellen Press, 1983), 131. Maxwell was charged with the appointment of ministers for these churches. Because Lady Glenorchy had been a Calvinist, Maxwell was concerned that as her executor she would be obliged to appoint Calvinist preachers to these posts, and she wrote to John Wesley for advice. "In his reply, Wesley earnestly chastises her for even thinking of appointing a Calvinist preacher with the money her friend has left: 'O let not any money or friend move you to propagate a lie, to strike at the root of Methodism, to grieve the holiest of your friends and to endanger your own soul!'" Letter of John Wesley to Lady Maxwell, September 30 1788, *The Letters of the Rev. John Wesley*, ed. John Telford (London: Epworth, 1931), 8:94–95.

10. Rowan Strong, "Coronets and Altars: Aristocratic Women's and Men's Support for the Oxford Movement in Scotland During the 1840s," in *Gender and Christian Religion*, ed. R. N. Swanson, Studies in Church History 34 (Woodbridge, U.K.: Boydell, 1998), 391.

followed a service of consecration and Holy Communion."[11] Having appointed
a chaplain who shared her High Church ideals, Lady Lothian insisted that he ·
use the Scottish Communion office for the church, a rite highly regarded by the
Oxford Movement, but unlawful in the Scottish Episcopal Church without the
permission of the bishop. Somehow she received this permission, even though the
bishop was on record for having said, "As to the Scottish Communion Office I
wish there were no such thing in existence."[12]

As the case of Lady Lothian suggests, women founders and patrons of churches
and monastery chapels had great influence over which forms and patterns of
worship took place there, and since the early Middle Ages, their rights were
safeguarded in law, to the extent that money given to a church might be reclaimed
if the clergy were "negligent in performing contracted services." In 1341 Margaret
de Roos sued the abbey of Creake in Norfolk to regain lands she had given them,
"because the abbot had failed to provide the services specified in the endowment
charter — including singing masses in the chapel of Margaret's foundation.... "[13]
Surely, not all churches wanted the gifts that were being given and the liturgical
changes they would require, but most probably remained silent if inappropriate
donations were made, not wishing to offend wealthy patrons. Queen Margaret
of Austria gave a substantial amount of money to the Church of St. Nicholas of
Tolentino in Brou, in order to transform the *pulpitum*, traditionally both a singers'
gallery and the location for the organ, into an overhead passageway leading from
her own lodgings on the south side of the church to a two-story oratory in the
north side, which was fitted with seating and a fireplace and from which it was
possible to see the High Altar. But no one seems to have raised any objections
to this plan. "There are many possible reasons to account for this silence. Those,
so to speak, in the institutional firing-line may well have found themselves in
a delicate position.... If the Brou Augustinians, deprived of their *pulpitum*, had
asked where they were supposed to put their organ, they would presumably have
been told that this was what the Emperor's daughter wanted and that they would
have to make other arrangements."[14] Likely those with authority over the church
at Brou knew that just as patronage could be given, patronage could be taken
away, and some benefactions came with explicit strings attached. In the fifth
century, Sosiana, widow of an official in the imperial court, gave the church
elaborately embroidered silk clothes, linens with designs in the weave, and fabric

---

11. Ibid., 398.
12. Ibid.
13. Aston, *Faith and Fire*, 126.
14. Andrew Martindale, "Patrons and Minders," in *The Church and the Arts*, ed. Diana Wood
(Oxford: Basil Blackwell, 1992), 168.

enriched with gold thread. "These were to be used as altar cloths and veils; she gave orders that they should not be sold for the benefit of the poor, in case a prostitute got them."[15]

The greatest number of women patrons and benefactors with interest in the liturgy have not been the wealthy and influential, but ordinary women who were not seeking self-promotion or power, but were simply trying to support under-resourced churches. Minnie Campbell, who grew up on the Kansas frontier in the last part of the nineteenth century, remembers, "We had no organ at our church, and no money to get one. My mother agreed to see there was an organ there, and she started a subscription paper. In a few days there was a good organ in the church and it was paid for."[16] On another occasion, after some interior decorating had been done in the church showing up the deficiencies of the liturgical furnishings, Campbell recalls that "no one liked the altar, and the man said he would put something there that would be much nicer if they could raise the money. My mother said, 'You fix the altar, and we'll see to the money.' And today when I see this beautiful altar I always think of the Mother who wanted her church to be as beautiful as her home."[17] In congregation after congregation, it has been as simple as this: women have wished to use whatever means available to them to make the liturgy of the church, and the setting in which it was conducted, "beautiful."

---

15. John of Ephesus, *Lives of the Eastern Saints*, 55; cited in Gillian Clark, *Women in Late Antiquity: Pagan and Christian Life-Styles* (Oxford: Clarendon, 1993), 111–12.

16. Joanna L. Stratton, *Pioneer Women: Voices from the Kansas Frontier* (New York: Simon and Schuster, 1981), 178.

17. Ibid.

Appendix Three

Deviating from Liturgical Norms and Standards

Although we have not paid a great deal of attention in these pages to the official rites, texts, and canonical legislation that have governed the common prayer of the various Christian communities, one should not conclude that women felt them inconsequential. Their absence is simply the result of the recognition that it is almost impossible to construct a women's history of Christian worship by looking at these kinds of materials. But many women have used the rites, rubrics, and liturgical legislation as a baseline for religious dissent; in their alternative worship practices, their theological interpretations of those practices, and their passive resistance to the liturgical status quo, women have carved a place for themselves in liturgical history in their own right. In dissenting from liturgical norms, women have withstood excommunication, imprisonment, physical punishment, violence at the hands of their neighbors, the scorn of their families, and even the threat of execution in order that they might engage in worship as they have seen fit. They have made their own independent judgments about the degree to which the official rites of the church were being scrupulously followed by those who had oversight over them. Dire warnings against deviance from liturgical standards have been enshrined not only in civil and canonical legislation, but in the *vitae* of the saints, the sermons of clergy, and the social wisdom of Christian communities. Gregory of Tours, for example, provided cautionary tales for women tempted to violate restrictions on activity during Sundays and feast days. (Vitalina, for example, washes her face on Good Friday and is excluded from the kingdom of heaven; another woman has her hand burned for hoeing a field on Sunday.[1]) As a result of this intricate network of sanctions, the courage required of women to deviate from prevailing liturgical norms and standards has at times been enormous; in nearly all periods of Christian history, the consequences have been great.

In every era of Christian history, the church's liturgy has been susceptible to two dangers: idolatry and clericalism. Women have always been enormously sensitive

---

1. *Libri Virtutibus Martini episcopus* 2.27; 2.24.

to both. Whenever worship has succumbed to the temptation to mistake the rites and symbols of worship for the experience of the living God it is meant to mediate, and whenever worship has succumbed to the temptation of insisting that God can only be experienced through rites controlled by designated experts, women have been there to speak out. In the year 1393, for example, Anne Palmer and four other Northampton women were accused by Bishop Buckingham of holding the belief that "it suffices every Christian to serve God's commandments in his chamber or to worship God secretly in the field, without paying heed to public prayers in a material building, lest conforming to the pharisees he is accounted a hypocrite."[2] Very often, it was debased ecclesiastical power politics and public strife among clergy that led women to seek alternative forms of liturgical organization, as we can see in the case of the thirteenth-century Guglielmites, a Milanese sect overseen by women, which began just after a fifteen-year period (1262–77) during which Milan's validly ordained archbishop was not allowed to enter the city because he was caught in a dispute between the pope and the Milanese ruling family.[3]

Women were often responsible for teaching one another deviant practices, in much the same way we have seen them teaching one another ordinary worship practices. In the first quarter of the sixteenth century, at least one young girl was brought for religious instruction to Lollard Alice Harding of Amersham, who, at the very least, taught her passages from the New Testament and the Ten Commandments and "to read her Bible loudly during Church services."[4] She also "dissuaded Joan Norman from going on pilgrimage, venerating the images of saints, fasting before going to mass, and going to confession."[5] We have seen how orthodox women used their domestic environment as settings for the liturgical formation of their social network, and dissenting women were no different. Historian of women in the Lollard movement Claire Cross says that "they made their houses stopping-places for Lollard travelers and meeting-places for worship and instruction; many were called to travel to other Lollard conventicles to recite the Scriptures they had learned by heart."[6] Ordinary family relationships, of course, also carried with them the power to communicate dissenting liturgical values. Thirteen-year-old Anabaptist Betkin van der Veste testified at her heresy trial in

---

2. Cited in A. K. McHardy, "Bishop Buckingham and the Lollards of Lincoln Diocese," *Studies in Church History* 9 (1972): 143.

3. Stephen E. Wessley, "The Thirteenth-Century Guglielmites: Salvation through Women," in *Medieval Women*, Studies in Church History, Subsidia, ed. Derek Baker (Oxford: Basil Blackwell, 1978), 289–303.

4. Claire Cross, "'Great Reasoners in Scripture': Women Lollards, 1380–1530," in *Medieval Women*, ed. Baker, 376–77.

5. Ibid. Harding also instructed men in the ways and means of liturgical dissent. In 1524, she advised Richard Bennett what to do to conceal his opinions from the priest.

6. Ibid., 373–74.

1558 "that she heard her father and mother say that they know better now, and that the baptism practiced here is not right, but they understood now that there is another baptism; people should be baptized when they understand and change their lives, when they no longer lie and deceive."[7]

Women not only held alternative points of view on liturgical matters, they have also engaged in alternative liturgical practices, and in active and passive resistance to forms of worship with which they disagreed. Resistance took many forms. Many women were charged with simply failing to attend services as required by both law and custom. In 1554, Anne Williamson of London was accused

> of not going on procession in St. Mary Magdalen Old Fish Street, nor witnessing the elevation of the host, and she confessed her scruples about receiving the eucharist.... [Earlier,] in 1553 she had, "contrary to womanhood," dared to enter the church without churching after childbirth, thereby breaking the old taboo and despising a Catholic rite. She refused to go from the church, to the horror of the "most devout and worthy of the parish," would not offer chrism for her child's baptism, and only left, and then contemptuously, at the sacring of the Mass.[8]

In this case, Williamson disrupted the church service simply by flouting liturgical convention, but other women seem to have intentionally disrupted the liturgy as a form of protest. When Margaret Brewster entered Boston's Third Church during a Sunday morning service in 1677, dressed in sackcloth, with her hair full of ashes and her face coated with soot, it "occasioned the greatest and most amazing uproar" according to Samuel Sewall, who witnessed the event. A Quaker from Barbados, Brewster was protesting the godless worship taking place in Massachusetts, and warning of the judgment that God would visit on the inhabitants if they failed to repent.[9] Rose Hickman was a staunch Protestant so deeply troubled by the return of the Catholic liturgy in the reign of Mary (that is, from 1542 to 1587) that she had "prayed earnestly to God to take wither her or me forth from the world." In order to " 'void popish stuff' so far as she could, Rose put sugar instead of the symbolic salt of the Catholic rite into the handkerchief she gave to the 'popish priest' at the baptism."[10] Earlier, during the reign of Henry VIII, young girls joined in "to profane the sacrament of the altar at their London parish church

---

7. A. L. E. Verheyden, *Anabaptism in Flanders 1530–1650* (Scottdale, Pa.: Herald Press, 1961), 117, citing "Testimony from the Proceedings against the Mennonites of Bruges, arrested June 24 and 29, 1558."

8. Susan Brigden, *London and the Reformation* (Oxford: Clarendon, 1989), 567.

9. For this timely warning, Brewster was "stripp'd and whipp'd." See Kenneth L. Carroll, "Early Quakers and 'Going Naked as Sign,' " *Quaker History* 67, no. 2 (Autumn 1978): 69–72.

10. Brigden, *London and the Reformation*, 626.

by throwing their caps at it during the elevation" on Corpus Christi day in 1548.[11] When Lydia Wright succumbed to a "leading of the Lord" which demanded that she "protest the wickedness of the minister and magistrates at Newbury, Massachusetts," she attended church stark naked as a sign of the pervasive "Ignorance and Persecution" in the church.[12]

But perhaps the most famous liturgical dissident was Jenny Geddes, who lives on in song and legend in the Scottish Church to this day.[13] When Charles I ascended the throne in 1625, he was determined to impose his views on the necessity of bishops and a set liturgy on the (Presbyterian) Church of Scotland. Year after year, ceremonial innovations were introduced, enforced by the Court of High Commission on the king's sole authority. The last straw was the imposition in 1637 of the Service Book, which to Scottish eyes was both redolent of popery and unlawfully imposed. The date was announced for the introduction of the new service book — July 23, 1637 — and it soon became clear that there would be trouble. That morning, St. Giles was crowded. "Long before the hour of worship 'servant women' with their 'creepie stools' had been making their way to the church to bespeak places for their mistresses, due to arrive somewhat later."[14] By the time the presider, Dr. David Lindsay, a royalist sympathizer and supporter of the king's religious views, arrived, the church was densely crowded with aristocrats, city officials, and ordinary people. The service began to murmurs of discontent, but when Jenny Geddes heard the officiant say the word "collect," she shouted aloud, "Take your 'colic' and get out! Out, thou false thief! Will you say mass at my lug [ears]?" Then, snatching up the stool on which she sat, she hurled it at his head. Others followed her example. "The Bishop sought in vain to quell the tumult that arose. The uproar increased. The magistrates were appealed to and cleared the church of the mob, who remained outside knocking at the door."[15] The dean continued on with the service, and when he was done the remaining congregation and participants were assaulted by the mob, and the bishop pelted with dung. Seldom has there been a popular uprising that had

---

11. Susan Brigden, "Youth and the English Reformation," in *Rebellion, Popular Protest, and Social Order in Early Modern England,* ed. Paul Slack (Cambridge: Cambridge University Press, 1983), 94–95. Later, Brigden reports, "When Dr. Browne preaches at Paul's Cross there was a 'gret up-rore and showtyng at ys sermon, at yt [were] lyke madpepull, watt yonge pepell and woman [as] ever was hard, as herle-borle, and castyng up of capes" (102).

12. David S. Lovejoy, *Religious Enthusiasm in the New World: Heresy to Revolution* (Cambridge, Mass.: Harvard University Press, 1985), 130.

13. "The Dean he to the altar went, and wi' a solemn look, / He cast his eyes to heaven, then read the curious-printed book. / In Jenny's heart the blood up-welled, with bitter anguish full, / Sudden she started to her legs and stoutly grasped the stool...." From a ballad by Professor J. S. Blackie, D.D.

14. J. C. Lees, "The Riot in St. Giles Cathedral in 1637: The Story of Jenny Geddes and Her Stool," in *Women of the Scottish Reformation: Their Contribution to the Protestant Cause,* ed. David P. Thomson (Crieff, Perthshire, Scotland: St. Ninian, 1960), 62.

15. Ibid., 61.

greater liturgical results than this one within St. Giles. This was not only the first and last time that the service was performed in its entirety, but gave impulse to the civil war in England, which ended in the overthrow of both church and monarchy.

Some women merely spoke out publicly against what they saw as deformed liturgical or sacramental practice. London matron Elizabeth Sampson admitted at her trial for the nonperformance of her religious obligations "using obscene words concerning various local pilgrimages and saints and having said 'I will not give my dog that bread that some priests minister at the altar when they be not in clean life,' asserting that she herself 'could make as good bread as that was; and that it was not the body of our Lord, for it is but bread, for God cannot be both in heaven and on earth.' "[16] A Norfolk woman arrested for being a Lollard was reported to have told a neighbor, "If you want to see the true cross of Christ, I'd like to show you here in your own house," upon which she stretched out her arms. "This is the true cross of Christ," she continued, "and this cross you can and ought to see and worship every day here in your own house, and so you labour in vain when you go to churches to worship or pray to any image or dead crosses."[17]

Many women were all too happy to be arrested for their deviant practice, and indeed saw it as an opportunity to spread their understanding of worship to a wider audience. Sister E. Sharp, an early Pentecostalist, was served with a summons to appear before the city magistrates on charges of disturbing the peace ("for praising Jesus with a loud voice") in 1920. She related the following experience:

> Oh, what glory filled my soul when I took that paper from the police constable for the sake of Jesus. The Lord was good to me; I danced around the constable in the Spirit. This brought Sister McPherson, who, when she saw me dancing, began to dance around them also. He went away remarking to others: "We cannot do one thing with these women." The Lord was with us in the Courtroom. . . . Of course, I had to plead guilty to the charges made by the scribes and the pharisees, some of them being Methodist Church people among whom I had been a worker for years.[18]

Others seem to have behaved in such a way as to invite arrest. In the first quarter of the seventeenth century, Magdalen, Viscountesse Montague, a Catholic aristocrat in Protestant England, made few attempts to avoid the civil penalties

---

16. Cross, " 'Great Reasoners,' " 376.

17. Cited in Margaret Aston, *Faith and Fire: Popular and Unpopular Religion, 1350–1600* (London: Hambledon, 1993), 24.

18. Cited in Aimee Semple McPherson, *This and That* (New York: Garland, 1985 [1923]), 259–60.

for deviant liturgical practice. "While she was present either at Masse or Sermon," her biographer tells us,

> she did not conceale herselfe for feare to be betrayed by some false brother, as it sometimes happeneth in England, but she did serve God publikely in the sight of all, that by her example she might encourage all; and when she walked abroad, by her Beads, or Crosse which she used to weare about her neck, she professed herselfe to be a Catholike, even to whatsoever Hereticall beholders; and so manifest was her religion, that scarce any in England had heard her name, who knew her not also be a Catholike.[19]

But of course the threat of arrest wasn't the only penalty to which women were subject for their deviant views and worship patterns. The [Exeter] *Morning Post*, May 16, 1745, reported on the anti-Methodist riots:

> In Exeter the Methodists had a meeting house behind the Guildhall, and on May 6th the mob gathered at the door, and pelted those who entered with potatoes, mud, and dung. On coming out, the congregation were all beaten, without exception. . . . Some of the women were lamed, others stripped naked and rolled most indecently in the kennell [gutter], their faces being besmeared with lampblack, flour, and dirt. The disgraceful mob consisted of some thousands of cowardly blackguards, and the disturbance was continued till midnight.[20]

Most of what we know of women's deviant views and practices in the matter of Christian worship comes from periods in which they were subject to arrest for liturgical noncompliance, and although these are very often reliable accounts, they probably represent only a very small proportion of women's deviant opinions and behavior.

Charges against Pastors

It was not only the liturgical misconduct of women parishioners, but the liturgical misconduct of their pastors that has often been at stake. Women frequently have joined in making both formal and informal complaints against the clergy of their churches on the grounds of liturgical impropriety, ineptitude, or malfeasance. All

---

19. This document is found in the British Library, catalogued as BL 4903, bb 47. See also Suzanne Trill, Kate Chedgzoy, and Melanie Osborne, eds., *Lay by Your Needles, Ladies, Take the Pen: Writing Women in England, 1500–1700* (London: Arnold, 1997), 125–30.

20. Quoted in Elijah Chick, *Reminiscenses of Methodism in Exeter and the Neighbourhood, From the Year 1739 until 1907* (Exeter: S. Drayton & Sons, 1907), 2, 4.

kinds of women made such complaints, demonstrating the demographic depth of knowledge of liturgical matters; although many of the women petitioners against clergy neglect and misconduct seem to be unable to write (making their mark, for example, in court documents, rather than signing their name), they all exhibit genuine interest in religious matters and an ability to express themselves in theological terms.[21] Such records also give evidence of women's knowledge of the official norms of the church's worship, and their unwillingness to have them breached by those who were appointed to have responsibility for them.[22] When parishioners in Manchester in the early 1640s petitioned against their minister Ralph Kirk because he failed to use the proper words at the communion service, "they were quite specific about his omissions, making their knowledge of the Prayer Book service clear: 'in the ministeringe of the Sacrament he doth not observe words sett downe in the booke of Common prayer, but doth omit these words, viz. 'the body of our lord Jesus Christ, etc.' until he come past 'preserve your bodye and soules unto everlasting lyffe.' "[23]

Women have been angry at their clergy on several accounts with regard to Christian worship. Sometimes clergy were too incapacitated by drink to fulfill their liturgical obligations. In Wells-next-the-Sea in 1747, women complained that their minister, Joseph Charles, was "too often and too much with Strong Liquors" and that he omitted the prayer for Parliament, and failed to conduct baptisms and funerals, to read prayers after announcing them of Wednesday in Holy Week, and to administer the sacrament on Easter Sunday.[24] The women of Charlton in Wiltshire were understandably distressed by the drunken behavior of their vicar, who sometimes fell " 'acrying and belching as though he would vomit and the like at the Administration of the Sacrament thereby making himself ridiculous.' Not surprisingly, such antics gave 'a great offense and discouragement to the congregation in soe much that ... divers ... cannot frequent the said church in time of divine service and participate of the sacraments with any comfort.' "[25]

At other times, a minister's undesirable personality traits affected the conduct of the liturgy. Women parishioners in Selsey, Sussex, were often in conflict

---

21. Judith Maltby, *Prayer Book and People in Elizabethan and Stuart England* (Cambridge: Cambridge University Press, 1998), 22.

22. For an account of the laity pointing out the liturgical errors of their parish priest, see Clare Cross, "Lay Literacy and Clerical Misconduct in a York Parish during the Reign of Mary Tudor," *York Historian* 3 (1980): 10–15.

23. Maltby, *Prayer Book and People in Elizabethan and Stuart England*, 49.

24. William M. Jacob, "A Practice of Very Hurtful Tendency," in *Church in Town and Countryside*, Studies in Church History 16 (Oxford: Blackwell, 1979), 321, citing Norwich Diocesan Records, "A Petition by the Churchwardens and Inhabitants of Wells to the Chancellor" (April 1747).

25. Cited in Donald Splaeth, "Common Prayer? Popular Observance of the Anglican Liturgy in Restoration Wiltshire," in *Parish Church and People: Local Studies in Lay Religion, 1350–1750*, ed. Susan J. Wright (London: Hutchinson, 1988), 132.

with their vicar, Thomas Kent, in the 1630s for his obnoxious behavior. Kent was described in the petition to have him removed from the parish, "a very bold audacious and impudent spirit," and was accused of having "struck and beaten several people of the parish and those who attempted to dissuade him from his 'lewd courses of life' he excluded from the sacrament,"[26] and of reviling his parishioners "with a very loud and extended voice," calling the men "base cheating knaves and their wives base stinking hussies ... to the great torment and fear of several people, especially women."[27] Women clearly have wanted pastors and their families to set a good example of liturgical piety to others in the parish, and Nathaniel Aske, mid-seventeenth-century rector of Somerford Magna in Wiltshire, certainly failed on this account. The women claimed that he and members of his family had not themselves received communion for over two years, and that as a result of this ("as well as the pastor's general attitude of contentiousness"), they now refused to take communion from the minister, "and rarely went to church, except to attend christenings and funerals."[28] Still other pastors seem to have been simply lazy. Margaret Gates (who is described in her petition against her minister as a "laborer") complained that he had "tried to sabotage his parishioners in their attendance at services by not giving notice that the service was about to begin." She claimed that her pastor " 'will not suffer the Clerke to ring the bell until such time as he is there himself' and then he 'doth make such haste that the prayers be half done before anie bodie can get to the church.' "[29]

As we have seen, women's interest in the official rites of Christian initiation and funerals has not always been high, but we do see it surface when clergy default on their duty in performing the rites. Complaints were lodged against the previously mentioned curate at Wells-next-the Sea that he "scorns to take children in his Arms but throws the Water on them as they are held by some Person."[30] Other ceremonial anomalies did not go unnoticed by women; in 1611 the vicar Richard Rowe of Bunbury, Cheshire, was accused by members of his parish "not only for not making the sign of the cross in baptism, but that he 'refuses to baptise any but on the Sabbath or holy day although it be in danger of death.' "[31] In a petition signed by several women in the parish of Folkingham in 1638, the rector was charged with "being absent from the parish on so many

---

26. Anthony Fletcher, "Factionalism in the Countryside," in *The Church in Town and Countryside*, 293.
27. Ibid.
28. Splaeth, "Common Prayer?" 130.
29. Maltby, *Prayer Book and People in Elizabethan and Stuart England*, 43–44.
30. Cited in William M. Jacob, *Lay People and Religion in the Early Eighteenth Century* (Cambridge: Cambridge University Press, 1996), 61.
31. Maltby, *Prayer Book and People in Elizabethan and Stuart England*, 53.

occasions that parents were forced to walk two miles to the next parish in order to have their children baptized, 'to their parents grief and danger and peril to their infants.' "[32] A similar petition in another parish complained "that parents had to walk several miles to a neighboring parish in order to procure infant baptism with Prayer Book ceremonies."[33] At the turn of the next century, a minister named Armitage was accused of being out of town when he was scheduled to conduct the funeral of Mary Hale. "He did not return until dusk, having kept the mourners and 'the whole parish also,' apprehensively waiting for his return."[34]

Both of these aspects of divergence from prevailing liturgical norms and standards — the divergent practices that women engaged in as a form of religious protest, and the divergent practices presided over by clergy that provoked women to seek redress — tell us a great deal about women's relationship to Christian common prayer. First, literate or illiterate, rich or poor, socially influential or socially marginal, women have felt the liturgy was their own possession and not the possession of the clergy or the larger church. This sense of ownership has meant that despite the myriad sanctions on deviant behavior, women have been willing both to challenge the liturgical status quo and to challenge the ordained to live up to their worship responsibilities. This evidence also leads us to the conclusion that women felt a sense of power in liturgical situations, power that they have exercised in different ways depending on the circumstances. They have absented themselves from the liturgy when they found it objectionable, they have taken their parish clergy to court, they have joined with other women in violent protest, and they have disrupted unacceptable worship services in various ways. They also demonstrate a considerable degree of liturgical knowledge, even if it is not always articulated in conceptual language. They know that the liturgy is meant to comfort, console, edify, and guide them into righteousness. They understand the relationship between liturgy and theology, and that changes in one necessitate changes in the other. They understand that the character of the presider is not incidental to the efficaciousness of the rite. The catalogue of women's deviation from liturgical norms and standards and of their responses to failures on the part of clergy to uphold liturgical norms and standards may never be complete. But if we are to understand the processes of liturgical change fully, work on such a catalogue must be high on the agenda of future liturgical scholars.

---

32. Cited in ibid., 53.
33. Ibid., 49.
34. Ibid., 57.

The Field-Matrons' Tale

In January 1908, two adventurous New Jersey women were appointed by the Indian Service of the Interior Department to serve as "field matrons" among the Karok Indians in the two-hundred-square-mile forest reserve around the fork of the Klamath and Salmon Rivers in northern California. For this work, Mary Ellicott Arnold and Mabel Reed were to receive thirty dollars a month and traveling expenses. Field matrons were not missionaries, but were rather employed by the government to bring a "civilizing influence" to the people among whom they lived, to "elevate them and introduce white standards," as their regional supervisor told them.[1] Arnold and Reed's only qualification for this task was that they were white and middle-class, with impeccable East Coast manners. But these social qualifications masked other, more personal qualities — qualities that in many ways made them entirely unsuitable for the work they were given to do. By nature, Arnold and Reed were curious, open, friendly, resilient, and utterly uncorrupted by racial prejudice. Their attitude toward the Karok was warm and welcoming, and in turn they were warmly welcomed by their neighbors. The Karok women taught them medical practices and manners, love songs and hunting songs; the Karok men asked them to settle quarrels. In the skirts they had split and resewn to create trousers, the two women rode miles and miles of trail on horseback and came to know every part of the land around them, as well as the ways of the inhabitants and the secrets of the wildlife. Their respect for and penetration into the lives of the people they had been sent to "civilize" was remarkable: "Living with Indians," they lamented, "is going to spoil us for living with white people." The story of Arnold and Reed is, however, more than just a story of two doughty and resourceful women. It is a story of the ways in which women, left to their own devices and without any particular ecclesial "charge," appropriated Christian worship as a part of their interactions with people of a different culture.

Both Arnold and Reed had been, in their words, "once considered the somewhat heathen members of the Episcopal Church of Somerville, New Jersey," and

---

1. Mary Ellicott Arnold and Mabel Reed, *In the Land of the Grasshopper Song: Two Women in the Klamath River Indian Country in 1908–09* (Lincoln: University of Nebraska Press, 1957, 1980), 24.

when the Episcopal bishop of California learned that the women were resident in his diocese, he sent them forty Bibles and twenty hymnals for distribution to the inhabitants. Unlike so many other women settlers of the period, Arnold and Reed never once lamented the absence of an established house of worship (although they do seem to have carried their prayer books with them when they came west), nor did they use traditional religious categories to interpret or describe the people and events around them. So it came as a genuine surprise to them when, after less than a month in residence, a rumor that they would be holding a "Sunday school" meeting began to circulate. "Everyone over to the store is talking about it," a neighbor said to them, "and the mailrider said he heard about it in Or-leans. They think it will be a big affair."[2] So, bowing to the local pressure, Reed and Arnold held their first "Sunday school" meeting in their own house in the Karok village Kot-e-meen. It was clear, however, that like so many of the women missionaries, they were using the term "Sunday school" to denote a fully formed service of Christian worship.

There had been some anxiety about the first service, not only because of their own liturgical inexperience, but also because it often happened that violence broke out at public gatherings: old grudges settled with knives and retribution exacted with fists and guns. Indeed, in the week before the first meeting was held, Arnold and Reed were called upon to act as mediators in a long-standing feud over some hogs before the two factions would agree to worship together. At that first service, Arnold and Reed led the congregation in collects and prayers from the *Book of Common Prayer*, in a number of hymns (beginning with the ones that the women knew by heart), and readings from scripture. (Although the women never say so explicitly, they likely followed the pattern of the service of Morning Prayer.) But then something happened that discloses the generous attitude of not only the "field matrons," but the members of the congregation as well. As the service was drawing to a close, one of the Native participants produced a drum, "painted with an Indian design and [with] a very clear, rich tone."[3] Arnold and Reed describe what followed: "The drum was received with marked favor by all the drummers present at the Sunday School. The rhythm was very quick, and the men sang 'ai-ai, ai-ai,' placing their voices differently than the way we do. As song followed song, the beat became more pronounced and the men swung in time to the music."[4] So peace reigned at the first meeting ("thirteen people came and nobody even got killed," the women wryly report[5]), and soon the "Sunday

---

2. Ibid., 74.
3. Ibid., 88.
4. Ibid., 44.
5. Ibid.

School" became a regular feature of the women's schedules, with services held in Kot-e-meen, in their second house at I-ees-i-rum, in the homes of local settlers, and in the other native villages in the region.

Mary Arnold and Mabel Reed offer more explicit details about the services that followed, and from these we get a strong sense of both their own liturgical sensibilities and the atmosphere they encouraged among the members of their congregations. The services, which were held in their own living room on Sunday afternoons, soon had so many in attendance that it "tries [the room] to its farthermost limits." Arnold and Reed set up their own furniture ("the large bench and the small bench and the three chairs and the two woodpiles"), and brought in planks laid on trestles so that seating occupied "all the available space in the room." The seating plan was entirely egalitarian, as can be seen in their description of one memorable service: "We have just seated Dora, Martha, and the Essie family from Kot-e-meen when there was a sound outside and all of Pich-pichi [village] boils in — two men, four women, three children, and a baby. They are followed by [white settlers] Pete Henry and Hackett and the two strange Indians who were here last week." Mary began this service with a collect and a reading from the Bible. Her mode of selection seems devoid of ecclesiastical constraint: "I love the collects and enjoy the freedom to choose the ones I like best," she reports. Having just begun to sing "From Greenland's Icy Mountains" on this occasion, two young Karok men, the Anglo shopkeeper from the town of Orleans, and two of the Orleans natives came in. "When the Orleans arrived, Mr. Hale courteously gave up his seat. . . . The Indians are able to squeeze themselves onto one of the benches, but the storekeeper and myself have to stand."[6] A prayer is said, and Mabel had begun to lead another hymn ("While Shepherds Watched Their Flocks by Night") when the entire congregation rushed to the windows to see "something uncommon" coming down the trail: "White dresses. Chiffon hats." The Hickoxes, who held the highest social standing in the region, had come to the service for the first time. Luther Hickox was accounted "the most dangerous man with a gun within a hundred miles," but Arnold and Reed's only comment is that his presence "makes the singing so much better." At the close of the service there was the heartwarming image of Mrs. Richards, the well-to-do wife of the manager of the local gold mine, helping the two Orleans natives sitting to her right and left to find the proper page in the hymnal for the singing of "Abide with Me."[7]

---

6. Ibid., 92.
7. Ibid.

By necessity, this service was not only democratic, but ecumenical as well. "We have our own infallible rule for discovering the church affiliations of the congregation," the women admit. " 'Come, Ye Disconsolate' brings out the Roman Catholics. 'Rock of Ages' goes strong with the Evangelicals. 'Lead, Kindly Light' is sure-fire with the Episcopalians." Having acknowledged the success of the singing at I-ees-i-rum, however, they turn their pastoral-liturgical eye on the Protestant Episcopal Church hymnal.

> The Lord have mercy on the people who wrote the words of the Episcopal hymnbook. They will not do. They simply *will not do*. "Veiled in flesh the Godhead see, Hail the incarnate deity." When the Indians are completely stampeded, we hold up everything and compose completely new words. The Lord Bishop better not try visiting this parish. He will think something is the matter with his hearing![8]

After some initial uncertainty about their competence to lead such services, Arnold and Reed soon are able to admit that "we have a masterful hand these days and Sunday School goes with a snap."[9]

One of Arnold and Reed's earliest friends in the Klamath region was "Papa Frame," and when he died the women were called upon to preside at his burial. They had arrived at the house just after he had succumbed, and they comforted his widow and three children. Mabel was asked to help "lay out" the body; she dressed him in his best suit and combed out his hair and beard. "You folks are real handy at funerals," one of his neighbors said to them. "Guess the folks here hope you'll stay around."[10] With a soaking rain beating on the windows, they went into the dining room where Papa Frame's coffin was laid on trestles. "I didn't have any prayer book," Mary explains, "but I read the psalms for the burial service from the great old Bible that Mama Frame brought me, and did my best with the prayers and a few words about what a good man Papa Frame had been." Then Mabel began the hymns that the widow had requested: "Rock of Ages" and "In the Sweet Bye and Bye," and all those gathered joined in. In the silence that followed, one person stepped forward to screw down the lid of the coffin; the daughter of the deceased screamed and grabbed hold of the handle of the coffin to keep the men from taking it away. "The old men listened to her in silence as they had listened to the prayers and the hymns." There was no time for prayers at the grave, since the rain came down in earnest as the coffin was lowered, and

---

8. Ibid., 173.
9. Ibid., 90.
10. Ibid., 287.

the women returned to the house with the mourners as the earth was shoveled into the grave.

In their description of their first Christmas in Klamath, Arnold and Reed show the sensitivity to the ceremonial ways of others that so endeared them to the native inhabitants. "The Indians are a musical peoples," they report. "Their intervals are different from ours and it is as hard for them to understand our music as it is for us to understand theirs. But once our music becomes familiar to them, all the passion and emotion of the Indian people goes into their singing."[11] The women's appreciation for the singing of the carols on this Christmas night is sincere and deep: "Steve [one of the Karok] leaned forward a little, his broad shoulders and clean-cut Indian features very clear in the firelight. His voice had depth and power, and rang out clear and strong. His silent drum was in his lap. His eyes were fixed on the blazing fire." The enthusiasm with which the native people embraced the carol singing introduced by these odd New Jerseyites is not difficult to explain when we recognize the field matrons' understanding of the underlying patterns of native singing: "We sang in the Indian way," Arnold and Reed reported. "Only one verse for each carol. But we sang that verse over and over, with mounting intensity, until 'Hark the Herald Angels Sing' had a passionate force." Later, they would describe Steve's dancing in the traditional Karok "Deerskin Dance" with the same kind of appreciative attention, clearly born out of a natural sense of the power of liturgy, in whatever form it takes.

Something is deeply compelling about the picture of Mary, riding her horse Sally over the rough terrain to a distant farmstead where a service will be held. "I am in the lead," she wrote, "and have in my hand my prayer book. It has just occurred to me that 'Lighten our Darkness' is not the appropriate prayer for Sunday morning and I am memorizing a collect while Sally with a clear trail ahead, moves at a sedate trot." Mary Ellicott Arnold and Mabel Reed only stayed in the Klamath region for fifteen months. But in that short time they showed themselves to be able pastoral liturgists, and natural practitioners of what would later come to be called among liturgical scholars the "inculturation" of Christian worship.

---

11. Ibid., 210–11.

Appendix Five

The Peasants' Tale

The conquest of the Maya people of Mexico was swift and bloody, and by the mid-seventeenth century the most significant elements of European Christian observance and ritual had usurped native religious practice. To all outward appearances, the colonization of the native liturgical imagination would seem to have been complete. But some Indian communities were less tractable than others, and Santa Marta, a Tzotzil pueblo in the Chiapas region, was described by the Dominican authorities as an "arrogant and disobedient" place. By 1711, the parish priest had already left in frustration, uttering threats of divine retribution, and the church had fallen into disrepair.[1]

Among the inhabitants of Santa Marta was twenty-three-year-old Dominica López, an orphaned Tzotzil woman who earned a meager living farming a small plot of land on the outskirts of the village. One evening, the worst of the day's heat having receded, Dominica went to work her land, and there she met a woman who spoke to her gently in her native language. The woman said her name was "Maria," and asked where Dominica's parents were; when Dominica said that she was an orphan, the woman told her that although she was also poor, she had come to help Dominica and her people. "Maria" directed Dominica to return to the pueblo, and to instruct the village overseers to build a shrine for her, "so that she might not die among the sticks and stones of the forest." Dominica did as she was told. When the shrine was completed, she returned to the site of the apparition with her husband and found the virgin wrapped in a *manta*, evidently ready to travel to her new home. They carried her to the shrine with great ceremony, accompanied by villagers playing drums, horns, and flutes, and singers carrying banners and torches. A niche was brought from the ruined parish church to the new shrine and the virgin was placed in it, while the people said the rosary and recited the creed. The village overseers appointed Dominica guardian of the shrine, but when she returned there she found that the virgin was no longer

---

1. For further information about the religious and social context of these events, see Kevin Gosner, *Soldiers of the Virgin: The Moral Economy of a Colonial Maya Rebellion* (Tucson: University of Arizona Press, 1992).

made of flesh and bone, but of wood. Even so, pilgrims to the shrine reported that prayers said before the image of the virgin resulted in miraculous cures, and they came with offerings: flowers, chickens, candles, and coins.

Word quickly spread in Santa Marta about the miraculous appearance, transformation, and healing power of the virgin, and men and women from other pueblos began to abandon regular services at their own parish churches in order to visit the shrine. When news of this reached the local bishop, he immediately sent an inquisitor, Fray Joseph Monroy, to investigate the claims. As soon as Monroy arrived at Santa Maria, the Tzotzil villagers graciously asked him to celebrate mass at the shrine, but he put them off, saying that he needed permission from the bishop in order to do so. He did visit the shrine, however, and interrogated Dominica López closely about the apparition. She told him her story, adding that she was able to explain neither the miraculous change in the virgin's material nature, nor her curative powers. Four days later, having sent an initial report to the provincial mayor, Monroy was ordered to bring Dominica López and the image of the virgin to the capital city, Ciudad Real.

Although the people of Santa Marta were understandably concerned that their virgin protector was to be disturbed, Monroy told them that if they would permit her to be taken without interference, she would be received in Ciudad Real with great honor. As a result of this assurance, they allowed the image to be removed, and more than two thousand Maya devotees accompanied it to the capital. Upon arrival in Ciudad Real, the statue was indeed set up in a honored place in the Dominican convent, but sometime during the night, while the people kept vigil in the graveyard outside, the authorities removed it from its place and destroyed it.

In the meantime, Dominca was taken into custody by church authorities and held for trial on the charge of promoting a false miracle and of aiding and abetting a work of the devil. She gave evidence for several days, seeking to persuade the inquisitors that she was a sincere believer acting in conformity with true Catholic doctrine, arguing that she and her people were simply doing what they had been taught by the church, venerating the Holy Mother Mary and saying the creed and the rosary. Other witnesses testified to the authenticity of her vision and of the healing power of the Santa Marta virgin. Despite their evidence, Dominica was convicted of heresy, and sentenced to two hundred lashes and ten years' exile from the province. When the lashes had been administered, she was carried through the streets of the capital and beaten so severely by the mob that the bishop intervened, fearing that she would be killed before the rest of the sentence could be carried out. Dominica ended her life in exile on the jungle coast of Honduras, far away from her mountain home and from the shrine of the virgin who had promised to help her.

But her story does not end there, even though it would be another young Mayan woman who would be the central actor in the second act of the drama initiated by Dominica. In the months that followed Dominica's exile, further apparitions were experienced in other pueblos, and in each case inquisitors were sent to suppress the religious enthusiasm that attended them. The turning point came in June 1712, when thirteen-year-old Maria López from the Tzeltal pueblo of Cancuc reported that she had met the virgin on the outskirts of town. She was given a similar message to the one given to Dominica: that the virgin was there to help her people and that in order to do that she needed a house provided for her. Everyone in the village went to the designated place to help construct the shrine, and the virgin continued to speak to Maria in a small room there.

When the inquisitors arrived in Cancuc, they immediately denounced the miracle as a fraud and young Maria was immediately given forty lashes. But she held fast to her story, and the townspeople continued to hope that a fuller investigation would result in the vindication of the young woman and the vision to which she testified. Some weeks later the bishop came to the pueblo and, finding the shrine flourishing, incarcerated Maria and the village overseers who had supported her, threatening to send troops to dismantle the shrine unless the townspeople did it themselves. But when he left, inhabitants of nearby pueblos, including Dominica's home village, Santa Marta, flooded into town to worship at the shrine. They released young Maria from jail and led her to the shrine where she and her family took up residence. Then they went to the parish church, tore statues from their accustomed places there and set them up around the altar of the shrine.

Within days, a full-scale pueblo revolt was in process, with the inhabitants of twenty-one villages taking up arms and converging on Cancuc. Another peasant visionary from a nearby pueblo, Sebastian Gómez de la Gloria, took up leadership of the virgin's devotees, claiming that St. Peter himself had invested him with the authority of a bishop. His first episcopal act was to ordain eight priests. But the profound subversiveness of Sebastian's liturgical acts lay not only in their lack of legitimate ecclesiastical sanction, but rather, like those of Dominica and Maria, in their establishment of the priority of Mayan religious authority over that of the colonizers. So, before they began their duties, the new priests were baptized by Sebastian, pronouncing "in the name of the Father, the Son and the Holy Spirit" not in Latin, but *in their mother tongue*. The rebels brought vestments and eucharistic vessels from the church, and celebrated mass at the shrine, with Maria serving at the altar dressed in an alb.

A general call to insurrection was issued to the inhabitants of all the Chiapas pueblos, who were told to bring all the silver, ornaments, and books from their churches. Five days of celebration followed, with the sort of processions and ritual dancing that had not been seen since pre-conquest days, and masses said by the native priests in their own language. Maria preached almost continuously at the shrine, testifying to the virgin's patronage of the Mayan cause, and stayed there throughout the rebellion, served by twelve appointed assistants.

The politico-liturgical revolution became increasingly violent, and when Spanish priests arrived in the pueblo insisting that they be allowed to say mass at the shrine, Maria allegedly had them shot dead before they reached the altar. Under her direction, additional Mayan priests from other pueblos were ordained and told to return to their communities to celebrate the sacraments there. But the Spanish counteroffensive was already under way, and soon thousands of troops from all over Central America had converged on the Chiapas region. By mid-November 1712, less that half a year since the virgin first appeared to Maria, the insurrection had been suppressed, and in the months that followed, the rebel leaders were chased down and either killed or captured. But Maria managed to escape to the mountains, continuing her devotion to the virgin in a small shrine until she died there two years later at the age of fifteen. Meanwhile, the authorities had driven the remaining inhabitants from the pueblos in a program of forced resettlement and had burned their houses to the ground.

The Maya effort to reclaim the rituals of faith from the colonizers had failed, and the promise of authentic Maya worship at the feet of the virgin was left unfulfilled. But to this day, rumors persist in the poor mountain villages of Chiapas that the Maya virgin will return to liberate her people, and that Dominica and Maria will rebuild her shrine and lead in the worship there.

BIBLIOGRAPHY

Abels, R. "Participation of Women in Languedocian Catharism." In *Medieval Studies* 16 (1979): 215–51.

Addleshaw, G. W. O. *The Early Parochial System and the Divine Office*. London: A. R. Mowbray, 1957.

Aghahowa, Brenda Eatman. *Praising in Black and White*. Cleveland: United Church Press, 1996.

"AHR Review: The Old History and the New." *American Historical Review* 94 (1989): 654–98.

Alderton, Nannie T., and Helena Huntington Smith. *A Bride Goes West*. Lincoln: University of Nebraska Press, 1969 (1942).

Allan-Olney, Mary. *The New Virginians*. 2 vols. Edinburgh: Blackwood, 1880.

Alldredge, Nick. "Loyalty and Identity in Chester Parishes, 1540–1640." In *Parish Church and People: Local Studies in Lay Religion, 1350–1750*, ed. Susan J. Wright, 85–124. London: Hutchinson, 1988.

Ames, Mary. *From a New England Woman's Diary in Dixie*. Springfield, Mass.: Plimpton Press, 1906.

Amussen, Susan Dwyer. "The Gendering of Popular Culture in Early Modern England." In *Popular Culture in England, c. 1500–1850*, ed. Tim Harris, 48–68. New York: St. Martin's, 1994.

Anderson, O. "Women Preachers in Mid-Victorian Britain: Some Reflexions on Feminism, Popular Religion and Social Change." *Historical Journal* 12 (1969): 467–84.

Andrews, William L. *Sisters of the Spirit: Three Black Women's Autobiographies of the Nineteenth Century*. Bloomington: Indiana University Press, 1986.

Anson, J. "The Female Transvestite in Early Monasticism: The Origin and Development of a Motif." *Viator* 5 (1974): 1–12.

Ariès, Philippe. *Essais sur la Histoire de la Mort en Occident du Moyen age à nos Jours*. Paris: Seuil, 1975.

Arnold, Eleanor, ed. *Voices of American Homemakers: An Oral History Project of the National Extension Homemakers Council*. Columbus, Ohio: NEHC, 1985.

Arnold, Mary Ellicott, and Mabel Reed. *In the Land of the Grasshopper Song: Two Women in the Klamath River Indian Country in 1908–09*. Lincoln: University of Nebraska Press, 1980 (1957).

Arnstein, Walter. "Queen Victoria and Religion." In *Religion in the Lives of English Women, 1760–1930*, ed. Gail Malmgreen, 88–128. Bloomington: Indiana University Press, 1986.

Arthur, Marilyn, et al., eds. *Conceptual Frameworks for Studying Women's History.* Bronxville, N.Y.: Sarah Lawrence College, 1975.

Astell, Mary. *The Christian Religion, as Professed by a Daughter of the Church of England.* London, 1705.

Aston, Margaret. *Faith and Fire: Popular and Unpopular Religion, 1350–1600.* London: Hambledon, 1993.

———. "Iconoclasm at Rickmansworth, 1522: Troubles of Churchwardens." *Journal of Ecclesiastical History* 40, no. 4 (1989): 524–52.

Avery, Myrtilla. *Exultet Rolls of South Italy.* Princeton, N.J.: Princeton University Press, 1936.

Badone, Ellen, ed. *Religious Orthodoxy and Popular Faith in European Society.* Princeton, N.J.: Princeton University Press, 1990.

Baker, Derek. "'A Nursery of Saints': St. Margaret of Scotland Reconsidered." In *Medieval Women.* Studies in Church History, Subsidia, ed. Derek Baker, 119–41. Oxford: Basil Blackwell, 1978.

———, ed. *Medieval Women.* Studies in Church History, Subsidia. Oxford: Basil Blackwell, 1978.

Balch, David, and Carolyn Osiek. *Families in the New Testament World: Households and House Churches.* Louisville: Westminster John Knox Press, 1997.

Barron, C. "The Golden Age of Women in Medieval London." *Reading* 15 (1989): 35–58.

Bateson, Mary. *Origin and Early History of Double Monasteries.* Royal Historical Society Transactions, n.s., 13 (London, 1889).

Baubérot, Jean. "The Protestant Woman." In *History of Women in the West,* vol. 4: *Emerging Feminism from Revolution to World War,* ed. Genevieve Fraisse and Michelle Perrot, 198–212. Cambridge, Mass.: Belknap Press of Harvard University Press, 1993.

Beale, John. *Public Worship, Private Faith: The Sacred Harp and American Folksong.* Athens: University of Georgia Press, 1997.

Beard, Madeline. *Faith and Fortune.* Leominster, U.K.: Gracewing, 1997.

Bednarowski, Mary J. "Outside the Mainstream: Women's Religion and Women Religious Leaders in Nineteenth-Century America." *Journal of the American Academy of Religion* 48 (1980): 207–31.

Bell, David N. *What Nuns Read: Books and Libraries in Medieval English Nunneries.* Kalamazoo, Mich.: Cistercian Publications, 1995.

Bell, Rudolf M. "Telling Her Sins: Male Confessors and Female Penitents in Catholic Reformation Italy." In *That Gentle Strength: Historical Perspectives on Women in Christianity,* ed. Lynda L. Coon, Katherine J. Haldane, and Elisabeth W. Sommer, 119–48. Charlottesville: University Press of Virginia, 1990.

Bell, S. G. "Medieval Women Book Owners: Arbiters of Lay Piety and Ambassadors of Culture." In *Sisters and Workers in the Middle Ages,* ed. J. M. Bennett, E. A. Clark, J. F. O'Barr, B. A. Vilen, and S. Westphal-Wihl, 135–61. Chicago: University of Chicago Press, 1989.

Bennett, J. M. "Medieval Women, Modern Women: Across the Gender Divide." In *Culture and History: Essays on English Communities, Identities, and Writings,* ed. D. Aers, 147–75. Detroit: Wayne State University Press, 1992.

————. *Women in the Medieval English Countryside: Gender and Household in Brigstock before the Plague.* New York: Oxford University Press, 1987.

Bennett, J. M., et al., eds. *Sisters and Workers in the Middle Ages.* Chicago: University of Chicago Press, 1989.

Beresford, B. "The Churchwarden's Accounts of Holy Trinity, Chester 1532 to 1633." *Journal of the Chester Archeological Society,* n.s., 38 (1951): 118–32.

Berger, Teresa. "The Classical Liturgical Movement in Germany and Austria: Moved by Women?" *Worship* 66 (1992): 231–51.

Berkin, Carol, and Leslie Horowitz, eds. *Women's Voices, Women's Lives: Documents in Early American History.* Boston: Northeastern University Press, 1998.

Berman, Constance H. "Women as Donors and Patrons to Southern French Monasteries in the Twelfth and Thirteenth Centuries." In *The Worlds of Medieval Women: Creativity, Influence, Imagination,* ed. Constance H. Berman, Charles W. Connell, and Judith Rice Rothschild, 53–68. Morgantown: West Virginia University Press, 1985.

Berman, Constance H., Charles W. Connell, and Judith Rice Rothschild, eds. *The Worlds of Medieval Women: Creativity, Influence, Imagination.* Morgantown: West Virginia University Press, 1985.

Berry, D. M., and R. S. Schofield. "Age at Baptism in Pre-Industrial England." *Local Population Studies* 25 (1971): 453–66.

Bessborough, Earl. *Lady Charlotte Guest, Journal, 1833–1852.* London: John Murray, 1950.

Bethell, Denis. "Two letters of Pope Paschal II to Scotland." *Scottish Historical Review* 49 (1970): 33–45.

Binfield, Clyde. "Architects in Connexion: Four Methodist Generations." In *Revival and Religion since 1700: Essays for John Walsh,* ed. Jane Garnett and Colin Matthew, 153–81. London: Hambledon, 1993.

Bird, Isabella L. *A Lady's Life in the Rocky Mountains.* Intro. Daniel J. Boorstin. Norman: University of Oklahoma Press, 1960.

Bodichon, Barbara Leigh Smith. *An American Diary 1857–8,* ed. Joseph W. Reed Jr. London: Routledge and Kegan Paul, 1972.

Bolton, Brenda L. "Mulieres sanctae." In *Sanctity and Secularity: The Church and the World.* Studies in Church History 10. Ed. Derek Baker, 77–95. Oxford: Blackwell, 1973.

————. "Vita Matrum: A Further Aspect of the Frauenfrage." In *Medieval Women.* Studies in Church History, Subsidia, ed. Derek Baker, 253–74. Oxford: Basil Blackwell, 1978.

Booty, John. "Preparation for the Lord's Supper in Elizabethan England." *Anglican Theological Review* 49 (1967): 131–48.

Bordin, Ruth. *Woman and Temperance: The Quest for Power and Liberty, 1873–1900.* Philadelphia: Temple University Press, 1981.

Børresen, Kari E. "Caritas Pirckheimer (1467–1532) et Vittoria Colonna (1490–1547)." In *Women's Studies in the Christian and Islamic Traditions: Ancient, Medieval and Renaissance Foremothers,* ed. Kari Børresen and Kari Vogt, 315–39. Dordrecht: Kluwer, 1993.

Børresen, Kari E., and Kari Vogt, eds. *Women's Studies in the Christian and Islamic Traditions: Ancient, Medieval and Renaissance Foremothers.* Dordrecht: Kluwer, 1993.

Borzello, Frances. *A World of Our Own: Women Artists since the Renaissance.* New York: Watson-Guptill, 2000.

Bossy, John. "Blood and Baptism: Kinship Community and Christianity in Western Europe from the Fourteenth to the Seventeenth Centuries." In *Sanctity and Secularity: The Church and the World.* Studies in Church History 10, ed. Derek Baker, 141. Oxford: Blackwell, 1973.

————. "Christian Life in the Later Middle Ages: Prayer." *Transactions of the Royal Historical Society* 6th series. London: RHS, 1991.

————. "The Mass as Social Institution." *Past and Present* 98 (1983): 27–61.

Boulton, J. P. "The Limits of Formal Religion: The Administration of Holy Communion in Late Elizabethan and Early Stuart England." *London Journal* 10, no. 2 (1984): 135–54.

Bourdua, Louise. "Friars Patrons and Workshops at the Basilica del Santo, Padua." In *The Church and the Arts.* Studies in Church History 28, ed. Diana Wood, 131–41. Oxford: Basil Blackwell, 1992.

Bowers, Roger. "Aristocratic and Popular Piety in the Patronage of Music in the Fifteenth-Century Nederlands." In *The Church and the Arts.* Studies in Church History 28, ed. Diana Wood, 195–224. Oxford: Basil Blackwell, 1992.

Boyer, Horace Clarence. "A Comparative Analysis of Traditional and Contemporary Gospel Music." In *More than Dancing: Essays on Afro-American Music and Musicians,* ed. Irene Jackson, 128–46. Westport, Conn.: Greenwood, 1985.

Boyle, Leonard E. "Montaillou Revisited: Mentalité and Methodology." In *Pathways to Medieval Peasants.* Papers in Medieval Studies 2, ed. J. A. Raftis, 119–40. Toronto: Pontifical Institute of Medieval Studies, 1981.

Branson, Ann, *Journal of Ann Branson, 1808–1891.* Philadelphia: W. H. Pile's Sons, 1892.

Bray, Anna Eliza. *A Description of the Part of Devonshire Bordering on the Tamar and the Tavy.* 3 vols. London, 1836.

Bridenthal, R., and C. Koonz, eds. *Becoming Visible: Women in European History.* Boston: Houghton Mifflin, 1977/1987.

Brigden, Susan. *London and the Reformation.* Oxford: Clarendon, 1989.

————. "Religion and Social Obligation in Early Sixteenth-Century London." *Past and Present* 103 (May 1984): 67–112.

Briggs, Robin. *Communities of Belief: Cultural and Social Tensions in Early Modern France.* Oxford: Clarendon, 1995.

Brock, Sebastian P., and Susan Ashbrook Harvey, trans. *Holy Women of the Syrian Orient.* Berkeley: University of California Press, 1987.

Brouard, Janine. *La Nassance, le mariage, la mort en Anjou dans la première moitié du XXe siècle.* Cahiers de l'I.P.S.A., no. 8, Angers: Université Catholique de l'Ouest, 1984. (interviews)

Brown, Andrew. *Popular Piety in Late Medieval England: The Diocese of Salisbury, 1250–1550.* Oxford: Clarendon Press, 1995.

Brown, Earl Kent. *Women of Mr. Wesley's Methodism.* Studies in Women and Religion 11. New York and Toronto: Edwin Mellen Press, 1983.

Brown, P. R. L. *Relics and Social Status in the Age of Gregory of Tours.* Stanton Lecture, 1977.

Brown, Stewart. " 'No More Standing in the Session': Gender and the End of Corporate Discipline in the Church of Scotland, c. 1890–1930." In *Gender and Christian Religion.*

Studies in Church History 34, ed. R. N. Swanson, 447–60. Woodbridge, U.K.: Boydell, 1998.

Brown, Theo. *The Fate of the Dead: A Study in Folk-Eschatology in the West Country after the Reformation.* Cambridge: Brewer, 1979.

Buel, Joy Day, and Buel, Richard. *The Way of Duty: A Woman and Her Family in Revolutionary America.* New York: W. W. Norton, 1984.

Buggeln, Gretchen Townsend. "Elegance and Sensibility in the Calvinist Tradition: The First Congregational Church of Hartford Connecticut." In *Seeing beyond the Word: Visual Arts and the Calvinist Tradition,* ed. Paul Corby Finney, 429–56. Grand Rapids, Mich.: Eerdmans, 1999.

Bulbeck, Chilla. *Australian Women in Papua New Guinea: Colonial Passages 1920–1960.* Cambridge: Cambridge University Press, 1992.

Bullough, David. *Friends, Neighbors, and Fellow-Drinkers: Aspects of Community and Conflict in the Early Medieval West.* Cambridge: Cambridge University Press, 1991.

Burgess, Clive. "'A Fond Thing Vainly Invented': An Essay on Purgatory and Pious Motive in Later Medieval England." In *Parish Church and People: Local Studies in Lay Religion, 1350–1750,* ed. Susan J. Wright, 56–80. London: Hutchinson, 1988.

———. "For the Increase of Divine Service: Chantries in the Parish in Late-Medieval Britain." *Journal of Ecclesiastical History* 36 (1985): 46–65.

———. "A Service for the Dead: The Form and Function of the Anniversary in Late Medieval Bristol." *Transactions of the Bristol and Gloucestershire Archeological Society* 105 (1987): 183–211.

Burke, Peter. *Popular Culture in Early Modern Europe.* London and New York: Temple Smith, 1978/1983.

Burlend, Rebecca. *A True Picture of Emigration: Or Fourteen Years in the Interior of North America; Being a Full and Impartial Account of the Various Difficulties and Ultimate Success of an English Family Who Emigrated from Barwick-in-Elmet, Near Leeds, in the Year 1831.* London: G. Berger, 1848; Chicago: Lakeside Press, R. R. Donnelly, 1936.

Burnim, Melonee V. "The Black Gospel Music Tradition: A Complex of Ideology, Aesthetic, and Behavior." In *More than Dancing: Essays on Afro-American Music and Musicians,* ed. Irene Jackson, 149–58. Westport, Conn.: Greenwood, 1985.

Bushman, Richard L. *The Refinement of America: Persons, Houses, Cities.* New York: Random House, 1993.

Bynum, Caroline Walker. *Holy Feast and Holy Fast: The Religious Significance of Food to Medieval Women.* Berkeley: University of California Press, 1987.

———. "Women Mystics and Eucharistic Devotion in the Thirteenth Century." In *Fragmentation and Redemption: Essays on Gender and the Human Body in Medieval Religion,* ed. Caroline Bynum. New York: Zone Books, 1992.

Byrne, Lavinia. *Women before God.* London: SPCK, 1988.

Caldwell, Nancy. *Walking with God: Leaves from the Journal of Mrs. Nancy Caldwell,* ed. James O. Thompson. Keyser, W.Va.: For Private Distribution, 1886.

Cameron, A. "The Empress and the Poet: Paganism and Politics at the Court of Theodosius II." *Yale Classical Studies* 27 (1982): 217–89.

Carey, Hilary. "Devout Literature: Laypeople and the Pursuit of the Mixed Life in Later Medieval England." *Journal of Religious History* 14 (1986–7): 361–81.

Carpenter, C. "Religion of the Gentry in Fifteenth-Century England." In *England in the Fifteenth Century,* ed. Daniel Williams. Woodbridge, U.K.: Boydell, 1987.

Carpenter, S. C. *Church and People, 1789–1889.* London: SPCK, 1933.

Carre, Beatrice. "Early Quaker Women in Lancaster and Lancashire." In Michael Mallett, *Early Lancaster Friends,* Lancaster Occasional Paper 5 (1978).

Carroll, Bernice, ed. *Liberating Women's History: Theoretical and Critical Essays.* Urbana: University of Illinois Press, 1976.

Carroll, Kenneth L. "Early Quakers and 'Going Naked as Sign.'" *Quaker History* 67, no. 2 (Autumn 1978): 69–72.

Carwardine, Richard. "The Second Great Awakening in the Urban Centers: An Examination of Methodism and the 'New Measures.'" *Journal of American History* 59 (1972): 327–40.

Catto, Jeremy. "Religion in the English Nobility." In *History and Imagination: Essays in Honour of H. R. Trevor-Rober,* ed. Hugh Lloyd-Jones, Valeria Pearl, and Blair Worden. New York: Holmes and Meier, 1982.

Chartier, Roger, ed. *A History of Private Life,* vol. 3: *Passions of the Renaissance.* Cambridge, Mass.: Belknap Press of Harvard University Press, 1989.

Chester Historical Society. *"Att a Society Meeting": The Records of the Fourth Ecclesiastical Society of Old Saybrook, 1741–1808.* North Chester, Conn.: Chester Historical Society, 1980.

Christian, William A., Jr. *Local Religion in Sixteenth-Century Spain.* Princeton, N.J.: Princeton University Press, 1981.

Clark, Alice. *The Working Life of Women in the Seventeenth Century.* New York: A. M. Kellogg, 1968.

Clark, Elizabeth A. *The Life of Melania the Younger: Introduction, Translation, and Commentary.* New York and Toronto: Edwin Mellen Press, 1984.

Clark, Gillian. *Women in Late Antiquity: Pagan and Christian Life-Styles.* Oxford: Clarendon, 1993.

Clark, Peter. "The Ownership of Books in England, 1560–1640: The Examples of Some Kentish Townsfolk." In *Schooling and Society,* ed. Lawrence Stone. Baltimore: Johns Hopkins, 1968.

Clarke, Margaret. "Northern Light? Parochial Life in a 'Dark Corner' of Tudor England." In *Parish in English Life, 1400–1600,* ed. Katherine L. French, Gary Gibbs, and Beat A. Kümin, 56–73. Manchester: Manchester University Press, 1997.

Clements, Mary, ed. *Correspondence and Minutes of the SPCK Relating to Wales, 1699–1740.* Cardiff: University of Wales Press, 1952.

Clifford, D. J. H., ed. *The Diaries of Lady Anne Clifford.* Stroud: Alan Sutton, 1990.

Clifton, Robin. "Popular Fear of Catholics in England, 1640–1660." In *Rebellion, Popular Protest, and Social Order in Early Modern England,* ed. Paul Slack, 129–61. Cambridge: Cambridge University Press, 1983.

Cloke, Gillian. *"The Female Man of God": Women and Spiritual Power in the Patristic Age, A.D. 350–450.* London: Routledge, 1995.

Coates, Simon. "Rendering Radegund? Fortunatus, Baudovinia, and the Problem of Female Sanctity in Merovingian Gaul." In *Gender and Christian Religion*. Studies in Church History 34. Ed. R. N. Swanson. Woodbridge, U.K.: Boydell, 1998.

Cobb, Buell E. *The Sacred Harp: A Tradition and Its Music*. Athens: University of Georgia Press, 1978.

Cochran, Louis, and Bess White Cochran. *Captives of the Word: A Narrative History of the Christian Church (Disciples of Christ), the Christian Churches (Independent), and the Churches of Christ*. Joplin, Mo.: College Press, 1987.

Cockburn, J. S., ed. *Crime in England, 1500–1800*. Princeton, N.J.: Princeton University Press, 1977.

Cohn, S. K. *Death and Property in Sienna*. Baltimore: Johns Hopkins, 1988.

Collinson, Patrick. *The Elizabethan Puritan Movement*. Oxford: Clarendon, 1967.

———. *The Religion of the Protestants: The Church in English Society, 1559–1625*. Oxford: Clarendon Press, 1982.

———. "The Role of Women in the English Reformation Illustrated by the Life and Friendships of Anne Locke." *Studies in Church History* 2 (1965): 258–72.

———. "Shepherds, Sheepdogs and Hirelings: The Pastoral Ministry in Post-Reformation England." In *The Ministry: Clerical and Lay*. Studies in Church History 26, ed. W. J. Sheils and Diana Wood. London: Blackwell, 1989.

———. "Windows on a Woman's Soul: Questions about the Religion of Elizabeth I." In *Elizabethan Essays*, ed. Patrick Collinson, 87–118. London: Hambledon, 1994.

Collinson, Patrick, and John Craig. *Reformation in English Towns, 1500–1640*. London: Macmillan, 1998.

Constable, Giles. "Aelred of Rivaulx and the Nun of Watton: An Episode in the Early History of the Gilbertine Order." In *Medieval Women*. Studies in Church History, Subsidia, ed. Derek Baker, 205–26. Oxford: Basil Blackwell, 1978.

Coon, Lynda L., Katherine J. Haldane, and Elisabeth W. Sommer, eds. *That Gentle Strength: Historical Perspectives on Women in Christianity*. Charlottesville: University Press of Virginia, 1990.

Corley, Kathleen E. *Private Women, Public Meals: Social Conflict in the Synoptic Tradition*. Peabody, Mass.: Hendrickson, 1993.

Coster, William. "Popular Religion and the Parish Register, 1538–1603." In *Parish in English Life, 1400–1600*, ed. Katherine L. French, Gary Gibbs, and Beat A. Kümin, 94–114. Manchester: Manchester University Press, 1997.

———. "Purity, Profanity and Puritanism: The Churching of Women, 1500–1700." In *Women in the Church*. Studies in Church History 27, ed. W. J. Shiels and Diana Wood, 335–87. Oxford: Blackwell, 1990.

Cott, Nancy F. *The Bonds of Womanhood: Women's Sphere in New England, 1790–1835*. New Haven: Yale University Press, 1977.

Cotton, Priscilla, and Mary Cole. *To the Priests and People of England, We Discharge Our Consciences*. London, 1655.

Cowman, Krista. "'We Intend to Show What Our Lord Had Done for Women': The Liverpool Church League for Women's Suffrage, 1913–1918." In *Gender and Christian*

Religion. Studies in Church History 34, ed. R. N. Swanson, 475–86. Woodbridge, U.K.: Boydell, 1998.

Cox, Jane. *Hatred Pursued beyond the Grave: Tales of Our Ancestors from the London Church Courts*. London: HMSO, 1993.

Cramer, Peter. *Baptism and Change in the Early Middle Ages*. Cambridge: Cambridge University Press, 1993.

Crawford, Anne. "The Piety of Late-Medieval English Queens." In *The Church and Pre-reformation Society: Essays in Honour of F. R. H. Du Boulay*, ed. Caroline M. Barron and Christopher Harper-Bill. Woodbridge, U.K.: Boydell Press, 1985.

Crawford, Patricia. *Women and Religion in England, 1500–1720*. New York: Routledge, 1993.

Cressy, David. *Birth, Marriage, and Death: Ritual, Religion, and the Life-Cycle in Tudor and Stuart England*. Oxford: Oxford University Press, 1997.

———. *Bonfires and Bells: National Memory and the Protestant Calendar in Elizabethan and Stuart England*. London: Weidenfeld and Nicolson, 1989.

———. *Literacy and the Social Order: Reading and Writing in Tudor and Stuart England*. Cambridge: Cambridge University Press, 1980.

———. "Purification, Thanksgiving, and the Churching of Women in Post-Reformation England." *Past and Present* 141 (November 1993): 106–46.

Crosby, Fanny. *Memories of Eighty Years*. Boston: James H. Earle, 1906.

Cross, Claire. *Church and People, 1450–1660: The Triumph of the Laity in the English Church*. Atlantic Highlands: N.J. Humanities Press, 1976.

———. "'Great Reasoners in Scripture': Women Lollards, 1380–1530." In *Medieval Women*. Studies in Church History, Subsidia, ed. Derek Baker, 359–80. Oxford: Basil Blackwell, 1978.

———. "'He-Goats before the Flocks': A Note about the Part Played by Women in the Founding of Some Civil War Churches." In *Popular Belief and Practice*. Studies in Church History 8, ed. G. J. Cuming and Derek Baker, 194–221. Cambridge: Cambridge University Press, 1972.

———. "Lay Literacy and Clerical Misconduct in a York Parish during the Reign of Mary Tudor." *York Historian* 3 (1980): 10–15.

———. "The Religious Life of Women in Sixteenth-Century Yorkshire." In *Women in the Church*. Studies in Church History 27, ed. W. J. Shiels and Diana Wood, 307–24. Oxford: Blackwell, 1990.

Cullinan, Edmond. "Forum: Women and the Diaconate." *Worship* 64 (1996): 260–66.

Cuming, G. J., and Derek Baker, eds. *Popular Belief and Practice*. Studies in Church History 8. Cambridge: Cambridge University Press, 1972.

Dahmus, J., ed. *The Metropolitan Visitations of William Courtenay*. Illinois Studies in the Social Sciences 31, no. 2. Urbana: University of Illinois Press, 1950.

Davies, J. G. "Deacons, Deaconesses, and Other Minor Orders in the Patristic Period." *Journal of Ecclesiastical History* 14 (1973): 1–15.

Davies, Stevan L. *The Revolt of the Widows: The Social World of the Apocryphal Acts*. Carbondale: Southern Illinois University Press, 1980.

Davis, Natalie Zeman. "City Women and Religious Change." In *Society and Culture in Early Modern France*, 2nd ed., ed. N. Z. Davis. Stanford: Stanford University Press, 1975.

————. "From 'Popular Religion' to 'Religious Cultures.'" In *Reformation Europe: A Guide to Research*, ed. S. Ozment, 321–46. St. Louis: Center for Reformation Research, 1982.

————. "Some Tasks and Themes in the Study of Popular Religion." In *The Pursuit of Holiness in Late Medieval and Renaissance Religion: Papers from the University of Michigan Conference*, ed. Charles Trinkhaus, with Heiko Oberman, 307–36. Leiden: Brill, 1974.

Davis, Natalie Zeman, and Annette Farge. "Women as Historical Actors." In *A History of Women in the West*, vol. 3: *Renaissance and Enlightenment Paradoxes*, ed. Natalie Zeman Davis and Annette Farge, 3–8. Cambridge, Mass.: Belknap Press of Harvard University Press, 1993.

Davis, Natalie Zeman, and Annette Farge, eds. *A History of Women in the West*, vol. 3: *Renaissance and Enlightenment Paradoxes*. Cambridge, Mass.: Belknap Press of Harvard University Press, 1993.

Dean, Beryl. *Ecclesiastical Embroidery*. London: Batsford, 1958.

Deasley, Margaret. "Vernacular Books in English in the Fourteenth and Fifteenth Centuries." *Modern Language Review* 15 (1920): 349–58.

DeLeeuw, Patricia Allwin. "The Changing Face of the Village Parish I: The Parish in the Early Middle Ages." In *Pathways to Medieval Peasants*. Papers in Medieval Studies 2, ed. J. A. Raftis, 311–22. Toronto: Pontifical Institute of Medieval Studies, 1981.

Del Giorgio, Michela. "The Catholic Model." In *History of Women in the West*, vol. 4: *Emerging Feminism from Revolution to World War*, ed. Genevieve Fraisse and Michelle Perrot, 166–97. Cambridge, Mass.: Belknap Press of Harvard University Press, 1993.

Dewey, Clive. *The Passing of Barchester*. London: Hambledon, 1991.

Dewhurst, C. Kurt, Betty MacDowell, and Marsha MacDowell. *Artists in Aprons: Folk Art by American Women*. New York: Dutton, 1979.

Dews, D. Colin. "Ann Carr and the Female Revivalists of Leeds." In *Religion in the Lives of English Women, 1760–1930*, ed. Gail Malmgreen, 68–87. Bloomington: Indiana University Press, 1986.

Dhuoda. *Handbook for William: A Carolingian Woman's Counsel for Her Son*, trans. Carol Neel. Washington, D.C.: Catholic University of America Press, 1991.

Dillard, H. *Daughters of the Reconquest: Women in Castilian Town Society, 1100–1300*. Cambridge: Cambridge University Press, 1984.

Dinn, Robert. "'Monuments Answerable to Men's Worth': Burial Patterns, Social Status and Gender in Late Medieval Bury St. Edmunds." *Journal of Ecclesiastical History* 46, no. 2 (April 1995): 237–55.

Dixon, C. Scott. *Reformation and Rural Society: The Parishes of Brandenburg-Ansbach-Kulmbach*. Cambridge: Cambridge University Press, 1996.

Dobson, Barrie, ed. *The Church, Politics, and Patronage in the Fifteenth Century*. Gloucester, U.K.: Sutton, 1984.

Doran, Susan. "Elizabeth I's Religion: The Evidence of Her Letters." *Journal of Ecclesiastical History* 51, no. 4 (October 2000): 699–720.

Dowling, M. "Anne Boleyn and Reform." *Journal of Ecclesiastical History* 35 (1984): 33.

Drew, C. *Early Parochial Organization in England: The Origin of the Office of Churchwarden*. London: St. Anthony's Press, 1954.

Driver, Martha W. "Pictures in Print: Late Fifteenth- and Early Sixteenth-Century Books in English for Lay Readers." In *De Cella in Seculum: Religious and Secular Life and Devotion in Late Medieval England*, ed. Michael G. Sargeant, 226–42. Cambridge: Brewer, 1989.

Dronke, P. *Women Writers of the Middle Ages: A Critical Study of Texts from Perpetua (203) to Marguerite Porete (1310)*. Cambridge: Cambridge University Press, 1988.

Duby, Georges. "Affidavits and Confessions." In *A History of Women in the West*, vol. 2: *Silences of the Middle Ages*, ed. C. Klapisch-Zuber, 479–83. Cambridge, Mass.: Belknap Press of Harvard University Press, 1992.

———. *A History of Private Life*, vol. 2: *Revelations of the Medieval World*. Cambridge, Mass.: Belknap Press of Harvard University Press, 1988.

Duffy, Eamon. "The Appropriation of the Sacraments in the Later Middle Ages." *New Blackfriars* 77 (January 1996): 40–57.

———. "The Parish, Piety, and Patronage in Late Medieval East Anglia: The Evidence of Rood Screens." In *Parish in English Life, 1400–1600*, ed. Katherine L. French, Gary Gibbs, and Beat A. Kümin, 133–62. Manchester: Manchester University Press, 1997.

———. *The Stripping of the Altars: Traditional Religion in England, 1400–1580*. New Haven: Yale University Press, 1992.

Eales, Jacqueline. "Iconoclasm, Iconography, and Altar in the English Civil War." In *The Church and the Arts*. Studies in Church History 28, ed. Diana Wood, 313–27. Oxford: Basil Blackwell, 1992.

Eichler, Lillian. *Book of Etiquette*. 2 vols. Oyster Bay, N.Y.: Nelson Doubleday, 1923.

Emmett, A. M. "An Early Fourth-Century Female Monastic Community in Egypt?" In *Maistor: Classical, Byzantine and Renaissance Studies for Robert Browning*, ed. A. Moffatt. Canberra: Byzantia Australiensia, 1984.

Ennen, Edith. *The Medieval Woman*. Oxford: Basil Blackwell, 1989.

Enright, D. J., ed. *The Oxford Book of Death*. Oxford: Oxford University Press, 1983.

Epstein, Dena J. "Lucy McKim Garrison, American Musician." *Bulletin of the New York Public Library* 67 (1963): 529–46.

———. *Sinful Tunes and Spirituals*. Chicago: University of Chicago Press, 1977.

Erikson, Carolly, and Kathleen Carey. "Women in the Middle Ages: A Working Bibliography." *Medieval Studies* 37 (1976): 340–59.

Erler, M., and M. Kowaleski, eds. *Women and Power in the Middle Ages*. Athens: University of Georgia Press, 1988.

Evans, Eifion. *The Welsh Revival of 1904*. Bridgend: Evangelical Press of Wales, 1969.

Evans, Joan. *Magical Jewels in the Middle Ages and Renaissance*. Oxford: Oxford University Press, 1922.

Ewing, George W. *The Well-Tempered Lyre: Songs and Verse of the Temperance Movement*. Dallas: SMU Press, 1977.

Fahy, Conor. "Three Early Renaissance Treatises on Women." *Italian Studies* 11 (1959): 30–55.

Fairfax-Lucy, A. *Mistress of Charlecote: The Memoirs of Mary Elizabeth Lucy*. London: Gollancz, 1983.

Farningham, Marianne. *A Woman's Working Life*. London: James Clarke, 1907.

Fatum, L. "Image of God and Glory of Man: Women in the Pauline Communities." In *Image of God and Gender Models in Judeo-Christian Tradition*, ed. K. E. Børresen, 56–137. Oslo: Solum Forlag, 1991.

Federal Writers' Project. *Slave Narratives: A Folk History of Slavery in the United States from Interviews with Former Slaves*. 1936–38. 17 vols. Washington, D.C.: Library of Congress. Reprint. St. Clair Shores, Mich.: Scholarly Press, 1976.

Ferrante, Joan M. "The Education of Women in the Middle Ages in Theory, Fact and Fantasy." In *Beyond Their Sex: Learned Women of the European Past*, ed. Patricia H. Labame. New York: New York University Press, 1984.

Fiennes, Celia. *The Illustrated Journeys of Celia Fiennes, 1685–1712*, ed. Christopher Morris. London: McDonald and Co., 1982.

Finney, Paul Corby, ed. *Seeing beyond the Word: Visual Arts and the Calvinist Tradition*. Grand Rapids, Mich.: Eerdmans, 1999.

Fisken, Beth Wynne. "Mary Sidney's Psalmes: Education and Wisdom." In *Silent but for the Word: Tudor Women as Patrons, Translators, and Writers of Religious Works*, ed. Margaret Hannay, 166–85. Kent, Ohio: Kent State University Press, 1995.

Fleming, Peter. "Charity, Faith and the Gentry of Kent." In *Property and Politics: Essays in Later Medieval English History*, ed. Tony Pollard. New York: St. Martin Press, 1984.

Fletcher, Anthony. "Beyond the Church: Women's Spiritual Experience at Home and in the Community, 1600–1900." In *Gender and Christian Religion*. Studies in Church History 34, ed. R. N. Swanson, 187–203. Woodbridge, U.K.: Boydell, 1998.

———. "Factionalism in the Countryside." In *The Church in Town and Countryside*. Studies in Church History 16. Oxford: Blackwell, 1979.

Flynn, Maureen. "Charitable Ritual in Late Medieval and Early Modern Spain." *Sixteenth-Century Journal* 16 (1985): 335–48.

Foote, Julia. *A Brand Plucked from the Fire: An Autobiographical Sketch by Mrs. Julia Foote*. Cleveland: W. F. Schneider, 1879.

Ford, Judy Ann. "Art and Identity in the Parish Communities of Late-Medieval Kent." In *The Church and the Arts*. Studies in Church History 28, ed. Diana Wood, 225–37. Oxford: Basil Blackwell, 1992.

Forrest, John. *Lord I'm Coming Home: Everyday Aesthetics in Tidewater North Carolina*. Ithaca, N.Y.: Cornell University Press, 1988.

Foster, Andrew. "Churchwardens' Accounts of Early Modern England and Wales: Some Problems to Note, But Much to Be Gained." In *Parish in English Life, 1400–1600*, ed. Katherine L. French, Gary Gibbs, and Beat A. Kümin, 74–93. Manchester: Manchester University Press, 1997.

Fox, Ruth. "Concelebration in Chapels of Women Religious." *Worship* 71, no. 5 (September 1996): 423–32.

Fox-Genovese, Elizabeth. "Religion in the Lives of Slaveholding Women of the Antebellum South." In *That Gentle Strength: Historical Perspectives on Women in Christianity*, ed. Lynda L. Coon, Katherine J. Haldane, and Elisabeth W. Sommer, 207–20. Charlottesville: University Press of Virginia, 1990.

Fraisse, Genevieve, and Michelle Perrot, eds. *A History of Women in the West*, vol. 4: *Emerging Feminism from Revolution to World War*. Cambridge, Mass.: Belknap Press of Harvard University Press, 1993.

Freedman, Sylvia. *Poor Penelope: Lady Penelope Rich, an Elizabethan Woman*. Bourne End, U.K.: Kensal Press, 1983.

French, Katherine. "Parochial Fund-Raising in Late Medieval Somerset." In *Parish in English Life, 1400–1600*, ed. Katherine L. French, Gary Gibbs, and Beat A. Kümin, 115–32. Manchester: Manchester University Press, 1997.

French, Katherine L., Gary Gibbs, Beat A. Kümin, eds. *Parish in English Life, 1400–1600*. Manchester: Manchester University Press, 1997.

Fulop, Timothy E., and Albert J. Raboteau. *African-American Religion: Essays in History and Culture*. New York: Routledge, 1997.

Gairdner, James, ed. *The Paston Letters, 1422–1590*. 4 vols. Westminster: A. Constable, 1900.

Gaitskell, Deborah. "Devout Domesticity? A Century of African Women's Christianity in South Africa." In *Women and Gender in South Africa to 1945*, ed. Cheryl Walker, 251–72. Cape Town: David Philip, 1990.

———. "Praying and Preaching: The Distinctive Spirituality of African Women's Church Organizations." In *Missions and Christianity in South African History*, ed. Henry Bredekamp and Robert Ross, 221–48. Johannesburg: Witwatersrand University Press, 1995.

Garcia, Celine Gremont. *Celine: Remembering Louisiana, 1850–1871*, ed. Frederick Geary. Athens: University of Georgia Press, 1987.

Garnett, Jane, and Colin Matthew, eds. *Revival and Religion since 1700: Essays for John Walsh*. London: Hambledon, 1993.

George, Suzanne K. *The Adventures of a Woman Homesteader: Life and Letters of Elinore Pruitt Stewart*. Lincoln: University of Nebraska Press, 1992.

Gerbet, Marie-Claude. "Les Confreries religieuses a Caceres de 1467 a 1523." *Melanges de la Casa de Velasquez* 7 (1971): 75–105.

Gerstel, Sharon E. J. "Painted Sources for Female Piety in Medieval Byzantium." *Dumbarton Oaks Papers* 52 (1998): 89–112.

Gibbs, Gary. "New Duties for Parish Communities in Tudor London." In *Parish in English Life, 1400–1600*, ed. Katherine L. French, Gary Gibbs, and Beat A. Kümin, 163–77. Manchester: Manchester University Press, 1997.

Gibson, Gail. "Churching as Women's Theater." In *Bodies and Disciplines: Intersections of Literature and History in Fifteenth-Century England*, ed. B. A. Hanawalt and D. Wallace, 139–54. Minneapolis: University of Minnesota Press, 1996.

Gifford, Carolyn de Swarte. " 'My Own Methodist Hive': Frances Willard's Faith as Disclosed in Her Journal, 1855–1870." In *Spirituality and Social Responsibility: Vocational Vision of Women in the United Methodist Tradition*, ed. R. Keller, 81–97. Nashville: Abingdon, 1993.

Gilkes, Cheryl Townsend. *If It Wasn't for the Women: Black Women's Experience and Womanist Culture in Church and Community*. Maryknoll, N.Y.: Orbis, 2001.

Gillespie, Vincent. "Vernacular Books and Religion." In *Book Production and Publishing in Britain, 1375–1475,* ed. Jeremy Griffiths. Cambridge: Cambridge University Press, 1989.

Gilley, Sheridan. "Victorian Feminism and Catholic Art: The Case of Mrs. Jameson." In *The Church and the Arts.* Studies in Church History 28, ed. Diana Wood, 381–91. Oxford: Basil Blackwell, 1992.

Gillis, John R. *For Better or Worse: British Marriages 1600 to the Present.* New York: Oxford University Press, 1985.

Gilman, Florence M. *Women Who Knew Paul.* Collegeville, Minn.: Michael Glazier/ Liturgical Press, 1992.

Gingrass, G. E. *Egeria: Diary of a Pilgrimage.* Ancient Christian Writers 38. New York: Newman Press, 1970.

Gittings, Clare. *Death, Burial, and the Individual in Early Modern England.* London: Routledge, 1988.

Goering, Joseph W. "The Changing Face of the Village Parish II: The Thirteenth Century." In *Papers in Medieval Studies,* 2, ed. J. A. Raftis, 323–33. Toronto: Pontifical Institute of Medieval Studies, 1981.

Gold, Penny Schine. *The Lady and the Virgin: Image, Attitude, and Experience in Twelfth-Century France.* Women in Culture and Society Series. Chicago: University of Chicago Press, 1985.

Goldberg, P. J. P. "Women's Work: Women's Role in the Late-Medieval North." In *Profit, Piety, and the Professions in Later Medieval England,* ed. M. Hicks. Gloucester, U.K.: Allan Sutton, 1990.

———. "Women in Fifteenth-Century Town Life." In *Towns and Townspeople in the Fifteenth Century,* ed. John A. F. Thomson. Gloucester, U.K.: Allan Sutton, 1988.

Goodfriend, Joyce D. *The Published Diaries and Letters of American Women: An Annotated Bibliography.* Boston, Mass.: G. K. Hall and Co., 1987.

Gordon, Beverly. *Bazaars and Fair Ladies.* Knoxville: University of Tennessee Press, 1998.

Gosner, Kevin. *Soldiers of the Virgin: The Moral Economy of a Colonial Maya Rebellion.* Tucson: University of Arizona Press, 1992.

Gottleib, Beatrice. *The Family in the Western World.* Oxford: Oxford University Press, 1993.

Gough, Richard. *The History of Myddle.* New York: Penguin, 1981.

Graham, E., ed. *Her Own Life: Autobiographical Writings by Seventeenth-Century English-women.* London: Routledge, 1989.

Greaves, R. L. "The Ordination Controversy and the Spirit of Reform in Puritan England." *Journal of Ecclesiastical History* 21 (1970): 225–41.

Green, I. "The Persecution of 'Scandalous' and 'Malignant' Parish Clergy during the English Civil War." *English Historical Review* 104 (1979): 527–43.

Greer, Germaine. *The Obstacle Race: The Fortunes of Women Painters and Their Work.* New York: Farrar, Straus, and Giroux, 1983.

Gregory, Jeremy. "Gender and the Clerical Profession in England, 1660–1850." In *Gender and Christian Religion.* Studies in Church History 34, ed. R. N. Swanson, 235–71. Woodbridge, U.K.: Boydell, 1998.

Gryson, Roger. *Ministry of Women in the Early Church.* Collegeville, Minn.: Liturgical Press, 1976.

Gueusquin, Marie-France. "Guardiennes et portefaix — De la preeminence de la femme dans le travail funeraire d'un commune rurale de la Nievre." *Ethnologie française* 13 (1983): 129–38.

Guibbory, Achsah. *Ceremony and Community from Herbert to Milton: Literature and Cultural Conflict in Seventeenth-Century England.* Cambridge: Cambridge University Press, 1998.

Gundersen, Joan R. "The Non-Institutional Church: The Religious Role of Women in Eighteenth-Century Virginia." *The Historical Magazine of the Protestant Episcopal Church* 51 (December 1982): 347–58.

Haigh, Christopher. "Communion and Community: Exclusion from Communion in Post-Reformation England." *Journal of Ecclesiastical History* 51, no. 4 (October 2000): 721–40.

Hall, Catherine. *White, Male, and Middle-Class: Explorations in Feminism and History.* New York: Routledge, 1992.

Hall, Suzanne W. *Chaste, Silent, and Obedient: English Books for Women, 1475–1640.* San Marino, Calif.: Huntington Library, 1982.

Hallett, J. P. *Fathers and Daughters in Roman Society: Women and the Elite Family.* Princeton, N.J.: Princeton University Press, 1984.

Hamilton, Bernard. "Women in the Crusader States: Queens of Jerusalem, 1100–1190." In *Medieval Women.* Studies in Church History, Subsidia, ed. Derek Baker, 143–74. Oxford: Basil Blackwell, 1978.

Hanawalt, Barbara A. "Medieval English Women in Rural and Urban Domestic Space." *Dumbarton Oaks Papers* 52 (1998): 19–26.

———. *The Ties That Bound: Peasant Families in Medieval England.* New York: Oxford University Press, 1986.

Hanawalt, Barbara A., and D. Wallace, eds. *Bodies and Disciplines: Intersections of Literature and History in Fifteenth-Century England.* Minneapolis: University of Minnesota Press, 1996.

Hanlon, Gregory. *Confession and Community in Seventeenth-Century France: Catholic and Protestant Coexistence in Aquitaine.* Philadelphia: University of Pennsylvania Press, 1993.

Hannay, Margaret, ed. *Silent but for the Word: Tudor Women as Patrons, Translators, and Writers of Religious Works.* Kent, Ohio: Kent State University Press, 1995.

Hansen, Karen. *A Very Social Time: Crafting Community in Antebellum New England.* Berkeley: University of California Press, 1994.

Hardesty, Nancy. *Women Called to Witness: Evangelical Feminism in the Nineteenth Century.* Nashville: Abingdon, 1984.

Hardesty, Nancy, and Adrienne Israel. "Amanda Berry Smith: A 'Downright, Outright Christian.' " In *Spirituality and Social Responsibility: Vocational Vision of Women in the United Methodist Tradition,* ed. R. Keller. Nashville: Abingdon, 1993.

Harris, Barbara. "City Women and Religious Change." In *Society and Culture in Early Modern France,* ed. B. Harris. Stanford: Stanford University Press, 1965, 1975.

Harris, Barbara, and Joann McNamarra, eds. *Women and the Structure of Society.* Durham, N.C.: Duke University Press, 1984.

Harris, Tim, ed. *Popular Culture in England, c. 1500–1850.* New York: St. Martin's, 1994.

Harte, N. B., and K. G. Ponting. *Cloth and Clothing in Medieval Europe.* London: Heinemann, 1983.

Hartman, Mary S., and Loos Banner, eds. *Clio's Consciousness Raised: New Perspectives on the History of Women.* New York: Octagon Books, 1976.

Haskell, Ann S. "Marriage in the Middle Ages, 3: The Paston Women in Marriage in Fifteenth-Century England." *Viator: Medieval and Renaissance Studies* 4 (1973): 460–71.

Hass, Louis. *The Renaissance Man and His Children: Childbirth and Early Childhood in Florence, 1300–1600.* New York: St. Martin's, 1998.

Head, Thomas. "The Religion of the Femmelettes: Ideals and Experience among Women in Fifteenth- and Sixteenth-Century France." In *That Gentle Strength: Historical Perspectives on Women in Christianity,* ed. Lynda L. Coon, Katherine J. Haldane, and Elisabeth W. Sommer, 149–76. Charlottesville: University Press of Virginia, 1990.

Heath, Peter. "Piety in the Late Middle Ages." In *The Church, Politics, and Patronage in the Fifteenth Century,* ed. R. Barrie Dobson. Gloucester, U.K.: Sutton, 1984.

———. "Urban Piety in the Later Middle Ages: The Evidence from Hull Wills." In *The Church, Politics, and Patronage in the Fifteenth Century,* ed. Barrie Dobson, 211–27. Gloucester, U.K.: Sutton, 1984.

Heeney, Brian. *The Women's Movement in the Church of England, 1850–1930.* Oxford: Clarendon, 1988.

Heilbrun, Caroline. *Writing a Woman's Life.* London: Women's Press, 1989.

Hempton, David. "Methodist Growth in Transatlantic Perspective." In *Methodism and the Shaping of American Culture,* ed. Nathan O. Hatch and John H. Wigger. Nashville: Kingswood Books, 2001.

Henderson, Katherine Usher, and Barbara F. McManus. *Half Humankind: Contexts and Texts of the Controversy about Women, 1530–1640.* Urbana and Chicago: University of Illinois Press, 1984.

Hero, Angel Constantine. *A Woman's Quest for Spiritual Guidance.* Brookline: Hellenic College Press, 1986.

Herrin, Judith. "In Search of Byzantine Women." In *Images of Women in Antiquity,* ed. A. Cameron. London: Routledge, 1983.

Herzel, Susannah. *A Voice for Women: The Women's Department of the World Council of Churches.* Geneva: WCC, 1981.

Hickeyu, Anne Ewing. *Women of the Roman Aristocracy as Christian Monastics.* Ann Arbor: University of Michigan Press, 1987.

Higgenbotham, Evelyn Brooks. *Righteous Discontent: The Woman's Movement in the Black Baptist Church, 1820–1920.* Cambridge, Mass.: Harvard University Press, 1995.

Higonet, Anne. "Images." In *History of Women in the West,* vol. 4: *Emerging Feminism from Revolution to World War,* ed. Genevieve Fraisse and Michelle Perrot, 166–97. Cambridge, Mass.: Belknap Press of Harvard University Press, 1993.

Hill, Rosalind. *Rolls and Registers of Bishop Oliver Sutton, 1280–1299.* Lincoln: Friends of Lincoln Cathedral, 1980.

———. "The Theory and Practice of Excommunication in Medieval England." *History* 42, pp. 1–11.

Hillsman, Walter. "The Victorian Revival of Plainsong in English: Its Usage under Tractarians and Ritualists." In *The Church and the Arts.* Studies in Church History 28, ed. Diana Wood, 405–15. Oxford: Basil Blackwell, 1992.

Hilton, R. *The English Peasantry in the Later Middle Ages.* Oxford: Oxford University Press, 1975.

Hindmarsh, D. Bruce. *John Newton and the English Evangelical Tradition: Between the Conversions of the Wesleys and Wilberforce.* Oxford: Clarendon, 1996.

Hogg, James. "Everyday Life in a Contemplative Order." In *Medieval Mystical Tradition in England,* ed. Marion Glasscoe. Cambridge: Brewer, 1992.

Holdsworth, Christopher J. "Christina of Markyate." In *Medieval Women.* Studies in Church History, Subsidia, ed. Derek Baker, 185–204. Oxford: Basil Blackwell, 1978.

Holifield, E. Brooks. *The Covenant Sealed: The Development of Puritan Sacramental Theology in Old and New England, 1570–1720.* New Haven: Yale University Press, 1974.

Holland, Mary Sibylla Lyall. *Additional Letters of Mary Sibylla Holland.* Ed. Edward Holland. Edinburgh, 1899.

———. *Letters of Mary Sibylla Holland.* Ed. Edward Holland. 3d ed. London, 1907.

Hollis, Stephanie. *Anglo-Saxon Women and the Church: Sharing a Common Fate.* Rochester, N.Y.: Boydell, 1992.

Holum, Kenneth G. *Theodosian Empresses: Women and Imperial Dominion in Late-Antiquity.* Berkeley: University of California Press, 1982.

Homans, George C. *English Villagers of the Thirteenth Century.* Cambridge, Mass.: Harvard University Press, 1941.

Hopkins, James K. *A Woman to Deliver Her People: Joanna Southcott and English Millenarianism in an Era of Revolution.* Austin: University of Texas Press, 1982.

Hopley, Catherine. "Two Sabbaths on the Atlantic." *The Sunday Home: A Family Magazine* 9 (November 8, 1862): 14–15.

Houlbrooke, Ralph. "Death, Church, and Family in England between the Late Fifteenth and Early Eighteenth Century." In *Death, Ritual and Bereavement,* ed. R. Houlbrooke. London: Routledge, 1989.

———. *English Family Life, 1576–1716.* Oxford: Oxford University Press, 1988.

———. "Women's Social Life." *Continuity and Change* 1 (1986): 171–89.

Howard, Dorothy. *Dorothy's World: Childhood in Sabine Bottom, 1902–1910.* Englewood Cliffs, N.J.: Prentice Hall, 1977.

Howarth, Glennys. "Professionalising the Funeral Industry in England, 1700–1900." In *The Changing Face of Death: Historical Accounts of Death and Disposal,* ed. Peter C. Jupp and Glennys Howarth, 120–34. New York: St. Martin's, 1997.

Howson, John Saul. *Deaconesses, or the Official Help of Women in Parochial Work and in Charitable Institutions.* London, 1862.

Hoywes, Anna. *Conversation of a Child with Its Mother on the Way to True Godliness.* London, 1628.

Hughes, Kathleen. *How Firm a Foundation: Voices of the Early Liturgical Movement.* Chicago: Liturgy Training Publications, 1990.

———. "Sanctity and Secularity in the Early Irish Church." In *Sanctity and Secularity: The Church and the World.* Studies in Christian Doctrine 9, ed. Derek Baker, 21–37. Oxford: Blackwell, 1973.

Hunt, E. D. *Holy Land Pilgrimage in the Later Roman Empire A.D. 312–460.* Oxford: Clarendon, 1982.

Huppert, George. *After the Black Death: A Social History of Early Modern Europe.* Bloomington: Indiana University Press, 1986.

Hutchinson, Ann M. "Devotional Reading in the Monastery and in the Household." In *De Cella in Seculum: Religious and Secular Life and Devotion in Late Medieval England,* ed. Michael G. Sargeant, 215–27. Cambridge: Brewer, 1989.

Hutchinson, Lucy. *Memoirs of the Life of Colonel Hutchinson.* London: Oxford University Press, 1973.

Hutton, Ronald. *The Rise and Fall of Merry England: The Ritual Year, 1400–1700.* Oxford: Oxford University Press, 1994.

Ingram, Martin J. "Communities and Courts: Law and Disorder in Early Seventeenth-Century Wiltshire." In *Crime in England, 1500–1800,* ed. J. S. Cockburn. Princeton, N.J.: Princeton University Press, 1977.

———. "From Reformation to Toleration: Popular Religious Cultures in England, 1540–1690." In *Popular Culture in England, c. 1500–1850,* ed. Tim Harris, 95–123. New York: St. Martin's, 1994.

Irvin, Dorothy. "The Ministry of Women in the Early Church: The Archeological Evidence." *Duke Divinity School Review* 45, no. 2 (1980): 76–86.

Jackson, Irene V. *More Than Dancing: Essays on Afro-American Music and Musicians.* Westport, Conn.: Greenwood, 1985.

Jacob, E. F. "Founders and Foundations in the Later Middle Ages." *Bulletin of Institutional History Research* 35 (1962): 29–46.

Jacob, William M. *Lay People and Religion in the Early Eighteenth Century.* Cambridge: Cambridge University Press, 1996.

———. "A Practice of Very Hurtful Tendency." In *Church in Town and Countryside.* Studies in Church History 16. Oxford: Blackwell, 1979.

James, Janet Wilson, ed. *Women in American Religion.* Philadelphia: University of Pennsylvania Press, 1980.

Jansen, Sharon L. *Dangerous Talk and Strange Behavior: Women and Popular Resistance to the Reforms of Henry VIII.* New York: St. Martin's, 1996.

Jarlbert, Anders. "From Private Counselor to Public Church Politician: Three Female Expressions of Conservative Urban Lutheranism in Western Sweden, 1810–1910." In *Gender and Christian Religion.* Studies in Church History 34, ed. R. N. Swanson, 295–307. Woodbridge, U.K.: Boydell, 1998.

Joceline, Elizabeth. *The Mothers Legacie to Her Unborne Childe.* London, 1624.

Johnson, Alexandra, and Sally-Beth MacLean. "Reformation and Resistance in Thames/Severn Parishes: The Dramatic Witness." In *Parish in English Life, 1400–1600,* ed. Katherine L. French, Gary Gibbs, and Beat A. Kümin, 178–202. Manchester: Manchester University Press, 1997.

Johnson, Dale A. *Women in English Religion, 1700–1925*. New York: Edward Mellen Press, 1983.

Jolly, Karen Louise. *Popular Religion in Late Saxon England: Elf Charms in Context*. Chapel Hill: University of North Carolina Press, 1996.

Joyner, Charles. *Down by the Riverside: A South Carolina Slave Community*. Urbana: University of Illinois Press, 1984.

Jupp, Peter C. "Enon Chapel: No Way for the Dead." In *The Changing Face of Death: Historical Accounts of Death and Disposal*, ed. Peter C. Jupp and Glennys Howarth, 91–104. New York: St. Martin's, 1997.

Jupp, Peter C., and Clare Gittings. *Death in England: An Illustrated History*. Manchester: Manchester University Press, 1999.

Jupp, Peter C., and Glennys Howarth, eds. *The Changing Face of Death: Historical Accounts of Death and Disposal*. New York: St. Martin's, 1997.

Karant-Nunn, Susan. "Churching." In *Oxford Encyclopedia of the Reformation*, 4 vols., ed. Hans Hillerbrand, 1:331–32. Oxford: Oxford University Press, 1996.

———. *The Reformation of Ritual: An Interpretation of Early Modern Germany*. London: Routledge, 1997.

Kastner, J. Ronald. "Eudokia." In *A Lost Tradition: Women Writers of the Early Church*, ed. Patricia Wilson-Kastner et al., 149–57. Lanham, Md.: University Press of America, 1981.

Keiser, G. "Patronage and Piety in Fifteenth-Century England: Margaret, Duchess of Clarence." *Yale University Library Gazette* (1985): 32–46.

Keller, Rosemary Skinner, ed. *Spirituality and Social Responsibility: Vocational Vision of Women in the United Methodist Tradition*. Nashville: Abingdon, 1993.

Kelly, Catherine E. *In the New England Fashion: Reshaping Women's Lives in the Nineteenth Century*. Ithaca, N.Y.: Cornell University Press, 1999.

Kelly, Henry Ansgar. "Marriage in the Middle Ages, 2: Clandestine Marriage and Chaucer's 'Troilus.' " *Viator: Medieval and Renaissance Studies* 4 (1973): 435–57.

Kelly-Gadol, Joan. "Did Women Have a Renaissance?" In *Becoming Visible*, ed. Renate Bridenthal and Claudia Koonz, 139–64. Boston: Houghton Mifflin, 1977.

———. "Notes on Women in the Renaissance and Renaissance Historiography." In *Conceptual Frameworks for Studying Women's History*, ed. Marilyn Arthur et al., 137–64. Bronxville, N.Y.: Sarah Lawrence College, 1975.

———. "The Social Relation of the Sexes: Methodological Implications for Women's History." *Signs* 1 (1976): 810–24.

Kelso, Ruth. "Doctrine for the Lady of the Renaissance." In *The Elizabethan Woman*, ed. Carroll Camden. Mamaroneck, N.Y.: P. P. Appel, 1975.

Kieckhefer, Richard. *Forbidden Rites: A Necromancer's Manual*. University Park: Pennsylvania State University Press, 1998.

Kienzle, B. M., and P. J. Walker. *Women Preachers and Prophets through Two Millennia of Christianity*. Berkeley: University of California Press, 1998.

King, Christine. "The Death of a King: Elvis Presley, 1935–1977." In *The Changing Face of Death: Historical Accounts of Death and Disposal,* ed. P. Jupp and G. Howarth, 164–76. New York: St. Martin's, 1997.

King, John N. "Patronage and Piety: The Influence of Catherine Parr." In *Silent but for the Word: Tudor Women as Patrons, Translators, and Writers of Religious Works,* ed. Margaret Hannay, 43–60. Kent, Ohio: Kent State University Press, 1995.

King, Margaret L. "Book-Lined Cells: Women and Humanism in the Early Italian Renaissance." In *Beyond their Sex,* ed. Patricia Labalme. New York: New York University Press, 1980.

———. *Women of the Renaissance.* Women in Culture and Society. Chicago: University of Chicago Press, 1991.

Kingford, C. L., ed. *The Stonor Letters and Papers, 1290–1483.* Series 3.1. London: Camden Society, 1900.

Kinzie, Juliette A. *Wau-Bun, The Early Days in the North-West.* Chicago: Lakeside Press, 1932.

Kirchberger, C. "Elizabeth Burnet, 1661–1709." *Church Quarterly Review* 148 (1949): 17–51.

Kirschner, Julius, and Suzanne Wemple, eds. *Women of the Medieval World: Essays in Honour of John H. Munday.* Oxford: Basil Blackwell, 1985.

Klapisch-Zuber, Christiane. *Women, Family, and Ritual in Renaissance Italy.* Chicago: University of Chicago Press, 1987.

———, ed. *A History of Women in the West,* vol. 2: *Silences of the Middle Ages.* Cambridge, Mass.: Belknap Press of Harvard University Press, 1992.

Kselman, Thomas A. *Death and the Afterlife in Modern France.* Princeton, N.J.: Princeton University Press, 1993.

Kümin, Beat. "The English Parish in a European Perspective." In *Parish in English Life, 1400–1600,* ed. Katherine L. French, Gary Gibbs, and Beat A. Kümin, 15–34. Manchester: Manchester University Press, 1997.

———. *The Shaping of a Community: The Rise and Reformation of the English Parish, c. 1400–1560.* Brookfield, Vt.: Scolar Press, 1996.

Kunze, Bonnelyn Young. "vessells fitt for the masters us[e]: A Transatlantic Community of Religious Women, The Quakers, 1675–1753." In *Court, Country, and Culture: Essays on Early Modern British History in Honour of Perez Zagorin,* ed. Bonnelyn Young Kunze and Dwight D. Brautigam. Rochester, N.Y.: University of Rochester Press, 1992.

Labalme, P. H., ed. *Beyond Their Sex: Learned Women of the European Past.* New York: New York University Press, 1984.

Lacquer, Thomas W. "Cemeteries, Religion and the Culture of Capitalism." In *Revival and Religion since 1700: Essays for John Walsh,* ed. Jane Garnett and Colin Matthew, 183–200. London: Hambledon, 1993.

Ladurie, E. Le Roy. *Montaillou, Village Occitan de 1294–1324.* Paris: Gallimard, 1975.

Laiou, A. E. *Society and Economic Life in Byzantium.* Aldershot: Variorum, 1992.

Lamb, Mary Ellen. "The Cooke Sisters: Attitudes toward Learned Women in the Renaissance." In *Silent but for the Word: Tudor Women as Patrons, Translators, and*

Writers of Religious Works, ed. Margaret Hannay, 101–20. Kent, Ohio: Kent State University Press, 1995.

Lambert, M. D. *Medieval Heresy: Popular Movements from Bogomil to Hus.* London: E. Arnold, 1977.

Lamberts, Josef. "Origins of the Corpus Christi Feast." *Worship* 71, no. 5 (September 1996): 432–46.

Lang, Judith. *Ministers of Grace: Women in the Early Church.* Middlegreen, U.K.: St. Paul, 1989.

Larson, Rebecca. *Daughters of Light: Quaker Women Preaching and Prophesying in the Colonies and Abroad, 1700–1775.* New York: Knopf, 1999.

Laurence, Anne. "A Priesthood of She-Believers: Women and Congregations in Mid-Seventeenth-Century England." In *Women in the Church.* Studies in Church History 27, ed. W. J. Sheils and Diana Wood. Oxford: Blackwell, 1990.

Lawson, Richard H., trans. *Brother Hermann's Life of the Countess Yolanda of Vianden.* Studies in German Literature, Linguistics, and Culture: Medieval Texts and Translations. Columbia, S.C.: Camden House, 1995.

Leader, Pauline. "The Historic Role of Women in the Society of Friends." *Friends Quarterly* (January 1986): 17–20.

Leaver, Robin, ed. *Studies in Liturgical Musicology.* Lanham, Md.: Scarecrow Press, 1974–.

Lees, James Cameron. "The Riot in St. Giles Cathedral in 1637: The Story of Jenny Geddes and Her Stool." In *Women of the Scottish Reformation: Their Contribution to the Protestant Cause,* ed. David P. Thomson, 58–66. Crieff, Perthshire, Scotland: St. Ninian, 1960.

Leigh, Dorothy. *The Mother's Blessing.* London: John Budge, 1621.

Levine, Lawrence. *Black Culture and Black Consciousness.* New York: Oxford University Press, 1977.

Lewis, Flora. "Rewarding Devotion: Indulgences and the Promotion of Images." In *The Church and the Arts.* Studies in Church History 28, ed. Diana Wood, 179–94. Oxford: Basil Blackwell, 1992.

Lewis, Thomas Taylor, ed. *Letters of Lady Brilliana Harley.* London: Camden Society, 1854.

Lindle, Susan Hill. *You Have Stepped Out of Your Place: A History of Women and Religion in America.* Louisville: Westminster/John Knox, 1996.

Litten, Julian. "The Funeral Trade in Hanoverian England, 1714–1760." In *The Changing Face of Death: Historical Accounts of Death and Disposal,* ed. Peter C. Jupp and Glennys Howarth, 48–61. New York: St. Martin's, 1997.

Lobody, Diane H. "A Wren Just Bursting Its Shell: Catherine Livingston Garrettson's Ministry of Public Domesticity." In *Spirituality and Social Responsibility: Vocational Vision of Women in the United Methodist Tradition,* ed. Rosemary Skinner, 19–38. Nashville: Abingdon, 1993.

Lockwood, Rose. "Potens et Factiosa Femina: Women, Martyrs, and Schism in Roman North Africa." *Augustinian Studies* 20 (1989): 165–82.

Lovejoy, David S. *Religious Enthusiasm in the New World: Heresy to Revolution.* Cambridge, Mass.: Harvard University Press, 1985.

Lyerly, Cynthia Lynn. "Religion, Gender and Identity: Black Methodist Women in Slave Society." In *Discovering the Women in Slavery: Emancipating Perspectives on the American Past,* ed. Patricia Manton, 202–26. Athens: University of Georgia Press, 1998.

Lynch, Joseph H. *Godparents and Kinship in Early Medieval Europe.* Princeton, N.J.: Princeton University Press, 1986.

MacDonald, Michael. *Mystical Bedlam: Madness, Anxiety, and Healing in Seventeenth-Century England.* Cambridge History of Medicine. Cambridge: Cambridge University Press, 1981.

Mack, Phyllis. *Visionary Women: Ecstatic Prophesy in Seventeenth-Century England.* Berkeley: University of California Press, 1992.

———. "Women Prophets during the English Civil War." *Feminist Studies* 8 (1982): 19–45.

Macurdy, G. H. *Hellenistic Queens: A Study of Women-Power in Macedonia, Selucid Syria, and Ptolemaic Egypt.* Chicago: Ares Publishers, 1985.

Maguire, Henry. "Garments Pleasing to God: The Significance of Domestic Textile Design in the Early Byzantine Period." *Dumbarton Oaks Papers* 44 (1990): 215–24.

Maigrot, Jean-Louis. "Le Gestes des Funerailles en Haute-Marne." *Ethnologie française* 6 (1976): 381–86.

Maison, Margaret. "'Thine, Only Thine!': Women Hymn Writers in Britain, 1760–1835." In *Religion in the Lives of English Women, 1760–1930,* ed. Gail Malmgreen, 11–40. Bloomington: Indiana University Press, 1986.

Malden, H. E., ed. *The Cely Papers, 1475–1488.* London: Camden Society Publications, Series 3.1, 1900.

Malmgreen, Gail, ed. *Religion in the Lives of English Women, 1760–1930.* Bloomington: Indiana University Press, 1986.

Maltby, Judith. "'By This Book': Parishioners, the Prayer Book and the Established Church." In *The Early Stuart Church 1603–1642,* ed. Kenneth Fincham. Stanford, Calif.: Stanford University Press, 1993.

———. *Prayer Book and People in Elizabethan and Stuart England.* Cambridge: Cambridge University Press, 1998.

Marshall, A. J. "Roman Women and the Provinces." *Ancient Society* 6 (1975): 108–27.

Marszalek, John F., ed. *The Diary of Miss Emma Holmes, 1861–1866.* Baton Rouge: Louisiana State University Press, 1982.

Martin, Mary Clare. "Women and Philanthropy in Walthamstow and Leyton, 1740–1870." *London Journal* 19 (1995): 119.

Martindale, Andrew. "Patrons and Minders." In *The Church and the Arts.* Studies in Church History 28, ed. Diana Wood, 143–78. Oxford: Basil Blackwell, 1992.

Mason, Emma. "The Role of the English Parishioner, 1100–1500." *Journal of Ecclesiastical History* 27 (1976): 17–29.

———. "A Truth Universally Acknowledged." In *The Church in Town and Countryside.* Church History Society 16, 171–86. Oxford: Blackwell, 1979.

Maultsby, Portia K. "West African Influences and Retentions in U.S. Black Music: A Socio-Cultural Study." In *More Than Dancing: Essays on Afro-American Music and Musicians,* ed. Irene Jackson, 25–57. Westport, Conn.: Greenwood, 1985.

McCleod, Hugh. "The 'Golden Age' of New York City Catholicism." In *Revival and Religion since 1700: Essays for John Walsh,* ed. Jane Garnett and Matthew Colin, 249–71. London: Hambledon, 1993.

McCree, Ben R. "Religious Gilds and the Regulation of Behavior in Late Medieval Towns." In *People, Politics and Community in the Later Middle Ages,* ed. Joel Rosenthal and Colin Richmond, 108–22. Gloucester, U.K.: Alan Sutton, and New York: St. Martin's, 1987.

McDannell, Colleen. "Marketing Jesus." In *Icons of American Protestantism: The Art of Warner Sallman,* ed. David Morgan. New Haven: Yale University Press, 1996.

———. *Material Christianity: Religion and Popular Culture in America.* New Haven: Yale University Press, 1986.

McGee, Gary B. " 'Latter Rain' Falling in the East: Early Twentieth-Century Pentecostalism in India and the Debate on Speaking in Tongues." *Church History* 68, no. 3 (September 1999): 648–64.

McHardy, A. K. "Bishop Buckingham and the Lollards of Lincoln Diocese." *Studies in Church History* 9 (1972): 131–46.

McIntosh, Marjorie Keniston. *A Community Transformed: The Manor and Liberty of Havering, 1500–1620.* Cambridge: Cambridge University Press, 1991.

McKechnie, Paul. "Women's Religion and Second Century Christianity." *Journal of Ecclesiastical History* 47, no. 3 (July 1996): 409–31.

McKee, Elsie A. *Reforming Popular Piety in Sixteenth-Century Strasbourg: Katharina Schütz Zell and Her Hymnbook.* Studies in Reformed Theology and History 2, no. 4. Princeton, N.J.: Princeton Theological Seminary, 1994.

McKinnon, James. *Music in Early Christian Literature.* Cambridge Readings in the Literature of Music. Cambridge: Cambridge University Press, 1989.

McKitterick, Rosamond. "Frauen and Schriftlichkeit im Frühmittelalter." In *Weibliche Lebensgestaltung im frühen Mittelalter,* ed. Hans Werner Goetz. Cologne: Böhlau, 1991.

———. "Nuns' Scriptoria in England and Francia in the Eighth Century." *Francia* 19, no. 1 (1992): 1–35.

———. "Women and Literacy in the Middle Ages." In *Books, Scribes, and Learning in the Frankish Kingdoms, Sixth–Ninth Centuries,* ed. Rosamond McKitterick. Aldershot: U.K.: Variorum, 1994.

McLaughlin, Mary Martin. "Looking for Medieval Women: An Interim Report on the Project 'Women's Religious Life and Communities, 500–1600 A.D.' " In *Monastic Studies: The Continuity of Tradition,* ed. Judith Loades, 273–85. Bangor, Wales: Headstart, 1991.

McLean, Ian. *The Renaissance Notion of Women: A Study in the Fortunes of Scholasticism and Medical Science in European Intellectual Life.* Cambridge Monographs on the History of Medicine. Cambridge: Cambridge University Press, 1980.

McMullen, Norma. "The Education of English Gentlewomen, 1540–1640." *History of Education* 6 (1977): 87–101.

McMullen, R. "Women in Public in the Roman Empire." *Historia* 29 (1980): 208–20.

McPherson, Aimee Semple. *This and That.* New York: Garland, 1985 (1919).

Meads, Dorothy M., ed. *Diary of Lady Margaret Hoby, 1599–1605.* London: Routledge, 1930.

Meale, Carol M. "'...alle the books that I have in latyn, englische, and frensch': Lay-women and Their Books in Late Medieval England." In *Women and Literature in Britain, 1100–1500,* ed. Carol M. Meale, 128–58. Cambridge: Cambridge University Press, 1993.

Mendelson, Sara Heller. "Stuart Women's Diaries and Occasional Memoirs." In *Women in English Society, 1500–1800,* ed. Mary Prior, 181–210. Cambridge: Cambridge University Press, 1985.

Mentzer, Raymond A., Jr. "The Reformed Churches of France and the Visual Arts." In *Seeing beyond the Word: Visual Arts and the Calvinist Tradition,* ed. Paul Corby Finney. Grand Rapids, Mich.: Eerdmans, 1999.

Mertes, R. G., and K. A. Mertes. "The Household as a Religious Community." In *People, Politics, and Community in the Later Middle Ages,* ed. Joel Rosenthal and Colin Richmond, 123–39. Gloucester, U.K.: Alan Sutton, and New York: St. Martin's, 1987.

Methuen, Charlotte. "'For Pagans Laugh to Hear Women Teach': Gender Stereotypes in the *Didascalia Apostolorum.*" In *Gender and Christian Religion.* Studies in Church History 34, ed. R. N. Swanson. Woodbridge, U.K.: Boydell Press, 1998.

———. "Widows, Bishops, and the Struggle for Authority in the Didascalia Apostolorum." *Journal of Ecclesiastical History* 46 (1995): 197–213.

Meyendorff, John. "Marriage in Byzantium: The Canonical and Liturgical Tradition." *Dumbarton Oaks Papers* 44 (1990): 99–107.

Middelditch, T. *The Youthful Female Missionary: A Memoir of Mary Ann Hutchins, Wife of the Rev. John Hutchins, Baptist Missionary, Savanna-la-Mar, Jamaica; and Daughter of the Rev. T. Middelditch of Ipswich, compiled chiefly from her own correspondence by her Father.* London: G. Whiteman and Hamilton Adams, 1840.

Mintz, Steven, and Susan Kellogg. *Domestic Revolutions: A Social History of American Family Life.* New York: Free Press, 1988.

Moffard, Juliet Haines. *And Firm Thine Ancient Vow: The History of North Parish Church of North Andover, 1645–1974.* North Andover, Mass.: Naiman, 1975.

Momigliano, Arnoldo. "Popular Religious Belief and the Late Roman Historians." In *Popular Belief and Practice.* Studies in Church History 8, ed. G. J. Cuming and Derek Baker, 1–18. Cambridge: Cambridge University Press, 1972.

Montcrief, Robert Scott, ed. *Household Book of Lady Gieselle Baillie, 1692–1733.* Edinburgh: Edinburgh University/Scottish History Society, 1911.

Montgomery, William E. *Under Their Own Vine and Fig Tree: The African American Church in the South, 1865–1900.* Baton Rouge: Louisiana State University Press, 1993.

Moody, Joanna, ed. *The Private Life of an Elizabethan Lady: The Diary of Lady Margaret Hoby, 1599–1605.* Stroud, Gloucester, U.K.: Sutton, 1988.

Moran, Gerald F. "Sisters in Christ: Women and the Church in Seventeenth-Century New England." In *Women in American Religion,* ed. Janet Wilson James. Philadelphia: University of Pennsylvania Press, 1980.

Morgan, David, ed. *Icons of American Protestantism: The Art of Warner Sallman.* New Haven: Yale University Press, 1996.

Morris, Joan. *The Lady Was a Bishop: The Hidden History of Women with Clerical Ordination and the Jurisdiction of Bishops.* London: Macmillan, 1973.

Mullen, Richard. *Birds of Passage: Five Englishwomen in Search of America*. London: Duckworth, 1994.

Mumm, Susan. *Stolen Daughters, Virgin Mothers: Anglican Sisterhoods in Victorian Britain*. London: Leicester University Press, 1999.

Murray, Alexander. "Piety and Impiety in Thirteenth-Century Italy." In *Popular Belief and Practice*. Studies in Church History 8, ed. G. J. Cuming and Derek Baker, 83–106. Cambridge: Cambridge University Press, 1972.

Myres, Sandra L. *Ho! for California: Women's Overland Diaries from the Huntingdon Library*. San Marino, Calif.: Huntingdon Library, 1980.

Neel, Carol, trans. *Handbook for William: A Carolingian Noblewoman's Counsel for her Son*. Lincoln: University of Nebraska Press, 1991.

Nelson, Janet. "Queens as Jezebels: The Careers of Brunhild and Bathild in Merovingian History." In *Medieval Women*. Studies in Church History, Subsidia, ed. Derek Baker, 31–78. Oxford: Basil Blackwell, 1978.

Newcomb, Harvey. *How to Be a Lady: A Book for Girls, Containing Useful Hints on the Formation of Character*. Boston: Gould and Lincoln, 1846.

Newman, Keith. "Holiness in Beauty?" In *The Church and the Arts*. Studies in Church History 28, ed. Diana Wood, 303–12. Oxford: Basil Blackwell, 1992.

Nicholson, Joan. "Feminae Gloriosae: Women in the Age of Bede." In *Medieval Women*. Studies in Church History, Subsidia, ed. Derek Baker, 15–29. Oxford: Basil Blackwell, 1978.

Nugent, Rosamond M. *Portrait of the Consecrated Woman in Greek Christian Literature of the First Four Centuries*. Washington, D.C.: Catholic University of America Press, 1941.

O'Brien, Susan. "Making Catholic Spaces: Women, Décor, and Devotion in the English Catholic Church, 1840–1900." In *The Church and the Arts*. Studies in Church History 28, ed. Diana Wood, 449–63. Oxford: Basil Blackwell, 1992.

O'Connor, Anne. "Listening to Tradition." In *Personally Speaking*, ed. Liz Steiner-Scott, 36–54. New York: Attic Press, 1985.

Oduyoye, Mercy Amba. *The Will to Arise: Women, Tradition, and the Church*. Maryknoll, N.Y.: Orbis, 1991.

Oliva, Marilyn. *Convent and Community in Late-Medieval England: Female Monasteries in the Diocese of Norwich, 1350–1540*. Woodbridge, U.K.: Boydell, 1998.

"One of Them." *What a Pastor's Wife Can Do*. Philadelphia: American Baptist Publication Society, 1893.

"The Ordeal of Community: Hagiography and Discipline in Merovingian Convents." *Vos Benedictina* 3–4 (1986): 293–326.

Orme, Nicholas. "Children in the Church." *Journal of Ecclesiastical History* 45, no. 4 (October 1994): 563–87.

Oseik, Carolyn. "The Widow as Altar: The Rise and Fall of a Symbol." *Second Century* 3 (1983): 159–69.

Otten, Charlotte, ed. *English Women's Voices, 1540–1700*. Miami: Florida International University Press, 1992.

Ovington, Mary White. *The Walls Came Tumbling Down*. New York: Harcourt, Brace, 1947.

Owen, Dorothy M. "Bacon and Eggs: Bishop Buckingham and Superstition in Lincoln-shire." In *Popular Belief and Practice*. Studies in Church History 8, ed. G. J. Cumming and Derek Baker, 135–42. Cambridge: Cambridge University Press, 1972.

———. "White Annys and Others." In *Medieval Women*. Studies in Church History, Subsidia, ed. Derek Baker, 331–46. Oxford: Basil Blackwell, 1978.

Palliser, D. M. "Introduction: The Parish in Perspective." In *The Age of Elizabeth: England under the Later Tudors, 1547–1603*. London: Longman, 1983.

Pantel, Pauline Schmidt, ed. *A History of Women in the West*, vol. 1: *From Ancient Goddesses to Christian Saints*. Cambridge, Mass.: Belknap Press of Harvard University Press, 1991.

Pantin, W. A. "Instructions for a Devout and Literate Layman." In *Medieval Learning and Literature*, ed. J. J. G. Alexander and M. T. Gibson, 398–422. Oxford: Oxford University Press, 1976.

Parker, Kenneth L. *The English Sabbath: A Study of Doctrine and Discipline from the Reformation to the Civil War*. Cambridge: Cambridge University Press, 1988.

Parvey, Constance. "The Theology and Leadership of Women in the New Testament." In *Religion and Sexism*, ed. Rosemary Ruether. New York: Simon and Schuster, 1974.

Pearson, Lu Emily. *Elizabethans at Home*. Stanford: Stanford University Press, 1957.

Pecklers, Keith F. *The Unread Vision: The Liturgical Movement in the United States of America, 1926–1955*. Collegeville, Minn.: Liturgical Press, 1998.

Perrot, Michelle, ed. *A History of Private Life*, vol. 4: *From the Fires of Revolution to the Great War*. Cambridge, Mass.: Belknap Press of Harvard University Press, 1990.

———. *Writing Women's History*. Trans. Felicia Pheasant. Oxford: Oxford University Press, 1984.

Perry, R. *The Celebrated Mary Astell*. Chicago: University of Chicago Press, 1986.

Peterson, Joan, trans. and ed. *Handmaids of the Lord: Holy Women in Late Antiquity and the Early Middle Ages*. Kalamazoo, Mich.: Cistercian Publications, 1966.

Plomer, H. L. "Books Mentioned in Wills." *Transactions of the Bibliographical Society* 7 (1902–4): 99–121.

Plummer, John F. *Vox Feminae: Studies in Medieval Women's Songs*. Studies in Medieval Culture 15. Kalamazoo, Mich.: Western Michigan University Medieval Institute Publications, 1981.

Pocock, W. W. *In Memoriam William Fuller Pocock, FRIBA, 1779–1849*. Privately printed, 1883.

Pollard, A. J. "Richard Clervaux of Croft: A North Riding Squire in the Fifteenth Century." *Yorkshire Archeological Journal* 50 (1978).

Pollock, Linda. *With Faith and Physic: The Life of a Tudor Gentlewoman, Lady Grace Mildmay, 1552–1620*. New York: St. Martin's, 1993.

Portefaix, L. *Sisters Rejoice: Paul's Letter to the Philippians and Luke-Acts as Received by First-Century Philippian Women*. Coniectanea Biblica New Testament Series 20. Stockholm: Almqvist and Wiksell International, 1988.

Porterfield, Amanda. *Female Piety in Puritan New England: The Emergence of Religious Humanism*. Oxford: Oxford University Press, 1992.

Postels, David. "Monastic Burials of Non-Patronal Lay Benefactors." *Journal of Ecclesiastical History* 47, no. 4 (October 1996): 620–37.

Pouncy, Carolyn Johnston, ed. and trans. *The Domostroi: Rules for Russian Households in the Time of Ivan the Terrible.* Ithaca, N.Y.: Cornell University Press, 1994.

Power, Eileen. *Medieval English Nunneries.* Cambridge: Cambridge University Press, 1922.

Powicke, Maurice. "Loretta, Countess of Leicester." In *The Christian Life in the Middle Ages and Other Essays.* Oxford: Clarendon, 1997 (1935).

Prince, Nancy. *A Black Woman's Journey through Russia and Jamaica: The Narrative of Nancy Prince.* New York: Markus Wiener, 1990.

Prochaska, F. K. *Women and Philanthropy in Nineteenth-Century England.* Oxford: Oxford University Press, 1980.

Prost, Antione, and Vincent Gérard, eds. *A History of Private Life,* vol. 5: *Riddles of Identity in Modern Times.* Cambridge, Mass.: Belknap Press of Harvard University Press, 1991.

Quasten, Johannes. *Music and Worship in Pagan and Christian Antiquity.* NPM Studies in Church Music and Liturgy. Washington, D.C.: National Association of Pastoral Musicians, 1983.

Quick, Howard E. *The Living Cathedral, St. John the Divine: A History and Guide.* New York: Crossroad, 1993.

Quinlan, Maurice J. *Victorian Prelude: A History of English Manners 1700–1830.* Hamden, Conn.: Archon Books, 1965.

Ragg, Laura M. *The Women Artists of Bologna.* London: Methuen and Co., 1907.

Rankin, Richard. *Ambivalent Churchmen and Evangelical Churchwomen: The Religion of the Episcopal Elite in North Carolina, 1800–1860.* Columbia: University of South Carolina Press, 1993.

Rapley, Charlotte. *The Devotees: Women and Church in Seventeenth-Century France.* Montreal: McGill-Queen's University Press, 1990.

Redstone, Dale, ed. *The Household Book of Dame Alice de Bryene, 1412–1413.* Bungay, Suffolk: Paradigm Press, 1984.

Reinburg, Virginia. "Liturgy and the Laity in Late Medieval and Reformation France." *Sixteenth-Century Journal* 23, no. 3 (1992): 526–46.

Richards, Mary. "Some Fifteenth-Century Calendars." *Archeologia Cantiana* 102 (1985): 71–85.

Richmond, Colin. "Religion and the Fifteenth-Century Gentleman." In *The Church, Politics, and Patronage in the Fifteenth Century,* ed. Barrie Dobson, 201–47. Gloucester, U.K.: Sutton, 1984.

Roche, John A. *The Life of Mrs. Sarah A. Lankford Palmer.* New York: George Hughes, 1898.

Rogal, Samuel. *Sisters of Sacred Song: A Selected Listing of Women Hymnodists in Great Britain and America.* New York: Garland, 1981.

Roos, Rosalie. *Travels in America, 1851–1855.* Carbondale: Southern Illinois University Press, 1982.

Roper, L. *The Holy Household: Women and Morals in Reformation Augsburg.* Oxford: Oxford University Press, 1989.

Rosenberg, Carol Beth. "The Female World of Love and Ritual: Relations between Women in the Nineteenth Century." *Signs: Journal of Women in Culture and Society* 1 (1975).

Rosenthal, Joel, and Colin Richmond, eds. *People, Politics, and Community in the Later Middle Ages*. Gloucester, U.K.: Alan Sutton, and New York: St. Martin's, 1987.

Rosser, Gervase. "Communities of Parish and Guild in the Late Middle Ages." In *Parish Church and People: Local Studies in Lay Religion, 1350–1750*, ed. Susan J. Wright, 29–55. London: Hutchinson, 1988.

Rousseau, Constance M. "Gender Difference and Indifference in the Writings of Pope Innocent III." In *Gender and Christian Religion*. Studies in Church History 34, ed. R. N. Swanson, 105–17. Woodbridge, U.K.: Boydell, 1998.

Rowlands, Marie B., ed. *English Catholics of Parish and Town, 1558–1778*. Catholic Record Society Monograph Series 5. Publications Series 3.29 and 30. London: Catholic Record Society, 1999.

———. "Recusant Women, 1560–1640." In *Women in English Society, 1500–1800*, ed. Mary Prior. Cambridge: Cambridge University Press, 1985.

Rubin, Miri. *Corpus Christi: The Eucharist in Late-Medieval Culture*. Cambridge: Cambridge University Press, 1991.

Ruether, Rosemary. *Women Church: The Theology and Practice of Feminist Liturgical Communities*. San Francisco: Harper, 1985.

Ruffin, Bernard. *Fanny Crosby*. Philadelphia: United Church Press, 1976.

Runciman, Steven. "The Empress Irene the Athenian." In *Medieval Women*. Studies in Church History, Subsidia, ed. Derek Baker, 101–18. Oxford: Basil Blackwell, 1978.

Rupp, Gordon. "A Devotion of Rapture in English Puritanism." In *Reformation, Conformity, and Dissent: Essays in Honour of Geoffrey Nuttal*, ed. R. Buick Knox. London: Epworth, 1977.

Sallmann, Jean-Michel. "Witches." In *A History of Women in the West*, vol. 3: *Renaissance and Enlightenment*, ed. N. Z. Davis and A. Farge, 444–57. Cambridge, Mass.: Belknap Press of Harvard University Press, 1993.

Sargeant, Michael G., ed. *De Cella in Seculum: Religious and Secular Life and Devotion in Late Medieval England*. Cambridge: Brewer, 1989.

Saul, Nigel. "Religious Sympathies of the Gentry." *Bristol and Gloucestershire Archeological Society Journal* (1990): 99–112.

Scarisbrick, J. J. *The Reformation and the English People*. Oxford: Oxford University Press, 1984.

Schen, Claire S. "Women and the London Parishes, 1500–1620." In *The Parish in English Life, 1400–1600*, ed. Katherine L. French, Gary Gibbs, and Beat A. Kümin, 250–68. Manchester: Manchester University Press, 1997.

Schmidt, Jean Miller. *Grace Sufficient: A History of Women in American Methodism, 1760–1939*. Nashville: Abingdon, 1999.

Schneider, Gregory. *The Way of the Cross Leads Home: The Domestication of American Methodism*. Bloomington: Indiana University Press, 1993.

Schofield, John. "Medieval Parish Churches in the City of London." In *Parish in English Life, 1400–1600*, ed. Katherine L. French, Gary Gibbs, and Beat A. Kümin, 35–55. Manchester: Manchester University Press, 1997.

Schulenbeurg, Jane Tibbetts. *Forgetful of Their Sex: Female Sanctity and Society, ca. 500–1100*. Chicago: University of Chicago Press, 1998.

Schultz, Nancy Lusiguan. *Fire and Roses: The Burning of the Charlestown Convent.* Minneapolis: Fortress Press, 2000.

Sedgwick, Alexander. "The Nuns of Port-Royal: A Study of a Female Spirituality in Seventeenth-Century France." In *That Gentle Strength: Historical Perspectives on Women in Christianity,* ed. Lynda L. Coon, Katherine J. Haldane, and Elisabeth W. Sommer, 176–89. Charlottesville: University Press of Virginia, 1990.

Shammas, Carole. "The Domestic Environment in Early Modern England and America." *Journal of Social History* 14, no. 1 (fall 1980): 3–24.

Shand-Tucci, Douglass. *The Art of Scandal: The Life and Times of Isabella Stewart Gardner.* San Francisco: HarperCollins, 1997.

Sharpe, J. A. *Defamation and Sexual Slander in Early Modern England: The Church Courts at York.* Borthwick Papers no. 58. York: University of York, Borthwick Institute of Historical Research, 1980.

Shiels, Richard. "The Feminization of American Congregationalism, 1730–1835." *American Quarterly* 33 (1981): 46–62.

Shiels, W. J., and Diana Wood, eds. *The Ministry: Clerical and Lay.* Studies in Church History 26. London: Blackwell, 1989.

———. *Women in the Church.* Studies in Church History 27. Oxford: Blackwell, 1990.

Shiman, Lillian Lewis. *Women and Leadership in Nineteenth-Century England.* New York: St. Martin's, 1992.

Shorney, David. " 'Women May Preach but Men Must Govern': Gender Roles in the Growth and Development of the Bible Christian Denomination." In *Gender and Christian Religion.* Studies in Church History 34, ed. R. N. Swanson, 309–22. Woodbridge, U.K.: Boydell, 1998.

Simmons, Thomas Frederick. *Lay-Folks Mass Book.* London: Early English Text Society, 1879.

Slack, Paul, ed. *Rebellion, Popular Protest, and Social Order in Early Modern England.* Cambridge: Cambridge University Press, 1983.

Smith, Amanda. *An Autobiography: The Story of the Lord's Dealings with Mrs. Amanda Smith, the Coloured Evangelist.* Chicago: Meyer and Brother, Publishers, 1893.

Smith, Julia M. H. "Gender and Ideology in the Early Middle Ages." In *Gender and Christian Religion.* Studies in Church History 34, ed. R. N. Swanson, 51–73. Woodbridge, U.K.: Boydell, 1998.

Smith, Karen E. "Beyond Public and Private Spheres: Another Look at Women in Baptist History and Historiography." *Baptist Quarterly* 34, no. 2 (1991): 79–87.

Smith, L. Toulmin, ed. *English Gilds: Original Ordinances of More than 100 Early English Gilds of the Fourteenth and Fifteenth Centuries.* London: Early English Text Society, 1870.

Smith, M. G. *Pastoral Discipline and the Church Courts: The Hexham Court, 1670–1730.* Bothwick Paper 62. York: University of York: Bothwick Institute for Historical Research, 1982.

Smith, Richard. *The Life of the Most Honourable and Vertuous Lady, the La. Magdalen, Viscountesse Montague.* London, 1627.

Smith, Steven R. "The London Apprentices as Seventeenth-Century Adolescents." In *Rebellion, Popular Protest, and Social Order in Early Modern England*, ed. P. Slack, 216–27. Cambridge: Cambridge University Press, 1983.

Snee, Rochelle. "Gregory Nazianzen's Anastasia Church." *Dumbarton Oaks Papers* 52 (1998): 157–89.

Sneyd, C. A., ed. *A Relation, or Rather a True Account, of the Island of England... about the Year 1500.* Ed. C. A. Sneyd. Camden Society, Old series, 37, 1847.

Sobel, Mechal. *Trabelin' On: The Slave Journey to an Afro-Baptist Faith.* Princeton, N.J.: Princeton University Press, 1988.

Splaeth, Donald. "Common Prayer? Popular Observance of the Anglican Liturgy in Restoration Wiltshire." In *Parish Church and People: Local Studies in Lay Religion, 1350–1750*, ed. Susan J. Wright, 125–51. London: Hutchinson, 1988.

Spreadbury, Jo. "The Gender of the Church: The Female Image of Ecclesia in the Middle Ages." In *Gender and Christian Religion*, ed. R. N. Swanson, 93–103. Cambridge: Boydell, 1998.

Springer, Marlene, and Haskell Springer, eds. *Plains Women: The Diary of Martha Farnsworth, 1882–1922.* Bloomington: Indiana University Press, 1986.

Spufford, Margaret. "Can We Count the 'Godly' and the 'Conformable' in the Seventeenth Century?" *Journal of Ecclesiastical History* 36, no. 3 (1985): 428–38.

———. "First Steps in Literacy: The Reading and Writing Experiences of the Humblest Seventeenth-Century Autobiographers." *Social History* 4 (1979): 407–35.

Spurr, Barry. *The Word in the Desert: Anglican and Roman Catholic Reactions to Liturgical Reform.* Cambridge: Lutterworth, 1995.

Stafford, Pauline. *Queens, Concubines and Dowagers: The King's Wife in the Early Middle Ages.* Athens: University of Georgia Press, 1983.

———. "Sons and Mothers: Family Politics in the Early Middle Ages." In *Medieval Women.* Studies in Church History, Subsidia, ed. Derek Baker, 79–100. Oxford: Basil Blackwell, 1978.

———. "Women and the Norman Conquest." *Transactions of the Royal Historical Society* (6th series) 4 (1995): 221–50.

Stannard, David E. *The Puritan Way of Death: A Study in Religion, Culture, and Social Change.* New York: Oxford University Press, 1977.

Stapleton, Thomas, ed. *The Plumpton Correspondence.* Original Series 4. London: Camden Society Publications, 1839.

Steele, Anne. *The Hymns of Anne Steele.* London: Gospel Standard Baptist Trust, 1967.

Stewart, Elinore Pruitt. *Letters of a Women Homesteader.* Boston: Houghton Mifflin, 1914.

———. *Letters on an Elk Hunt by a Woman Homesteader.* Lincoln: University of Nebraska Press, 1979 (1915).

Stock, N., ed. *Miss Weeton's Journal of a Governess, 1811–1825.* Newton Abbot, U.K.: David and Charles, 1969.

Stone, Lawrence. *The Family, Sex, and Marriage in England, 1500–1800.* New York: Oxford University Press, 1979.

Strahorn, Carrie Adell. *Fifteen Thousand Miles by Stage: A Woman's Unique Experience during Thirty Years of Path Finding and Pioneering from the Missouri to the Pacific and from*

Alaska to Mexico. New York: Knickerbocker Press, 1911; reprint: Lincoln: University of Nebraska Press, 1988.

Stratton, Joanna L. *Pioneer Women: Voices from the Kansas Frontier.* New York: Simon and Schuster, 1981.

Straubhaar, Sandra B. "The Forgotten Skáldkonur and Their Place in Early Skandinavian Literature." In *The Worlds of Medieval Women: Creativity, Influence, Imagination,* ed. Constance H. Berman, Charles W. Connell, and Judith Rice Rothschild, 14–23. Morgantown: West Virginia University Press, 1985.

Strong, Rowan. "Coronets and Altars: Aristocratic Women's and Men's Support for the Oxford Movement in Scotland during the 1840s." In *Gender and Christian Religion.* Studies in Church History 34, ed. R. N. Swanson, 391–403. Woodbridge, U.K.: Boydell, 1998.

Sullivan, Richard E., ed. *"The Gentle Voices of the Teachers": Aspects of Learning in the Carolingian Age.* Columbus: University of Ohio Press, 1995.

Sutton, Lillian Lewis. " 'Changes Are Dangerous': Women and Temperance in Victorian England." In *Religion in the Lives of English Women, 1760–1930,* ed. Gail Malmgreen, 193–215. Bloomington: Indiana University Press, 1986.

Swanson, R. N. "Liturgy as Theatre: The Props." In *The Church and the Arts.* Studies in Church History 28, ed. Diana Wood, 239–53. Oxford: Basil Blackwell, 1992.

———, ed. *Gender and Christian Religion.* Studies in Church History 34. Woodbridge, U.K.: Boydell, 1998.

Taft, Robert. "Women at Church in Byzantium: Where, When — and Why?" *Dumbarton Oaks Papers* 52 (1998): 27–88.

Taft, Zechariah. *Biographical Sketches of the Lives and Public Ministry of Various Holy Women.* 2 vols. London: Kershaw, 1825, and Leeds: Cullingworth, 1828.

Taitz, Emily. "Kol Ishah — the Voice of Women: Where Was It Heard in Medieval Judaism?" *Conservative Judaism* 38, no. 3 (spring 1986): 46–61.

Talbot, Alice-Mary. "Women's Space in Byzantine Monasteries." *Dumbarton Oaks Papers* 52 (1998): 113–28.

Tanner, Norman. *The Church in Late-Medieval Norwich.* Toronto: University of Toronto Press, 1984.

———. "The Reformation and Regionalism." In *Towns and Townspeople in the Fifteenth Century,* ed. John A. F. Thomson. Gloucester, U.K.: Allan Sutton, 1988.

———, ed. "Heresy Trials in the Diocese of Norwich, 1428–31." London: Camden Society, 4th series, xx (1977): 41–49.

Taylor, Brian. "Church Art and Church Discipline Round about 1939." In *The Church and the Arts.* Studies in Church History 28, ed. Diana Wood, 489–98. Oxford: Basil Blackwell, 1992.

———. "Gender in Sarawak: Mission and Reception." In *Gender and Christian Religion.* Studies in Church History 34, ed. R. N. Swanson, 461–73. Woodbridge, U.K.: Boydell, 1998.

Taylor, Jane H. *Dies Illa: Death in the Middle Ages.* Liverpool, U.K.: F. Cairns, 1984.

Taylor, Suzie King. *Reminiscences of My Life in Camp with the 33rd US Colored Troops, Late 1st South Carolina Volunteers: A Black Woman's Civil War Memoirs*, ed. Patricia Romero and Willie Lee Rose. Princeton, N.J.: Markus Weiner, 1988.

Tentler, T. N. *Sin and Confession on the Eve of the Reformation*. Princeton, N.J.: Princeton University Press, 1977.

Theissen, Gerd. *Sociology of Early Palestinian Christianity*. Philadelphia: Fortress, 1978.

Thomas, Keith. *Religion and the Decline of Magic*. New York: Oxford University Press, 1997.

———. "Women and the Civil War Sects." *Past and Present* 13 (1958): 42–62.

Thompson, A. H. *The English Clergy and Their Organisation in the Later Middle Ages*. Oxford: Clarendon, 1947.

Thompson, Sally. "The Problem of Cistercian Nuns in the Thirteenth Century." In *Medieval Women*. Studies in Church History, Subsidia, ed. Derek Baker, 227–52. Oxford: Basil Blackwell, 1978.

Thomson, David Patrick. *Women of the Scottish Church*. Skinnergate, Perth: Munro and Scott, 1975.

———. *Women of the Scottish Reformation: Their Contribution to the Protestant Cause*. Crieff, Perthshire, Scotland: Book Department, St. Ninians, 1975.

Thomson, John A. F. *Towns and Townspeople in the Fifteenth Century*. Gloucester, U.K.: Allan Sutton, 1988.

———. "The Well of Grace: Englishmen and Rome in the Fifteenth Century." In *Church Politics and Patronage*, ed. Barrie Dobson, 99–114. Gloucester, U.K.: Sutton, 1984.

Thurston, Bonnie Bowman. *Widows: A Women's Ministry in the Early Church*. Minneapolis: Fortress, 1989.

Tillson, Christina. *A Woman's Story of Pioneer Illinois*. Chicago: Lakeside Press, 1919.

Tracy, Patricia J. *Jonathan Edwards, Pastor: Religion and Society in Eighteenth-Century Northampton*. New York: Hill and Wang, 1979.

Trill, Suzanne, Kate Chedgzoy, and Melanie Osborne, eds. *Lay by Your Needles, Ladies, Take the Pen: Writing Women in England, 1500–1700*. London: Arnold, 1997.

Uitz, Erika. *Women in the Medieval Town*. Trans. Shiela Marnie. London: Barrie and Jenkins, 1990.

Underhill, Frances. "By Their Works Ye Shall Know Them: Elizabeth de Burgh and Clare College, Walsingham Friary, Ballinrobe...." In *The Worlds of Medieval Women: Creativity, Influence, Imagination*, ed. Constance H. Berman, Charles W. Connell, and Judith Rice Rothschild, 86–96. Morgantown: West Virginia University Press, 1985.

Utterback, K. T. "Worship at the Church of Your Choice: Church Attendance in Mid-fourteenth Century Barcelona." *Journal of Medieval History* 17, no. 3 (1991): 245–33.

Valenze, D. *Prophetic Sons and Daughters: Female Preaching and Popular Religion in Industrial England*. Princeton, N.J.: Princeton University Press, 1985.

Van Houts, Elizabeth. "The State of Research: Women in Medieval History and Literature." *Journal of Medieval History* 20 (1994): 277–92.

Venarde, Bruce. *Women's Monasticism and Medieval Society, 890–1215*. Ithaca, N.Y.: Cornell University Press, 1997.

Verbrugge, Vera. "Margaret More Roper's Personal Expression in the Devout Treatise on the Pater Noster." In *Silent but for the Word: Tudor Women as Patrons, Translators, and Writers of Religious Works,* ed. Margaret Hannay, 30–42. Kent, Ohio: Kent State University Press, 1995.

Veyne, Paul, ed. *A History of Private Life,* vol. 1: *From Pagan Rome to Byzantium.* Cambridge, Mass.: Belknap Press of Harvard University Press, 1987.

Vickery, Amanda. "Golden Age to Separate Spheres? A Review of the Categories and Chronology of English Women's History." *Historical Journal* 36 (1993): 383–414.

Vlasto, A. P. *The Entry of the Slavs into Christendom.* Cambridge: Cambridge University Press, 1979.

Voaden, Rosalynn. *Prophets Abroad.* Cambridge: Brewer, 1996.

Vodola, Elisabeth. *Excommunication in the Middle Ages.* Berkeley: University of California Press, 1986.

Vogt, Kari. "The Desert Mothers." In *Women's Studies in the Christian and Islamic Traditions: Ancient, Medieval, and Renaissance Foremothers,* ed. K. Børresen and K. Vogt. Dordrecht: Kluwer, 1993.

Von Arx, Waltar. "The Churching of Women after Childbirth: History and Significance." *Concilium* 112 (1979): 63–72.

Wabuda, Susan. "Shunamites and Nurses of the English Reformation: The Activities of Mary Glover, Niece of Hugh Latimer." In *Women in the Church.* Studies in Church History 27, ed. W. J. Shiels and Diana Wood, 335–44. Oxford: Blackwell, 1990.

Wakefield, Priscilla. *Reflections on the Present Condition of the Female Sex.* London: J. Johnson, 1798.

Walker, Cheryl, ed. *Women and Gender in South Africa to 1945.* Cape Town: David Philip, 1990.

Wall, Alison. "Elizabethan Precept and Feminine Practice: The Thynne Family of Longleat." *History* 75 (1990): 23–38.

Wallace, Charles, Jr. *Susannah Wesley: The Complete Writings.* Oxford: Oxford University Press, 1997.

———. "Susannah Wesley's Spirituality: The Freedom of a Christian Woman." *Methodist History* 33 (1983–84): 138–73.

Wallace-Hadrill, John Michael. *The Frankish Church.* Oxford: Oxford University Press, 1983.

Walsh, W. *The Religious Life and Influence of Queen Victoria.* New York: E. P. Dutton, 1902.

Walter, John, and Keith Wrightson. "Death and Social Order in Early Modern England." In *Rebellion, Popular Protest, and Social Order in Early Modern England,* ed. Paul Slack, 108–28. Cambridge: Cambridge University Press, 1983.

Wandel, Lee Palmer. *Voracious Idols and Violent Hands: Iconoclasm in Reformation Zurich, Strassbourg, and Basel.* Cambridge: Cambridge University Press, 1995.

Ward, W. R. *The Protestant Evangelical Awakening.* Cambridge: Cambridge University Press, 1992.

Warner, Julia Stewart. *The Primitive Methodist Connexion: Its Background and Early History.* Madison: University of Wisconsin Press, 1984.

Warnicke, Retha M. "Lady Mildmay's Journal: A Study in Autobiography and Meditation in Reformation England." *Sixteenth Century Journal* 20 (1989): 59–68.

———. *Women of the English Renaissance and Reformation*. Contributions to Women's Studies 38. Westport, Conn.: Greenwood Press, 1982.

Watt, Diane. *Medieval Women in Their Communities*. Toronto: University of Toronto Press, 1997.

Weaver, F. Ellen. *The Evolution of the Reform of Port-Royal: From the Rule of Cîteaux to Jansenism*. Paris: Éditions Beauchesne, 1978.

Webb, Pauline. *She Flies Beyond: Memories and Hopes of Women in the Ecumenical Movement*. Geneva: WCC, 1993.

Weiner, Marli F., ed. *A Heritage of Woe: The Civil War Diary of Grace Brown Elmore, 1861–1868*. Athens: University of Georgia Press, 1997.

Weinstein, Minna F. "Reconstructing Our Past: Reflections on Tudor Women." *International Journal of Women's Studies* 1 (1978): 133–40.

Welch, Edwin. *Spiritual Pilgrim: A Reassessment of the Life of the Countess of Huntingdon*. Cardiff: University of Wales Press, 1995.

Wemple, Suzanne Fonay. "Women from the Fifth to the Tenth Century." In *A History of Women in the West*, vol. 2: *Silences of the Middle Ages*, ed. Christiane Klapisch-Zuber, 169–201. Cambridge, Mass.: Belknap Press of Harvard University Press, 1992.

———. *Women in Frankish Society: Marriage and the Cloister, 500–900*. Philadelphia: University of Pennsylvania Press, 1981.

Wessinger, Catherine. *Women's Leadership in Marginal Religions: Explorations Outside the Mainstream*. Urbana and Chicago: University of Illinois Press, 1993.

Wessley, Stephen E. "The Thirteenth-Century Guglielmites: Salvation through Women." In *Medieval Women*. Studies in Church History, Subsidia, ed. Derek Baker, 289–303. Oxford: Basil Blackwell, 1978.

Westerkamp, Marilyn. *Scots-Irish Piety and the Great Awakening, 1625–1760*. Oxford: Oxford University Press, 1988.

———. *Women and Religion in Early America, 1600–1850: The Puritan and Evangelical Traditions*. New York: Routledge, 1999.

Whaley, Joachim, ed. *Mirrors of Mortality: Studies in the Social History of Death*. New York: St. Martin's Press, 1981.

White, W. J. "Changing Burial Practices." *Ricardian* 4, no. 63 (1978): 23–30.

Whiting, Robert. *The Blind Devotion of the People: Popular Religion and the English Reformation*. Cambridge: Cambridge University Press, 1989.

Wiesner, M. E. *Women and Gender in Early Modern Europe*. Cambridge: Cambridge University Press, 1994.

Wilberforce, William. *A Practical View of the Professing Christians in the Higher and Middle Classes in This Country Contrasted with Real Christianity*. London, 1797; Peabody, Mass.: Hendrickson, 1966.

Willen, Diane. "Godly Women in Early Modern England: Puritanism and Gender." *Journal of Ecclesiastical History* 43 (1992): 561–80.

Williams, E. M. "Women Preachers in the Civil War." *Journal of Modern History* 1 (1929): 561–69.

Wilson, Linda. "The Spirituality of Non-Conformist Women, 1825–1875." In *Gender and Christian Religion*. Studies in Church History 34, ed. R. N. Swanson, 347–59. Woodbridge, U.K.: Boydell, 1998.

Wilson, Stephen, ed. *Saints and Their Cults: Studies in Religious Sociology, Folklore and History*. Cambridge: Cambridge University Press, 1983.

Wilson-Kastner, Patricia, et al. *A Lost Tradition: Women Writers of the Early Church*. Lanham, Md.: University Press of America, 1981.

Winegarten, Ruthe. *Black Texas Women: A Sourcebook*. Austin: University of Texas Press, 1996.

Winter, Bruce W. *Seek the Welfare of the City: Christians as Benefactors and Citizens*. Grand Rapids, Mich.: Eerdmans, 1994.

Witherington, Ben. *Women in the Earliest Churches*. Cambridge: Cambridge University Press, 1988.

Wittenmyer, Annie. *Women's Work for Jesus*. New York: Nelson and Phillips, 1871.

"Women and the Word in the Later Middle Ages." *Studies in Church History* 27 (1991): 53–78.

Wood, Diana, ed. *The Church and the Arts*. Studies in Church History 28. Oxford: Basil Blackwell, 1992.

Wood, Jeryldene. *Women, Art and Spirituality*. Cambridge: Cambridge University Press, 1966.

Wood, Susan. *English Monasteries and Their Patrons in the Thirteenth Century*. London: Oxford University Press, 1955.

Wood-Legh, K. L. *Perpetual Chantries in Britain*. Cambridge: Cambridge University Press, 1965.

Wright, Susan J. "Catechism, Confirmation, and Communion: The Role of the Young in the Post-Reformation Church." In *Parish Church and People: Local Studies in Lay Religion, 1350–1750*, ed. Susan J. Wright, 203–28. London: Hutchinson, 1988.

———. "Easter Books and Parish Rate Books: A New Source for the Urban Historian." *Urban History Yearbook* (1985): 30–31.

———, ed. *Parish Church and People: Local Studies in Lay Religion, 1350–1750*. London: Hutchinson, 1988.

Wyman, Lillie B. Chase. "Colored Churches and Schools in the South." *New England Magazine* 3 (February 1891): 787–88.

Yarborough, A. "Christianization in the Fourth Century: The Example of Roman Women." *Church History* 45 (1976): 149–64.

Yates, Nigel. *Buildings, Faith, and Worship: The Liturgical Arrangement of Anglican Churches, 1541–1871*. Oxford: Oxford University Press, 1991.

Zell, Katharina. *Von Christo Jhesu Lobgsäng*. Strasbourg, 1534/35.

Zinserling, Verena. *Women of Greece and Rome*. New York: Abner Schram, 1972.

Index